THE TREATMENT OF THE HOLOCAUST IN TEXTBOOKS

The Federal Republic of Germany,
Israel,
The United States of America

Edited by

RANDOLPH L. BRAHAM

SOCIAL SCIENCE MONOGRAPHS, BOULDER
and
INSTITUTE FOR HOLOCAUST STUDIES OF
THE CITY UNIVERSITY OF NEW YORK
DISTRIBUTED BY COLUMBIA UNIVERSITY PRESS, NEW YORK

1987

Holocaust Studies Series

Randolph L. Braham, Editor
The Institute for Holocaust Studies
The Graduate School and University Center
The City University of New York

Previously published books in the Series:
  Perspectives on the Holocaust, 1982
  Contemporary Views on the Holocaust, 1983
  Genocide and Retribution, 1983
  The Hungarian Jewish Catastrophe
    A Selected and Annotated Bibliography, 1984
  Jewish Leadership During the Nazi Era:
    Patterns of Behavior in the Free World, 1985
  The Holocaust in Hungary—Forty Years Later, 1985
  The Origins of the Holocaust
    Christian Anti-Semitism, 1986
  The Halutz Resistance in Hungary, 1942–1944, 1986
  The Tragedy of Hungarian Jewry: Essays, Documents, Testimonies, 1986

The Holocaust Studies Series is published in cooperation with the Institute for Holocaust Studies. These books are outgrowths of lectures, conferences, and research projects sponsored by the Institute. It is the purpose of the Series to subject the events and circumstances of the Holocaust to scrutiny by a variety of academics who bring different scholarly disciplines to the study.

The first three books in the Series were published by Kluwer-Nijhoff Publishing of Boston.

Copyright © 1987 by Randolph L. Braham
ISBN 0-88033-955-1
Library of Congress Catalog Card Number 87-60633
Printed in the United States of America

Contents

Introduction vii

Part I: Federal Republic of Germany:
Germans, Jews and Genocide
Walter F. Renn 1

1. Introduction.. 3

2. Textbooks: Development and Production................... 5

   The Conditions of Textbook Production 5
   The Influence of the State on Textbook Production........ 6
   The State and the Textbook Depiction of the Holocaust..... 7
   State Guidelines for the Treatment of the Third Reich
      and the Jews 10
   Criticism of the Educational Role of the State........... 12
   Agencies and Institutions Supporting Textbook
      Education 15
   The Georg-Eckert-Institut für internationale
      Schulbuchforschung 17

3. Textbooks: Treatment of the Holocaust and
   Related Themes 21

   General Criticisms of Textbooks 21
   The Sense of Obligation Toward the Jews 22
   Scope of the Study..................................... 23
   Motives and Background of Anti-Semitism 25
   The Religious Roots of Anti-Semitism................... 26
   Economic Motives of Anti-Semitism..................... 29
   Racial Anti-Semitism 33
   The Functions of Anti-Semitism 41

The Presentation of Negative Images of Jews 57
Persecution of the Jews, 1933–1939 61
"Aryanization" and Plunder of Jewish Property 72
Humiliations and Deprivations 75
Forced Emigration 77
Advanced Warnings of the Holocaust 83
The Order and Planning of Genocide 87
The Agony and Murder of the European Jews 96
Killing Centers and Mass Murder....................... 101
The Number of Victims................................ 108
The Significance of the Event.......................... 113

4. Conclusions... 125

   Notes 131
   Appendix I: List of Textbooks, Workbooks and
        Teacher-aids Consulted 149

Part II: Israel
Ruth Firer 153

5. Introduction.. 155

6. The *Mikra'ot* 161

   The Maintenance of the Human Image................. 162
   The Armed Resistance 164
   The Ritual Angle..................................... 166
        The Vengeance Issue.............................. 166
   The Commandment to Remember 167
   The Commandment to Implement
        the Zionist Vision............................... 167
        The Consolation.................................. 167
        The Imaginative Escape to Israel.................. 169
        On the Way to Eretz-Israel........................ 170
        In Eretz-Israel................................... 170
   Conclusion... 170

7. The Holocaust in History Textbooks.................... 177

   The Holocaust—A Proof of Zionist Truth................ 177
   The Holocaust as a Stimulus of Humanistic Education.... 182

From 1983 On: A New Period?........................ 185
Evaluation of the Treatment of the Holocaust in History
    Textbooks, 1948–1984: An Overview................. 187

8. The Research Textbooks............................... 193

    The German-Centered Research Textbooks.............. 194
    The Judeo-Centered Research Textbooks................ 200
    Some Reasons for Changes in Approach 204

9. Conclusion.. 207

    Notes 213
    Bibliography 223

Part III: The United States of America
Glenn S. Pate.. 231

10. The Selection of Textbooks........................... 233

    Elementary and Secondary Levels 233
    College Level 237

11. The Holocaust in American Textbooks................. 239

    Elementary Social Studies Textbooks 240
    Secondary Level Textbooks........................... 243
        United States History Textbooks.................. 243
        World History/Western Civilization Textbooks 260
        Government and Civics Textbooks 282
        Sociology Textbooks 283
        Psychology Textbooks............................ 285
        World Geography/Area Studies Textbooks............ 287
        Social Studies Textbooks 288
    College Level Textbooks 288
        History—College Level 288
        Political Science—College Level 297
        Sociology—College Level......................... 299
        Religious Studies—College Level.................. 302
    Humanities—College Level.......................... 305

12. Conclusion.. 307

    Notes 311
    Bibliography 323
    Contributors 333

Introduction

The linkage between anti-Semitism and the Holocaust has now been thoroughly documented. The postwar years have seen an encouraging trend in both the secular and religious spheres to combat the scourge of anti-Semitism. The measures adopted by the ecclesiastical and state authorities in many parts of the world appear to vary in terms of stringency and effectiveness. In some parts, especially Western Europe and North America, anti-Semitism, while present and subdued, is no longer pervasive; in others, it is exploited—openly or subtly—as an important component of domestic or foreign policy.

The effort to contain and gradually eliminate this age-old scourge has taken many forms, ranging from legislation to education. It is generally believed that the ultimate hope for victory in the battle against anti-Semitism—and other forms of prejudice—lies with the schools. It is also widely believed that an awareness of the nature and consequences of anti-Semitism, culminating in the Holocaust, will motivate students to improve the world.

The effectiveness with which these objectives might be achieved depends to a large extent on the textbooks teachers use at all levels of education. Even with commitment and enthusiasm, teachers cannot fulfill the mission of education unless they have suitable textbooks at their disposal. It is very distressing to note the paucity with which anti-Semitism and the Holocaust are treated in history textbooks the world over. The notable exception is, of course, Israel. Although it was one of the most awesome events in world history, the Holocaust—the assembly line murder of six million Jews in the broad daylight of the Twentieth Century—is given little, if any, space in most textbooks.

The purpose of this volume—the tenth in the Holocaust Studies Series of the Institute for Holocaust Studies of The City University of New York—is to present an overview of the treatment of the Holocaust in the textbooks used in the Federal Republic of Germany,

Israel, and the United States. (A subsequent volume will deal with other countries, including France, Hungary, and the USSR.)

The selection of these three countries was based on historical, political, and state administration criteria. While all three are democratic, they vary in terms of history, heritage, and educational system. The Federal Republic of Germany is of special interest. It is one of the two successor states of the Third Reich, and has made considerable progress in coming to grips with Nazism. It has a democratic federal system of government in which educational policy, including the selection of textbooks, is determined by the states (*Laender*). Israel, the home of many of the survivors of the Holocaust, is a special case. A democratic country, Israel has a centralized system of government in which the power of textbook selection is shared with many social organizations and institutions, including the *Kibbutzim*. The United States, a former member of the Grand Alliance, has a constitutionally and politically federal state structure in which education is the primary responsibility of the states. Consequently, the selection of textbooks is the primary responsibility of the state and local governments acting through their boards of education. In several states, the selection of textbooks at the higher levels of education is left to the discretion of the instructors.

Each section in this volume presents an overview of the country's postwar system of education with emphasis on the agencies and authorities responsible for the selection, production, and distribution of textbooks. A special effort is made to differentiate between the textbooks used at the various levels of education in the treatment of anti-Semitism, Nazism, and the Holocaust. The bibliographies appended to each of the three essays provide additional sources for the interested reader.

The views expressed by the authors are theirs alone and do not necessarily reflect those of the editor or of the Institute for Holocaust Studies.

This volume was prepared with the aid of many people who gave their time, energy, and material support. First and foremost, I thank the contributors for sharing their expertise. I also thank President Harold M. Proshansky and Dean Solomon Goldstein of the Graduate School and University Center of The City University of New York for their unfliching support of the Institute for Holocaust Studies. Finally, I would like to express my gratitude to the Holocaust Survivors Memorial Foundation and especially to the contributors to the Special Holocaust Studies Research and Publication Fund, without whom the publication of the Holocaust Studies Series would not be possible. Special mention should be made of the generosity of Valerie and Frank Furth, Doris and Louis Glick, and Susan and Marcel Sand.

Randolph L. Braham
August 1987

PART I

Federal Republic of Germany: Germans, Jews and Genocide

Walter F. Renn

1
Introduction

The teaching of the Holocaust and its related subjects in the West German education holds a special interest to the Western world. Of all nations the Federal Republic of Germany seems to have the most direct stake in coming to grips with the legacy of National Socialism. Indeed, overcoming the barbarous history of the Nazi era has engaged the efforts of many West German educators and government leaders since World War II. In the past 30 years, they have responded with varying degrees of intensity and success to the challenge posed by the *unbewältigte Vergangenheit*—the unmastered past. The record of their confrontation with this recent past is reflected in the textbooks' treatment of the Nazi era, and especially the persecution and murder of the European Jews.

Because most German educators recognize textbooks as significant in shaping each generation's view of its collective past, the examination of the treatment of the Holocaust may be expected to contribute to an understanding of the achievements and shortcomings which have accompanied West Germany's attempt to make sense of its recent past. Some understanding may be attained also of the attitudes and methods of West German educators in seeking to overcome racial and class prejudice, their attempts to teach civic responsibility for opposing government wrongdoing, as well as the efforts to educate students in democracy in a nation with a relatively short democratic tradition. It will be of interest also to learn how questions of anti-Semitism are treated in West German texts. More indirectly, the examination of West German textbooks reveals much about how the West Germans see themselves, and their society, in relation to the

I would like to express my thanks to Denise Battista, Lisa Hines, Susan McMannis, Karen Johnston, and Andy Nice for their technical assistance in bringing this manuscript to completion. I also owe my wife, Rose Gatens, a debt of gratitude for her organizational and editing skills.

Nazi past and to the crimes committed by the National Socialist
government in the name of the German people.

West German textbooks have in the past been regularly criticized
for deficiencies in various aspects of the depiction of the origins and
history of the Third Reich. Many texts showed signs of repression,
guilt projection, minimization of Nazi crimes, apologetics, rational-
ization of wrongdoing, and sometimes even an apparent sympathy
with certain aspects of National Socialist philosophy or deeds. The
length and balance of treatment of these topics, however, have improved
in each decade since the war's end, and the most recent textbooks
treat the subject with great sensitivity and fairness to the victims of
Nazi aggression.

Though today's texts are by no means free of weaknesses, these
shortcomings are not so grave as those of the past. Many of the
worst deficiencies have been reduced or eliminated. This analysis will
present the strengths and the weaknesses perceived in contemporary
textbooks of West Germany, focussing where necessary on shortcomings, but with due regard also to exceptionally well-done subjects.
It is the author's hope that this study will contribute to the improvement
of future textbook editions in dealing with this sensitive and difficult
subject.

The weaknesses which remain in the contemporary textbook treatment of National Socialism and the Holocaust may be instructive to
other peoples to show the difficulties a society faces in its effort to
reeducate and resocialize its citizens toward the acceptance and
appreciation of others in a pluralistic society. These efforts and the
challenge they pose may be of value to other nations seeking to
discover a "usable past" which does not shrink from confronting the
darker and less palatable side of their people's own history.[1]

2
Textbooks: Development and Production

The Conditions of Textbook Production

Before examining the textbooks themselves, some remarks about textbook writing and production are in order, especially since in West Germany these processes are intimately connected and interdependent.

In 1982, Karl-Ernst Jeismann took note of the vital importance of examining "the conditions under which textbooks are produced and the actual constraints under which their authors live"[2] in order to understand how their contents are produced. The production of textbooks in West Germany involves authors, publishers, schools, and the state in complex processes of writing, editing, certifying, managing, marketing, and teaching techniques. Authors and publishers play a pivotal role in textbook production and have a strong mutual economic and educational interest in developing successful products. Publishers closely guard their relationship with authors, and seek to minimize outside influences in developing their materials. As the representative of the Task Force of German Schoolbook Publishers, Wolfram Schultze-Fieltz, stated at a conference on "The Jewish Problem in Historical Instruction," "The schoolbook publishers give assurance that they will undertake the solution of the problem with a great sense of responsibility, but publishers and authors must be left with a free hand, since any sort of regimentation is inappropriate."[3]

Regimentation would not be easily accepted by textbook authors, most of whom are pedagogical specialists, university professors, or secondary-school faculty working together as teams.[4] Such author-teams may produce a text on their own or in response to a publisher's initiative. In either case, they develop the concept of the book as a team, then divide the tasks of production between them; some members resolve didactical problems, while others concentrate on research, selection of content, writing, or editing. As the individual parts of the book are completed, they are tested by teachers in schools as the

5

manuscript is readied for the publisher.[5] When the manuscript is complete and all parts have been successfully tested, it is submitted to one of more than 80 textbook publishers in the Federal Republic.

The purchase of texts by the schools is supported for the most part by state tax allocations; the balance is financed by the personal purchases of texts by parents. Theoretically, the use of public funds to purchase textbooks should assure that their production is primarily in the public interest. Since book publishing is private enterprise, the publishers, of course, support the principle of letting the market decide what texts are to be offered.[6] But, just as obviously, the public obtains only texts that are profitable to produce. Although state-published textbooks—such as these sold in the Socialist countries— would cost about 50 percent less, polls of West German teachers indicate that the majority prefer privately published teaching materials. Among other things, they believe that private publication facilitates the process of textbook correction.

Publishers negotiate with education administrators, educators, and various other public officials through two lobbying and public relations management associations: the *Verband der Schulbuchverlage* (*Association of Schoolbook Publishers*) and the *Institut für Bildungsmedien* (*the Institute for Educational Media*), both of whose task it is to defend the interests of the publishers against their critics.[7] The most powerful institution they must deal with is the government itself.

The Influence of the State in Textbook Production

At the primary and secondary school levels, the selection of history, social science and social studies textbooks is decisively influenced by the *Kultusministerien* (Permanent Conference of the Ministries of Education). The *Kultusministerien* is composed of representatives from each of the eleven German states (*Länder* and Berlin), and acts as the highest level of federal authority. Although the recommendations of the *Kultusministerium* are not binding on the individual states, most states accept their general recommendations. These, in turn, have had a unifying influence on textbooks and curricula in West Germany.

Below the Permanent Conference, the individual State Ministers of Education are charged with responsibility for the political education of German youth, and play a significant role in shaping the textbook treatment of subjects.[8] The individual State Ministries closely follow the recommendations of the Permanent Conference of the Ministries of Education. The State Ministries issue general guidelines on subjects to be included in teaching. Though the Constitution prohibits the state from prescribing specific teaching content, State guideline recommendations may suggest how subjects are to be handled as well as the emphasis to be placed on certain areas of the subject. Guidelines are often brief, stating only general aims and goals of instruction without entering into specifics. However, this does not diminish their considerable influence in structuring the treatment of subjects; indeed, authors and publishers consider the State guidelines to be a decisive standard which must be followed carefully if they are to obtain state authorization of their textbooks.

Publishers must submit for approval all schoolbook proposals to the state Ministries of Education before they may be accepted for general classroom use. Individual states require from four months to sometimes two or more years to process requests for textbook authorization.[9] One of the criteria for authorization is that the text correspond in content with the individual guidelines and curriculum plans of the ten states of Germany and Berlin, which also structure the teaching in the schools. Each year the ministries send newly updated lists of approved textbooks to the schools, from which teachers select the school books for their classes.[10]

The State and the Textbook Depiction of the Holocaust

The ministries have carried on a long struggle since the late 1950s to assure that textbooks treat adequately the Nazi persecution of the Jews and the Holocaust. In the early postwar period, they were hindered by national suppression of the past in Germany, by the lack of a didactical model for handling such sensitive material, and by a generally conservative social and political system which only gradually gave way to democratic attitudes and a wholehearted condemnation of the Nazi era and all its works. Over the years, the ministries have intervened frequently, issuing curriculum guidelines which call for a more intensive handling of the Third Reich, and especially of the Nazi terror, concentration camps, and the Holocaust. Though they have acted often in the wake of renewed outbreaks of neo-Nazi activity,[11] gradually they have taken the lead in assuring that textbooks include the treatment of even the most brutal elements of the Nazi dictatorship and terror which make condemnation of the Third Reich clear and unequivocal.

Until the 1950s, little had been done to ensure the discussion of Jews, anti-Semitism and the Nazi "Final Solution" in textbooks.[12] The earliest textbook conference, with the theme "The Jewish Problem [sic] in Historical Writing," was conducted in 1954 in Düsseldorf. Educators and publishers discussed questions of content, methodology, and treatment of the Jews in history textbooks.[13] Though all participants expressed a special commitment to the subject, changes came slowly in the textbooks and often seemed to wait for state guidelines to take the lead. As late as 1956 there was still no mention of the destruction of the European Jews in the guidelines of some leading German states.[14]

In 1957 and 1958, a rise in the frequency of anti-Semitic incidents led Chancellor Konrad Adenauer, at the urging of German resistance organizations and groups of victims of Nazism, to petition ministries to increase their efforts to assure that "special attention be devoted to historical instruction in the recent past."[15] By 1959 other voices were raised. The Interior Minister of North-Rhine Westphalia recalled to that state's legislators that in the name of the German people millions of Jews had been murdered through National Socialism, and declared, with the lively support of the representatives, "We may not allow our conscience to rest comfortably in relation to this gruesome history. We owe it to the victims of the past, to the survivors, and to ourselves to confront the unmastered past. The home, the school, the church and the state are all being addressed here with equal seriousness."[16] But there were also in the Federal Republic many who had not broken with the past, and for whom such attestations were "deemed to be the private matter of a few politicians as a more or less necessary evil, [so as] above all not to displease the Americans."[17]

In 1959, responding to increased incidents of anti-Semitic outbreaks in Germany, the Permanent Conference and the respective state Ministries of Education issued guidelines calling for the treatment of the Jews in two areas: ancient Israel and the persecution of the Jews under Nazism.[18] Before these directives could be implemented, however, a wave of anti-Semitic attacks took place in late 1959 and early 1960. Swastikas and grafitti were painted on the Jewish synagogue in Köln and on gravestones in Jewish cemeteries throughout West Germany. A number of the culprits were caught and were found to be youths. This called attention to anti-Semitic attitudes among German school children, to their profound ignorance of the fate of the Jews in Nazi Germany, and the lack of adequate treatment of these subjects in German textbooks.

Although the *Deutsche Ausschuss für das Erziehungs- und Bildungswesen* (Committee of the German Education System) published a declaration "On the Occasion of the Anti-Semitic Excesses,"[19] which absolved the State Ministers of Education of neglect in political education, worldwide indignation alarmed the German government, and the State Ministers were called upon to renew their efforts and to devote more attention to these matters.

Since the events of 1959–60 the Permanent Conference of the State Ministries of Education and Cultural Affairs has regularly issued directives concerning the treatment of National Socialism in the educational system. These directives have strongly influenced the handling of the persecution of the Jews in German textbooks. In February 1960, the Permanent Conference instructed that Nazism be scrutinized in depth at the highest grade of all schools.[20] In a resolution of July 1962, they issued "Guidelines for the Treatment of Totalitarianism in Classroom Teaching," specifying, among other things, that the Nazi system of terror, "including extermination of Jews and destruction of 'worthless lives,'" be treated.[21]

In July 1962, the Ministers supplemented their instructions with a set of "Recommendations for the Preparation of Textbooks for Instruction in Recent and Contemporary History." This guideline placed considerable added emphasis on the period since 1917, and admonished that a "mere exposition of facts and correlations will not suffice." Additionally, they intended that

> Germany's present political situation and the causes thereof must be made clear. Without an in-depth coming to grips with Nazism, political education is impossible in Germany. Furthermore, in dealing with wars in history, descriptions of military events are to be subordinated . . . and the sufferings of the nations involved are to be particularly stressed.[22]

By the 1970s the curriculum guidelines of all German States required that the German Jews, Judaism, and the Holocaust be treated and textbook authors increasingly used the format of these guidelines to outline their textbook treatment.[23]

In 1978, the State Ministries of Education extended their initiative, calling for nationwide anti-Fascist commemorative ceremonies. On the suggestion of the State Committee for Schools, they recommended that the fortieth anniversary of the 1938 German pogrom against the Jews, called "Reich Crystal Night" by the Nazis, be commemorated in a manner consistent with its meaning. The *Bundeszentrale für politische Bildung* (The Federal Center for Political Education) was asked to prepare appropriate materials. The Ministries on this occasion again pointed to the need for mounting an "active opposition to uncritical acceptance or presentations which even glorify the Third Reich, characterized as it was by dictatorship, genocide and inhumanity" and called upon the schools to treat this theme with "particular intensity."[24]

State Guidelines for the Treatment of
the Third Reich and the Jews

The individual German state guideines follow and elaborate the directives of the *Kultusministerium,* so it will be of interest to examine a sampling of the state guidelines which treat the Third Reich and the Jews. Lower Saxony's guidelines are considered a model of excellence for treatment of National Socialism and Fascism at the *Gymnasium* (high school) level. They are one of the few to connect the Nazi past with the possibility of present Fascist threats in German society. As formulated in its introduction,

> The state and society of the Federal Republic of Germany developed after the collapse of the National Socialist Fascistic state system and have carried out a conscious turning away from the past, [and] not merely in their Constitution. However, the continuing power of the earlier dominant political, social and ideological tendencies is greater than frequently presumed, for every present is co-determined by the past. Herein lies the justification for the treatment of this theme in instruction. The decisive question is whether today the danger of a revival of Fascism still exists.[25]

The Lower Saxony guidelines include strong support for teaching about resistance to National Socialism and the study of totalitarianism. The Ministry wrote:

> The attitude which the men and women of the resistance displayed under totalitarianism is to be honored as exemplary in lessons and school celebrations. Instruction should awaken in young people the desire to participate in a responsible manner in the shaping of a democratic and lawful order and to contribute to the rejection of totalitarianism. Success—especially in the treatment of National Socialism—depends above all on the openness of the encounter between teacher and student.[26]

Many textbooks include the treatment of certain aspects of resistance, but at the end of 1980 the Permanent Conference of Ministries, at the suggestion of the Federal Ministers of Justice, issued another resolution to emphasize the need for stronger treatment of the resistance.

While the recommendations of the Permanent Conference of Ministers tend to unify state curriculum plans, there are, nevertheless, major differences between various state guidelines and even to some extent within States. In a study of the curriculum plans of five states,

Marhild Hoffmann[27] found a number of interesting variations and peculiarities. In Berlin, for example, equal space is devoted in the curriculum plan to the "Problem of Reparation to the Jews" and "The Resistance Movement and Jewish Policies." The plan includes different concepts subsumed under common headings: "The Right of Resistance—Anti-Semitism—Unconditional Surrender." Still other curriculum plans betray glaring anti-Communism in the directives for treating Nazi ideology, with the virtual twinning of Communism and Nazism under the rubric of totalitarianism. For example, the curriculum plan of North Rhine Westphalia emphasizes the Nazi-Soviet "alliance" during the first two years of World War II: "Hitler's foreign policy—conquest of Europe by Hitler—Germany in alliance with the Soviet Union (1939–1941)."[28]

Some curriculum plans are quite sketchy as, for example, the Lower Saxony guidelines for tenth grade, where educators are given only the following schemata:

a. the origins of the authoritarian and fascist systems,
b. the totalitarian system of domination of National Socialism in Germany and Europe,
c. the Second World War in Europe and Asia.[29]

Because the German constitution prohibits prescribing specific school content, state education ministers often write curriculum plans in the form of learning goals and qualifications of various levels. However, since some learning qualifications are recognized as being very close to content directives, they are frequently offered as suggestions.

There is also a wide variation in the learning goals for treating the Third Reich, including cases where none are stated. For example, the North Rhine Westphalia guidelines contain no learning goals for the ninth and tenth grades—when National Socialism is taught—even though learning goals are discussed in the introductory section. Where learning goals exist, they may be very general and sweeping, as those of Berlin, for instance, which require that students attain "insight into the juxtaposition of continuity and discontinuity in political culture and socio-economic structure from Wilhelmine Germany through the Weimar Republic to the Third Reich."[30]

Most learning goals for National Socialism are more cognitive than value oriented. Despite the German commitment to "education for democracy," curriculum plans rarely refer to values or attitudes to be fostered. In the same manner, few connections are made between the historical past and contemporary issues. While comparisons with present day events occasionally appear in curriculum plans for the periods before 1919, few allusions to the present are made in any topics—including National Socialism—after 1919. For example, in outlining the theme "Historical Basis of Modern Democracy" in the *Lower Saxony Guidelines for Eleventh Graders,* no reference is made to democratic developments in Germany since 1919.

One result of these guideline generalizations is that German textbooks treat the Nazi era overwhelmingly as a closed event, with no legacy in the present. It is, of course, preposterous to write as if there were no relationship between the Nazi past and the postwar era. As Hoffmann points out, historical references which compare the past with the present show students the relationship of history to contemporary life, and liberate the student from presentist views. Teaching historical continuities makes the present more meaningful by its relation to the past, and the past more comprehensible by its comparison with the present. As the guidelines of Lower Saxony put it: "Every present becomes history and every historical appearance is conditioned respectively by its past and the present."[31] Indeed, the Lower Saxony guidelines suggest that a unit be taught about the possibilities and circumstances which might lead to a revival of fascism in Europe. However, this is a recent development and the exception to the rule; thus far, only a few new texts have followed this suggestion.

If only a few guidelines recommend that connections be made between the National Socialist past and present-day Germany, the same is true of guidelines for handling contemporary Germany. In outlining the coverage of the Federal Republic, guidelines rarely refer to the Third Reich. When questions are raised about present threats in the Federal Republic, neo-Nazism is not mentioned as an example, if any dangers are stated at all.[32] Again, an exception may be found in the Berlin guidelines for social sciences in the *Gymnasium* or college preparatory secondary schools, where the threat of totalitarianism arising within a democratic society is described, referring to the defeat of the Weimar Republic by the National Socialists.

Criticism of the Educational Role of the State

The extensive powers of the government in educational affairs have not gone unnoticed by educators. As Marhild Hoffmann wrote, "the use of guidelines and lesson plans set up by state decree is a political act,"[33] and in carrying out its mission the Permanent Conference of State Ministers imposes the political priorities of the state on its educational institutions. Even though the Permanent Conference has taken strong initiatives to improve and elaborate the treatment of

National Socialism, many educators object on principle to the role of the state in influencing instructional content.[34]

Dr. Frank Hennecke, in his *Staat und Unterricht: Die Festlegung didaktische Inhalt durch den Staat im öffentlichen Schulwesen* (State and Instruction: The Determination of Didactical Content by the State in the Public School System),[35] harshly criticized the state's role in approving educational content. While his concern in this instance is the ideologically lopsided treatment of the Soviet Union, his condemnation is a general one: "There is an obvious, far-reaching danger arising from policies in which the function of educational-content is placed in the service of the state."[36] This criticism is echoed by Eckehardt Stein,[37] who argues that state institutions should not be the final judge over curricular matters. Gerd Stein warns as well that the state "becomes a danger to educational freedom if the cultural possessions of humankind are transmitted (selectively and tendentially) to the youth of a state only in accordance with what the *Kultusministerium* considers best."[38]

In the light of Nazi *Gleichschaltung* of education during the Third Reich, such concerns are understandable. However, government control over education preceded the Nazi era. In both the Wilhelmine Reich and the Weimar Republic the state had the authority to examine and certify textbooks for classroom use.[39] Moreover, while the issuance of guidelines and curriculum plans in the Federal Republic may be perceived as onerous, it is still a looser form of control than is exercised in the German Democratic Republic, where the State approves only one text in each subject for each grade level.

After the Federal Republic has issued what it regards as appropriate curriculum guidelines, expert evaluators are appointed to examine manuscripts from publishers. The State certifies these textbook appraisers, who use State guidelines as their yardstick. "With cavilling meticulousness," declares Horst Gies, "experts determine everything which has not been taken into consideration, without considering that particular cuts and editing which have occurred are caused by [limitations set by] authorization authorities themselves (length of text, price)."[40]

Because of space limitations and other state specifications, Margarete Dörr has concluded that the texts can scarcely be better than the curriculum guidelines which govern their production: "Any criticism which faults only the selection of materials can be a useful contribution to the development of curriculum, but it applies only indirectly to the textbook."[41]

Such criticisms reflect the tension arising from state intervention, particularly in subjects where political education is involved. Intervention by means of state guidelines applies increasingly to politically relevant subjects such as social science, history and German instruction. "In all three sectors," wrote Alfred Baumgartner, "for years attempts at reforms have collided—one can scarcely characterize it otherwise— with a virtual wall of suspicion of manipulation."[42] Critics accuse state authorities of being fearful that political education might alienate students from their present society.

The tension between education reformers and government administrators has dampened the spirits of innovative textbook writers. Publishers usually defer to state authorities, because the government is strong and publishers seek to remain on good terms with the education ministries to keep textbook authorizations. Privately, however, they complain bitterly. The contents of a few textbooks approved in the 1970s were later declared by the *Kultusministerium* to have been against the German constitution and revoked by some ministries, costing publishers and authors considerable profit.[43] There is always the fear among publishers that a text may be rejected in one or more of the states. "There exists for the products of schoolbook publishers only 11 customers, and the loss of any one of them would truly be a calamity."[44] There have been cases in which only six of the states authorized a text and the other five rejected it.[45] There also have been cases in which heavy criticism of a textbook has led to the loss of authorization. A history textbook from Germany's largest textbook publisher, Klett Verlag, was removed from the roster of authorized textbooks in two states following a strong attack by a French journalist in a Berlin newspaper.[46]

The sometimes long and difficult process of obtaining state authorization for textbooks has led to criticism not only by schoolbook publishers, but also by strong faculty organizations such as the *Gewerkschaft Erziehung und Wissenschaft* (Union of Education and Science), which has protested that in some states, such as Rhineland-Pfalz and the Saarland, books are required to undergo two authorization processes, one by the federal Permanent Conference of Ministers of Education and a second by the state ministries.[47]

In order to challenge the tradition of mere dissemination of facts, some authors have written innovative textbooks which incorporate the latest pedagogical techniques and scientific knowledge. But such progressive treatments are not very often reflected in the guidelines and can actually work against authorization by traditionally minded state administrations. Problems rapidly arise in situations where the advance of scientific knowledge and school reforms accelerates the rate of school development to such a degree that the administration of the *Kultusministerium*—having necessarily a slow apparatus—cannot keep up.[48]

The consequences of the tension between textbook producer and state authority, as Thomas Berger has said, is "a sport without winners, because a school book which survives the hurdles of internal publisher censorship and the 11 state ministry authorization authorities will be printed so long as there is a market—regardless of the correctness of its contents."[49]

Agencies and Institutions Supporting Textbook Education

In addition to the *Kultusministerium*, a dense network of related agencies supports the task of education, including, as part of their overall responsibility, the teaching of the Third Reich and the Holocaust. In the sphere of political education, the *Bundeszentrale für Heimatdienst* (Federal Center for Domestic Service) publishes and disseminates political information on a broad range of topics, including studies on Holocaust instruction. The *Institut für Zeitgeschichte* (Institute for Contemporary History), in Munich, a federally supported agency, is the nation's most prestigious research center for National Socialism, and has carried out numerous studies on the Third Reich, including studies on various aspects of the Holocaust. These have served over time to strengthen textbook accounts of the Jewish tragedy under the Nazi dictatorship. In addition, the *Deutsche Ausschuß für das Erziehungs- und Bildungswesen* (German Committee for the Educational System) for many years was the highest advisory body to the State Education Ministries. From 1953 to 1965 it was highly influential in the education policies of the state ministries especially as these dealt with political education in the schools. Its 1955 *Report on Political Education* shows that the Committee was still wrestling with the attitude it would adopt toward the Nazi past:

> We have not yet succeeded in establishing the relationship of our present situation to German history. Among broad sections of people, in particular, no consensus has yet been achieved in the evaluation of National Socialism and the Resistance. [Further], the lack of clarity in the constellation of international politics makes sketching out any vision of our political future more difficult.

The report concludes, however, that such uncertainties should "not be allowed to serve as excuses."[50]

Consensus on the interpretation of National Socialism has never been easily achieved, but several periodicals, such as *Geschichte in*

Wissenschaft und Unterricht (History in Research and Instruction), *Blickpunkt Schulbuch* (Viewpoint Schoolbook), and *Internationale Schulbuchforschung* (International Schoolbook Research), the periodical of the *Georg-Eckert-Institut*, play important roles in disseminating the main trends of historical theory and interpretation which later find reflection in West German history, political science, and social studies textbooks. Equally influential are such institutions as the *Georg-Eckert Institut für internationale Schulbuchforschung* (George Eckert Institute for International Schoolbook Research), the State Education Ministries, the *Landesverbände* (State History Association), and German universities, which cooperate on various long-range projects relating to the way textbooks deal with various aspects of the Third Reich.

The *Geschichtslehrerverband* (Organization of History Teachers) is also important in the structure of history textbooks, and many schoolbook authors are counted among its members. The Organization reviews and analyzes many texts and curriculum plans in its publications.[51] The *Geschichtslehrerverband*, in turn, cooperates with the *Historikerverband* (Historians' Association), in part through comembership of many of their leading professionals, which serves to homogenize some aspects of political education in the textbooks. The effect of these bodies has been to ensure that political presentations in textbooks support democracy and capitalism and condemn totalitarianism and Soviet communism.

The *Institut für Bildungsmedien* (Institute for Educational Media) based in Frankfurt, and the prestigious *Max-Planck-Institut für Bildungsforschung* (Max Planck Institute for Educational Research) in Berlin, also conduct important textbook projects focussing on various aspects of National Socialism, and during the past decade have been increasingly active in this sphere of education research.

Many German academic conferences have also included sessions on National Socialism, but until the 1980s relatively few were devoted to the Holocaust. In 1983, Dieter Vogel, the director of a private firm in Frankenthal, the *Pegulan-Werke* near Mannheim, held a highly successful symposium on the Holocaust;[52] and in May 1984, a major conference was convened in Stuttgart to discuss the theme "The Genocide of the European Jews During the Second World War." The Stuttgart conference featured international speakers dealing with the question of Hitler's order for the Holocaust and his degree of involvement in the genocide. Such conferences have had an indirect influence on textbooks over time, especially as new areas of research are publicized and new findings or interpretations are made known.

The Georg-Eckert-Institut für internationale Schulbuchforschung

Of special importance in reducing distortions found in instructional materials and in revising textbooks is the prestigious *Georg-Eckert-Institut für internationale Schulbuchforschung* (The Georg Eckert Institute for International Schoolbook Research) located in Braunschweig. Founded in 1954 by Dr. Georg Eckert, it concentrated first on history textbook studies; it has slowly expanded to incorporate other subjects. Renamed after its founder in 1975, it has become a comprehensive international schoolbook institute, equipped with the largest schoolbook library in the world. It is financially supported in part by the Volkswagen Foundation and seven states. Its task is textbook research and convening international conferences aimed at improving schoolbooks around the world.[53]

Its investigations and conferences focus particularly on texts with political content—history, political science, geography, and social science—and its considerable work has gradually come to be known throughout the world of education.

Because teachers are rarely specialists in any single period of history, they cannot readily evaluate the quality of textbooks as a whole. The *Georg-Eckert-Institut* specializes in convening educators, pedagogues, social scientists, and textbook authors to examine schoolbooks and curriculum plans with respect to their goals and conditions of origin, in order to understand the circumstances in which textbooks are created and to make suggestions for their improvement. By the 1980s it had conducted hundreds of international educators' conferences to improve textbooks from all over the world.[54]

Many aspects of National Socialism, including the Holocaust, have been treated in the conferences and investigations of the Institute. As the Director of the *Georg-Eckert-Institut*, Karl-Ernst Jeismann, declared, "instruction is challenged to leave the ghettos of national prejudices and distortions,"[55] and "to transmit a provocative impulse to the pedagogical as well as the political realm."[56] With the development of new analyses in the area of fascist ideology, the Institute periodically has reviewed the coverage of National Socialism in textbooks and made numerous recommendations to school authorities and publishers for its improvement.

The Holocaust is viewed as a particularly challenging and difficult subject. Dr. Jeismann quotes Elie Wiesel's famous dictum: "The question of questions that we faced then and shall face forever is: What does one do with such knowledge?"[57]

While the *Georg-Eckert-Institut* has not taken the lead in analysis of the textbook presentations of the Jews and the Holocaust, on an international level the Institute has called attention to problems of national attitudes and distortions which arise in textbooks because of inequitable coverage of various periods of history. Its director has recognized that "basic questions of international schoolbook research are posed by the specially emphasized and sensitive example of the Holocaust."[58]

Thus, for example, the Institute has revealed that the treatment of contemporary Germany is distorted in French and U.S. textbooks by the fact that the Weimar era is edited to play the role primarily of preparation for the Hitler era. In these texts, German history reaches a climax in the National Socialist era, which is the last period treated in detail. The whole postwar history of the Federal Republic of Germany, from its founding in 1948 to the present, is hardly treated in a systematic manner.[59] Thus, the aim of the Institute will be to establish greater balance in the treatment of the epochs of German history, instead of treating the National Socialist period as the pinnacle of coverage at the expense of other periods. At the same time, it recognizes the significance of an understanding of the Nazi era and its central place in the textbooks.

The Institute cooperates with various state and federal ministries[60] and makes its recommendations to them; in turn, the authors of the state guidelines place considerable emphasis on the recommendations of the Institute.[61] There are many who would like to see the Institute give greater weight to its recommendations and exercise a more direct effect on textbooks by mandating the submission of texts for its scrutiny.[62] However, its leadership rejects any such direct influence on schoolbooks. Dr. Jeismann prefers the voluntarism of an "autonomous adapting to and adoption of recommendations by the authors of guidelines and textbooks."[63] The gradual revision of textbooks to reduce nationalistic, chauvinistic, revanchist, racist, and ethnic prejudices is understood as necessarily a voluntary process—especially internationally—as well as an ongoing one, since new directions in research, new knowledge, and new historical circumstances change awareness and sensitivity, resulting in new evaluations of the past.[64] In short, as Dr. Jeismann notes,

> Prejudices and mistakes, stereotypes and distortions, the placing of accents and meanings [in textbooks] are not simple errors which will be replaced with a pure truth, thereby simply eliminating these errors.

They are themselves the integral ingredients of perceptions and meanings, constantly in motion, emerging ever anew and in ever-changing form. . . . We will have to accept that new understanding and insight, as it corrects old errors, will itself fashion new errors, one-sidedness and distortions.[65]

3
Textbooks: Treatment of the Holocaust and Related Themes

General Criticisms of Textbooks

Schoolbook critics fault publishers and authors especially in the selection of materials, the brevity of treatment, omissions, and superficiality. Space restrictions, based on the inevitable necessity of selection and exclusion, may account for some deficiencies. As one text author, seeking to explain the omission of Jewish thematic materials in her textbook, plaintively wrote: "Unfortunately, many questions of a political, sociological, cultural, historical and ethnological nature dealing with Judaism have had to be excluded. Hopefully, they will receive attention in other school subjects or courses."[66] But while space limitation is a genuine problem, there are also cases of poor judgment in the allocation of space.

There is inadequate liaison between university professors and schoolbook authors. The need for greater cooperation between the scholarly and textbook world is apparent when one considers that annually there are more than 3,000 publications in the area of the Third Reich and World War II.[67] Textbook authors can be expected to keep abreast of only a fraction of the most important historical literature. Though recent texts reflect major trends in German historical and didactical research, all are far more sensitive to the directives of state guidelines than to new directions of historical scholarship. This prefiguration of texts by state guidelines is most evident in the similarity in content of many textbooks in treating the Nazi era and the persecution of Jews.

An array of related political, economic, and social forces act upon textbook authors when they write about the Third Reich: the standard of their research, pedagogical and didactical considerations, the needs of publishers, the state guidelines, the wishes of classroom teachers, and the desires of society as expressed by parents, colleagues, students, the media, and other interest groups.

In view of all this, it is important to emphasize the degree of consensus among educators that the Holocaust must be taught, because of the need to overcome past injustice and tragedy and to carry out a special commitment to the Jewish people.

The Sense of Obligation Toward the Jews

Many German educators have attested the sense of moral obligation they feel toward the Jewish people. Alfred Schickel characterizes the "more than six million dead of Auschwitz, Treblinka, Buchenwald and the other National Socialist annihilation camps" as "constituting the heaviest of moral debts."[68] Romano Guardini, a distinguished German educator, addressed the German people soon after the war on the attitude they would take toward the crimes of their government and of fellow Germans. In terms reminiscent of *Volksgemeinschaft* (National Community), he reminded Germans that they were members of a family community gone astray:

> When a member of my family has committed an injustice, I may say: I am not guilty of this, but I may not say that this is not my concern. I am guilty only of that which I myself do or fail to do, but I am concerned with everything which the members of my family do. For, I exist as a part of them and their honor is—in partial measure—my honor. If the family thrives, as a matter of course I share their good fortune. . . . Thus, must I also share responsibility for injustice which takes place within the family; otherwise, I am a parasite. I must from deep within come to terms with this [responsibility], and do whatever I possibly can to make it right again.[69]

Dietrich Goldschmidt saw in the struggle of the Jews "necessarily the common struggle of the Germans"; the price of German freedom, he said, was Jewish freedom: "When we become aware of the danger [and] feel the disgrace of our unwilling co-responsibility with the anti-Semites which has turned all of us into hangmen, perhaps then we will realize that we must fight for the Jews no less than we would fight for ourselves."[70]

The German educator Walter Hofmann saw in loyalty to the Jewish people no more than loyalty to Germany's own sense of humanity: "Nothing humane is alien to me: We are able to understand the works of the most distant times and peoples. Humanity is a normative concept which . . . requires full human respect be accorded to every other person."[71]

A similar vision of the German relation to the Jews is stated by the religious educator Heinz Kremers, who believes the Germans owe "spiritual restitution" (*geistliche Wiedergutmachung*)[72] to the Jews; the German duty to remember what happened is simply the fundamental "obligation of the living to the dead."[73]

The sense of obligation to treat the tragedy of German Jews is shared by virtually all German educators. The attitude of textbook authors toward this subject is an emphatic condemnation of the genocide and of the perpetrators; an unequivocable condemnation of fascism, and an attitude of sympathy toward the Jewish victims. This does not mean that texts are thereby free of distortion, defective phrasing of specific points, or noteworthy omissions in depicting the Holocaust; it means, simply, that the deficiencies to be found in the treatment of the Jews and the Holocaust are less in evidence than the positive features. The focus on critical aspects of the textbook treatments sometimes may tend to obscure this fact.

Scope of the Study

The textbooks depicting the Holocaust—the persecution and genocide of the European Jews under National Socialism—primarily deal with political education: history, social studies, and civics at the secondary-school level. There are a large number of such textbooks in the free-market-oriented Federal Republic of Germany; the government does not authorize a single, state-approved text in each subject. At the same time, the state exercises general control by requiring authorization by state educational authority of all reading materials for school use.

The handling of education materials at the university level, on the other hand, is more complex. German universities do not have the equivalent of the American "course textbook" for subjects in history and politics, and no state authorization is required for education materials. German university professors assemble bibliographies of scholarly works choosing freely from the available literature to assign to students. In courses dealing with National Socialist ideology and the Third Reich, professors assign reading materials from a variety of primary and secondary sources in a number of languages. A survey of the scholarship used for the study of the Holocaust in the university setting would involve the whole range of postwar scholarship on the subject. Such a comprehensive study, even of German language Holocaust scholarship, would have to consider such factors as the wide variety of courses which include the Holocaust (history, political science, sociology, theology and others), the diverse scholarly works assigned in these sources, the variety of course offerings at the 51 German universities, the longevity of these courses in the curriculum (some last no more than two or three years), and the frequency of such course offerings in the curriculum.

Such a comprehensive undertaking, while never before undertaken in the Federal Republic, would be of value. No conclusions, however, may be drawn about university treatment of the Holocaust in the limited space of this study. A survey of university catalogs does indicate a remarkable number of offerings—98 courses—dealing directly with anti-Semitism or the Holocaust. In all, about 360 university courses treat some aspect of Jewish history, anti-Semitism, persecution, or the Holocaust. Such an array of offerings constitutes something of an explosion in the number of higher education courses dealing with aspects of Nazi Germany. In 1979, the Director of the *Institut für Zeitgeschichte*, Martin Broszat, surveyed about half of the German universities for the period 1970–1978. He described the findings as "astonishingly positive" in the *Vierteljahreshefte für Zeitgeschichte* (Quarterly for Contemporary History).[74] In the nine years included in the survey, more than 650 courses, practica, and seminars were offered on German history of the National Socialist era. Most of these courses were taught in Germany's larger universities: Berlin (75), Hamburg (61), Frankfurt (60), while some smaller universities offered a higher than average number of courses in this area, such as Mainz (59), Tübingen (40), Freiburg (36), Bonn (35), Göttingen (34) and Marburg (31). Of the 650 courses treating the Nazi era, 46 dealt with the subject of Resistance and Persecution in the Third Reich; 22 courses examined the history of anti-Semitism and German and non-German Judaism in the nineteenth and twentieth centuries; 6 treated the subject of National Socialist racial theory or its ideological predecessors; and two dealt entirely with "Jewish History during the Second World War" and "The National Socialist Policy of the Final Solution." Broszat's conclusion about university course offerings is that: "The 'Final Solution of the Jewish Question' is by no means left out, but treated overwhelmingly in the context of general presentations of the history of the Third Reich, that is, for the most part, it is treated with relative brevity and only rarely is it the subject of a detailed examination."[75]

In the secondary schools of Germany young Germans usually make their first encounter with the Third Reich in history courses required of students between the eighth and tenth grades. Texts used in these courses constitute the primary educational instruction from which students are to obtain an early understanding of the Holocaust and related subjects. In these texts, students study Nazi Germany and World War II as a part of the history of modern Europe since the eighteenth century. This is the only general requirement course on this subject which *all* students must take. In addition, many students may enroll in advanced-level history, social studies, and political science courses, though these courses are offered primarily as electives (*Leistungskurz*). In such courses the themes are treated within the context of the methodologies and learning goals of social science, political science, or historical science. Though not all students take these courses, the textbooks used in them are included in this study, since they add to the understanding of what West Germans teach about anti-Semitism, the persecution of the Jews, and the Holocaust in the German education system.

This study analyzes what German students learn in their texts about the origins of anti-Semitism, the Nazi persecutions and the Holocaust. A total of 49 textbooks have been examined, 27 of them at the intermediate history level, and 22 at the advanced level of history, social studies, and political science. An additional 10 teacher manuals and supplementary workbooks were examined.

When possible, the texts and supplementary sources have been allowed to speak for themselves. To simplify citation of sources, the full citation is stated the first time it is used. In all subsequent citations of materials, the author(s) or editor(s) name(s) will be used to identify the education book cited. A list of the textbooks, readers, workbooks, and teacher manuals examined in this study may be found in Appendix I. They comprise the texts, supplementary reading, and teaching aids in use in more than 95 percent of the West German schools, and may be viewed as representative of the standard school presentation of the subject in the late 1970s to the mid-1980s.

Motives and Background of Anti-Semitism

In his teacher manual, Wolfgang Hug asks the challenging question, "Auschwitz: How is this outbreak of barbarism in the Europe of the twentieth century to be explained?"[76] Textbook answers to this question often take the form of descriptions of nineteenth- and early-twentieth-century racial and political anti-Semitism. This emphasis on the modern antecedents of Nazi racial ideology offers a necessary background explanation of Nazi racial anti-Semitism. However, the long-term origins of anti-Semitism are rooted in a centuries-long tradition of religious and economic competition, envy, and intolerance toward the European Jews.

To adequately understand modern forms of anti-Semitism, it is necessary to study this tradition. However, it receives only brief treatment in many of the textbooks. Moreover, such material as is found in texts is primarily descriptive and often merely transmits to students the libels and stereotypes of anti-Semitic canon. In almost all textbooks, the problem is compounded by the absence of even a summary history of the Jewish people in Europe. Indeed, Nazi anti-Semitic persecutions and the Holocaust must appear to students as incomprehensible and adventitious historical eruptions if textbooks do not adequately analyze the religious and economic roots of prejudice which fed National Socialist racial anti-Semitism. Many Nazi anti-Semitic symbols, practices, and forms can only be understood with knowledge of the religious and economic attitudes which sustained National Socialist prejudices against the Jews.

The pattern of textbook analysis of anti-Semitism, usually takes the following form: (1) a brief mention of religious anti-Semitism; (2) an abbreviated treatment of economic anti-Semitism; (3) a relatively detailed description of racial anti-Semitism; (4) a partial analysis of the functions which anti-Semitism serves for political groups and individuals.

These topics will be analyzed below.

The Religious Roots of Anti-Semitism

In treating the origins of modern anti-Semitism, the large majority of intermediate-level history texts and workbooks (Secondary I level) do not discuss its longevity or roots in Christianity. Those which mention the duration of anti-Semitism root it in Roman times,[77] or, Otto Boeck's *Damals und heute* (Then and Today), mention simply that the defamation of Jews preceded the National Socialist seizure of power.[78] Hans Döhn, in *Erdkunden und erkennen* (Earth Studies and Understanding), in fact, introduces anti-Semitism as "a core point of the National Socialist program," without presenting any historical background.[79] The text by Joachim Hoffmann disposes of the problem by assigning students the task of looking up an encyclopedia account of how anti-Semitism has been manifested in the past. Hans Muggenthaler's *Geschichte für Realschulen* (History for Secondary School) refers to the duration of anti-Semitism in a manner which especially reveals the problems of omitting its origins. He comments that "In this matter it was by no means a new phenomenon. Since the expulsion of the Jews from their homeland and the minority status which they took on in foreign states, there have been repeated anti-Semitic movements."[80] Without treatment of the history of anti-Semitism, such statements may lead the student to believe that, if so many outbreaks of hostility against the Jews have occurred, they must somehow have been justified.

The enduring religious tradition of anti-Semitism does not receive much space in the 27 textbooks used in the German intermediate schools. Only a half dozen mention it, usually in combination with economic opposition to the Jews.

Joachim Hoffmann's *Spiegel der Zeiten* (Mirror of the Times), Wolfgang Hug's *Geschichtliche Weltkunde* (Historical World Study) and Hans Heumann's *Unser Weg Durch die Geschichte* (Our Path through History) mention Christian anti-Semitism only incidentally. Schmid states additionally that Jews in the Middle Ages were deemed an alien body and charged by the Christian Church with the sacrifical death of Christ.[81] Helmut Kistler and Werner Stroppe in *Harms Arbeitsmappen Geschichte* (Harm's Workbook of History) note that religious differences were one of the main reasons for opposition between Christianity and Judaism, and that the Jews were accused of "murdering Christ."[82] Nowhere is the deicide libel countered or criticized.

Friedrich Lucas, in his sensitive text, *Menschen in ihrer Zeit. In unserer Zeit* (People in Their Era: Our Era), actually presents cases of Christian, Good Friday "Jew hunting"—while noting Church disapproval—and points to the economic circumstance that, "with the emancipation of the Jews in the nineteenth century, Jews, Catholics and Protestants first encountered one another in daily competition."[83]

Another text touches upon the fateful connection between anti-Semitism and Christian belief. Eduard Steinbügl's *Geschichte. Neueste Zeit* (Contemporary History), cites Hitler's allusion in *Mein Kampf:* "I believe I act in the spirit of the almighty creator when I defend myself against the Jews. I am fighting for the work of the Lord."[84] The author makes no comment, however, on the relationship between Christian historical anti-Semitism and Hitler's anti-Semitic ideas.

The advanced history, political science, and social studies texts omit mention of the long-standing duration of anti-Semitism. Christian roots of anti-Semitism are alluded to in only four texts, two of which merely gloss over religious anti-Semitism; the other two contain more extensive, but certainly far from satisfactory discussion. The first, Friedrich Deuschle, *Du und die Politik. Lehrbuch für die politische Bildung* (You and Politics. Teacher Manual for Political Education) contains passages which are anti-Semitic in content or overtone, as indicated in the following excerpt:

In the Middle Ages the causes of anti-Semitism were primarily religious questions. The descendants of those who had nailed Christ on the cross and stubbornly resisted conversion were persecuted, above all, in Spain and Germany.[85]

Deuschle's harsh and cynically stated writing certainly gives the impression of lack of sympathy for religious difference, if not of downright anti-Semitism:

> In all countries at all periods there have been expressions of anti-Semitism. A minority which defends its cultural and religious heritage must reckon, rightly or wrongly, with repeated attacks, especially if, by their material success, they call forth envy. To this extent the Jews confront the fate of any minority which is not prepared to integrate itself fully.[86]

It should be added that Deuschle does not repeat these sentiments in his textbook, and although his text lacks warmth, it is not so anti-Semitic or harsh in its evaluation of the Jews as is his teacher manual. Moreover, both books are exceptions among texts, and not characteristic of the normal tone. However, the text was approved by the state ministries and represents a kind of text which earlier was frequently used in the schools.

The second is Hans-Georg Fernis's and Andreas Hillgruber's *Grundzüge der Geschichte. Sekundarstufe II. Vom Zeitalter der Aufklärung bis zur Gegenwart* (Principles of History. Secondary Level II. From the Age of the Enlightenment to the Present). In their section on anti-Semitism, Fernis and Hillgruber link Christianity and Judaism. In a manner different from what one might expect, they point out that "the conversion to Christianity of the ancestors of the Germans now appeared as a fateful event, due to the historical connection of Christianity with Judaism." For, in consequence of nineteenth century anti-religious teachings of Nietzsche and Marx, "Christianity had been designated as an inferior religion. A renunciation of Christian teaching and reversion to pre-Christian heroic values was to be sought."[87] Thus, Fernis and Hillgruber in a section about *anti-Semitism* expound on the threat *to Christianity* of its historic association with Judaism—while the historic threat to Jews of Christian anti-Semitism is omitted.

Thus, neither the intermediate nor the advanced texts develop (or in many cases even mention) the centuries-long "teaching of contempt" (Jules Isaac) fostered by parish and pulpit. Without such background the teaching of Nazi anti-Semitism remains distorted and, as in the case of materials such as Deuschle's teacher manual, is counterproductive.

Economic Motives of Anti-Semitism

Economic factors in anti-Semitism are only slightly better handled than religious factors. Again, only a half-dozen or so intermediate history textbooks deal even in passing with economic motives. For example, Muggenthaler, in a brief retrospective on medieval anti-Semitism simply cites Christian envy and indebtedness to Jews without explanation.[88] Tenbrock and Kluxen stress in their teacher manual that during the Middle Ages, in addition to religious grounds for anti-Semitism, "material motives of course, were often equally decisive; [and] in the modern era [Christian] prejudice and envy at times predominated in the field of significant Jewish achievements as well as in the economic and cultural sphere."[89]

Binder and Burkhardt, in their teaching manual for *Damals und heute* (Then and Now) also devote some attention to economic anti-Semitism. They point out that during the nineteenth century the word "Jew" was used as a "term of abuse for a kind of business spirit of the Jewish minority"; they then cite extensively, but without comment, the writings of Karl Marx against the Jews.[90]

In his critique of capitalism, Marx, of course, did attack Jews as well as other elements of the bourgeoisie, but there seems to be no discernable pedagogical purpose in citing Marx—one of the greatest enemies of greed—to present economic stereotypes of Jews. In his war against capitalism, Marx was sometimes not immune from breathtaking categorical generalizations, and did not usually transcend typical nineteenth-century expressions of economic anti-Semitism. Since Marx is much admired among many educated persons in Germany, however, the uncritical citation of this authority could have the effect of strengthening negative stereotypes. Quoting the calumnies of famous men against the Jews is not a common practice in texts, and is the more remarkable in this case because Binder and Burkhardt elsewhere clearly condemn all aspects of anti-Semitism.

Heinz Dieter Schmid's *Fragen an die Geschichte* (Questions of History), on the other hand, is one the best texts of general presentation of the background of Jewish history in Germany. In a tightly argued historical essay on anti-Semitism, Schmid assesses the significant economic factors connected with the prohibition against Jews practicing most "Christian occupations"; their having been "pushed into trade and financial professions by the Christian taboo against taking interest on money"; the recruitment of Court Jews in the seventeenth and eighteenth centuries to "finance court and state undertakings which led to hatred against them"; and the "access of Jews to the independent professions during the nineteenth century, which brought on increased economic envy."[91] Although brief—as are most accounts—Schmid handles the economic aspects of anti-Semitism with mastery and understanding.

Another text, *Die Reise in die Vergangenheit* (Travel Into the Past) by Hans Ebeling and Wolfgang Birkenfeld, also makes it clear that Jews suffered economic disabilities: Jews were "not allowed to own land, and were limited to the professions allowed them; those of money exchange and selling used articles. Thus, they were persecuted for their belief as well as for their business."[92] Lucas, in an otherwise empathetic treatment, asserts erroneously that, after emancipation in the first half of the nineteenth century "Jews who had had themselves baptized were no longer subject to limitations."[93] In reality, even after conversion and considerable assimilation, German Jews were still excluded from military and government careers during most of the nineteenth century.

Eugen Kaier's text, *Grundzüge der Geschichte* (Foundations of History) contains one of the better economic treatments, citing Christian envy of Jewish success in professions opened to them by emancipation. But even Kaier concludes on a strangely apologetic note: "*Indeed, it cannot be denied* that by comparison with their neighbors they held many important positions in economic and cultural life. But along with these prosperous Jews we may not overlook those Jewish citizens who eked out a miserable existence as junk and old-clothes dealers."[94]

When seen in the context of Kaier's general treatment this is merely a slip, none too rare in texts, into inappropriate pedagogical language— for, why should anyone need to be apologetic about the status a minority group has attained by contributing service through the major professions? In a pluralistic society, special honors would be accorded to a minority group that had made such achievements. Kaier recovers his sense of balance when writing of nineteenth-century farmers, who "got into a fatal dependence on Jewish—and also Christian— dealers and money lenders," and of cities, in which "the Jews were made responsible in the competition offered small shops and businesses by the large emerging enterprises, factories and department stores."[95]

In the textbook sections on National Socialist persecutions, there are also occasional references to economic motivations of anti-Semitism. For example, Robert Tenbrock's *Zeiten und Menschen* (Times and People) alludes to anti-Semitic economic exploitation when he writes: "Jewish sworn testimony counted for less than that of non-Jews: contracts made with Jews could be much more easily evaded or broken.''[96] The statement, however, is made in relation to persecution of the Jews, and not as part of the economic motives of anti-Semitism, which, as noted, is represented in only a few of the intermediate history texts.

The advanced level history and political science texts also emphasize economic envy and the benefits to Jews after emancipation because of their alleged "special economic-mindedness." Some advanced history and political science textbooks carry sophisticated economic analyses of the consequences of emancipation for Jews during the nineteenth century, as with Robert Tenbrock and Kurt Kluxen, *Zeiten und Menschen. Zeitgeschichte: 1917 bis zur Gegenwart* (Times and People. Contemporary History: 1917 to the Present). There, the authors make a connection between medieval Jewish economic experience and the economic envy Jews endured in the nineteenth century:

> After the Jews were emancipated as a consequence of the Enlightenment and had largely assimilated, they were reproached for not separating themselves more from the society; and it was later noted with envy that—supported by their own past and not confined by restrictive class [*ständischen*] or economic traditions—they frequently grew strongly in the areas of the economy to which they applied themselves. Thus, the economic envy stemming from the Middle Ages was newly revived. (In the Middle Ages and beginning of the modern Era, Jews, as non-Christians, were allowed to charge interest; the growing requirements of the economy for money and the small amounts of capital offered for use permitted some of them to become rich through high interest rates.)[97]

The analysis, while correct, does not rise above an ambiguous attitude toward these economic developments pioneered by the Jews which have largely transformed contemporary economic society. Far from an appreciation of the historic role played by many Jews in the modernization of the European economy, many texts come near to reproducing the attitudes of the time about these achievements. Hermann Meyer and Wilhelm Langenbeck, for example, in their text, *Grundzüge der Geschichte. Sekundarstufe II. Historisch-politisches Arbeitsbuch. (Quellenband II) Vom Zeitalter der Aufklärung bis zur Gegenwart.* (Principles of History. Secondary Level Historical-Political Workbook, Source Volume II. From the Age of the Enlightenment to the Present), normally a very satisfactory text on the Holocaust, leave a curious impression when they assert that the Jews have a special aptitude for business: In describing the "economic grounds" for anti-Semitism, they refer to the "embittered competitive struggle in the economy of free trade" of the nineteenth century, during which Jews "brought a special 'economic-mindedness' (*Wirtschaftsgesinnung*) to the economy of free trade and everywhere were active as capitalistic pioneers."[98]

Han-Georg Fernis and Heinrich Haverkamp, in their one-volume text, *Grundzüge der Geschichte: Von der Urzeit bis zur Gegenwart* (Principles of History: From Primeval Times to the Present), seem to recognize, though without genuine appreciation, the unique role which some Jews played as "capitalistic pioneers" in the development of modern economic relations. They do describe, however, how militant nineteenth century anti-Semites sought to push the Jews out of the economy and make them economic scapegoats, "laying the burden for all defects of economic life one-sidedly on the Jews."[99]

One other text has a relatively extensive analysis of historical economic anti-Semitism. Helmut Altrichter and Hermann Glaser, *Geschichtliches Werden. Oberstufe, IV: Vom Zeitalter des Imperialismus bis zur Gegenwart* (Historical Development. Advanced Level, IV: From the Age of Imperialism to the Present) broach the issue of economic envy, calling attention to conflicts which arose in the Middle Ages and early modern times due to religious differences, to peculiarities associated with religious usage, and "the role of the Jews as money-lenders." Again, in dealing with the emancipation of the Jews during the nineteenth century, Altrichter and Glaser discuss economic questions informatively:

> In the case of the Jews, they developed a historically conditioned aptitude for specific tasks and activities. As a minority which was always looked upon with suspicion, over centuries they accommodated themselves skillfully [*geschickt*] to the limitations in trade and money lending relations in order to secure their existence. In the age of industrialization, the abilities which they had developed began to serve them in good stead.[100]

The analysis is excellent so far as it goes, but suffers from over generalization. Many Eastern Jews, for instance, continued to live in abject poverty and squalor and did not share in this emancipation; at the same time, there are many examples of comparable economic success among Christian Europeans, exemplified in such novels as Thomas Mann's *Buddenbrooks*.

Altrichter and Glaser continue their analysis:

> Further, the sons of the Jewish houses which had become affluent after emancipation pressed inexorably from the life of business into the

cultural professions, so that *"within a few decades not only the professions of doctors and attorneys were filled and overfilled with Jews, but in Germany as well as also Austria, a greater part of the culture industry, the newspaper, publishing and theater system came into Jewish hands."* (H. Arendt). . . . Some Jews came to the fore as sharp critics of existing conditions (Borne, Heine, Karl Krause) and especially as promoters of social transformation (Marx, Lassalle, Rosa Luxemburg, Trotsky). [*However,*] *"the vast majority of Jews, especially in Germany, and perhaps even more so in the old Danubian monarchy, remained quite decisively conservative, definitely clung to the existing order, the protection of property, [and depended] entirely on the protection which the state offered them."* (Golo Mann)[101]

As seen above, the authors employ the practice of quoting a respected Jewish source (as Binder and Burkhardt earlier cited Marx's criticism of capitalist Jews) to make a point which otherwise might sound critical of Jewish behavior. What needs to be emphasized here is that no one considers a profession to be "filled and overfilled" by a group in the society if that group is in the majority, that it was normal that Jews would tend to dominate occupations shaped by restrictive history as outlets to their activity; Jews are as likely to gravitate to certain occupations open to them as Christians were likely to establish guilds open only to themselves; finally Jews and Christians *alike* were economically conditioned more by highly competitive business practice commonplace in the nineteenth century than by their Christian or Jewish identity.

Altrichter and Glaser achieve greater even-handedness in the latter part of the passage above, when they balance the observation that Jews were especially active as revolutionary transformers of society with a quotation from Golo Mann that the vast majority of Jews were traditional, conservative *Burgers* like most of their fellow German citizens. The passage reveals one of the bases upon which anti-Semitic accusations rest: the double standard accorded the same or comparable actions in one group as compared with the other. Altrichter and Glaser, it may be noted, are sympathetic scholars, and have demonstrated their understanding elsewhere in their writings. What is noteworthy here is how difficult it is to attain an independent position in the analysis of economic or other prejudices when generalizations are made about groups, and how easy it is to slip into double standards of judgment.

Racial Anti-Semitism

Textbook authors generally consider the antecedents of the Holocaust mainly in nineteenth-century anti-Jewish racism rather than in religious or economic anti-Semitism. Therefore, the coverage of nineteenth-century and National Socialist racial concepts is more differentiated in intermediate history texts. A few texts, such as Grassmann, Kaier and Lucas, include the major personalities associated with the genesis of nineteenth-century racial thought. Kaier describes the roles of Arthur Gobineau and Houston Stuart Chamberlain, noting that "with such fuzzy, unscientific racial teaching, it was only a short way to the persecution of the Jews as an inferior race."[102]

Many texts reflect an awareness of the threat to Jews implicit in Social Darwinism as it was assimilated into racial ideology. The shift from traditional religious and economic to racial anti-Semitism during the nineteenth century was a new development with profound implications for Jews. Until the middle of the nineteenth century, Jews had been regarded as a cultural, religious and ethnic group, but not as a separate race. With the decline of Enlightenment values and the advent of Social Darwinist concepts in the last half of the century, Jews gradually were assigned relatively permanent characteristics. The new racial teachings ascribed the most negative biological features and character traits to Jews *as a race*; conversely, these teachings attributed to the mythological "Aryan" race the most positive characteristics. Such racial lore was widely believed in the late nineteenth and first half of the twentieth century. The Germans were thought to belong, as the most exemplary core, to the "Master Race."

The enormous threat to Jews posed by the assimilation of Social Darwinian thought by ideologies of the Right, notably National Socialism, is reflected in many intermediate texts. Ebeling and Birkenfeld, for example, present a well-developed account of the racial component of anti-Semitism. Beginning with the transition from religious and economic anti-Semitism and then tracing developments through the period of equality of rights during emancipation, they call attention to the new teachings of the inequality of races, and trace the antecedents of Hitler's racial thought. In the Social Darwinian biological teaching, they point to "a new *racial* root [which] strengthened anti-Semitism."[103] Authors such as Hoffmann, for example, make it clear that the traditional economic and religious prejudice against Jews "was transformed into a racial anti-Semitism in the nineteenth century."[104]

Other authors express awareness of the threat posed by the new anti-Semitism: "Until modern times the Jews had a way out in baptism, [but] with the racial anti-Semitism of the National Socialists, this last step was also blocked."[105] Kistler and Stroppe ask that students explain, "Why was persecution based on 'racial' grounds far more threatening than that based on religious grounds?—What threatened the Jews?"[106] Hug grasps this essential point in his question to students: "Wherein do you see the fateful injustice in the transfer of Darwin's teaching of the 'struggle for survival' to politics?"[107] Hug also states, in his section entitled *"Social Darwinism: The Right of the Stronger,"* that "the connection between Social Darwinism and racial anti-Semitism had to become a deadly threat, and not only to the Jews."[108] Joachim Hoffmann arrives at the same conclusion in his text[109] and, in his teaching manual *Lernziele und Lernschritte. Handreichung für den Lehrer* (Learning Goals and Learning Steps. Teacher Manual), he explains the broader implications of the threat: "The student should recognize the principles of the National Socialist 'world view': an aggressive ideology of 'race war' and 'living space' based on Social Darwinistic conceptions. They should recognize that this ideology represents a deadly threat to democracy and to the peace of the world."[110]

Another text, Grassmann's *Zeitaufnahme* (Perception of an Era), points to the further threat which racial teachings pose to women. In a section entitled "Racial Madness and the *Führerprinzip*," Grassmann takes note of Hitler's views of the biological inferiority of women: "Hitler wanted to deny to unmarried women the right of full citizenship, to forbid by law their entering the professions of judgeships or state prosecuting attorneys, and to reduce the number of females who could study at the university to 10 percent of the student body."[111]

Occasionally, authors write in an overcondensed manner or too abstrusely to make their point. Muggenthaler, for example, states that "during the nineteenth century the aversion to the members of the Mosaic faith was extended to all who were of Jewish ancestry."[112] Here, the word "aversion" should read "prejudice" or "intolerance." Further, the sentence is misleading, since many assimilated Jews in Europe experienced few disabilities because of their Jewish heritage. But the primary difficulty is that few students will recognize that the author's prime purpose was to point out that there had been a shift from religious to racial prejudice in the nineteenth century which inescapably affected all Jews.

Virtually all authors devote a special section to the presentation and condemnation of Nazi racial theory. Heumann, for example, allocates considerable space to National Socialist racial teaching. After citing a long relevant passage from *Mein Kampf*, he presents an extensive explanation of how the term "Aryan" gradually came to be extended "in false generalization" to all Indo-Germanic speaking peoples. He explains the relationship between "Aryan" and "Nordic," and notes that the two terms, "Aryan" (from linguistics) and "Nordic" (from anthropology), were gradually combined, "especially when it came to distinguishing them from the Jews." The *Deutsche Volk* were held to be racial descendents of the Germanics. The racialists made the claim that the Germans were a "Master race" or "Master people" to be served by inferior races.[113]

In this extensive (37-line) exposition on race, Heumann's main critical statement is the declaration that "National Socialist racism cannot be scientifically demonstrated," though he vitiates even this by declaring, first, that modern anthropologists claim the existence of three main races, and then, nevertheless, stating that there are other "individual races" subsumed under these categories, concluding lamely: "However, anthropology comes to secure results here only with difficulty."[114] Another author, Hug, reprints a passage from a 1941 German field manual of the *OKW* (Armed Forces High Command) which claims, among other things, that the Jews were made up of the "colored of the Near East and the Oriental races."[115] Such passages apparently are considered so absurd that authors most often do not challenge them.

Some texts neither describe nor analyze racial anti-Semitism, but simply cite racial and Nazi quotations, repeating verbatim the lore of "Aryan" and "non-Aryan" teachings. For example, Hug introduces racial anti-Semitism by describing nineteenth-century ideas of Social Darwinism—"Survival of the Fittest," "Capitalist and Imperialist" attitudes about the right of the stronger to rule—and cites long passages from Nazi wartime texts and Hitlerian quotations.[116] He offers no criticism nor rebuttal to these ideas, except to denounce them because they led to conquest and genocide.

In many cases, it appears that the authors no longer take seriously Nazi racial teachings, and therefore expend little effort in arguing against them. In view of the tragic legacy and continued threat posed by such teachings, it would seem that authors should present a decisive critique of racial ideas, making it clear why such ideas are scientifically untenable and ethically repugnant. Since a modified form of Social Darwinist thinking continues in the contemporary West, it appears prudent that students should read critical analysis and counter-arguments to Social Darwinian ideas in the textbooks.

It appears also, at times, that authors continue to view the Jews as a separate race, though not an inferior one. Steinbügl, for instance, asks "Why is the thesis of the inferiority of the Jewish race out of place?—In answering, think about the achievements of the new Jewish state of Israel."[117] Obviously, the author is concerned more with countering the notion of an allegedly inferior "Jewish race" than with leaving the impression with students that Jews are a separate race.

Other texts, such as Grassmann's *Zeitaufnahme*, do place more emphasis on correcting racial misconceptions. Grassmann defines the Jews as the "descendents of the former people of Israel who comprise, not a biological, but a socio-religious unit." He emphasizes that "one cannot speak of the Semitic race since [the term] Semite is a concept belonging to linguistic science."[118] The clarifications of Robert Tenbrock and K. Kluxen in their teacher manual, *Didaktische Grundriss für den Geschichtsunterricht zu Zeiten und Menschen* (Didactical Foundations for Historical Instruction to Times and People), are even more helpful. They state: "It should be stressed very strongly that the Jews are not a race, but rather a community of belief which . . . is comprised of many different peoples."[119]

There are also texts in which the treatment of racial anti-Semitism is far too abbreviated to be understood. Consider, for example, Han Heumann's summary in *Geschichte für morgen, Arbeitsbuch für bayerische Hauptschulen* (History for Tomorrow. Workbook for the Bavarian Junior High School), in which he condenses the factors of racial teaching, scapegoating, and economic prejudice into a short passage: "The hatred of the Jews was based primarily on the racial teachings of National Socialism. Hitler claimed that the Jews were responsible for Germany's misfortunes in the First World War and during the Weimar Republic."[120]

Without prior knowledge, the student would think from the preceding passage that hatred of Jews was a consequence of their poor performance (as an inferior race) in World War I and during the Weimar Republic.

The most superficial accounts confine the phenomenon of racial anti-Semitism far too much to the Nazi era and to Hitler. Döhn, for example, presents no background information whatever and treats anti-Semitism exclusively as "Hitler's obsessive idea."[121] Steinbügl writes that "Hitler lived in the delusion that the Jews belonged to an inferior race," that "they sought to destroy the German people."[122] Interestingly, the purpose of the passage is to show that, contrary to Hitler's views, there were many famous and creative Jews. In fact, in Steinbügl's entire text there is only the barest mention of nineteenth-century racial anti-Semitism.[123]

Some authors make effective use of the racial sections of the NSDAP 25-Point Program. Grassmann, as some others, for example, prints sections 4 and 5 of the Party program, which note with Nazi logic that: (4) only *Volksgenosse* (fellow-citizens) can be citizens of the state; that only those of common German blood can be *Volksgenosse* and that therefore no Jew can be a *Volksgenosse;* and (5) whoever is not a citizen of the state shall be allowed to live only as a *guest in*

Germany and must live under the laws applying to aliens.[124] The racial threat against Jews is made clear by this use of materials, and the student is prepared for the Nazis' political manipulation of race theory during the 1930s to deprive German-Jewish citizens of political and civil rights.

While the racial antecedents of the Holocaust are handled in more texts and in greater detail than any other aspect of anti-Semitism, authors often exhaust themselves in repeating old racial slanders, and then simply dismiss them as unscientific nonsense. All texts need to take seriously the thread of racial anti-Semitism in German thought; all texts need to examine the phenomenon carefully and offer energetic and closely argued criticisms.

More challenges need to be made against Social Darwinism as well. Gerhart Binder and Hermann Burkhardt, in their text *Damals und heute. Vom Ersten Weltkrieg bis heute* (Then and Now. From the First World War to the Present), for example, pose the astute question: "Can one transfer the relations of the animal world to those of human beings?,"[125] and in their teacher manual they cite Darwin in this connection—the only text to do so—pointing out that: "Darwin himself was cautious, and emphasized that even in the case of animals there was, along with the struggle for existence, a form of community (symbiosis). In the case of humans, the struggle and the will to succeed is combined with the capacity to work in cooperation with one's fellow man."[126] The author Hoffmann also makes the excellent point that in *Mein Kampf* Hitler took as his standard of superiority the victory of the strongest instead of recognizing the value of those best able to adapt successfully to the conditions of life on this earth.[127]

Texts could argue that societies have achieved far more by cooperation than by war and conquest, more by mutual assistance than by ruthless competition, and greater progress by adaptation than by willfullness and rigidity of thought. It should be recalled to students that the belief in a Social Darwinian "struggle for existence" and "survival of the fittest" is the opposing side of the nineteenth-century liberal-humanistic heritage which in turn has its roots in the humane teachings of the Judeo-Christian tradition. Social Darwinian racial thought is in fundamental opposition to the values of compassion, tolerance, the rights and welfare of the individual, respect for and belief in the sanctity of all human life.

Turning to the advanced secondary history, political science and social studies texts, there are again certain similarities to the intermediate level texts. The antecedents of racialism in Gobineau's and H. S. Chamberlain's writings are more often delineated in advanced history texts; in addition, Hans-Hermann Hartwich, editor of *Politik im 20. Jahrhundert* (Politics in the Twentieth Century) includes the works of the virulent nineteenth-century anti-Semite, and enemy of Karl Marx, Eugen Dühring.[128] Tenbrock and Kluxen allude to the countless leaflets and pamphlets which circulated in late-nineteenth-century central Europe, which Hitler read so avidly.[129]

In addition to Gobineau and Chamberlain, Altrichter and Glaser mention Richard Wagner's obsessive anti-Semitism and invoke the influence of the writings of Henri Bergson on the cult of irrationality, without noting that Bergson (1859–1941) himself was a Jew who died just before he would have had to wear the Jewish Star. Altrichter and Glaser are also excellent in weaving together the views of Treitschke, Theodor Mommsen, and Wilhelm Marr on the racial question, and quote Mommsen's teaching of tolerance about the Jews: "Their peculiarites are . . . to be judged like those of the various German Tribes,"[130] referring to the many Germanic regional groups— Prussians, Bavarians, Saxons, etc.—which had such ethnic differences that they could not understand each other's dialects. Apart from the authors' good intentions, it is questionable whether Jews or any other "tribe" should be categorized as a separate German group. There is plenty of German regional and provincial prejudice which speaks against this. One can only say that the Jews were as German as any of the ancestral Germanic "tribes."

Like the intermediate texts, the advanced history and social science texts largely neglect the shift from the traditional to the new racial anti-Semitism associated with Social Darwinism. Only Tenbrock and Kluxen, in fact, discuss the shift to racial anti-Semitism.[131] At the same time, more texts include some treatment of anti-Semitic racial teachings, again, however, with the sole *caveat*, as in Fernis and Hillgruber, that such teachings are "entirely without scientific foundation."[132]

Deuschle's section on racial teaching, which is utterly inadequate, describes the Nordic-Germanic race to which Nazi racial teaching prescribes a conquering role. He contrasts this Nordic race with the non-Aryan, of which the Jews were members. Following the logic of this development, Deuschle writes, "The Jew as a fellow-citizen was unthinkable." In the preceding section, describing the economic "grounds" for anti-Semitism, Deuschle states apologetically, "there has at no time been proof, however, that Jewish fellow-citizens have damaged (*geschadet*) their host people (*Gastvolk*)."[133] Such categorization of the Jews as "guests" of the German host nation is a mode of thought reminiscent of the Nuremberg Laws!

The only other mention of racial anti-Semitism in the advanced texts is a brief excerpt from *Mein Kampf* found in Hermann Meyer's,

Probleme des Totalitärismus. Materialien für die Sekundarstufe II (Problems of Totalitarianism. Materials for Secondary Level II). Curiously, Meyer makes no other mention of Jews, anti-Semitism, the persecutions of the 1930s, or the Holocaust in his entire text![134]

A number of political science texts, such as Herbert Baumann's *Politische Gemeinschaftskunde* (Political Social Studies) discuss neither Darwinism nor Social Darwinism. Baumann cites the standard racial teachings of National Socialism, and is satisfied merely to condemn them as a *"confused mixture of half-truths, conscious lies, national megalomania* and a *barbaric glorification of the rights of the stronger."*[135] The only critical comment of Hartwich's political science text about Nazi racial theory is that it was based on "the principle of eternal struggle derived from a perverted Darwinistic teaching. . . ."[136]

Two advanced-level history texts stand above the rest for their clear critique of Social Darwinism and thoughtful presentation of a humanistically based challenge to Social Darwinist thought. The first of these, Tenbrock and Kluxen, designates Social Darwinism as a "vulgar pseudo-science," and emphasizes the threat it poses to democratic humanism:

> The mechanism of biological selection was used to explain the course of history, equating humans and animals, culture with nature. The slogans, "struggle for existence" and "the right of the stronger," could be used to justify war and force. According to Social Darwinism, humans were imprinted by "natural selection" and inheritance; not, however, for example, by efforts of social assistance, tolerance, understanding and education. This [Social Darwinism] contradicted the democratic understanding of people and society as well as the value system of the European cultural tradition.[137]

Altrichter and Glaser are equally effective in writing about the implications of Social Darwinist ideology. They make a close connection between the atrocities associated with imperialism and the rationalizations provided by Social Darwinism, linking the justifications used for slave hunting, conquest, and decimating colonial peoples with similar ideological arguments taken from Social Darwinism for the extirpation (*Ausmerzung*) of the Jews in the Holocaust. They show that the most despicable deeds were often combined with the greatest hypocrisy—naked aggression frequently covered by the fig-leaf of ideology. The authors point out that the so-called superior imperialist powers themselves were often rampantly corrupt despotisms. Hitler and National Socialist racial teachings were merely "a simplified, late form of imperialistic Darwinism."[138]

The Functions of Anti-Semitism

Probably no other teaching is more important to the treatment of the antecedents of National Socialism than a discussion of the psychological and sociological mechanisms which motivate anti-Semitic behavior and the political purposes for which the state uses anti-Semitism. While analysis of the religious, economic, and racial motives for anti-Semitism is necessary for the students' *historical* understanding of Nazi persecution of the Jews, such motives do not explain anti-Semitism as a mental prejudice, or how prejudice is often used to justify destructive human behavior based upon fear, greed, envy, and scapegoating. Without such analysis, students cannot be expected to understand the underlying motive forces behind anti-Semitic behavior.

A characteristic weakness of most German texts is that they do not even treat anti-Semitism as a prejudice, nor very often designate it by that term. It is described, instead, as racial illusion, or mania—*Rassenwahn*. In fact, the German word comes close to connoting racial madness in German. The consequence of such a view is that it renders unnecessary an analysis of the sociology of prejudice in explaining anti-Semitic susceptibilities. To present as an analysis a textbook treatment which merely describes the hatreds and classic libels themselves is merely to transmit the words and deeds against Jews as they appeared to the anti-Semites at the time. This perpetuation of the terminology of the persecutors may be seen, for example, in Ebeling and Birkenfeld's teacher manual. A text illustration of anti-Semitic prejudice features a box in the center of the page labeled "The Roots of Hostility toward Jews." Arrows radiate to three boxes around it, entitled: (1) "The Jews as Murderers of Christ"; (2) "The Jews as Money-lenders and Business Dealers"; (3) "The Jews as Carriers of Inferior Characteristics."[139] The boxes convey the religious, economic, and racial roots of anti-Semitism in the language of the prejudices they describe. The boxes might instead have been entitled, (1) "The Libel of Deicide"; (2) "Economic Prejudice and the Role of Envy"; (3) "Racial Prejudice." The central box might have stated: "Historical anti-Semitic Prejudices." Such phraseology casts the theme in a new intellectual framework which escapes the vocabulary and mental framework of anti-Semitism.

To cite another example, Heumann asks students, "What are the *grounds for hostility* toward Jews during the Middle Ages and during National Socialism?"[140] The thrust of the question causes the learner to seek *legitimate reasons* for such hostility. The phrase "grounds for hostility" should instead read "anti-Semitic prejudices against Jews." This would lead the learner to approach the subject with greater detachment and begin to analyze human attitudes instead of either sympathizing with or rejecting the prejudices described in the textbooks. Even Lucas, usually an effective teacher on this subject, uses the introductory heading *"Racial Madness"* to deal with the causes of prejudice, and writes about "the mad ideas of 'racially valuable' and 'racially inferior' peoples." He recites the whole catalog of libels against the Jews, along with the standard textbook defense of the Jews: a listing of prominent Jewish leaders as evidence of their worthiness. Not until he has completed this does he finally take up "the real causes of racial madness."[141] In this regard Lucas's book is typical of many textbooks, except that he at last does conclude with a genuine analysis of the causes of anti-Semitism.

With few exceptions though, the tendency is to treat racism as a form of mania or madness instead of analyzing prejudice as a form of thought. Tenbrock, for example, while designating anti-Semitism as a prejudice—and making a fair case that "Hitler's struggle against Judaism was founded entirely on prejudices against a minority, and was not justified by anything"[142]—makes no attempt to analyze prejudice or to explain German susceptibility to anti-Semitism.

In treating the anti-Semitic background and dynamics of National Socialism it is necessary that authors analyze the actual causes underlying anti-Semitic behavior rather than skating the surface of the phenomenon, taking explanations and behavior at face value, and discussing the various "grounds" of anti-Semites for "hostility toward Jews."

The great German historian Theodor Mommsen long ago spoke of the essentially irrational character of anti-Semitism. His insight is cited in one of the teacher manuals. Mommsen declares:

> You deceive yourself if you believe that we can do anything with rationality. I used to think that, too, and protested over and over again against the sinister disgrace called anti-Semitism. But it is useless. It is completely futile. What I could state to you—what anyone at all can state in this matter—is certainly only reasons, logical and traditional arguments. No anti-Semite ever listens to them. They listen only to their own hatred, to their own envy—to the most shameful instincts. Nothing else matters to them. They are deaf to reason, justice and morality. No one can have any effect on them. . . . Anti-Semitism is the opinion of the *Canaille*. . . . Those who are accessible to reason and argument can never be anti-Semites. Those, however, who follow their barbarous hatred of education, freedom, and humanity, will not be converted by proofs.[143]

The irrational basis of anti-Semitism requires that it be taught by emphasizing the functions it serves for the individual and the society. Peter Furth, in his teacher manual, *Menschen in ihrer Zeit, volume 5, Handreichung für den Lehrer* (People in their Era, volume 5, Teacher Manual), echoing Mommsen's insights, warns teachers of the limits of rational argumentation in discussing the merits of anti-Semitic accusations:

> As much as one desires to fight anti-Semitism in subjects [i.e., in students] one shouldn't expect too much from reference to facts, which often do not lend themselves to application or are neutralized by being made the exception. Rather, one should turn the argumentation onto the subjects being addressed. One should make them conscious of the mechanisms which cause racial prejudice in themselves.[144]

Furth clarifies why philo-Semitism is no more desirable a goal than anti-Semitism, since both are based equally on irrational mental constructs: "To place emphasis on the genesis [of anti-Semitism], avoids the danger of an irrational philo-Semitism becoming, if not the vehicle, then at least the accompaniment of other negative forms of behavior."[145]

While seeking historical "grounds for hostility against Jews" is a fundamentally flawed pedagogy, students may profitably analyze the psychological mechanisms and motives of anti-Semites. For this reason, the inclusion of such an analysis in texts is one of the most essential ingredients for teaching the background of anti-Semitism.

A number of texts—though not enough—treat anti-Semitism partly in functional terms. In Hoffmann's teacher handbook on learning goals, for example, the author stresses that a study of the National Socialist dictatorship is particularly suited for "making clear social connections: the situation of the social outcast; the search for guilty parties for one's own inadequacies and for social problems (Marxism and Judaism)."[146] In his teacher's guide, Furth emphasizes the broader aspects of studying the causal mechanisms of anti-Semitism: "The mechanisms which trigger anti-Semitism should be recognized as those which operate in the rejection, oppression or persecution of every minority. The learner should recognize that anti-Semitism is not only about the Jews, but about the right of life of each and every minority."[147] Furth looks upon the mass atrocities of the National Socialist past as a warning addressed to present generations against the consequences of future unbridled prejudice.

A leading German educator, Dietrich Goldschmidt, cautioned in 1960 that "anti-Semitism, presently a potential, perhaps slumbering or suppressed [danger], will be activated as soon as a new objective occasion presents itself—for example, a particularly competitive economic situation—or a subjective occasion—such as a renewal of widespread political or economic difficulties. The degree to which anti-Semitism can be enlisted by political leaders or ideological seducers in a campaign will no doubt play an important role."[148] Furth and Goldschmidt challenge textbook authors to analyze anti-Semitism as a serious mental prejudice with dangerous implications.

Though only a few textbooks meet the challenge of analyzing anti-Semitism as a mental aberration, many of them incorporate in their historical presentations at least some of the conclusions reached by modern social analysis.

Such an approach may be observed in the way racialism is presented as an accompaniment of modern nationalism and imperialism. As Bodo von Borries observed in *"Geschichte lernen—mit heutigen Schulbüchern?"* (*"Learning History—with Today's Schoolbooks?"*): "The presumed dominance of the 'Whites' (the 'Europeans,' 'Western peoples') has contributed most particularly to their self-security and self-understanding."[149]

The role of white racism in the history of European imperialism and nationalism is incorporated in some textbooks. For example, Hoffmann in his teacher manual states the learning goal: "How does one explain the origin of the thesis of 'biological superiority of the white race'?—What role did it play during the era of imperialism?"[150] He answers these questions in his text: "The imperialistic expansion of the industrial states was based on [the concept of] the biological superiority of the 'white race' which supposedly had maintained at its core the 'Aryan' as the only pure race. Racial teaching and Social Darwinism established the basis for the most brutal forms imaginable of National Socialist and imperialistic activities."[151]

Hug follows Hoffmann in this passage verbatim (as in many other passages). Hug's discussion of nineteenth-century imperialism and nationalism also contains comments on the results of Darwin's teaching of a "war for survival" as applied to peoples and nations: "With the 'right of the stronger,' [the German nationalists] wanted to justify their national claims of importance to the outside world while at the same time denigrating everything un-German as inferior (for example, the Jews)."[152]

Hug also includes some highly offensive racial materials from *Mein Kampf* which could be expected to have negative effects on students, though he does accompany them with effective analytical questions. Based on readings from *Mein Kampf*, he asks the students (1) to investigate Hitler's attitude toward people whom he sought to influence politically; (2) to describe Hitler's characterization of his followers and the "opposition"; and (3) to indicate the kind of behavior he demands of his racist adherents.[153] These are appropriate questions to explain the function of prejudice in political movements. If crude quotations of anti-Semitic ravings *must* be presented to students, perhaps this type of specific function may help to justify them.

One of the best texts on the Holocaust is Friedrich Lucas, *Menschen in ihrer Zeit*, volume 4, *In unserer Zeit* (People in Their Epoch 4: In Our Epoch), a model of clear, concise instruction designed for young people. Explaining the conclusions of modern science on the question of race, Lucas cites a political psychology book which asserts that: (1) there are no pure races; (2) that giftedness is conditioned not by racial membership, but by cultural conditions and opportunity; and (3) that all races have their share of geniuses and idiots. In a section charmingly entitled *"An Attempt to Render the Text so that Young People can Understand, too!"* Lucas summarizes the basic mechanisms of anti-Semitism, which turn out to be the basis of all prejudice: Fear. His passage merits full presentation:

> Science has today come to understand what the *causes* of anti-Semitism have been in the last century. They are the same as the causes for the suppression and persecution of minorities everywhere and at all times:
> The powerful transformation of the relationships of life and work because of the industrialization of the nineteenth century led people to seek to shift their distress, their economic problems, their fears onto something or someone [else]. Someone had to be responsible for the fact that they were economically threatened and powerless—and for this purpose, there were always "those people"—frequently people of a group which was not too large, but which everyone recognized and from whom everyone could distinquish themselves. Everything evil took place where these people were to be found—and at that time this was the Jews—and everything good was to be found on one's own side. Already in the Middle Ages people in their fear blamed the Jews, for example, for the plague. In the nineteenth century, it was primarily the middle class and lower middle class who, because of their economic difficulties and powerlessness, in unjustified fear of the workers who sought to fight for their own rights, surrendered themselves to anti-Semitic catch-phrases.[154]

Lucas' text demonstrates how much may be said briefly and clearly. This is a far better use of precious text space than belaboring the pseudo-scientific racial teachings of the National Socialists. Models of the brief rendition of anti-Semitic motives have existed in pedagogical literature for some time. To cite one example, Theo Fruhmann,

in an insightful article, *"Überwindung des Antisemitismus"* (Conquering
Anti-Semitism), in 1949, presented a list of six brief, comprehensive
motives for this prejudice:

1. The mere fact that the other person is "other" may be seen as
   a threat to one's existence and to one's own power status;
2. persons with unfulfilled needs of self-assertion may see in
   "others" the sufficient reason why they have not been able to
   reach the goals they are seeking;
3. envy is metamorphized into a suspicion of the "alien" manner
   in which the "other" has an instinct for achieving superiority;
4. one sees the "other" as a competitor who, an intractable personality type himself, by working with others outflanks and
   defeats one;
5. the "other" is seen simply as a hindrance in one's way; the
   other [thus] invokes aversion and loathing;
6. there may be hatred against morally superior persons by con-
   sciously—though more often unconsciously—morally inferior
   people.[155]

Fruhmann is an early example of the insightful understanding by
postwar German educators of the psychological role played by fear
and envy. Such synopses of the psychology of hatred in textbooks
could help to clarify the fear-inspired prejudices which attached to
Jews in the nineteenth and twentieth centuries.

It would also provide a valuable accompaniment in discussing the
great insecurity aroused by the historical forces of accelerating modernization in the nineteenth century. Ebeling and Birkenfeld, for
instance, write well about this transformation. They describe the
gradual achievement in theory of equality before the law during the
eighteenth century and the advancement of many Jews into respectable
and influential positions, especially in banking and the independent
professions during the nineteenth century.[156] But the sort of analytical
perspective presented by Ebeling-Birkenfeld and Lucas is presently
still limited to teacher manuals. Burkhardt, for example, does a
creditable job in his teacher manual, interpreting anti-Semitism as
part of the critique on nineteenth-century liberal change, and as a
protest against modernity itself by those who would turn the clock
back on the ideas of 1789:

> Anti-Semitism is . . . at once a symptom and consequence of the fact
> that the value system of the liberal middle class world had begun to
> lose its compelling force. [Anti-Semitism] is an ideology of dissatisfaction

with modern society. . . . The insecurity of the German national consciousness and the constant striving to intensify the certainty of national identity find partial expression in anti-Semitism.[157]

This kind of historical perspective is needed in the analysis of events if textbooks are to escape merely describing anti-Semitic accusations merely to condemn them and the lethal persecutions which followed.

The psychological concept of the Scapegoat—the most obvious function served by anti-Semitism—is well-represented in many of the texts. Schmid mentions that Jews were blamed for all the "difficulties, guilt, and distress"[158] of society; Kistler and Stroppe discuss in greater detail persecutions from pre-Crusade to late Middle Ages, pointing out that "during wars, epidemics and economic hard times, the Jews had to bear the brunt as [scapegoats]: expulsions, alienation of property and murder were the consequences."[159]

Binder and Burkhardt in their teacher manual also use scapegoat theory: "After the defeat of the First World War, 'latent anti-Semitism— in the form of the search for a scapegoat—[became] current.' . . . The necessary 'scientificness' was achieved by the construction of a radical racial theory. The Jew became the most important anti-symbol of National Socialist propaganda."[160] Muggenthaler as well alludes to scapegoats and to the practice of making Jews responsible for all ills confronting Germany, including the Nazi assertion that "Jews were made responsible for diminished respect for Germany abroad."[161] Gerhard Jaacks in his teacher manual, *Damals und heute*, Band 4, *Geschichte für Hauptschulen, Lehrerbegleitheft*, (Then and Today, volume 4, History for Junior High Schools. Teacher Supplement) treats scapegoats in his discussion of National Socialist anti-Semitic propaganda: "The enemy against which the 'Final Solution' was aimed, in the meantime, had been made into a demon of mythological proportions: the Jew." It may be noted that Jaacks slips when he refers to the Jews as "the enemy."[162]

In a few instances, the only motive an author offers for anti-Semitism is that of scapegoat: "The National Socialists designated the Jews as 'subhuman.' By turning Jews into devils, they benefited by the fact that there were many followers of anti-Semitism after the First World War."[163]

Once the mental aberration of the scapegoat had a secure hold in the psychic economy of the anti-Semite, the next step in the pathology of prejudice was the development of the scapegoat into a universal threat, into conspirators bent upon world conquest and responsible for all disasters in the world. The concept of a universal Jewish conspiracy in National Socialism is well represented in a large proportion of the textbooks, although individual texts treat only selected aspects, and no analysis treats it as an outgrowth of the scapegoat mentality. Heumann declares that "all condemnations of the Jews culminate in the accusation that they plotted 'world conspiracy,' with the goal of destroying the 'Aryans' and especially the Germans."[164] Schmid stresses that Jewry was:

> stamped as an alien, racially inferior body which sought the destruction of the German race, the undermining of German culture and, above all, strove for world conquest, while simultaneously seeking to commit . . . Jewish journalists and politicians (viz. Marx, Lassalle, Bernstein) to the liberal parties and Social Democracy, in support of democracy and the workers' movement.[165]

In his discussion of National Socialism, Schmid also cites the Nazi assertion of an "international conspiracy of Judaism with intentions of world conquest." In his teacher manual, Heumann stresses the role Jews had come to play by the time of the Weimar Republic:

> For Hitler the Jews are the incarnation of all evil in the world, stated simply, the negative principle. Everything Hitler thought worthy of hatred he identified with the Jews: the "November criminals," the Weimar Republic, Bolshevism, American Capitalism, Marxism, "international high finance." Judaism was made into a gigantic bogey, an enemy which it was only a matter of destroying.[166]

A few texts cite original sources, such as this quote from a 1935 SS tract: "Thus, the Jew today is the great instigator of the complete destruction of Germany. Wherever we read of attacks on Germany in the World, Jews are the fabricators."[167]

The preceding examples show that the scapegoat function and international conspiracy theory are well represented in intermediate-level history texts. Indeed, these factors are more frequently cited as causal antecedents of the Holocaust than any other cause except, perhaps, Hitler's "racial madness" or mania.

Since anti-Semitism does not necessarily lead to persecution, much less genocide, the unique role played by the state apparatus and its use of anti-Semitism is essential to an adequate presentation of the Holocaust. In part, references to scapegoats and conspiracy theory cited above already suggest how the government utilized anti-Semitism. But the essential function anti-Semitism served for the state is featured variously in different textbooks and teacher manuals. Jaacks, for example, analyzing the Nazi pogrom of 1938, in his conclusion observes that "dictators are all too accustomed to camouflaging their atrocities as the indignation of the people."[168]

A brief account of the role played by German Jews in Nazi state policy is found in Hermann Burkhardt's *Damals und heute. Von der Zeit des Imperialismus bis heute. Geschichte 9 Baden Württemberg* (Then and Today. From the Era of Imperialism to Today. History 9 Baden Württemberg.) He begins by calling attention to Hitler's cynical awareness of the political uses of anti-Semitic incitement: "Hitler as early as 1920 stated how he would exploit anti-Semitism: 'It must be our concern to awaken and incite the instinctual opposition to Judaism in our people' ";[169] and in another textbook, Gerhart Binder and Hermann Burkhardt's, *Damals und heute, volume 5, Vom Ersten Weltkrieg bis heute* (Then and Today, volume 5, From the First World War to the Present) the authors point to the State's persecution of German Jews:

> There were reasons why the National Socialists turned against the Jews earlier and more severely than against the Christian churches. First, for a long time there had been in Germany an anti-Semitic attitude of hostility toward Jews which could be used. It extended well back into the period before the First World War. . . .
>
> It is a proven means of dictatorship to divert internal tensions and difficulties outward. Thus, the National Socialists were able to divert public attention from the arbitrary measures against the Jews in 1938/ 39, when Union with Austria and Germany as well as the dismemberment of Czechoslovakia were taking place.[170]

To demonstrate the rabble-rousing character of the propaganda used by the state, Hug in his Workbook prints a front page from *Der Stürmer* bearing the headline: "Jewish Murder Plan Against Non-Jewish Mankind Discovered."[171] Hoffmann notes in his text that "it turned out that it was not only Hitler for whom the vision of a 'Jewish World Conspiracy' was suitable as an excuse for one's own failures and defeats." Hoffmann, as do many other authors, uses *Mein Kampf* to illustrate the exploitation of sexual fears by the party and state, here used in relation to the dark, irrational fear of many people concerning interracial sex. Hoffmann cites a venomous passage which combines concepts of rape, seduction, race-mixing, libels of blood poisoning, bastardization, destruction of the white race, a network of conspiring enemies, and so on, in a chilling display of Hitler at his most lurid. Hoffmann also cites a passage from a military manual which proclaims the special rights conferred by following the racial anti-Semitic creed proclaimed by the Nazi State: "There are no equal rights for everyone. The superior has the right to be advanced, the inferior does not have this right. . . . Those who follow racial hygiene [measures] have to adapt themselves to the laws of nature."[172]

Following the logic of conspiracy theory, one of the more bizarre functions National Socialist government leaders sought to make the Jews serve was as hostages to guarantee the good behavior of foreign states, and as a source of booty. Binder and Burkhardt cite a Goebbels speech of 1933: "If they begin to incite abroad again . . . the Jews [cannot] run away from us. Their property is also here. This is very good that it's here. It could be that one day—in a coming difficult conflict—it can serve as a very good pledge."[173]

The authors ask the student to explain, "What did Goebbels have in mind by 'pledge'?" The answer in the teacher manual makes it clear how far the Nazis were prepared to go in their cynical use of Jew-hatred: "The Western powers could be placed under pressure, using the 'possessions' of the Jews in Germany, much as criminals do with hostages. For example, during the war, SS functionaries offered the 'sale' of Jews abroad in return for trucks."[174]

Elsewhere, Burkhardt presents the crowning example of the extent to which Hitler believed in conspiracy theory. In a discussion of Hitler's wartime goals, Burkhardt cites the *Führer's* declaration that one of his fundamental assumptions had been that "in England's democracy, the Jews had not yet—as in France—won the upper hand." Hitler envisioned a bitter struggle going on in all democratic governments between the "poisonous" forces of international Jewry and the forces of the defending peoples. It was a question he had earlier posed in *Mein Kampf* of whether the forces of traditional British statecraft could "break the enormous Jewish influence or not." Hoffmann cites Hitler's answer to the question in 1945 of why catastrophe was closing in on all sides of Germany: "One thing I myself underestimated," Hitler remarked, February 4, 1945, shortly before the end, "the degree of Jewish influence on the Englishman Churchill."[175]

The anecdote powerfully illustrates the connection between state policy and the most radical anti-Semitic myth. However, it must be remarked that Hoffmann's context was, as noted, a discussion of Hitler's strategic wartime goals, not the functions of anti-Semitism. The impression made by the vignette leads one to wonder what purpose is served by citing Hitler's anti-Semitic conspirational ponderings in the context of foreign policy goals unless they are clearly harnessed to some pedagogical point, such as, in this case, the uses of scapegoating in the mind of an utterly reductionist, simplistic megalomaniac. Despite this occasional odd note, Hoffmann's teaching manual in many respects is an excellent tool which stresses the analytical side more than most teacher manuals.

The upper-division history as well as political science and social studies texts offer far more variety of interpretation in treating the causes and functions of anti-Semitism. The advanced-level history and political science texts, especially, present a more sophisticated level of analysis. Altrichter and Glaser, for example, analyze anti-Semitism in relation to the nineteenth-century economic, social, political, and spiritual upheavals which transformed European society and threatened the stability of the German conservative classes. The authors conclude that the new anti-Semitism was based on the response to the accelerating pace of change rather than to the old religious and social prejudices, and "thus, this hostility, springing from an internal insecurity, is to be distinguished from the hatred of Jews in epochs gone by."[176]

How different the new anti-Semitism was from previous epochs is explained in the excellent analysis by Tenbrock and Kluxen in which they point to the relationship between anti-Semitism and the fear of change connected with modernization processes. In a section entitled *"Susceptible Social Classes,"* they describe the threat as perceived by the conservative German middle class of increasing industrialization and the rise of the worker class. In a section entitled "Direct Prerequisites," they note the tendencies in late-nineteenth-century German society—exaggerated nationalism, Social Darwinism, and anti-Semitism—"which caused a particular susceptibility to Fascism." The authors point to the special utility of anti-Semitism as a defensive, conservative and nationalist ideology: "Frequently anti-Semitism entered into close association with nationalism and conservatism; it could be anti-capitalist and anti-socialist at the same time; and it was always against internationalism and cosmopolitanism. It lent itself well for use as a defensive ideology."[177]

The authors connect hostility toward Jews with its general scapegoat function in European society: "As with every hatred of strangers, [anti-Semitism] served as a diversion from one's own unresolved problems, as was the case with the great pogroms of Russia, 1881–1882, the Dreyfus Affair in France, 1894–1906, and the postwar [I] period in Germany and Austria. . . . As a defensive ideology, it adapts itself well against everything."[178]

Since "Jews had played a large role in Liberalism and Socialism, the two most important movements of emancipation in the nineteenth century," this provided material for the myth of a Jewish conspiracy, which was soon designated as capitalist, internationalist, or communist.

In this way, a reason had been found for the political, social and economic dislocations associated with the transformations of the modern world.

Hermann Meyer and Wilhelm Langenbeck, in their text, *Vom Zeitalter der Aufklärung bis zur Gegenwart. Grundzüge der Geschichte. Sekundarstufe II. Historisch-Politisches Arbeitsbuch. (Quellenband II.)* (From the Age of the Enlightenment to the Present. Principles of History. Secondary Level II. Historical-Political Workbook. Source book II.), analyze the secularization trends of nineteenth-century society which, according to the authors, made semi-educated people susceptible to new, secular ideologies of salvation:

> The secularization of many areas of life led the average person to unbelief and doubt, and therewith to increasing helplessness. He was tossed back and forth between many possibilities. He was seeking some security, and found it in that century of faith in science and education. But, for many, this remained only a smattering of eduation which merely made them vulnerable to propaganda. People, in making personal judgments, were all too easily made victims of false, pseudoscientific teaching. . . .
>
> As justified as were the workers and petty middle class in striving for an improved material and spiritual standard of living, in their striving for something "higher," they became typical representatives of the semi-education which presumed to comprehend the way of the world. Increasingly, politics had to reckon with these masses as the most decisive factor in the play of forces among peoples. Politicians were led, each according to the degree of their sense of responsibility, to influence the voting public in a democracy with arguments no longer based on reason. [Such factors] could offer success to a determined politician. The more primitive an ideology, the greater the chance it would be accepted by the masses. The fewer the demands an ideological element makes on understanding or morality, and the more directly it promises the "liberation of the instincts," the more easily it is accepted.[179]

Whatever the merit of this comprehensive and highly interpretive thesis, certainly Meyer and Langenbeck have given the student a thought-provoking analysis, not only of susceptibilities to anti-Semitism in salvation ideologies, but of some of the assumptions about democracy and education as well. The authors add a final insight, again challenging the presumptions of democratic majorities: "Majorities always incline to self-justification and see only inadequacies in minorities."[180]

If Jewish conspiracy theory was to be made plausible, it had to explain the disconcerting fact that Jews—as individuals and as groups—

were not homogenous, but manifested the greatest diversity of views, social status, and characteristics. The conspiracy theory was to find its unifying factor in the racial assumptions of Social Darwinistic biological determinism:

> The picture of "Jews" was ultimately biologically determined; sociological discrepancies could thus be easily ignored, for the biological cliché of Jewish descent veiled all historically and individually determined differences: the rich West European (for example, Rothschild) and the completely impoverished East European Jew[s]. Men such as Karl Marx on the one hand, and, for instance, the conservative theoretician of State, Friedrich Julius Stahl on the other, had something in common only if seen through these glasses.
>
> [Now] human beings were distinguishable by purely racial characteristics. Individual, historical, social [and] political differentiation was entirely eliminated.[181]

In the above statement, Tenbrock and Kluxen have provided an explanation of anti-Semitism based on its historical role as a defensive ideology against change and modernization, cloaked with scientific respectability by the application of theories of biological determinism. This kind of functional analysis is precisely what is needed in texts.

The racial stereotyping of Jews provided a unifying factor, but did not directly point to a Jewish World Conspiracy. This would require that anti-Semites construct a bold assertion of such intent. Hartwich furnishes an analysis of the important role in conspiracy theory played by the early-twentieth-century tract, "The Protocols of the Elders of Zion."

> Racial hatred received its political accent by the conjuring up of an alleged "Jewish World Conspiracy." . . . For the National Socialists the program of this "World Conspiracy" was contained in the so-called "Protocols of the Elders of Zion," a piece of writing many times revised and long ago proven to be a forgery. Notwithstanding this, it played a significant role in anti-Semitic propaganda. The anti-Semitic component of National Socialist thought represented *the* panacea by which the leadership of the "Third Reich" pretended to explain all problems and to fight all emergencies. The nebulous existence of an international secret group which sought world domination was magnificently suitable as a propagandistic explanation of all afflictions and worries of the "little man."[182]

Hartwich emphasizes that though all international entities such as "Judaism, the Freemasons, the Catholic Church, and so on" presented only a "fictive danger" to totalitarian regimes, the National Socialists, on the one hand, secretly admired these alleged "'international organizations,' whose real or presumed organization they sought to emulate, while, on the other hand, passionately fighting it."[183]

Another text, Hans-Georg Fernis and Andreas Hillgruber, *Grundzüge der Geschichte. Sekundarstufe II. Historich-politisches Arbeitsbuch*, vol. 2, *Vom Zeitalter der Aufklärung bis zur Gegenwart*. (Principles of History. Secondary Level II. Historical-Political Workbook, vol. 2, From the Age of the Enlightenment to the Present) presents an analysis depicting Nazi thought processes, which used the Jewish racial and conspiracy theory to rationalize genocide:

> The counterpole to the Nordic race was "the Jew" who purportedly had set himself the task of conquering the world and exterminating the Nordic race. For this reason, World-Jewry should be radically fought and the Jews one could get one's hands on should be suppressed and exterminated. The Jews were condemned as the instigators of all disasters which befell the German Reich. . . .
>
> [Anti-Semites] made the Jews responsible for every political or economic misfortune. Propaganda simply stamped "the Jews" as the incarnation of evil from which everything bad in the world originated, including wars.[184]

Werner Ripper's text, *Weltgeschichte im Aufriß. Der europäische Faschismus und das Dritte Reich* (World History in Outline. European History and the Third Reich), contains an interesting discussion of the impact of the nineteenth-century belief in scientific deterministic principles on the thought of leading ideologues. Basing his comparisons on the work of August Nitschke, Ripper notes that Hitler, Marx, and Lenin, share some common mental constructs in their assumption of scientific determinism. He cites Hitler's autobiographical statement in *Mein Kampf* that, from a very early age, he had a fixed view from which to interpret all history, and that he had sought to discover the motivating forces behind history in the causes and effects of historic events:

> As August Nitschke in his analysis, 'Der Feind' [The Enemy] (1964), correctly observed, the emphasis of [Hitler's] sentence lies in the principle of causality, a sentence which can almost be taken as [expressing] a creed of natural science. It shows quite clearly how Hitler approached ideological problems: from his point of view, coolly, clearly, and free of feelings, or, as he would put it, "ice cold." . . . Thus, just as Marx and Lenin postulated an economic determinism, Hitler postulated— though on a far less scientific basis—a biological determinism.[185]

Ripper makes clear how far deterministic, reductionist thought can be taken in his reconstruction of Hitler's belief in a great, world conspiracy behind the outbreak of World War II. Basing his passage on H. W. Koch, *"Die Rolle des Sozialdarwinismus"* (The Role of Social Darwinism) in *Zeitschrift für Politik*, Ripper explains that:

> From Hitler's point of view, the war which broke out in 1939 was neither necessary nor expedient. In view of the German-Russian treaty, Poland couldn't defend itself in any case; thus, logically, they should have accepted German demands, especially since neither England nor France could give any aid to their ally. That Poland did not surrender to the German demands, that England and France continued the war was, from Hitler's point of view, against all human understanding. Thus, it required an explanation; this was fashioned in the form of a "conspiracy of World Judaism," to clarify the incomprehensible. From this conspiracy theory was drawn the ultimate conclusion: the mass murder of a race.[186]

Bernd Hey and Joachim Radkau's text, *Politische Weltkunde II. Themen zur Geschichte, Geographie und Politik. Nationalsozialismus und Fascismus* (Political World Studies II. Themes for History, Geography and Politics. National Socialism and Fascism) does not mention conspiracy theory specifically, but includes a Goebbels speech which expresses the Nazi paranoic vision of general destruction. In that speech may be heard a disguised reference to the genocide which Goebbels knew the SS was carrying out in the East: "The danger before which we stand is enormously large. . . . Everyone knows that if we lose this war it would destroy us all. And here the people with its leadership now is determined to grasp the most radical [measures of] self-help."[187]

Hartwich asserts that the need for scapegoats and alibis is typical of totalitarian thought: "One of the typical characteristics of totalitarian systems is that, for the maintenance of their dictatorship, they need a counter-pole toward which, for tactical reasons, they can direct the attention of the people."[188]

In *Grundriß der Geschichte für die Oberstufe der Höheren Schulen,* vol. 3, *Von 1850 bis zur Gegenwart* (Principles of History for the Upper Level of Advanced Schools vol. 3, From 1850 to the Present), E. D. Gallmeister points out that the systematic persecution of real or imagined enemies "belongs to the practice of every totalitarian state."[189]

One social science textbook, Henning Eichberg's *Minderheit und Mehrheit* (Minority and Majority), deals entirely with minority groups and their relationships to majorities. This optional, upper-level reader treats prejudices against Jews, Irish, North American Indians, and foreign laborers working in various countries, including Germany. The section on the Jews is extensive, constituting about one-third of this 125-page book, and portrays the Jewish people from antiquity to the foundation of Israel and the postwar American, Soviet, and German diaspora.

Eichberg's treatment of the Jews as a minority is often so detached that at times he seems unsympathetic. He does not often analyze or pass judgment, but rather describes. He does not present the situation of the Jews from the perspective of a persecuted minority, nor seek to explain the effects of social status and history on the Jews he presents. To cite a few samples, he uses such phrases as "cosmopolitan tendencies" in explaining the effects of the Enlightenment on Jews; declares the Jews to have been "highly overrepresented" in many professions in Berlin, and uses statistical tables of the proportion of Jews in various professions in which Jews in the professions add up to well over 100 percent![190]

For all that, however, Eichberg excels in clear and brief exposition of historical, psychological and sociological interpretations of anti-Semitism. He lists eight categories of interpretations, many of which will be seen to have been presented in texts already discussed:

1. The secularization of Europe, causing a new search for secular creeds;
2. The racial, Social Darwinistic "scientificization of demonization" of a people as carriers of negative traits and an "inferior" race;
3. Psychological explanations based on projection and scapegoats;
4. The interest of leading political groups in using anti-Semitism as a safety valve for social tensions;
5. Sociohistorical explanations in which anti-Semitic disturbances are attributed to the degree of difference between the Jews' social structure and mores and those of the rest of the population;
6. Marxist explanations of anti-Semitism as a manifestation of the response to dissimilarity of economic class: the Jews representing capitalism; and the states of Prussia, Austria and Russia representing declining social classes trying to salvage themselves in a modernizing world;
7. Socioeconomic interpretations of anti-Semitism emphasizing the search for a scapegoat during the downside of the boom-and-bust business cycle of modern capitalism;
8. Sociological interpretations of anti-Semitism, presenting it as an expression of forces, a form of criticism and protest against the tendencies of modernism: capitalism, the commercialization of life, and/or contemporary social values in general.

Eichberg's list of anti-Semitic interpretative constructions provides students with a summary of the spectrum of current understanding of the historical, psychological and sociological clarifications of the sources from which these mental processes arise. It may also serve to remind the reader how many of these analyses have been found in the German textbooks. Every model except for 5, 6, and 7 has been represented in the texts. Number 7 will appear in a following section on the persecutions of the 1930s. Number 6, a Marxist explanation, is excluded. Number 5 is considered inapplicable, since German Jews were largely assimilated and had adopted the social structure and mores of the majority of non-Jewish Germans.

The Presentation of Negative Images of Jews

In the course of presenting the racial teachings of the anti-Semites and National Socialists, many textbook authors repeat, at times in detail, the most insidious traditional charges, libels, and infamies against Jews. Many texts rely heavily on excerpts from primary sources. The purpose may be to illustrate the hate-filled prejudices of the Nazis in order to expose and condemn them as irrational. However, in the absence of the presentation of the actual character and history of German Jews in the texts, this caricature of a demonized Jewry becomes imprinted to some degree on young minds, and remains a mental association with Jews, thereby perpetuating a distorted image. German students have relatively few contacts with Jews (only 30,000 Jews now live in the Federal Republic), a reality which also contributes to this problem.

One of many offending texts is Heumann's. In portraying Jews of the Weimar Republic, he uses a blatantly racist and anti-Semitic document of Weimar Minister of the Interior Severing, which reports the domestic situation of 1929. The Minister complains of "Negro music," of continuous "uproar in Berlin," as well as "ten years of the Republic of the Jews; ten years of betrayal of the people; ten years of stock-market swindling; ten years of bitter struggle against these rogues and criminals who in 1918 stabbed the German front in the back and sold and betrayed us into international Jewish finance for the sake of base Mammon."[191]

Heumann's only textual comment is the question, "What does the Minister of the Interior note in this summary?" Invoking the un- challenged authority of a State Minister of the Weimar Republic cannot fail to produce a distorted, stereotyped view of German Jews of the Weimar era, especially in the absence of counter testimony. Like most other texts, Heumann writes almost nothing about the real Jews of Germany to oppose the negative impression left by his sections on racism and anti-Semitism in which Jews are depicted in demeaning caricature. Heumann entitles this section "Why Hitler Persecuted the Jews," and the language and vocabulary of his explanation is that of the persecutors. He provides scarcely any analysis of the documents he uses, nor is anything said about prejudice, so that the reader can hardly avoid a distorted answer to "Why Hitler Persecuted the Jews."[192]

Kaier writes in a similar vein in treating the national and ideological roots of anti-Semitism. For background he quotes, without comment, a conservative 1892 German party program: "We are fighting . . . Jewish influence in our national life. We demand for the Christian people a Christian leadership and Christian teachers for Christian students."[193]

While adults may easily see the bigotry and insularity in this remark, without education, parochialism is natural to young people, and such intolerance may appear less outrageous to them than we would expect.

Kaier also briefly discusses Weimar Jews under the heading "The Position of the Jews in the Republic." While it is a much better treatment than Heumann's, it is not without problems. In discussing the influx of East European Jews into Germany, the author inadequately explains the plight of these Jews. They are depicted as "problems" because they are foreigners. "The government and the older native Jewish citizens had to control the problem of the so-called 'Eastern Jews.' During and after the war, approximately 100,000 Jews, primarily from Poland, had immigrated to Germany. They came as armament workers or as propertyless refugees." During the time it took them to assimilate, Kaier notes, "their own co-religionists as well as Christian citizens were in a relationship of mistrust toward them."[194]

Kistler and Stroppe cite nineteenth-century anti-Semitic literature to horrify students and arouse indignation. But it is questionable whether statements such as the following achieve this goal: "The Jews are the lowest and most unsuccessful creation of nature" (1881); "The Jews are a vermin which must be stepped on. There is no discussion with *trichina* and *bacilli,* nor are they bred; they are destroyed as fast as possible and as far as possible" (1887). Unless such vicious statements have some clear pedagogical purpose beyond that of showing the vicious vulgarity of the extreme anti-Semitic mentality, they have no place in textbooks.

At least Kistler and Stroppe have the intention of wanting students to compare such rabid pronouncements with similar ones made in the Nazi area: "What the pestilence and tuberculosis means for the health of all mankind Judaism means traditionally for the white people. . . . Only those who are persistent and tough will conquer Judaism. We may begin with half measures, but eventually this struggle will have to end with the use of ruthless brutality by the Nordic peoples."[195]

Materials of this kind may perhaps have a minor place in textbooks. They may, as above, be needed to reveal the historical pedigree of Nazi racists, to show the assimilation of biological concepts by anti-Semites, or to act simply as a warning of the dangers of such thought processes. But the mere reproduction of Nazi descriptions of Jews as *Untermenschen* (subhumans) without comment on the political uses made of such hate-mongering by the National Socialists, the effects on the lives and self-esteem of German Jews, or the reaction of non-Jewish Germans, may simply be harmful. Pelzer, Hug, and Schmid all include such passages; the latter, for example, employs a potent quotation about the "subhuman Jew," again, without comment.[196]

Kaier, on the other hand, uses the concept of *Untermenschen* to explain, with chilling effect, the aims of Nazi racial biology:

> The National Socialist racial fanatics considered the peoples of Europe to be like irrationally laid-out plants, overgrown with weeds, in which order finally had to be created. The valuable elements would be promoted while letting inferior elements become stunted or exterminating them. The final goal of this process was the genesis of a new, biologically ordered, sensible European society. To this insane idea is ascribed the most horrifying atrocities of the NS-regime: the murder of the sick and the old and the mass murder of the European Jews.[197]

Elsewhere, however, Kaier simply restates the poisonous Nazi slander, with only rare reminders that these are radical anti-Semitic prejudices:

> In Hitler's eyes, the Jews were the global enemy of the Aryan master race. In them was manifested everything dark, bad and evil. They were "sponges," "parasites," the "well-poisoners of world history." There was a world-wide conspiracy which had as its goal the destruction of the Aryan race, and especially the German people. They incited the First World War against Germany and unleashed the Revolution of 1918. Versailles had been their triumph. The Jewish element was dominant in "world-capitalism" and "world-Bolshevism," the two main enemies of the coming greatness of a new Germany: "The Jews are our misfortune."
>
> According to Hitler, the suffering of Germany could be explained by the German defeat in the First World War, by "Jewish foreign infiltration"; [and] by the Weimar "System." . . . For him the German people had to be welded into a solid society. This would be possible only by the "elimination of everything Jewish from the body of the nation."[198]

Grassmann, who has written one of the better recent texts, also has a long, negative section on Nazi racial teachings, dubiously entitled "Superior and Inferior Races?" But Grassmann makes clear that those who cherish radical, racial, hierarchial values may arrive at conclusions which justify mass murder:

> [The "Aryans"] are called upon to rule over the allegedly cultureless Negroes, Indians and Jews [*sic!*]. The Jews and also the Slavs (Poles, Russians and others) and gypsies are not really humans but only appear to be: In reality they are subhuman or human-animals. Since they are nearer to animals than to humans, they may also be used like animals—bred or exterminated. In the extermination camps of the National Socialists, these mad ideas, in fact, were realized.[199]

Although the effect of Grassmann's passage is negative, with only one qualifier—"allegedly"—to interrupt the description, the author has made the valuable point that Nazi racial theory was not irrational: National Socialists lived in a rational if terrifying world in which, by the simple amoral device of defining certain groups as out of the protective circle of being human, they may be used exactly as humans use animals. Grassmann is also one of the few textbook authors to describe Nazi racial propositions in his own language, rather than simply reprinting anti-Semitic slurs.

Schmid does not escape this weakness. Like many German text authors, he exhibits Nazi anti-Semitic documents. In Schmid's case, he has chosen to publish the anti-Semitic portions of Hitler's Last Testament: The Jews started the war; the Germans are to resist the "world poisoners of all people, International Jewry," and fight them with pitiless resistance.[200] The negative effect is heightened by the fact that it is printed, without comment, as the *final* paragraph of the chapter on World War II. Here is a case of negative teaching, both by the force of its being Hitler's final testament, and by its positioning in the text.

If properly analyzed, the virulently anti-Semitic language of Hitler and other Nazis may be used effectively, as can be seen in Burkhardt, who uses Hitler's words in his final weeks to provide evidence that he ordered the genocide of the Jews. A few weeks prior to his death, Hitler said: "People will be eternally grateful to National Socialism that it wiped out the Jews in Germany and Central Europe."[201] Burkhardt also asks that students "take a position on this statement," thus providing an opportunity for a class discussion on the meaning of the loss of the European Jews to Germany and Europe.

In teaching the Nazi era, the textbooks need to find a way to examine Nazi anti-Semitic diatribes and slanders without reinforcing prejudice. It is not enough for authors to adopt the terminology of the Nazis and reproduce anti-Semitic smears; in effect, this merely asks the murderers to describe their victims. Care needs to be taken when presenting propagandistic materials so that, as much as possible, students are not simply left with the negative effects of such views. One of the best ways to present radical anti-Semitic views may be to clearly integrate them within the framework of the functions they served for Nazi ideology, and as illustrative of the destructive power of prejudice both on the mind of the bigot and on the victims of prejudice.

Upper-division history, political science, and social studies texts are largely free of negative descriptions of Jews except within the context of making such pedagogical points. Tenbrock and Kluxen is the only text which, in an otherwise well-presented treatment, makes a small slip in wording: "Latent anti-Semitism had been present within the citizenry in consequence of the strong Jewish elements in politics, economy and culture during the Weimar era."[202]

Apart from the fact that there was not a strong Jewish element in Weimar politics, it is *not* adequate to treat the presence of Jews in politics as in itself an explanation of anti-Semitism.

Wolfgang Scheffler, in Hartwich, is the only author who, in presenting Hitler's racial teachings, continually reminds the reader that these were Hitler's views. Using such simple literary divices as "He made the assumption that" or "He believed," or, "For Hitler" such was the case, "For him," and "According to his belief, people were,"[203] Scheffler presents Nazi racial material without the negative stereotyping of Jews.

Persecution of the Jews, 1933–1939

All textbooks have a separate section presenting the Nazi persecution of the Jews during the Nazi prewar era. In scarcely any other section is the influence of state guidelines so evident as in the coverage of the Nazi measures against the Jews. Almost without exception, textbooks mention the following major points, often in similar manner: (1) The boycott of Jewish businesses on April 1, 1933; (2) the expulsion of Jews from government posts in 1933; (3) the Nuremberg Laws of 1935; (4) the Nazi pogrom of 1938; (5) "Aryanization" and plundering of Jewish property; (6) expulsion of Jews from jobs and German economic life; (7) removal of Jews from German public and cultural life; (8) Jewish deprivations and humiliations; and (9) the forced emigration of Jews.

Though these sections convey much factual information about the persecutions, they are generally short and in many respects remarkably uniform from book to book. They are also largely descriptive, containing little analysis or evaluation except for a general tone condemning the events reported. They also contain general information on the attitude of the German people toward the Nazis and the Jews.

Most books mention the boycott of Jewish businesses. Wolfgang Hug reprints a full page article about the boycott from the *Völkischer Beobachter*, the Nazi press organ, in his source book, *Geschichtliche Weltkunde. Quellenlesebuch. Band 3. Von der Zeit des Imperialismus bis zur Gegenwart.* (Historical World Studies. Source Readings, vol. 3. From the Era of Imperialism to the Present).[204] Many books illustrate the boycott with pictures of SA men standing guard in front of Jewish shops exhorting Germans not to buy from Jews. Burkhardt points out that the signs, "Defend Yourselves," were a "conscious misrepresentation of the facts," and that the Nazis "thus treated the Jews as hostages: the more that foreign countries criticised the policies of the National Socialist rulers, the more the Jews should feel the power of National Socialist might."[205] Only one text, Schmid's, nuances the presentation, making the remarkable assertion that, "in the case of Jewish department stores, however, measures of support were taken, at first, for reasons of national economy and the politics of employment,"[206] presumably by the National Socialist government.

The expulsion of Jews from government positions, including teaching, is also recounted in virtually all texts, but without commentary. Only Karl Menzel and Fritz Textor, in their textbook *Staatensystem und Weltpolitik* (Systems of States and World Policy), offer the rather self-evident comment that the measure "was to offer a lever whereby unwanted civil servants could be dismissed."[207]

The Nuremberg Laws of 1935 are described in detail in all textbooks, again without significant interpretation or comment. Grassmann notes that, along with other measures, it "created the prerequisites for persecution and deportation."[208] Tenbrock presents the Nuremberg Laws particularly well, defining *"Mischlinge"* (Persons of "mixed race"), which not many other intermediate texts do, and reporting the Nazi threat of the death penalty for *Rassenschande* (Racial sexual violations). In previous editions of the text, Joachim Immisch, the author of this section of Tenbrock's text, ends with the fascinating and scathing observation that, "since 'Aryan' membership could not be proven by one's appearance, religious confession [of German citizens] therefore became the criteria." He continues.

A great storming of Church registries began. Everyone needed the Christening document of his forebears. The most frightful scenes were enacted in the presence of the pastor. After looking in the Church registry, it was sometimes forcefully brought home to a searcher—who until then had never bothered about his family tree—that he was no longer a *Reich* citizen; that he had to give up his profession; or that he was prohibited from marrying his financé.[209]

This impressive passage unfortunately has been omitted from the latest edition of Tenbrock, yet it is just the sort of anecdotal supplement needed in texts. The passage explains the harsh and arbitrary impact of the discriminatory laws enacted against the Jews as represented in the shocked reactions of "Aryan" Germans when they find themselves suddenly the victims of racism.

Heumann asks of the Nuremberg Laws—"What new concept has been introduced here?"[210]—designed to teach that racial discrimination had been embodied in the laws of citizenship. Hug prints a "Report on the Proclamation of Misdeeds between Aryans and Jews, 1933" in his documentary source book.[211]

Though the provisions of the laws are faithfully recorded in the texts, little is stated about what the loss of citizenship meant for the Jews, or about their pseudo-scientific character; nor is there an emphasis on the necessity of government recourse to *religious* confession as proof of *racial* membership (because the Nazis could not produce evidence based on racial science to support their claims for race discrimination). Only Erich Kosthorst in his Curriculum Materials text, *Geschichte. Politik. Unterrichtseinheiten für ein Curriculum. Das nationalsozialistische Regime* (History. Politics. Instructional Units for a Curriculum. The National Socialist Regime), includes the remark of Reinhard Heydrich at the Wannsee Conference that, in determining the number of European Jews, "we are dealing only with religious Jews, since in this respect the conceptual determination of Jew according to racial principles is still partially inadequate."[212]

The Nuremberg Laws of 1935 transformed Nazi racial doctrine into German law. As such, the textbook depiction of these laws could be used to show (1) the perversion of the law to serve the purposes of a criminal regime; (2) the threats which accompany loss of the rights of citizenship; (3) the indefensibility of laws denying citizenship on the basis of racial criteria; (4) the anguish, suffering, and deprivation caused the Jews as a consequence of these laws; (5) the Nuremberg Laws as only the preliminary shock which set in motion an avalanche of further decrees, ordinances, and decisions culminating in the Holocaust.

However, scarcely any intermediate texts discuss these issues. Only Tenbrock and Kluxen in their teacher manual impute a wider significance to the Nuremberg Laws. They inform the teacher that: By means of the law, the longstanding symbiosis which till then had existed between Germans and Jews finally had been broken and rendered impossible.[213]

In the allocation of space, the Nuremberg Laws take second place only to the Nazi pogrom of November 1938 against German Jews. No book omits it and most give it prominence. It is used to emphasize the ruthlessness of the regime in persecuting Jews, to highlight Nazi duplicity and cynicism, and the suffering and desperate situation of German Jewry.

Many books also stress that German citizens did not approve of the pogrom, nor did they—as portrayed by Nazi propaganda— participate in terrorizing the Jews. Many texts correctly point out as well that German citizens, despite their shame and revulsion, did not publicly protest the outrages because they were intimidated by Nazi strength and ruthlessness.

All textbooks treat the following elements: the Paris shooting which served as the pretext for the 1938 pogrom; the Nazi incitement of the pogrom; the pretense that it was a spontaneous act of an aroused German people; the destruction of Jewish life and property throughout Germany; the arrests and deportation of tens of thousands of Jews to concentration camps; and the collective fine imposed on the Jews for the damage, cynically called an "atonement" by the Nazis. In some cases, the treatment is too brief and general not to be misleading about some aspects of this complex series of events.

Grassmann presents one of the best treatments of the background of the shooting by Herschel Grynszpan, explaining that the National Socialist government had arrested some 15,000 to 17,000 Polish Jews in order to deport them to Poland, that the Polish government had refused to accept them, that they had wandered about in a German-Polish no-man's-land, and that among these Jews was the family of the young Jew, Herschel Grynszpan. In Paris, as an act of revenge, on November 7, 1938, Grynszpan assassinated the German emissary, Ernst vom Rath. This assassination was then used by the NSDAP as a welcome pretext for a stage-managed pogrom against the Jews.[214]

Kaier also has written a model account of the origins of the pogrom, presenting the background of the "great mass arrest action in June" which led,

during the Fall, to more than 15,000 Jews of Polish nationality [being] pushed across the border but, not being immediately accepted by the

Poles, they wandered around for some time in the no-man's-land between the borders. The seventeen-year-old son of one of the affected families shot a German diplomat in Paris, fatally wounding him. This assassination, the desperate act of a youth, was used as grounds for a great Jewish pogrom on the night of November 9–10.[215]

These excellent descriptions explain the important background of the fatal shooting. However naïve and confused Grynszpan may have been—and there are aspects of his action and motives which defy speculation[216]—Grassmann and Kaier have satisfactorily identified Grynszpan's Polish nationality, his youth, his suggested motive. In view of the use the Nazis made of this assassination and their attempt to make his act the proof of an "international Jewish conspiracy," this background information to Grynszpan's shooting of the third Secretary of the German embassy in Paris is necessary.

Various texts identify Grynszpan (inadequately) as "a Jew,"[217] (adequately) as "a Polish Jew,"[218] and (most adequately) as "a young Polish Jew."[219] Some texts, such as Kistler and Stroppe's, are entirely too brief about the pretext for the Nazi pogrom, stating simply that: "The murder of a German diplomat in Paris by a Jew was used by the National Socialists to organize a campaign of destruction and persecution throughout Germany."[220]

Heumann, also too brief, states that: "When a German diplomat in Paris had been murdered by a young Jew, the National Socialists plotted violent activities against the Jews on the night of November 9th to 10th throughout the Reich." Ebeling and Birkenfeld make no mention of the shooting in their textbook, treating it only in their teacher manual, *Die Reise in die Vergangenheit. Westermann Lehrerband* (Travel into the Past. Westermann's Teacher Volume).[221] Pelzer does not mention Grynszpan, so that there is no logical connection between the murder and the pogrom: "When a German diplomat in Paris was murdered, Goebbels had the synagogues set on fire in revenge against the Jews. Jewish businesses were devastated and partially plundered."[222]

Hannelore Lachner's *Geschichte für Realschulen. 4 Neueste Zeit* (History for High School. 4 The Contemporary Era) is almost as vague: "The assassination of a member of the German embassy in Paris by a young Polish Jew was used by Hitler as a welcome reason."[223]

Hug, on the other hand, treats the background of the Paris murder with greater nuance and sensitivity: "In 1938, in consequence of the exclusion of physicians and attorneys from practicing their profession, selective measures of arrest and deportation followed. When the son of one of those affected shot a member of the German embassy in Paris, this was a welcome signal for a pogrom of the greatest extent: Reich Crystal Night."[224]

Hoffmann also deals clearly with Grynszpan's motives: "When the son of one of those affected [by the deportations] shot a member of the German embassy in Paris, this was a welcome signal for a *pogrom of the greatest extent* which was stage-managed by the Party as 'Reich Crystal Night.'"[225]

Joseph Schwander, in his text *Geschichte* (History), settles the issue of the motive for the murder by simply juxtaposing the assertions both of Grynszpan and the Nazi press: "According to the statement of the murderer, the real motive for the act had been the increasing persecution of the Jews in Germany. German propaganda presented it as a first great blow by the 'Jewish instigators of world conflagration.'"[226]

Schmid, on the other hand, states unambiguously that the broader motive for Grynszpan's act was "to call attention of world opinion to the fact that his parents had just been deported from Germany to Poland, but that they had not been accepted by the Poles."[227]

All texts emphasize that the pogrom was planned and carried out by organized groups of *SA*-personnel and other Nazis, and that it was not the spontaneous outbreak of an enraged German populace as presented by Nazi propaganda. It is made clear that the pogrom was "staged by the party,"[228] that it was, "in reality, carefully organized,"[229] or at least that "the party organized 'the people's indignation.'"[230] Many texts print original documents of *SA* orders and accounts, police reports, and Heydrich's report on damage. Burkhardt in his teacher manual characterizes the Nazi propaganda about German indignation as "a masterpiece of Goebbels' hypocrisy."[231]

The destruction of the pogrom is treated in accurate detail by nearly all texts, many authors presenting the destruction of synagogues, businesses and homes, and the murder or injury of Jews with a sense of its horror. Grassmann, for instance, writes that men, women, and children were kicked, beaten, and murdered, that thousands of men were sent to concentration camps, where "many hundreds of Jews died of maltreatment."[232] Binder and Burkhardt point out that: "All synagogues, many Jewish old age homes, hospitals, businesses and houses were burned down, partially plundered, and thousands of Jews, often after mistreatment, were dragged off to jails and concentration camps."[233] Lucas, curiously, reports only that after the Paris shooting "a dreadful persecution of the Jews"[234] followed.

The number of Jews arrested and sent to concentration camps and the number of murdered and injured varies considerably from text to text, perhaps because of the varying figures presented in official contemporary documents. The lowest death toll, 36, is accepted by Kaier, Muggenthaler, and a few others, whereas most of the rest of the texts report the more accurate figure of 91. The figure for Jewish men arrested or sent to concentration camps varies from 20,000, given in most texts, to 35,000 cited by Hug and others.[235] Kistler and Stroppe report that "20,000 rich Jews" were placed under arrest, which creates a peculiar impression.[236] In fact, the SS seized many prosperous German-Jews to extort as much wealth as possible, forcibly deport them, and then lay hands on their assets. Thus, the authors while not inaccurate, are so brief as merely to perpetuate a stereotype.

The collective payment of one billion *Reichmarks* imposed by Hermann Göring and other party members on the German Jewish community is described in all texts, but designated by the cynical Nazi term *"Büsse"* (atonement) or *"Sühneleistung"* (expiation offering). Though the term is placed within quotation marks, no text points out the Nazi cynicism involved in the handling of Jewish insurance claims, or the financial ruin which the collective extortion payment meant for German Jewry.

As indicated above, almost all texts use the term *Reichskristallnacht* (Reich Crystal Night) for the events of November 9–10, 1938, although most of them place it within quotation marks. Only Grassmann points out that the term is a cynical usage of the Nazis, lamenting that, "unfortunately, this concept is still frequently and uncritically used today."[237] Some other texts offer alternative explanations for the origin of the term. Binder and Burkhardt declare that the impression made by the "countless shattered shop windows of Jewish businesses found popular expression in Berlin with the term 'Reich Crystal Night.' "[238] Heumann states, less specifically, that "because during this night the sound of breaking and shattering glass and crystal was heard, it has since been called 'Reich Crystal Night.' "[239]

Whether originally Nazi or popular, the term Reich Crystal Night renders the 1938 Nazi pogrom sufficiently innocent and innocuous sounding, that, like the term "Final Solution of the Jewish Question," it deserves to be treated as a part of the phraseology of Nazi propaganda: terms designed to camouflage the measures it describes and to manipulate public opinion by its terminology. Though it is deeply embedded in the literature, steps need to be undertaken to replace this vocabulary with terms which more accurately describe the real horror of the 1938 pogrom.

The persecutions of the 1930s in the advanced history, political science and social studies books is presented similarly to the intermediate texts, except that the former often carry more interpretative and evaluative judgments.

Most advanced texts mention the boycott of 1933, although only one enlarges on the subject: Wanda Kampmann's *Politik und Gesellschaft, Gründlagen und Probleme der modernen Welt. Lehr- und Arbeitsbuch für den historisch-politischen Lernbereich (Sekundarstufe II)* (Politics and Society. Foundations and Problems of the Modern World. Teaching and Workbook for the historical-political Subject Areas. Secondary Level II). She notes that Julius Streicher directed the Nazi boycott and that, "despite a profound and broadly based anti-Semitic mood, at least among labor and the educated middle class, their measures found little response, so that thereafter the Party changed to so-called 'spontaneous' activities against the Jews."[240]

The expulsion of the Jews from government positions is mentioned only by about one-third of the advanced history, social studies, and political science texts. Tenbrock and Kluxen add the comment that Jewish World War I veterans were exempted from these dismissals.[241]

In treating the Nuremberg Race Laws of 1935, in sharp contrast with the intermediate texts, many advanced history and some political science books call attention to the pseudo-scientific character of Hitler's racial teachings. Hartwich, for instance, stresses that:

> as soon as these concepts were confronted with reality, their scientific indefensibility became clear. Thus, after the Nuremberg Laws (1935) and the measures for their implementation [were enacted], the proof of *biological* ancestry—the determination of who is a Jew—had to be demonstrated with the help of *confessional membership.*[242]

Hartwich reminds students further that "only an infinitesimal number of the German people corresponded to the Aryan-Nordic ideal of big, blue-eyed, and blonde." Tenbrock and Kluxen make the point that as soon as "religious membership was proclaimed to be the criteria for racial membership . . . , the arbitrariness and senselessness of racial ideology become evident."[243] Eichberg stresses this teaching: Despite the racial principle embodied in the Nuremberg Laws, those "who belonged to the Jewish religious community were considered to have been of Jewish ancestry. Here, the contradiction between racial teaching and religious criteria lay clearly revealed."[244]

Altrichter and Glaser also teach the point, but in such an off-hand manner that it is questionable whether it can be recognized that they are depicting the irrational and hypocritical nature of Nazi racial ideology: "In regard to [the Nuremberg Racial Laws], the characteristic which determined one as a 'Jew' [was] current or earlier membership of German citizens or their ancestors in the Jewish religion; apparently 'racial characteristics' for this were not usable."[245]

There are other ways in which texts reveal the contradictions involved in racial teaching. Werner Grütter's *Hinweise und Interpretation* (Directives and Interpretation) to *Zeiten und Menschen* (Times and People) is the only text to state the implications of the requirement that all Jews take the first names of Israel and Sarah.: "The ordinance on the first names was enacted before 'Reich Crystal Night' and was supposed to make all Jewish citizens recognizable. Apparently, they were not really so sure all Germans could be outwardly distinguished from Jews, as a broadly disseminated and ugly propaganda would have it believed."[246]

In a later section, Grütter calls attention to the inability of the SS to distinguish *Mischlinge*, and that most persons of mixed parentage were not included in the mass murders: "The authorities opposed this [since] the technical difficulties of distinguishing them were too great. [Thus,] only people in this category who were taken into custody in concentration camps were murdered in the extermination camps."[247]

Werner Ripper, in his text *Weltgeschichte im Aufriß. Der europäische Faschismus und das Dritte Reich* (World History in Outline. European Fascism and the Third Reich), points to the significance of such laws in facilitating more and more radical measures:

> From the perspective of history, there can be no doubt that the social isolation and moral stigmatization of the Jews which [the Nazis] sought to accomplish—or complete—by instituting a law based purely on biological criteria, provided a psychological impetus for the later, radical persecution measures of the Party leadership, for whom these laws had meaning only as stages of their Jewish policies.[248]

Hans Ritscher and Alfred Krink, in their political science text, *Welt der Politik II: Lehrbuch der Zeitgeschichte* (World of Politics, II: Teaching Book for Contemporary History), draw a clear line of connection between the Nuremberg Laws and the ensuing stages of persecution policy. The enactment of the Nuremberg Laws, they declare,

> became the basis for thirteen implementation ordinances and 250 specific ordinances which also made clear the ideological background of National Socialist anti-Semitism, and gradually made unbearable the life of the Jewish population in Germany: They intervened in personal life, tore families apart, forbade marriages between Aryans and Jews, distin-

guished Aryan Reich citizens from Jewish members of the state, who thereby became second class people.[249]

Gallmeister concludes that the Nuremberg Laws and other ordinances "left the Jews without rights and delivered them over to totally arbitrary action."[250]

The most devastating of these prewar arbitrary actions was the German pogrom of 1938. In treating the pogrom, the upper-level history, political science and social studies texts display many of the strengths and weaknesses of their intermediate counterparts. Once again, many do not adequately identify Herschel Grynszpan, who remains merely "a Jew" who murdered a German diplomat in France;[251] Ripper describes Grynszpan curiously as "a Jewish refugee."[252] Only Grütter has the sensitivity to refer to Grynszpan as "a desperate Polish Jew."[253] Further, almost all texts refer to the victims of the 1938 pogrom simply as "Jews." Only Elmar Krautkrämer and Eberhard Radbruch's text, *Wandel der Welt* (The Changing World) for adult education, refers to the victims as *German*-Jews![254]

Most texts content themselves with teaching merely that Grynszpan's assassination was a welcome pretext for violence against the Jews. Few texts trace the real origin and background of the pogrom such as do Fernis and Hillgruber: "Jews of Polish origin were expelled. When the 17-year-old son of one of the deported Jews shot an embassy advisor of the German embassy in Paris, Goebbels took this as grounds to carry out organized, violent activities."[255]

Kampmann and Mickel say only that, since the Nazis "couldn't drive the Jews out of [German] economic life by legal means, they seized upon terror."[256]

A few texts, such as Ripper's, provide an excellent analysis of the genesis of the pogrom. Ripper poses the question: "To what extent did the assassination by Herschel Grynszpan of November 7, 1938, promote the intentions of the radical anti-Semites within the National Socialist leadership?" Ripper reports—his is the only textbook to do so—a meeting in the Reich Air Ministry of October 14, 1938, concerning the Four Year Plan, in which Göring declared that "the Jewish question must be settled using all possible means—for they must be pushed out of the economy." Ripper notes that, by the murder of the legation secretary vom Rath in Paris on November 7, "the desired lever was offered." He also presents portions of Goebbels' speech inciting the Germans to riot, November 9.[257] Ripper states that, based upon an internal Nazi court report sent to Göring, Goebbels gave an oral directive for the pogrom. Furthermore, Ripper declares that, most certainly "Hitler himself had co-knowledge and, indeed, was the responsible originator of the allegedly 'spontaneous reaction of the German people,' although he was smart enough to remain in the background."[258]

Willi and Margret Frank, in *Politik heute* (Politics Today), also attest that Goebbels, "certainly in agreement with Hitler, incited the Germans to 'spontaneous' measures of revenge. Indeed, such spontaneous revenge actions scarcely took place anywhere."[259]

One text in particular, Kurt Gönner and Rolf Krug's, *Politik in unseren Tagen* (Politics in our Day), makes excellent use of Goebbels' November 9 speech, in which he ascribes the pogrom to an "outraged" German citizenry. The authors cite the relevant portions of Goebbels' speech, then refute them, using internal Nazi documents. According to the authors, Goebbels stated in the *Völkischer Beobachter* that, "indeed, [while] it had gone to the extreme of dynamiting Jewish property, nowhere had it gone so far as plundering." Goebbels continues: "It is our opinion that the reaction of the German people to this cowardly, treacherous murder in Paris must be explained in terms of the ruthless brutality of the deed. The reaction was neither organized nor prepared, but rather broke out spontaneously within the nation."[260]

This document is followed by a dispatch sent by Heydrich to Göring reporting that "plundering of Jewish shops and businesses" had, in fact, taken place "in numerous cities," and that 174 persons had been arrested to prevent further plundering. This document, in turn, is followed by a report from an SA brigade chief who refers to the previous order of his *Gruppenführer* (Group Leader) that his brigade dynamited or set fire to fifty or more synagogues.[261] Here is a fine example of the use of Nazi documents to indict the regime, revealing its own lies and hypocrisy.

In their account of the events of the 1938 pogrom, Fernis and Haverkamp, surprisingly, make no mention whatever of the roles of Göring and Goebbels in the pogrom.[262]

The suffering of the victims of the pogrom is made special mention of in only a few upper-division texts. Baumann tells of "hordes of SA-men who violently broke into houses and businesses . . . killing men, women and children"; he reports the "outrage abroad," the fact that "the U.S.A. even recalled its ambassador and threatened to break off diplomatic relations with the Reich."[263] Altrichter and Glaser explain with feeling that the "Jewish people were tortured, murdered or delivered over to concentration camps, where they only rarely survived the tortures of the brutal guard overseers."[264] Ritscher and Krink explain that the more than 20,000 Jews sent to concentration camps "were mistreated there until they promised to leave Germany immediately."[265]

The cynically imposed collective "fine" on the Jewish people for the damages of the pogrom is also usually discussed. In the same manner as the intermediate texts, all upper-division books use the term *"Büsse"* (atonement), or *"Sühneleistung"* (expiation payment) to refer to this criminal extortion; in some cases they do not even place the term within quotation marks. Only Gallmeister adds the important information that the *"Sühneleistung"* meant "financial ruin for thousands of Jewish families."[266]

Some texts also use the popular Nazi designation for the pogrom. Only Ripper comments that the term *Reichsckristalnacht* "was invented in Berlin as a bitterly ironic and critically intended designation."[267]

In summary, all textbooks, intermediate and advanced, describe the November pogrom, sometimes in considerable detail. However, scarcely any evaluate its larger meaning as a turning point in the Nazi persecution of German Jews: The pogrom was a clear signal from the public that they would not stand up for the Jews; it also offered further demonstration that the magisterium of the law had been seized and subverted by a criminal regime. As such, the November 9th pogrom represents an important milestone on the road to Auschwitz.

"Aryanization" and Plunder of Jewish Property

German text authors devote little attention to the looting of Jewish property. Neither in presenting the persecution and murder of the Jews, nor in reporting restitution (*Wiedergutmachung*) to Jewish survivors, does the gigantic Nazi plunder of the Jews receive more than passing attention. A number of textbook analyses have criticized this deficiency,[268] but the accounts have not changed.

When the enrichment of the Nazis and occasionally other Germans is mentioned, it is done in connection with the 1938 pogrom or the Holocaust itself. In an earlier edition of his text, R. H. Tenbrock published an excellent commentary on the subject in the form of a 1934 newspaper article entitled "Expropriation in the New Reich":

> To the dangers which can justify expropriation of property by the government in an emergency belong also some threats which only now perhaps are being recognized as such, namely the danger to blood and race. Thus, expropriation proceedings are underway against foreign racial elements and do not require legal empowerment in so far as they pertain to German ground and land. We must do away completely

with liberalistic ideas of the "just state." Our highest law is, What serves the German People: that is just.[269]

Unfortunately, this source has been deleted from the most recent edition of Tenbrock and, like most all others, the text contains no discussion of the economics of anti-Semitism.

Menzel and Textor are among the few authors who point out the Jewish loss of contractual protections before the law: "The Jews, in addition [to the loss of freedom of movement], lost the protection of the law [*Rechtsschutz*]: one could take their dwelling from them and break all contracts."[270]

Ebeling and Birkenfeld in their teacher manual allude to the "beginnings of forced Aryanization of the economy amid threats and blackmail."[271] The term "Aryanization" used here, however, is a Nazi euphemism which renders innocuous the extortion and theft of helpless victims' property and personal belongings. In the few texts which discuss "Aryanization," not only is the massive expropriation passed over in silence, but in most cases the Nazi term is not even explained. Hoffmann deals incidentally with the subject, writing that in 1938 "compulsory Aryanization of all Jewish enterprises" took place, in the course of which "many who could now acquire Jewish economic enterprises for little money enriched themselves."[272] Hug, using almost the same language as Hoffmann, states laconically that "many enriched themselves."[273] Lachner mentions the German takeover of Jewish assets in the wake of the 1938 pogrom: "Jewish property owners therefore had to close their doors or sell, naturally, at giveaway prices";[274] and Kaier writes of party functionaries extorting Jews and forcing them to "place their property in German hands at prices far below the value of the property."[275] In no text, however, is there an inquiry into the extent and use made of Nazi economic extortion of the Jews, the degree of German awareness of these gangster-like shakedowns, or their atttude toward them.

Kistler and Stroppe mention only that Jewish business owners had to place non-Jewish business mangers in charge of their enterprises.[276] Kaier is clearer in explaining that "Aryanization" of Jewish businesses meant that "Jewish enterprises were transferred to German hands by means of threats and extortion by local Party functionaries at prices far below the true value," and he reports the "plundering of German Jews by the state," listing among the extortions the required sale of security bonds, jewels, artwork, increased taxation, and the "forced Aryanization" of all Jewish businesses.[277]

As part of the persecution of the Jews, most texts at least briefly treat the final exclusion of the Jews from the German economy in the last years before the war. Some, such as Bernhard Heinloth's *Geschichte* (History), state only that "Jews were expelled from the German economy,"[278] others, such as Boeck, Döhn and Burkhardt, identify some of the professions from which Jews were expelled, noting that they could not be lawyers, doctors, judges, writers, or druggists.[279] Heumann cites the loss of employment, adding that after the Nuremberg Laws, "those who remained behind could only earn their subsistence with great difficulty."[280]

Upper-level history, political science, and social studies texts place no more emphasis on the plunder of the Jews than the intermediate texts. In most, economic aspects are treated as part of the general persecutions. Eichberg, for example, in dealing with the Nuremberg Laws and pressure to emigrate, notes incidentally that the Nazis "did not at first intervene against the Jews in the economy in order not to get into difficulties with the 'Four Year Plans' and abroad."[281] He states that after "Crystal Night" the process of "Aryanization" was begun—which he defines as "the dispossession of the Jewish economic enterprises"[282]—but makes no further mention of the subject. A single advanced textbook, Tenbrock and Kluxen, alludes to the loss of contractual protections before the law, noting that "previously acquired rights such as pension claims were lost." In discussing the aftermath of the 1938 pogrom, the authors report that the Jews "had to sell their property to 'Aryans' at ruinous prices."[283]

The most finely nuanced treatment of the economic question in advanced texts is developed by Ritscher and Krink. They note that hundreds of professors and thousands of lawyers, doctors, officials, and artists were expelled from their positions within the economy. Then,

> In the next three years, from 1935 to 1937, this process of expulsion was significantly broadened so that the Jews finally disappeared from almost all professional groups. A last refuge remained for them yet in the business world. Here, Hitler granted them, under pressure from Schacht [the *Reichsbank* President and financial wizard of Germany], a brief reprieve because he needed their knowledge and experience until qualified replacements could be educated.[284]

The final economic ruination of the Jews took place, Ritscher and Krink report, when the Jews were expelled entirely from the economy soon after the pogrom of 1938, and were no longer allowed even to be managers or salesmen.

Humiliations and Deprivations

Between 1933 and 1939 the Nazis subjected the German Jews to an endless array of humilations and deprivations which gradually deprived them of the means of life itself. In addition to the major persecutions presented in all texts—the Nuremberg Laws, the pogrom of 1938, the expulsion of the Jews from their jobs, and the expropriation of their property—the Nazis passed a series of more than 250 laws, decrees, ordinances, and directives calculated to devastate the Jews of Germany. Here, above all, is a rich source of materials for students who are attempting to understand how the Nazis corrupted the law to destroy a people by subjecting them to great suffering before finally stripping them of life itself.

Most textbooks present only a brief selection of these degradations and humilations, limited to an average of three or four significant examples. Virtually all texts mention the expulsion of Jewish children from German schools. Quite a number of texts mention as well the prohibition of Jews from public transportation, cultural events, and public facilities of one kind or another, such as swimming pools or heated shelters. Others, such as Kistler and Stroppe, also include lists of personal possessions which Jews were forbidden to own, such as record players, typewriters, bicycles, heaters, vacuum cleaners, irons, cameras, radios, and other electrical appliances, although the texts do not disclose that the Jews had to surrender these belongings without compensation. Karlheinz Pelzer's, *Geschichte für die Hauptschule* (History for High School) presents an impressive list of deprivations and exactions made of Jews within the period 1938–1942. Except for the texts cited above,[285] most texts list only three or four prohibitions, though the collective listing from all text sources constitutes an imposing inventory: In addition to the disabilities mentioned above, the NS-regime forbade Jews from walking in parks, forests, and on certain streets; they were prohibited from attending all sports events, theaters, movies or museums; from possessing driver's licenses, electric razors, or household pets; and Jews were required to live in segregated housing and to observe strict curfew ordinances. Ebeling and Birkenfeld's text also includes an illustration of a placard which states, "Jews will not be served here," which, the authors report, was displayed in German retail stores.[286]

The cataloging of belongings which many young people take for granted, but which Jews were forbidden to possess, is a valuable aid to teaching about the persecution of the Jews and, properly emphasized, more could be done to present this aspect effectively.

Almost all texts report that Jews were required to wear the star of David attached to their clothing. A few further note that it was required of children of six years and older; others note the date when the decree was put in force (September 1, 1941). Kaier notes, moreover, that "the houses of Jews were also identified in this manner."[287] Schmid provides the information that German Jews had to have the letter "J" stamped in their passports.[288] But none of this information is used to emphasize that the requirement for wearing the identifying star further demonstrates the inadequacy of Nazi racial doctrine, which contended that Jews were distinguishable by their physical racial appearance from the surrounding population. The texts do not take this opportunity to emphasize that European Jews were indistinguishable from other Europeans except by characteristics prescribed by their faith. Even circumcision, vulgarly relied upon by the Nazis as an identifying mark, is based upon religious practice. The texts make little note of the fact that the Germans had no reliable means of identifying Jews by physical characteristics, and that the star of David and other measures *had* to be introduced to facilitate identification.

Advanced history, political science, and social studies texts do not differ markedly from their intermediate-level counterparts in interpreting this subject. However, many more of them cite a longer list of ordinances which humiliated and finally destroyed German Jewry.

Baumann begins his description of Jewish losses with a moving introduction, noting that in the years after 1938, "there followed more than 250 laws and ordinances which gradually made life for the Jews a hell, and finally took from them all possibility for existence."[289] His inventory of disabilities includes some pre-1938 privations as well as many subsequent ones: expulsion from the civil service, medicine, the law, business leadership, the educational system; the imposition of the given name of Israel or Sarah; curfew; the wearing of the Star of David; exclusion from films, theaters, swimming pools; confiscation of electrical appliances, typewriters, and bicycles. And these inhumane laws, Baumann declares, were "a chicanery which was only the beginning."[290] To the list of Nazi "chicaneries," Ripper adds the particularly hypocritical Nazi directive prohibiting the names of Jewish military dead from being inscribed on future monuments erected to honor the fallen of World War I.[291]

While both intermediate and advanced texts report the humiliations and deprivations of the Jews in sufficient detail to convey that German-Jews were hounded, mortified, and deprived of basic human rights, they do not examine the persecutions in a way which examines the perpetrators even as a group, much less as individuals. Except for the occasional mention of Hitler, Himmler, Heydrich, and Hoess, the executors of the killings are depicted mainly as organizations (*SS, Gestapo, Einzatzgruppen*), rather than people. Were the processes of this degradation depicted in greater detail, the textbooks would perhaps become involved in a discussion of German complicity in these events, something which very few texts are prepared to do. As Martin and Eva Kolinsky have noted, while most texts treat the persecution of the German Jews, they still "fail to present how and with whose ideological support and physical assistance these policies were carried out."[292]

Forced Emigration

The largest wave of expulsions of German Jews took place following the 1938 pogrom and most textbooks treat the subject at that point, summarizing Jewish emigration for the period 1933 to 1939. Although the majority of German Jews fled the country before the outbreak of war, a significant number remained in Germany or other European countries, later to be murdered in the death camps. The task of authors in discussing the expulsions of German Jews is to clarify to students that this was a case of Germans driving fellow Germans from their homeland; to explain further why many Jews, despite the hostile atmosphere remained in Germany; and to make clear that leaving Germany was not *Auswanderung* (emigration), as Nazi propaganda proclaimed, but more accurately described as *Austreibung* (expulsion).

In reporting the aftermath of the 1938 pogrom, Kaier comments: "Fortunate were the Jews who already at this time read correctly the signs of the times and decided to emigrate in good time."[293] The statement introduces a prophetic note into history: that of avoiding a catastrophic fate by correctly foreseeing the signs of the times. None of those who left Germany, of course, even remotely foresaw the Holocaust, nor did they think themselves "fortunate" in becoming refugees from their homeland. It would be better to emphasize the suffering that accompanies such decisions to leave home, relatives, friends—all that is familiar—and to portray how German Jews felt about leaving the land which had been their home for centuries.

The tragedy of the 1930s German Jewry was precisely that they *were* so rooted in home and hearth, so assimilated, so fundamentally *German* that they could scarcely conceive of expatriation from a country which for many of them had been for centuries the land of their ancestors.

Most textbooks do make reference to the difficulties of German-
Jews leaving their country, and some texts present the subject quite
well. Kistler and Stroppe, for example, present a geneological table
and family tree of Moses Mendelsohn, including many illustrious
family members and their professions. The student is asked to identify
the birthplace of these family members, and is informed that many
of Mendelsohn's descendants lived in the time of the Third Reich,
though their fate is not discussed. The authors ask the student to
answer: "Why would they legitimately feel themselves to be German?—
Why did the decision to emigrate appear so difficult to them and to
other German Jews?" The text provides further information on the
financial and other difficulties involved in emigration.[294]

Tenbrock inserts an excellent quotation from the great German
dramatist Max Reinhardt, which expresses how difficult it was for
Jews to emigrate. Reinhardt wrote in 1933:

> The decision finally to separate myself from the German theater is not
> easy for me. I lose the possession not only of thirty-seven years of
> activity but, even more, I lose the land on which I have built for a
> lifetime and on which I myself grew up. I lose my homeland. I need
> not say what this means to those who place this concept above everything
> else.[295]

To Tenbrock's account may be added that of Menzel and Textor, who
treat emigration with balance and sympathy:

> The Jews were struck by a plethora of edicts, ordinances and directives
> which took from them almost all freedom of movement. Many lived
> from the remainder of their means; others had to do forced labor. [To
> emigrate], they had to leave behind the bulk of their assets [*Vermögen*].
> Many countries refused to take them. Those Jews who, in spite of
> everything, remained in Germany, could not imagine the fate which
> yet threatened them.[296]

Menzel and Textor also ask the student to recount why the Jews
were not allowed to take their valuables with them. Although the
text provides no direct answer, the student may surmise the material
motives of the NS-government, and its satisfaction in finding that
countries were reluctant to receive impoverished Jewish immigrants
during the worldwide depression of the 1930s.

Binder and Burkhardt discuss emigration before they treat the 1938
pogrom. They view emigration as "the first stage of the 'Final
Solution,'" noting that "the National Socialists at first sought to solve

the 'Jewish Problem' by means of expulsion of the Jews from Germany." This is followed by the important information—the only text to mention it—that most Jews "became fully without means since a Reich Flight Tax [*Reichsfluchtsteuer*] was levied upon them. This amounted to 99% for property amounting to DM 1,000 and 99.9% for property valued at DM 10,000 and above, and so forth. . . . It thus became ever more difficult for the plundered refugees to find acceptance abroad."[297]

Grassmann, in reporting the number of Jews who left Germany between 1933 and 1938, stresses that "Many Jews were too poor, however, to pay to leave the country. Additionally, it was very difficult to find a country which took in immigrants."[298] Though Grassmann's is one of the better textbooks on the Holocaust, he does not explicitly mention the connection between the impoverishment of the Jews and the reluctance of countries to accept them during the economic crisis of the 1930s. While anti-Semitism did play a role in many countries, certainly the plight of the Jews was exacerbated by the fact that the NS-regime confiscated virtually all of their possessions before allowing their departure. Lachner, to her credit, refers to this in her excellent presentation on emigration:

> The Gestapo themselves were interested in the emigration of the Jews, to be sure, only if they left behind a great portion of their means. Many older Jews did not want to give up their homes, especially since they still believed that in a civilized country like Germany their lives were not in danger. For Jews who no longer had any means, leaving the country was made even more difficult by the fact that only a few states accepted them. Thus, some 280,000 German Jews remained as a pawn in the hands of Hitler when on January 30, 1939, he declared in a Parliamentary speech that a future war would bring about the destruction of the Jewish race in Europe.[299]

This is relatively extensive coverage of emigration as compared with most texts. Heumann, for example, does not even treat the theme in the text section, and only casually alludes to it in his chapter summary: "At first Hitler wanted to force the Jews to emigrate."[300]

Burkhardt devotes more space to it, emphasizing its compulsory nature ("This expulsion, which the National Socialists called emigration") but then twice refers to the expulsions as "emigration," using quotation marks to suggest irony. He also calls attention to the relationship between the Nazi theft of Jewish possessions and their difficulty in leaving the country: "For Jews without means, it was always more difficult to find acceptance abroad."[301]

Tenbrock handles the expulsions well. In a passage dealing with the pre-1938 emigration, he stresses that these were *German* exiles, that many, and especially the elderly, did not want to give up their homes for an uncertain fate as refugees, and that they clung to the hope that

> a nation with the culture of Germany would give them a chance to live, even if under conditions of reduced rights, and would never rob them of life itself. Also the readiness of foreign countries to accept [Jews] was small. With the effects of the world economic crisis, the entry of additional manpower was not desired. The British occupation force limited *emigration* to Palestine. Thus, only about a quarter of the emigrants succeeded in getting there. Jewish assistance organizations abroad, of course, accepted refugees, but many of them lived in impoverished conditions.[302]

In his post-1938 pogrom section, Tenbrock returns briefly to the expulsions:

> Now a mass flight set in. Approximately 150,000 Jews left the Reich in 1938/39. Those remaining moved toward their terrible destiny.[303]

Heinloth (after the briefest treatment of the persecutions), states only that, of the 200,000 Jews left in the country, "those who did not emigrate from Germany were condemned to a shadowy existence," without mentioning how they continued to exist. In his section on the Holocaust, he returns briefly to the expulsions: "After the beginning of the war, the authorities at first permitted the emigration (*Auswanderung*) of Jews to continue—of course under severe conditions, such as the loss of their entire domestic wealth and payment for departure in the currency of the country of acceptance."[304]

Many texts compare the number of Jews living in Germany in 1933 with those of the Jews remaining after forced emigration. The figures for German Jewry in 1933 range from 500,000 to 540,000. The number of Jews who departed Germany between 1933 and the outbreak of war in 1939 is reported with considerable variation in texts, ranging from 125,000 (Schwander) to 300,000 (Grassmann), a range of difference too broad to be accounted for by unreliable sources.[305]

In all the textbooks, the exercise questions asked at the end of the section on the prewar persecutions lack imagination and clear pedagogical purpose, especially when it is remembered that these persecutions were the direct antecedents of the Holocaust. Many texts ask the student merely to recite various measures against the Jews; some ask slightly more, as, for example, Heinloth, who requests that the student use the textbook to "evaluate and judge how the Jews were treated" from 1933 to 1939.[306] On the other hand, authors such as Boeck, who includes thirteen review questions in his section on the prewar NS regime, has no questions relating to the persecution or any other aspects of German-Jewish relations during the 1930s.[307]

Advanced history, political science, and social studies texts do not markedly differ in tone or comment from the intermediate history texts. They, too, focus on the obstacles which made it difficult or impossible for German Jews to leave, and they report the loss of economic means of Jewish emigrés which added so much to their plight.

A sympathetic and effective presentation is done by Krautkrämer, who stresses the assimilation and integration of German Jews:

> Germans of Jewish ancestry feel and act as Germans. German cultural and spiritual life owed much to them. They know that Hitler hates them, but few can understand how brutally Hitler is going to proceed against them. The poet Jochen Klepper, who is married to a Jew, describes the situation of the German Jews: If anyone leads the life of a German family, it is us. . . , The most difficult thing for a Jew of this educational class is that they are absorbed to such a degree in Germany—they love only German landscapes, language, music, literature; love only German festivals; and find not the slightest solace or substitute in their own ancestry![308]

On the other hand, some texts, such as Fernis and Hillgruber, state little more than that the Jews "felt themselves to be German."[309]

Many texts stress the Jewish sense of unreality about the danger of remaining. Kampmann and Michel make this point, explaining also that the Jewish exodus from Germany was not a decision to emigrate, but an expulsion:

> Many could not believe in a genuine life-threatening situation; they considered the excesses of the early thirties to be a transitional phenomenon; indeed, there were even returnees who had experienced how difficult it is to make a new start abroad. The increased emigration after 1938, which was more like expulsion—for it cost the emigrants their possessions—met with considerable difficulties in the potential lands of acceptance and in the area of money exchange.[310]

Though Gönner and Krug are too brief, they more accurately note that the German Jews "either emigrated or were driven out." Deuschle refers only to a "mass flight" of Jews after 1938.[311]

Ritscher and Krink discuss conditions of Jews between 1938 and 1939, when: "It was sought, above all, to force them to emigrate and at the same time thereby to enrich themselves on their property."[312]

After the 1938 pogrom, the emigration statistics doubled over the preceding years, "although the conditions of emigration had significantly worsened. Many European countries . . . required high immigration fees. . . . By the beginning of the war, already more than half had gotten clear of the pressure. The remainder were comprised mainly of poor and older Jews; half of them were over 65 years of age."[313]

Hey raises the important question: "Why did foreign governments make immigration of Jews into their countries more difficult?," and, referring to the war period, he asks the related question: "Why will the emigration program now be given up?" From the text documents, it becomes clear, however, that Hey expects the student to use *the Wannsee-Protocol of Reinhard Heydrich's speech* to answer these questions![314] To be sure, the SS officer expresses his views on why foreign governments did not take in more Jews—and declares further that, "in view of the new possibilities of the East," further emigration is forbidden due to war—but this is hardly an adequate textbook approach to such questions!

Bernd Hey and Joachim Radkau, in their teacher manual, *Politische Weltkunde II, Nationalsozialismus und Faschismus, Handreichung für den Lehrer* (Political World Studies II, National Socialism and Fascism, Teacher Handbook), provide a carefully balanced answer to why German Jews had difficulty in finding acceptance in foreign lands:

> The massive emigration of German Jews also placed their new host countries in difficulties. Since the German Jews frequently could not take their possesions with them, they caused expenses in part for the countries receiving them at the outset. It was not always easy to create jobs for them; [and] problems in mentality and language made their incorporation more difficult. Further, there was fear of alienation and a latent anti-Semitism, which also existed outside of Germany.[315]

Gallmeister reports that only about half of the original half-million German Jews "succeeded in emigrating," without citing the difficulties thrown in their way. On the other hand, he does comment on how difficult life was for those remaining, who had to "eke out a living in forced labor assigned to them."[316]

Ritscher and Krink also make a good case for why many German Jews, despite the threat to them, remained in Germany:

> Many Jews hoped . . . that the National Socialist outbreaks would finally come to an end if only one showed oneself to be patient and good-willed. They did not want to leave their homeland prematurely; this applied especially to the older among them.
>
> Apart from the fact that many lacked the means or strength to emigrate, they also felt themselves deeply attached to Germany. Almost 20% of the Jewish population had taken an active part in the First World War.[317]

Generally, upper division political science and social studies texts are devoid of review questions about any aspect of the persecutions of the 1930s. Only Frank asks the general question: "What consequences are to be derived from the persecution of the Jews?"[318]

Advance Warnings of the Holocaust

Remarkably, many texts include Nazi statements warning or prophesying the destruction of the German Jews. There does not appear to be a requirement in the state guidelines that such statements be included, nor is there much evident purpose for including them beyond the terrifying prophetic quality they possess and perhaps for the warning function they may serve. The Nazis, it seems, did publicly proclaim their murderous intentions in general terms on various occasions—though sane and civilized people simply did not heed them.

Most of the texts which emphasize these prophesies use Hitler's words. Hoffmann, for example, takes *Mein Kampf* as the source of his warning—although he does not choose the best citation he could have made. In his learning goals for teachers, he states that the core of Hitler's thought was racial teaching bound up with Social Darwinist ideas of a constant struggle for existence, a relentless, merciless struggle for total domination by one group, and "the extirpation of all people, groups, and nations declared to be enemies." Hoffmann points out that "as early as 1927, Hitler published his extirpatory goals in all clarity in *Mein Kampf*." In his exercise question, Hoffmann explains why he includes Hitler's prophetic warnings: "How do we explain the fact that for a long time Hitler's statements, disseminated in millions of copies, apparently were not taken seriously?"[319] The text does not answer the question, but the purpose of the question seems to be to emphasize that threats and warnings, no matter how sinister, were simply not believed.

Boeck cites an undated Hitler speech which, in hindsight, seems to hint of coming disaster: "The National Socialist government will remove the unhealthy influence of the Jews. No Jew in the future will any longer be allowed to exploit the honest, hard-working German people and corrupt them by word and example in the Jewish spirit. No Jew will be able to be a citizen of Germany. Long live Germany! *Sieg Heil!*[320]

Many texts quote or describe Hitler's notorious speech before the *Reichstag* on January 30, 1939, in which he "publicly announced the destruction of the Jewish race in Europe" in case a new war broke out in Europe.[321] Referring to Hitler's 1939 *Reichstag* speech, Heumann asks students: "On whom is placed the responsibility for the Second World War?"[322]

Binder and Burkhardt's is the only text which points out that Hitler made the same prophetic threat on three different occasions: originally in the *Reichstag* speech of January 30, 1939, marking the sixth anniversary of the Nazi seizure of power; again on September 1, 1939, marking the outbreak of World War II; and again on January 30, 1942, the ninth anniversary of Hitler's seizure of power.[323]

Other texts employ statements of such lesser Nazi leaders as Goebbels or Göring. Döhn cites a 1932 speech of Goebbels in which he "demanded that the Jews be eradicated like vermin."[324] In his teacher manual, Jaacks cites a Goebbels' speech made soon after the 1938 pogrom, declaring it a prelude to the Holocaust: "The entire removal of the Jews from Europe is not a moral question, but one of state security. . . . Just as the potato-bug destroys the potato, indeed, has to destroy it, so the Jew destroys states and peoples. Against this, there is only one measure: fundamental removal of the danger!"[325]

Other authors cite utterances made after the November pogrom. Kistler and Stroppe, for example, quote Göring's statement of November 12, 1938, which, in retrospect, can be recognized for its prophetic character: "If the German Reich enters into an external political conflict at any time in the forseeable future, there is no question that in Germany we will also carry out a great reckoning with the Jews."[326]

In treating Nazi elections and terroristic measures, Kaier cites a Göring speech wherein the *Reichsmarschall* proclaims the purpose of concentration camps: "Here I am not practicing justice. I have here only to destroy and exterminate, nothing else."[327] Boeck cites the same statement in connection with Sachsenhausen.

While the above statements are made in connection with German prewar concentration camps, they and the Hitler prophesies evoke a sinister and foreboding atmosphere, preparing the student for the section on the Holocaust.

Only one text, Grassmann's, uses a Jewish source of prophetic warning. Its author was none other than Rabbi Leo Baeck. Though in his darkest moments he could not have foreseen the horrors of the Holocaust, Rabbi Baeck already saw matters with sharp insight in 1933. The text states: "Only a few Jews had a foreboding of the imminent tragedy of German-Jewish life together. To them belonged the Berlin Rabbi, Dr. Leo Baeck, who said in 1933: 'The thousand year history of German Judaism is at an end.'"[328]

In upper-division history texts, as well as some social studies and political science books, the prophetic warnings by Nazis of their intentions are stressed with even greater emphasis. Many of these texts contain short passages which suggest that Nazi leaders publicly threatened genocide long before they actually carried it out. Again, the emphasis is on Hitler's utterances. In a section on Nazi racism, Fernis and Haverkamp, for example, state that, in accordance with Nazi racial theory and Adolf Hitler, "the Jews, above all, as members of an allegedly inferior race, were to be oppressed or exterminated."[329] On the other hand, the authors add,

These radical goals, of course, were familiar only to those who took the trouble to read the writings of the National Socialists. Most people after their experiences with the numerous parties of the Weimar Republic were not inclined to take party programs seriously. For the majority of voters, the decisive role was played by the hope for a political, economic and social New Order.[330]

In a similar vein, Fernis and Hillgruber mention Hitler's prophetic warnings of murder, but emphasize even more strongly why the warnings were not widely known or, when they were known, were not heeded by Germans:

Of course, at first these radical world views [and] long-range goals were familiar only to those who went to the trouble of reading National Socialist writings such as Hitler's *Mein Kampf* and Rosenberg's *Myth of the Twentieth Century*. In public propaganda, the masses of the National Socialist electorate were addressed primarily in terms of a political, economic and social New Order. Many Germans welcomed . . . these ideas . . . [but], the radical core of the National Socialist world view remained hidden from many behind the goals being pursued.[331]

Baumann also emphasizes that the threats contained in Hitler's writings and program simply were not taken seriously, by Germans, or by other nations: "Many intelligent people, even abroad, by no means believed in the seriousness of such a lunatic program. The 55 million deaths of the Second World War as well as the gas chambers and crematoria of the extermination camps should make clear to the world how seriously Hitler took his program."[332]

Textor and Kluxen consider that the prophetic statements about the Jews in *"Mein Kampf* (1925–1927)" were "formulated in such a manner that the National Socialists putting into practice the destruction of the Jews and [their] occupation policies during the war could not have surprised [anyone]. (*Mein Kampf* was disseminated in almost 10 million copies, but was taken less seriously than it was intended.)"[333] Thus, the authors conclude their section on the 1930s persecutions of the Jews with the statement: "The often announced 'Final Solution,' which could only be mass murder, approached visibly nearer."[334]

Gönner and Krug, Ritscher and Krink, Altrichter and Glaser, and Gallmeister all cite Hitler's dire threat of January 1939, against the Jews.[335] Ritscher and Krink also cite Gauleiter Wilhelm Kube's ominous remark of May 1934, that "One can begin with half-measures, but this fight will finally have to end with ruthless brutality carried out by the predominantly Nordic peoples."[336] Eichberg alludes to Göring's warning, without mentioning the *Reichmarschall*'s name, when he states that "threats by National Socialist leaders already held out the prospect 'of a great final reckoning with the Jews' in case of war."[337]

One of the most remarkable of the Hitlerian death threats has been quoted by Werner Ripper in his thematic text on European Fascism and the Third Reich. It is worth citing in its entirety to show the emphasis placed on the advance warnings in texts and for its historic significance in its own right. Ripper claims that

The way in which Hitler imagined further developments [for the Jews after the Nuremberg laws of 1935] may, indeed, be foreseen in statements he made within his most initmate circle after the [1936 Nuremberg] Party Day, in which he declared regarding the Jews: "Eliminated from all professions; enclosed in a territory where they can indulge themselves as corresponds to their manner, while the German people look on— as one looks at wild animals." Perhaps, however, his most deeply felt attitude and the most infernal consequences of his Jewish policy are demonstrated in the unpublished statement which Hitler made to Party District leaders on April 29, 1937, where he expressed himself with almost unprecedented hideous clarity in his tone and choice of words. Taking note of an article from a provincial newspaper in which the editor "demanded" that Jewish businesses be identified [publicly], Hitler remarked, "Of whom is he making this demand? Who can order it? Only me, alone. Thus, the *Herr* editor is demanding of me, in the name of his readers, that I carry this out. In the first place, long before this editor ever had any idea about the Jewish problem, I had already occupied myself with it very thoroughly, indeed. . . . The final goal of our policy, of course, is quite clear to all of us. For me it is always a matter of taking no step which later, perhaps, may have to be reversed, and of taking no steps which will do harm to us. You know I go to the very brink of what may be risked, but not beyond that point. One has to have a nose for such things, as if to smell out: 'What can I yet do; what can't I do?' In the struggle against an enemy, as well, I certainly don't want to challenge an enemy to a violent fight: I don't say: 'Let's fight!' because I desire to fight, but, instead say (now shrieking even louder): 'I want to destroy you!' And now, Wisdom help me to maneuver you into the corner so that you do not get in another punch; and then you will receive a stab in the heart."[338]

After Auschwitz, the speech's chilling and prophetic meaning is unmistakable. Apart from the teaching value of such a powerful document, Ripper has publicized a source of obvious scholarly value in the discussion of Hitler's order of genocide.

The Order and Planning of Genocide

While all textbooks treat the processes of the Holocaust in some detail, they by no means mention even all major aspects of the tragedy of the Jews. Only slightly more than half, for instance, discuss the genesis of the Holocaust order or the planning of the genocide, and some of them mention these aspects only in passing. It may be said, of course, that the textbook rendering of Hitler's virulent anti-Semitism and the Party and SS persecution of the Jews makes perfectly clear who was responsible for the Holocaust. Nevertheless, it is disturbing that so many texts omit discussion of the order and planning of a tragedy of such dimension. Indeed, only a few texts devote attention to it at all.

Kistler and Stroppe indicate only that "from 1942 onward the destruction of the Jews was carried out according to plan." Hug is vague about the genesis of the genocide, merely stating that, "with the conquest of large parts of Europe, it appeared to the leaders of National Socialism that the time had come for a 'Final Solution of the Jewish Question.' "[339] Binder and Burkhardt introduce the Holocaust as "the most hideous act of destruction in history, the 'Final Solution of the Jewish Question,' "[340] but they do not raise the issue of the order or planning of the genocide. Burkhardt, in another text,

is only slightly less vague in his reference to the source of the order
for the Holocaust: "From 1941 onward, the National Socialist rulers
began systematically to murder Jewish men, women, and children
within their sphere of influence."[341]

Boeck, on the other hand, is specific in designating Hitler as the
source of the Holocaust order. Under two separate headings, *Hitler's
War of Destruction against the Jews* and *Hitler Orders the "Final Solution
of the Jewish Question,"* Boeck states that "the most horrifying event
of all occurred . . . when Hitler ordered the Final Solution of the
Jewish Question (January, 1942)." In his second treatment, he states
that, "after the attack on Russia, Hitler issued the order for the *Final
Solution of the Jewish Question* to Reichsführer of the SS Himmler
(1941).[342] Boeck at least is decisive about the genesis of the Holocaust
order, though his repeated use of Nazi terminology for the Holocaust
is objectionable: At times he does not even place the Nazi designation—
"Final Solution of the Jewish Question"—within the standard quotation marks.

Döhn, too, is decisive about the order of the Holocaust. Moreover,
he cites some circumstances surrounding the decision:

> Hitler decided on the "Final Solution of the Jewish Question." Until
> the beginning of the war, the National Socialists sought to solve the
> "Jewish Question" by means of promoting emigration to Palestine. The
> war, however, made it impossible to carry out this undertaking to the
> end. Therefore, Hitler decided on the "Final Solution to the Jewish
> Question." The Jewish race was to be completely exterminated.[343]

Like Boeck, Döhn also makes use of Nazi terminology ("Final
solution," "Jewish Question," "the Jewish race," "exterminated") when
discussing the genesis of the order. He also leaves a highly dubious
impression when he indicates that the war, had "made impossible"
the seemingly legitimate NS-program of "promoting emigration to
Palestine." The reality was that European Jews were being expelled
from their homelands.

Lucas states forthrightly that it was merely a matter of time before
the Nazis attempted genocide against the Jews and that only the need
to consider foreign opinion prevented Hitler from acting earlier. In
his well-titled section "The Final Phase of Inhumanity," Lucas assesses
the influence of the war on Hitler's decision. "Consideration of foreign
countries was scarcely any longer necessary. The victories of the first
years of war made the *Führer* secure. After 1943, the pressure of
danger led to measures of ever increasing severity."[344]

On the other hand, Grassman thinks that the killing measures were not linked simply to an increasingly doubtful German war situation, as demonstrated by the euthanasia murder program and Nazi policies in Poland, ordered at the beginning of the war. Grassmann states, "Terror and crimes were not primarily the consequences of the desperate war situation. At the very beginning of the war, Hitler decreed 'that the incurably sick, in the critical judgment of their situation of illness, and according to all human standards of measurement, can be accorded a mercy death.' He wanted to remove 'useless eaters.' "[345]

Grassmann stresses that this was only the first killing action, and was accompanied by Hitler's "destructive work on the Jews in Poland shortly after the beginning of the war." Thus, war developments cannot be blamed for the brutality of the government's deeds, though it was also nonetheless true that "the worse the military situation became, the sharper the dictator made the terror."[346]

The most detailed commentary on the order and planning of the Holocaust is found in Binder and Burkhardt. These authors are the only ones to discuss the absence of a direct order linking Hitler to the genocide. In clarification of this absence, they point out that in the case of Hitler's order for the euthanasia program to kill the mentally and physically incurably ill, "The 'Führer and Reich Chancellor' of the German Reich signed the murder order on a simple sheet of note-paper [*Briefbogen*] which cost countless victims. The Reich Minister of Justice did not learn of it until a year later. It was not a law which decreed the 'mercy deaths,' but merely a directive, an order."[347]

With regard to the genesis of the Holocaust order, Binder and Burkhardt state that "Göring received from Hitler a strictly secret instruction [*Weisung*] empowering the Secret Police with these activities." The authors cite Göring's decree of July 31, 1941, which called for "the preparation in the near future of a complete plan for carrying out the 'Final Solution of the Jewish Question.' "[348] Grassmann, citing Göring's clear order to Heydrich, observes that Göring was the "intimate confidant of Hitler"[349] to reinforce the indubitable lineage of the Holocaust order to Hitler. The same purpose is served by the information provided about the origins of the mobile gassing vans used during the initial phase of the Holocaust: "At this time [the end of 1941], victims were already being killed in portable gas vans. The 'Chancellery of the *Führer*' participated in providing these gas vans."[350]

While there is no reason to doubt that Hitler ordered (in all likelihood, *orally*) the mass murders of the European Jews and was thoroughly aware that the slaughter was taking place, the absence of a written document confirming this has led some historians[351] to express doubts about Hitler's order or even of his direct knowledge of the Holocaust. The subject has received increasing scholarly attention in Germany during recent years. In May 1984, a major conference was convened in Stuttgart entitled "The Genocide of the European Jews during the Second World War: Decision and Realization." Some leading German scholars of Third Reich history participated in it.[352] Thus, Grassmann's text creditably reflects some of the concerns of recent German Third Reich scholarship.[353]

One of the few texts which deals with the question of Hitler's knowledge and order of the Holocaust at length is Kosthorst in his Curriculum Materials text. He cites extensively a number of remarkable documents which, taken as a whole, certainly provide *prima facie* evidence of Hitler's knowledge and responsibility for ordering the destruction of the European Jews. Kosthorst, for example, cites a November 8, 1942, speech of Hitler in Munich to the trusted "Old Fighters" of the Party. In a chilling display of paranoia, Hitler seems to allude obliquely to the genocide then taking place:

> Meanwhile, another Power which was also once very expectant in Germany, has learned that National Socialist prophecies are not phrases. This is the leading Power which we have to thank for all misfortunes: International Jewry. You will all still recall the meeting of the *Reichstag* in which I declared: If Jewry imagines perhaps that an international world war will lead to the extermination of the European race, then the result will not be the extermination of the European race, but rather the extermination of Jewry in Europe. They have always laughed at my prophecies. Of those who once laughed, today countless of them no longer laugh; and those who yet laugh will perhaps in a short while no longer do so. This knowledge will be disseminated from Europe throughout the entire world.[354]

Kosthorst also published pertinent excerpts from the writings of Goebbels which strengthen the view, that not only did Hitler and Goebbels know of and instigate the Holocaust, but that the German public could not help but have surmised a great deal even if they read only the newspapers.

Kosthorst's source documents are the most extensive found in a textbook on Goebbels' revealing remarks about Hitler, Göring, and himself in connection with the Holocaust. Kosthorst has done a service also by reprinting Goebbels' article from *Das Reich*, a remarkably candid public declaration which hints strongly of the annihilation campaign.[355] As valuable as these documents may be to students, it should be pointed out that Kosthorst's Curriculum Materials is an optional source book supplementing main texts, and therefore is by no means read by all students.

In discussing the circumstances of the genocide, it is remarkable how few authors bear in mind the original racial motives which lay behind the killings. An exception to this is Burkhardt who, in his teaching manual, cites K. D. Erdmann's insightful judgments, contrasting the Holocaust with other outbreaks of terror during revolutions:

> The genocide of the Judaic peoples was not a terror measure. The Terror, as practiced in either the French Revolution or Bolshevik Revolution, and whose victims in the Soviet Union numbered many millions, was directed against enemies. It was carried out in public as a means of intimidation. The guillotine stands in the middle of Revolutionary Square. Around the Killing Camps, however, there stretched forth a zone of silence. What occurred there, no one—including the German people—was supposed to learn. Here people were murdered who—apart from whether they in the least way represented a political factor—were considered inferior. Therefore, the National Socialist destruction activities are not to be compared with elementary outbreaks of Jew-hatred which erupted time and again in European history, based on religious, political, or economic grounds . . . ; this mass murder was the sinister consequence of the theory of biological materialism translated into practice.[356]

Depiction of the actual planning of the Holocaust most often begins with the citation of Adolf Eichmann's minutes of the Wannsee Conference of January 20, 1942, in which Reinhardt Heydrich, Head of Reich Security Service, laid out the plan of genocide. Many of the text authors simply quote the document, making no further comment. A few authors insert explanatory notes so that the student understands the camouflaged Nazi jargon of the period: "By words, 'appropriately treated' was understood extermination."[357] "The participants knew that by the phrase 'correspondingly handled' killing them was meant." Heumann also calls attention to the banality of the bureaucratic language by asking the students: "What do you say to the language in which such a monstrous event is being treated?"[358] Jaacks in his teacher manual stresses the "inhuman administrative style" of language which allows "the participants . . . to have no feeling whatever of responsibility, [and] which was confirmed with horrifying clarity by the Eichmann trial."[359] Grassmann notes also that it was understood by all concerned that camouflaged terminology "should be used in the correspondence to veil the factory-like genocide of Jews, Poles,

Russians, and Gypsies."[360] Grassmann also stresses the involvement
of the many government offices represented at the Wannsee meeting,
including Hitler's Reich Chancellery, adding the comment: "There is
no record of a protest against this monstrous plan. On the contrary,
Secretary of State, Dr. Bühler, requested that the Jewish Question in
Occupied Poland 'be resolved as soon as possible.' "[361]

In his Curriculum Materials book, Kosthorst lists the participants,
and includes a long excerpt from the protocol of Heydrich's speech
to the conferees.[362] Most authors who cite the Wannsee protocol,
however, use only a brief, though highly relevant, portion of this
long and crucial document on the planning of the Holocaust.

It will have been noted in the preceding analysis that many authors
use the Nazi designation "The Final Solution of the Jewish Question"
for the mass murder of the European Jews. More than a dozen texts
use the designation "Final Solution of the Jewish Problem." Only
one teaching manual points to the fact that this was *the Nazi term*
for the organized mass murder of the European Jews,[363] and no text
calls attention to its propaganda effect of downplaying the reality of
the mass murder of the European Jews. The designation is so firmly
entrenched in texts and scholarly literature that it will probably never
entirely be replaced; but its use is no less objectionable since it
renders harmless the unspeakable reality of the Holocaust and continues to use the terminology of the murderers. Perhaps, most important, it subtly perpetuates the idea that there was a *Jewish* problem—
instead of an *anti-Semitic* problem—and conveys the obscene notion
that genocide may be referred to legitimately as a "solution." Nothing
could be less edifying than, in effect, making the killers the final
judges for designating the terms of description for what they did to
the Jews of Europe. The term was Hitler's, and its use is a posthumous
victory.

In marked contrast to the intermediate-level history textbooks
(except for Kosthorst), the great majority of upper-level history, political
science, and social studies textbooks discuss the genesis of the Hitler
order, the circumstances surrounding the decision, and the camouflaged
language of the SS bureaucracy designed to maintain the secrecy of
the killing operations. Tenbrock and Kluxen consider that, based upon
the prewar pattern of persecutions, the complete elimination of the
Jews of Europe was only a matter of time and opportunity. They
explain that the Jews "were systematically denied their rights and
oppressed as pariahs until the outbreak of war—their complete removal
being held in abeyance for the time being only for tactical reasons."[364]

Hey in his teacher manual expresses some of these tactical considerations. He concludes that the cloak of war made it unnecessary any longer to worry about the kind of protests which would accompany the revelation of such massacres in peacetime. In war, "their comprehensive European program of extermination could be carried through without the sensation it would have stirred up in peacetime, and without having to take individual protests into account."[365]

Similarly, Altrichter and Glaser believe that the reasons for delaying the mass killings were based on considerations of national and world opinion: "After 1939, when the German population was increasingly preoccupied with the effects of the war [and] the attitudes of world opinion had become unimportant, the Jewish minorities, first of the Occupied countries, then of Germany, were rounded up, deported and [either] massacred, gassed or tortured to death."[366]

Frank makes Hitler responsible for the genocide, though without actually attributing the order to him. He begins his section on the persecution of the Jews with the words: "Hitler was not only a conquerer who, like other conquerers, shed a lot of blood; he was also a mass murderer who had millions of innocent people (primarily Jews), brutally murdered." In the following section, Frank reports, rather confusedly, that Hitler's decision was based on his calculation that he could no longer win the war, and yet now no longer needed to consider the reaction of England to his deeds: "Hitler began the great mass murder actions at the end of 1941 when apparently he came to the conclusion that the war was no longer to be won. He no longer had to consider England, whom he had always sought to win over to his politics."[367]

Other texts do not mention the specific origin of the genocide order. Gönner and Krug, for example, state only that "After the beginning of the war, when the 'Final Solution of the Jewish Question' had been decided, the number of people increased who were delivered [to concentration camps] for racial reasons (mostly Jews)."[368]

Fernis and Haverkamp, however, are decisive in asserting who gave the order: "Before the beginning of the Russian campaign, Hitler ordered the destruction of all Jews in the German sphere of control."[369]

Gallmeister also thinks that "Hitler had decided on the '*Final Solution of the Jewish Problem*,' that is, the Jews in Germany and the Occupied regions—using the deception of relocation—were to be shot or gassed."[370] Krautkrämer is brief, but also decisive about Hitler's order: "Hitler used the war to exterminate the Jews. Hitler ordered the Final solution."[371] It may be noted that Krautkrämer, as many others, does not vary much from the Nazi's own denigrative and camouflaged terminology.

Fernis and Hillgruber state that Hitler not only issued the command, but also its approximate time. They also emphasize that he made the war against the Jews his first priority: "The Second World War for Hitler was not only a fight for the 'expansion of space,' but rather, the war possessed for him at the same time an interior 'Front' which was actually the 'decisive' one in his eyes: the destruction of European Jewry." Hitler briefly considered a plan to remove the Jews to the island of Madagascar, "but, before the beginning of the Eastern Campaign, he set in motion the extermination of all Jews in the German area of control."[372]

Most texts mention the Madagascar project, but only Ritscher and Krink point out that this scheme also envisioned a general plan of destruction: "There was no lack of suggestions for suitable extermination methods. Among the numerous plans was to be found the so-called Madagascar project: All Jews were to be concentrated on the island of Madagascar as on a penal colony, where they would gradually be worked to death for the Master Race."[373]

In an excellent source originating in Helmut Krausnick, *Anatomie des SS Staates* (Anatomy of the SS State), Kampmann and Michel cite Himmler's reference to the "difficult order" Hitler had given him of "freeing the East of Jews." The source also indicates Himmler's awkwardness about the inadequate racial grounds even for determining who Jews were:

> Since apparently difficulties arose as to who was to be considered a Jew, Himmler decreed an energetic directive on July 26, 1942: "I would like urgently to request that no ordinance be issued on the concept 'Jew.'" With all these foolish stipulations we are only tieing our hands. The Occupied areas of the East will be cleared of Jews. The accomplishment of this hard order the *Führer* has laid on my shoulders. No one can release me from this responsibility in any case."[374]

Grütter, also citing Krausnick, presumes an oral order by Hitler sometime in March, 1941:

> Krausnick assumes that Hitler gave the execution order, which was never put in writing, in March, 1941, at the same time as the decision to attack the Soviet Union. According to oral statements by those who participated, the order . . . was never distributed in writing. (An order of Heydrich, the Commander in chief of the *Einsatzgruppen*, in fact, has been preserved, but it does not contain the whole truth. The true magnitude of the extermination activity was apparently made orally.)[375]

Eichberg does not enter into a discussion of who made the decision, but dates it considerably later than Krausnick. Eichberg points out that after the Madagascar plan was abandoned, "the extermination of all Jews within the area of power of German troops—'the Final Solution of the Jewish Question'—was decided in December, 1941."[376]

The decision to change the killing method from the semi-public shootings by SS troops to more concealed and systematized gassings, Baumann suggests, was made by three Nazi leaders: "For Hitler, Göring and Himmler these methods of murder were, however, too inconvenient and noticeable."[377] Baumann follows this brief notice with the decisions made at the Wannsee Conference.

The Wannsee Conference is discussed in many texts in connection both with its role in the planning of the genocide and the camouflaged language of the murderers. Kampmann and Michel call it "the point of departure for the 'Final Solution of the Jewish Question,'" and present a half page of relevant sections from the conference protocol.[378] Grütter rightly notes that the genocide decision was made, not at the Wannsee Conference in 1942, but well before: "When the Wannsee conference began, the extermination program had already begun long before; therefore, it is not correct to state that the decision for mass extermination was not made until 1942."[379]

Grütter uses the protocol to teach how the Nazis used camouflaged language ("evacuation," "work activities," "Final Solution") to cover their atrocities. "The SS developed a special language which would be worthy of its own research."[380] Though the language was disguised and indirect, Grütter explains, "the text is clear enough. . . . Eichmann stated in Jerusalem that by the [phrase] 'Final Solution'" killing had been meant. Grütter carefully deciphers such phrases as work in the East under "corresponding control measures," and "in an appropriate manner," where "doubtless," a great part of the Jews would be "decimated by natural diminution." Grütter continues:

> One can assume that most of the "evacuated" Jews are to be worked to death by the fact that "road construction" is not normally associated with "natural diminution," and, thus, the quoted places on control measures and the manner of work activities say enough about the meaning of the Final Solution. The true intentions are quire unmistakably revealed when "a remaining stock" is referred to, "which . . . must be handled accordingly."[381]

Grütter carefully analyzes the meaning behind the camouflaged language and the difficulties encountered even by Heydrich and Eichmann in trying to avoid revealing their murderous intentions openly. Slips of the tongue and inconsistencies appear in the Wannsee text of the proceedings which make their intentions apparent, especially when the fate of those deemed unfit to work—women, children and old people—are being discussed in as euphemistic language as possible.[382] Grütter also points to the "alibi function" for the SS of a camp like Theresienstadt, which Heydrich designated for the purpose of opposing " 'the many interventions' on behalf of Jews too prominent to be 'evacuated' without it coming to world attention. Theresienstadt itself was a camouflage measure, and letters and postcards were fabricated to serve this purpose."[383]

Hey includes a long section of the protocol, which no other text contains, outlining the tasks assigned to the various representatives of the government departments who participated in the Wannsee Conference. In this way he underscores their active role in the genocide. Heydrich stated that the goal until now had been to "cleanse German living space of Jews by legal means." In elegant, cool, and bureaucratic language, Heydrich outlined the plan for the mass murder of millions of Jews, the destruction of Jewish communities all over Europe. At the end of the section containing the conference protocol, Hey asks students to clarify the meaning behind such euphemisms as "natural reduction of the Jews in work activities," and "appropriate treatment" of the "remaining remnant."[384]

Ritscher and Krink briefly paraphrase some of the most relevant sections of the Wannsee protocol and describe its meaning and message. Ripper also explains the Wannsee protocol and its bureaucratic language of death, and asks students a question about the camouflaged vocabulary before turning to the Holocaust itself.[385]

The Agony and Murder of the European Jews

It may be said that the texts, though brief, generally depict the agony and extreme horror of the killing installations and murder factories of the East. All texts include discussions of the concentration camps, killing centers, and gas chambers; and many mention the SS *Einsatzgruppen*—the Deaths' Head squads which roamed the East behind German military lines systematically murdering Jews.

The only intermediate-level history text to devote space to the horror of the preceding deportation process is Schmid's, using an excerpt from the diary of the German writer Jochen Klepper, a non-Jew with a Jewish wife:

August 24, 1942: Again and again the heavy, heavy terrifying nightmare of forced separation, deportation and SS, which so easily could become reality at any time, often weighs [me] down the whole day. We go frightened and timid not only through the day, but also through the night, and start up in horror. How hard and alien my life has become. . . .

September 28, 1942. Deportations, deportations—the old, the sick. And no longer rumours, but human beings whom we know.[386]

The diary is a moving tribute to the couple's love, and its inclusion in Schmid's text demonstrates what may be done with even a brief passage from a sympathetic witness.

Heinloth briefly mentions the world of pain and dread experienced by the Jews in their transport East: "Thousands were already starving in the dreadful conditions of transportation and life during the evacuation and in the camps along the way."[387] Others mention only that the Jews were shipped "in cattle cars to the East,"[388] that "the Jews remaining in Germany were loaded into railroad cars and transported to Poland,"[389] or that "day and night trains rolled toward Poland with Jewish men, women and children."[390] Curiously, Heumann writes of "Jews who had previously escaped destruction (*Vernichtung*) in Germany"[391] now being rounded up and sent to ghettos in the East. In their teacher manual, Ebeling and Birkenfeld mention only that the first deportees from Germany were sent to Poland and Southern France;[392] Grassmann, usually a sensitive witness, mentions transportation only in relation to its lack of military expedience: "Frequently the transportation of soldiers, wounded, and war materials was sidetracked for countless trains carrying off people to the extermination camps."[393]

Hug includes a horrifying and moving three-page German account, "Report on the Deportation of Jews from Stettin," but Hug's choice of a German source exemplifies a characteristic of German texts: despite effective and moving testimony by Jewish survivors available in German, text authors appear to prefer mostly non-Jewish witnesses to portray the brutality of Holocaust.

An exception is Grassmann's recent textbook, which includes a number of Jewish sources. He incorporates, for example, the very moving account of a 15-year-old Jewish boy's experience of the 1938 pogrom, the loss of his family in Auschwitz (he saw them arrive and could not even acknowledge them), and the murder of camp inmates by injection. The inclusion of such accounts may indicate a change in this area, though even Grassmann's report was based upon a newspaper account![394]

The accounts of surviving Jews are able to better recapture the sense of pain, dread, and anguish of the victims, necessarily reminding students again that the victims were human, that once they were much more than the grotesque shapes to which they were reduced by the Nazis and which students now encounter as text illustrations.

German documents or accounts, while they may shock and horrify, retain—in tone at least—the attitude of the perpetrators, or the clinical detachment of the observer. Lucas, for example, has a strong excerpt taken from a London exile document of life in a concentration camp. It cites a camp order which depicts the incredible devaluation of Jewish life by the SS:

> The guard has orders to shoot without warning anyone who moves in his direction. Every bullet costs 12 *pfennige;* this is exactly the sum a Jew is worth, no more and no less.

The document then describes an inspection:

> The commander inspects. He treats the healthy ones immediately with his swagger stick in the presence of the others. "Jews do not get sick." The commander decides simply by looking at you who is ready for the doctor. . . . The others must return to work details with the assistance of shoves and the swagger stick. The doctors declare the sick to be either "sick" or "healthy." In the latter case, they are punished in the evening for "lying." There are only the healthy or the dead. . . . The work consists of breaking rocks a quarter of an hour away from the roadway which was being built. . . . Many brought their suffering to an end by feigning an escape attempt in order to be shot.[395]

The limitations of German sources are made apparent in a document used by Burkhardt to depict Jewish life in the ghetto. The scenes evoked are of muddy, dirty streets; emaciated masses of people in rags and tatters crowding the streets of the Warsaw ghetto; of bodies lying on the sidewalk covered only with newspapers and laid there by the inhabitants of the buildings "to save the cost of a funeral"; of persons without shelter who died in the street; of Jews forced by guards, for their sadistic pleasure, to dance, do exercises, or wallow in filth.[396]

Burkhardt's powerful source for describing the Nazi degradation of the Jews, focusses so relentlessly on conditions so awful, humilations so terrible, that the emotions aroused are more of revulsion than of sympathy.

Four decades after the event, major Jewish accounts of the sufferings, fears, triumphs, and tragedy in the Holocaust remain inexplicably underrepresented in the great majority of German textbooks. It is important that, before students are introduced to the unavoidable horrors of the Holocaust, the Jews become flesh and blood people with whom young people can empathize as fellow human beings. Some of the best introductory materials include the writings of Jewish children.[397]

In reporting the killing activities of the *Einsatzgruppen*, where eyewitness reports are used, the texts again cite German witnesses. Hug, in his source book, prints the "Report of a Corporal on the Killing of Jews, 1941" and the "Report of [Hermann] Friedrich Gräbe on the Massacre near Dubno, 1942." Gräbe was a German engineer for a German construction firm.[398] His report, while terrifying, is almost detached as he recalls what he saw one day in 1942. The texts scarcely utilize any of the accounts of the *Einsatzgruppen* massacres by Jewish survivors or Russian eyewitnesses, and which have been published in German and other languages.

Most texts reveal little more than that "*Einsatzgruppen* raged in Poland and in the occupied Soviet regions, supported in part by local anti-Semitic militia units."[399] In many cases, the texts do not make clear that the primary victims were Jews ("shooting one million people from June 1941 to June 1943");[400] they do not indicate the magnitude of the killings ("so called *Einsatzgruppen* of the SS raged among the Jewish population of Poland. Jews were shot, especially in the small villages in the country");[401] or they make the death of the Jews appear as simply one of several possible fates for Jews ("*Einsatzgruppen* of the SS took over the seizure, deportation, and shooting of Jews in areas occupied by German troops.").[402]

Heinloth writes a more detailed account. He explains that, notwithstanding the aborted Madagascar Plan, "In the Eastern theater of war, *Einsatzgruppen* set up by Himmler were already carrying out radical solutions: immediate shooting of Jews [and] the incitement of pogroms."[403] He explains that the *Einsatzgruppen* were divided into four units totaling about 3000 men who killed approximately one million "people" between 1941 and 1943. Lachner mentions the killings by the *Einsatzgruppen*, without referring to them by name; Burkhardt refers to "Special Action Commands made up primarily of members of the SS and the Gestapo," who began the shooting of Jews in the East before the Death Camps were erected.[404] Grassmann refers to "*Einsatzgruppen* made up of the SS, the police, and Field Military Units [who] carried out mass shootings in the Soviet Union." Grassmann also pointedly mentions that reports of the operations as well as eyewitness accounts survived the war.[405]

As may be seen from the foregoing, *Einsatzgruppen* are represented in many texts, an improvement over just a few years ago, yet still only about half of the intermediate-level history texts include these incredible and horrifying massacres of the Jewish people.

Political science, social studies, and upper-level history texts pass over the deportations in silence. Nor is ghetto life discussed in the texts. Only Gönner and Krug mention ghettos even in passing:

> At first, the Jews, as, for example, in conquered Poland, were housed in ghettos and work camps. Many were killed by excesses and shooting, in part with the help of native police forces.[406]

A few pages later, they again mention ghettos:

> Within the framework of the "Final Solution of the Jewish Question," the Jews were housed in ghettos and work camps and ultimately murdered in concentration camps, in part, in great gassing facilities.[407]

But, as seen from the above, ghetto life is not the subject under discussion. The same is true of other authors.[408]

About one-third of the social studies, political science, and upper-level history texts mention the activities of the *Einsatzgruppen* in Russia and Poland. Those which do so are usually accurate as to the basic killing tasks, zones of operation, and composition of the forces. Some texts, such as Grütter's, make a point of mentioning that local militia units took part in the mass shootings,[409] the purpose of which seems to be to share the burden of responsibility. Grütter also makes the contribution of describing the psychic effect on the killers: "The *Einsatzkommandos* were not always up to the atrocious mass murders psychically, so that most of them were issued a special ration of spirits after executions. There were also cases of personal enrichment."[410]

Very little is said about the mass shootings themselves, and even less than the intermediate texts do the advanced and social science texts use Jewish sources, or even German ones. Baumann stands out because, after the usual brief treatment, he includes this tragic additional detail: "The victims themselves had to dig their own graves and then, standing on the edge of the ditch, were mowed down with machine guns. In this bestial way one million people were murdered."[411]

Little wonder that the SS, according to Fernis and Hillgruber, "at the end of 1941 developed less visible methods."[412]

Killing Centers and Mass Murder

Essentially all intermediate history texts treat the mass murder of the Jews, mentioning concentration camps and the main killing centers. The treatment is frequently brief, concentrated, and powerful, though the authors often describe the killings by using the documents of the perpetrators. Indeed, some of the documents effectively re-create the authentic atmosphere of sinister inhumanity and detachment of the killers. Again, the eyewitness accounts are overwhelmingly those of non-Jews, and more often evoke a response of shock and horror than of sympathy with the victims, all of whom remain shadowy and anonymous figures, as they were for the National Socialists and SS killers.

Almost all intermediate-level history textbooks describe the concentration camp system at some length, while many texts treat the killing camps in Poland in a special section, invariably indicating the importance of Auschwitz-Birkenau and naming, on an average, two other killing centers, such as Belsec, Treblinka, Maidanek, Kulmhof, or Sobibor. The mass gassings of the Jews are mentioned in all texts, either by indicating the gassings, the gas chambers or both. A few texts, such as Kaier's, identify Cyclon B in the text. Some texts name all major concentration camps and killing centers by including a map. Burkhardt's map designates the main killing camps with stars of David.[413] Kistler and Stroppe include a detailed color map naming all killing centers and major concentration camps, with the numbers of victims for each country signified by variable sized type and + symbols. Kistler and Stroppe ask the students to count the number of the large and small concentration camps, write the names of the main concentration camps and killing centers and total the number of Jews killed in each of the countries.[414] Schmid briefly discusses the concentration camps and killing centers in two places, under the heading "Persecution and Destruction of the Jews," and in a section on "German-Polish Relations,"[415] indicating sensitivity to the fact that a major part of the genocide was carried out on Polish soil.

Heumann asks this exercise question: "Where are the Killing Camps located?"[416] which could tend to reinforce an assertion frequently found in texts that, because all the main killing centers were located outside Germany, the Germans had little chance of learning about the Holocaust while it was taking place.

Textbook illustrations of the Holocaust are often the same, and perhaps appropriately appear to be selected for their power to shock. For the most part, they are photographs to be found in standard studies of the Holocaust.

The large majority of intermediate texts describe the killing process almost entirely by the use of primary documents. A few, such as Boeck's, add brief statements by the author, such as, "Those unfit to work, the old and sick, any women and children went to the annihilation camps." Another author reports that the gold in the victims teeth was broken out and the hair was cut from the dead before cremation.[417] Menzel and Textor write that "Great annihilation camps arose in which millions of Jewish men, women, and children were murdered," but though they identify Auschwitz and the gas chambers, they do not describe the killing process even by the use of excerpts from documents.[418]

Almost all texts depend heavily on primary sources to tell the detailed story of the SS process of killing and utilizing bodies. The source most often used is the account by Rudolf Hoess, Commandant of Auschwitz, written immediately after the war when he was a prisoner in Poland. Others use the Gerstein Report,[419] the account of an SS man, Felix Gerstein, a sympathetic eyewitness. Both documents are shattering, and powerful enough to remain memorable to a young person for years. From these grim, detailed accounts, the student learns of the herding of men, women, children, and infants-in-arms into the changing rooms; of them being driven into the gas chambers disguised as showers; of the process of gassing; of the agonies of the victims; of *Sonderkommando* who removed the bodies and stripped the dead of valuables; of the process of cremation; of the slave labor of the temporarily fit in the camps and their being worked to death. The excerpts vary in length, but most of them contain the above information.

A few mention certain aspects of the mass murder process. Steinbügl points out that young children were always destroyed since they were unable to work[420]; Schmid states that women with children went to the gas chambers first, to be followed by the men.[421] Though Döhn mentions gassings only in relation to carbon monoxide killings, he relates the process to its predecessor, the euthanasia program, and asserts that the surrounding population knew what was going on at Asuchwitz because of the burning of the bodies in the great crematoria.[422] Kosthorst, in his materials book, publishes the longest excerpts from the Hoess report, describing the killing process, Hoess's observations regarding his feelings, as well as an analysis of Hoess by Martin Broszat, Director of the *Institut für Zeitgeschichte* and one of the foremost authorities on National Socialist Germany.[423]

A common denominator in virtually all textbook treatments of the Holocaust is the swift and abrupt closure of the subject. This is done using a document, usually on the killing process itself, to end the section. Though the document and subject cry out for comment and evaluation, the authors make no attempt to place this most ghastly event in German history in any perspective. No attempt is made to state any larger meaning of the Holocaust, to interpret its significance, its lessons, its portent. Nor is any particular emphasis placed on the historical enormity—the simple awesomeness and historic dimension of the deed—of the destruction of the European Jews for European or Jewish history. Here the authors appear to suffer a general discomfiture in the presence of the event and a common unwillingness to evaluate its significance.

Another characteristic of the treatment, noted earlier, is the tone and language which stresses the horror of events more than sympathy, compassion, mourning, or remorse for the victims. Such accents, of course, are a matter of the individual temperament of authors, but when it is lacking in *all* texts, it is a matter for remark. It should be stressed that, almost without exception, authors and editors of texts make it unequivocally clear that they have no sympathy for the National Socialist government, and are shocked, indignant, dismayed, and shamed by what was done to the European Jews in the name of the German people.

The reason the element of sympathy and mourning of the tragedy of the Jews appears to be absent from the texts may be due in part to (1) the omission of modern Jews or recent Jewish history in the texts except as objects of persecution viewed primarily through the documents of the persecutors; and (2) the failure to attempt an evaluation of these events at the end of the Holocaust section, a place in which a note of tragedy and identification would be most appropriate. Words alone, of course, cannot measure the magnitude and significance of the Holocaust, least of all in the brief space allocated for such assessments in textbooks. Nevertheless, words must be spoken, for silence, the ally of the perpetrators, is indefensible.

The texts carry little comment about the perpetrators, either as individuals or as sociological types. Two texts, Lucas's and Grassmann's make brief mention of the murderers. In his section on "Organized Manhunts in Germany," Lucas includes an excerpt from "Documents on the Treatment of German Citizens" written in 1940 in London. It carries a brief analysis of some of the concentration camp prisoner hierarchy: "The men who are guards are older prisoners. Professional criminals were mixed in as supervisors among the political prisoners."[424] Grassmann has a similar analysis though written with different emphasis: "Although the SS preferred as much as possible to use criminals as camp functionaries, in fact, they were often dependent on the more able and intelligent political prisoners."[425]

Although both excerpts deal with the issue of how the machinery of the killing centers was made to work, neither suggests who carried out the gruesome details of mass murder, or what system of coercion was devised by the SS to allow them physically to avoid most of the cruder aspects of mass murder and the system they devised to compel others to carry out the ghastly tasks of mass gassings, looting corpses, and cremation.

Kaier's is one of the few texts to comment on the subject. In discussing the concentration camps, he states: "The Jews and the political prisoners were humiliated the worst. On the other hand, criminals were preferred by the SS for camp administration as foremen, as 'Kapos' (Work Commando Leaders) and as block elders." In the succeeding section on the Holocaust, Kaier identifies some of the groups who carried out the killings themselves and characterizes the SS personnel as perpetrators:

The million-fold murders took place according to general staff-like planning with bureaucratic precision, using factory-like technology. Ukrainians, Poles, Lithuanians, and Jewish forced labor were compelled to carry out the crude activities under threat of death. The SS were placed in positions as administrative, supervisory, technical, and medical personnel. Now and then there were devilish torturers. [But] the majority were simple, upright [biedere] family fathers, correct in their private life, citizens obsessed with duty, who convinced themselves that their dirty "work" was in the service of the people and the fatherland.[426]

Kaier's effort to characterize the perpetrators, while well-intentioned, makes clear the inadequate results of uncritical generalization on the subject. No sociological categories are used in his depiction and the German SS-men emerge as decent family men gone wrong because of overzealous efforts to carry out patriotic duties in service of *Volk* and *Vaterland*.

In reality, the motives of SS personnel were far more differentiated and less noble. German supervisors, administrators, and guards may be classified according to some five overlapping sets of characteristics: (1) fanatical Nazis who hated Jews because of ideological prejudice; (2) purely destructive types who reveled in the chance to torture and murder; (3) looters, who sought to enrich themselves on the booty of the victims; (4) ambitious opportunists at all levels, who saw in their murderous work a means of gaining a better income and higher status than they ever could have expected in normal occupations; and, (5) at all levels, conformists who merely took lines of least resistance, went wherever they were directed, doing whatever they were told.

Kaier's depiction of "upright family fathers" underscores the need for a more differentiated textbook analysis of the psychological types of those who served in these camps and clear treatment of the SS administrative and operational techniques which allowed German "citizens, correct in their private life," seemingly guilty of no more than excessive nationalism and an uncritical sense of duty, to organize and administer the murder of millions of people "with bureaucratic precision, using factory-like technology," and with only "now and then" a "devilish torturer" among them.

The political science, social studies, and advanced history textbooks share with the intermediate texts an almost unrelieved emphasis on the brutal horror of the camps and killings, a dependence on German primary documents instead of the author's or Jewish presentations, and an abrupt closure of the subject, without judgment or evaluation. Also, these texts add nothing to the analysis of the perpetrators or the SS methods of coercion.

Again, an average of two or three of the killing camps are mentioned, sometimes fewer. Deuschle, for example, mentions only Auschwitz and, even this is in the caption to an illustration.[427] Some of the texts mention the killing centers in a casual manner as, for instance, Fernis and Haverkamp's, which places the names of the camps in parentheses, and diminishes their significance further by adding "etc." to the list, thus: "(Auschwitz, Treblinka, Maidenek, etc.)."[428] Fernis and Hillgruber do much the same thing, except that Maidenek is replaced by Sobibor within the parentheses.[429] The authors mention the gassings and burnings which took place in the camps. Gallmeister, although he does print an excerpt from the Hoess report, is too brief, completing the discussion of the killing centers with only a six-line mention of the gassings of Auschwitz.[430]

Although the above selections are the worst examples of brevity, none of the text narratives are very long on the subject of the killing centers, all preferring to supplement brief introductory remarks with primary documents. Thus, Grütter lists five killing camps, supplemented with statistics about each, in place of a meaningful treatment of these places of death.[431] It is almost as if their existence were not an uncommon thing being reported, and treated as dryly as some military episode or treaty provision. Ritscher and Krink, otherwise so excellent in their treatment, become notably brief in describing the gas chamber killings, stating only that "Gassing [was done] by means of diesel exhaust or cyclon B. The victims went into the millions."[432] Tenbrock and Kluxen identify four killing centers, commenting laconically that "immediately after arrival, most of the prisoners were killed in factory-like, managed gassing facilities."[433]

Michel and Kampmann also emphasize the automatic nature of the killings, characterizing "the gas chambers and burning ovens of the largest extermination camps, Auschwitz, Maidanek, and Treblinka" as "the greatest technical murder apparatus created in history."[434] Baumann thinks that "indeed, the most hideous destructive work of all time" was carried out in the gas chambers, and includes a short passage by Rudolf Hoess describing the number of victims of the gassings and other murders at Auschwitz.[435] Gönner and Krug mention "among others" only Auschwitz and Treblinka, "to which entire trainloads of Jews were carried from the German occupied regions, and millions of them murdered in great gassing facilities."[436]

The above are the *final lines* of a very brief, sketchy account, in which no perpetrators are mentioned, no numbers of victims are reported, and no perspective or closing comment on events is carried out.

As with the intermediate books, these texts also conclude their sections with documents about the killing operations instead of meaningful perspective. The great majority of texts again use Hoess's report of his activities as Commandant of Auschwitz. Altrichter and Glaser include a brief but effective 16-line excerpt from Hoess on the processes of killing and utilizing bodies.[437] Hey incorporates a full page of Hoess's revealing report on operations at Auschwitz as well as interesting sidelights describing his attitude toward his crimes, his sense of guilt and obedience, and his remarkable declaration that he sought a "more humane way to kill the masses," and was very "relieved" when he found Cyclon B, "for now the victims could be spared until the last moment."[438]

Grütter's documentation incorporates the findings of Felix Gilbert, the court psychologist at the International Military Tribunal at Nuremberg, who examined Hoess's mental state while in custody. Gilbert found Hoess to be sane, but noted his virtual absence of feeling about his deeds, his lack of any human contacts or friends, his marked lack of empathy and generally apathetic temperament. Gilbert associates this with his religious upbringing in a parental home which required strict obedience. Grütter concludes the document by comparing Hoess's psychogram with similar problems of repressed persons in contemporary society, calling particular attention to the My Lai Massacre in the Vietnam War and Stanley Milgram's experiments involving test subjects in simulated application of deadly currents. Such evocation may be a welcome signal that a beginning is being made at last to place this material in an evaluative context.

A few texts cite other Holocaust witnesses, again, all of them German sources. Eichberg uses the Hermann Gräbe report, based upon Gräbe's important sworn testimony of November 10, 1945.[439] Gallmeister contains a long and powerful citation from the Gerstein Report: ". . . Mothers with infants at their breasts approach, hesitate, enter into the death chamber! . . . The majority know; the smell announces to them their fate. . . . One hears crying, sobbing."[440]

The report details the murder process in full, including the cleansing of bodies fouled in death, the exploitation of the corpses "by two dozen dentists," and cremation operations. The author, however, uses this document to close the subject. Without transition, the text takes up the subject of Resistance to the National Socialist regime, a characteristic theme (required by state guidelines) taken up by most texts after the presentation of the Holocaust.

Only two texts, one political-social studies, the other an upper level history, mention persons and groups who carried out the killing processes. In both cases—while Hitler, Göring and Himmler are mentioned as having ordered the genocide, and the SS are named as having established the killing camps—Jews are named as having had to carry out the details of disposing of the bodies. In his introduction to the Hoess document, Grütter notes that

> If one is able to read the description of the murders with only scarcely concealed indignation, the robbing of the bodies—expressly ordered by Himmler—shocks the reader even more. A Special *Kommando* of Jews was entrusted with this as well as with "help" in the mass murders. The burning of the bodies . . . was carried out by the inmate *Kommando* as well.[441]

Baumann also mentions Jews in this connection: "Jews themselves had to remove the bodies, marked by their struggle with death, from the gas chambers, and operate the crematoria."[442]

In the absence of information about SS methods of coercion, the state of fear and desperation which existed in the camps, or the supreme desire of the *Sonderkommando* to live to tell the tale of the Holocaust, these bare facts of the Jewish role in the killing processes will seem incomprehensible to young people.

On the whole, the texts present no more than a brief overview of the concentration camps and killing centers. They deal even more briefly with specifics of the killing operations, and either close the subject without discussion or revert to the language of mechanistic processes. They are hampered from a discussion of human relations and organization in describing the activities of these camps partly by inhibition, but also by the lack of adequate scholarship on human interaction in these camps.

It is interesting to note that while funds have been raised and research carried out for multivolumed comprehensive histories of German experiences in all Allied prisoner-of-war camps, as well as for enormous collective volumes of experiences documenting the tragedy of the German expulsions from Eastern Europe at the end of the war, there have been neither enough funds nor interest to document and write a comprehensive history of the concentration camp system of the National Socialists. The Director of the *Institut für Zeitgeschichte*, Martin Broszat, in his *Studien zur Geschichte der Konzentrationslager* (Studies in the History of the Concentration Camps), in 1970, wrote of "the impossibility of carrying out a complete collective work of the type planned within a foreseeable time, with the limited personnel assistance and financial means of the Institute."[443] With the exception of Falk Pingel's excellent recent study, *Häftlinge unter SS-Herrschaft: Widerstand Selbstbehauptung und Vernichtung im Konzentrationslager* (Hamburg, 1978) (Prisoners Under SS Control: Resistance, Self-Assertion and Destruction in Concentration Camps), as Wolfgang Scheffler stated in 1979, "the situation has scarcely changed till now."[444]

The Number of Victims

Virtually all texts provide figures for the number of victims of the Holocaust. However, texts have not been left untouched by disputes which have arisen at times about the total number of victims, and this is reflected in the variation in numbers stated. In 1974, Martin and Eva Kolinsky in *Yad Vashem Studies*, criticized textbooks for vagueness about the number of victims killed in the Holocaust.[445] Two years after their article appeared, the German educator Alfred Schickel, in an article in *Israel Forum*, warned about lack of exactitude in such figures:

> In view of the doubts nourished by some right-wing groups about the correctness of the figures of gassed Jews, it appears particularly important to allow no unclarity whatever to arise in presenting the figures, so as not to strengthen the mistrust sown in various quarters. It would be desirable that such figures be supported by reference to their source, so as to remove those doubts which extremist groups seek to engender.[446]

Schickel urged further that uniform figures be accepted: "It would be very desirable to use a reliably researched, uniform number in all history books and teachers handbooks."[447]

Some texts, such as Menzel and Textor's, have heeded Schickel's advice and begun citing sources for their figures.

> At the begining of 1946, the World Jewish Council calculated the figures at 5,721,800; thus, the figure 6 million has often been used. Another Jewish calculation later arrived at the figure 4.2 and 4.6 million, among them 3.8 million from Poland, Romania and the Soviet Union. In the event that further research leads to different figures, the overall picture is changed very little. The destruction of all Jews was planned without distinction of age or sex; on Heydrich's list was written the figure "more than 11 million."[448]

Ebeling and Birkenfeld base their figures on Reimund Schnabel, *Macht ohne Moral*, and list the number of victims by country with a total figure of 5,978,000. In their teacher manual, Ebeling and Birkenfeld further note that the figures came from the Institute for Jewish Problems, New York, and also cite the estimates of Gerald Reitlinger and others, ranging from 4.2 to 5.7 million dead.[449]

The most extensive documentation on the number of victims appears in Kosthorst's Curriculum Materials book, which presents the analysis of Georges Wellers', *"Die Zahl der Opfer der 'Endlösung' und der Korherr-Bericht,"* ("The Number of Victims of the 'Final Solution' and the Korherr Report") which appeared originally in *Aus Politik und Zeitgeschichte*, a leading German political and education weekly. Wellers evaluates various studies made by scholars since the war, and neo-Nazi apologetic literature which denies the Holocaust. They note that "for those who mourn this [Nazi] regime, there is nothing they can do but deny the abominations inasmuch as they are unable to find any justification for the crimes."[450]

Most texts, despite Schickel's urgings, do not cite sources for their figures, nor is there much uniformity in numbers. Slightly less than half of the texts use the figure of 6 million for the number of Jewish victims of the Holocaust. The second largest segment of texts—about 30 percent—use figures of from 4 to 6 million; and a few texts use figures of 5 to 6 million. One text, Hug's, actually publishes the figures of a Polish pamphlet, "Kennen Sie Polen?" (Do You Know Poland?), which discusses the annihilation of "more than 6 million human victims, 1.8 million of whom were children and young people up to 14 years of age, . . . a figure supplemented by nearly 600,000 invalids and many hundreds of thousands of Poles."[451] While this is moving testimony, a brochure is hardly a source document for figures of such importance, nor, be it noted, are Jews specifically mentioned in the document nor is the fact that Poland once had a large Jewish population.

The most conservative estimates are in Heinloth, who cites the murder of "at least 3 million Jews,"[452] Lucas, who places the figure at "more than 4 million from all Europe,"[453] and Burkhardt, who in his teacher manual presents a detailed breakdown of the figures, followed by this statement: "Recent investigations have determined that the number of victims, in any case, amounts to more than 4 million."[454]

Some texts contain anomalies. Schmid, for instance, gives an estimate of 5 to 6 million Jewish victims in the text, but has no heading for the Jews, the Holocaust, or Genocide in a detailed summary of war victims of all types at the end of his chapter. The sole relevant headings are 300,000 "Racially and Religiously Persecuted," and 2,251,500 "Losses due to Expulsions and Deportations,"[455] the last of which could well include Germans expelled from Eastern Europe at war's end. Heumann, too, includes an extensive balance sheet of casualties for World War II in which Jews have no category. Presumably they are incorporated within the broad classification of "10 million from expulsion areas, forced [labor] camps, and forced work."[456] However, in his Holocaust section, Heumann provides the figure of 5 to 6 million Jewish victims, and asks the student to "make the numbers meaningful by comparing them to the number of inhabitants in cities familiar to you."[457]

Long ago, Eberhard Quester wisely pointed out that the issue of textbook presentation of the Holocaust and the Jews "is far more profound than the mere examination of such matters as whether—and what—figures are to be stated for the Jewish victims."[458] Schickel as well has observed that whatever the precise figures, the moral question takes precedence over the statistical issue:

It cannot be determined whether further research will arrive at other figures and from the moral point of view this is of no consequence. It will remain a horrifyingly high number of victims, and the accompanying circumstances of this unparalleled persecution and the apathy of so many who knew or suspected something about these events forever shames us.[459]

Perhaps one of the best summations of the numbers dispute is found in Ebeling and Birkenfeld's teacher manual:

The numbers will never be known exactly and ultimately are of no consequence when compared with the basic fact that, although there had often been persecutions of Jews in the course of history, there had never been one like *the* persecution—ordered by the state, carried out with such diabolical, cold, systematic planning and execution, with such shocking dimension and results—which the National Socialist regime undertook in its sphere of influence, with all administrative and machine-technical means.[460]

Since the number of victims is usually treated at the conclusion of the Holocaust section, this would be an appropriate place to take note of the dimensions of the event. Only a few texts, however, do any more than affirm that the murdered Jews came from countries all over Europe. Boeck, for example, states that: "6 million, from no less than 30 nations" were killed.[461] Binder and Burkhardt are among the few authors who merit attention for placing some emphasis on the magnitude of disaster:

> The most hideous was the mass destruction in Poland, the Baltic States and the Soviet Union. In those places, the majority of Jews living there were destroyed. Also, in the Balkan countries—from Romania, Yugoslavia, Hungary and Greece—most of the Jewish inhabitants had to take the death trip to the destruction camps of the East.[462]

Though not all countries are named, the authors at least give a sense of the sweep and enormity of this immeasureable tragedy.

The figures presented in upper division history, social studies, and political science texts offer a spectrum as broad as intermediate-level texts, ranging from 6 million in most texts to an implied minimum of 3.6 million in Eichberg's text. Eichberg arrives at his figures by stating the losses of Jewish world population between 1931 and 1949. He states that the number of Jews in that period declined from 15.1 million (1931) to 11.5 million (1949), though he does not cite his sources.[463]

Using a similar subtractive method, Fernis and Hillgruber arrive at a figure of about 6 million: "The number of victims," they state, "cannot be exactly transmitted. They amount to about 6 million . . . total in the world." They adduce this figure by subtracting the estimated world Jewish population of 9 million in 1945 from a 1939 Jewish world population figure of 15 million; they also cite parallel European Jewish population figures of 9 million in 1939 reduced to 3 million in 1945.[464] Again, the authors do not cite sources. Gönner and Krug, in the 1978 edition of their text, conclude only that "millions" of Jews were murdered in the great gassing installations of the Holocaust.[465] In the 1981 edition, they conclude a brief but powerful account of the murder of the Jews in Auschwitz and Treblinka and by *Einsatzgruppen* in Poland and Russia, with this statement: "In 1939, 9.2 million Jews lived in Europe. In 1945, there were 3.1 million left. Eighty-one percent of the German Jews were murdered."[466] Thus, using the subtractive method, they arrive at the figure of 6.1 million Jewish victims of the Holocaust.

Hey, on the other hand, provides a country by country breakdown, based on figures from the Institute for the Jewish Problem, New York, with a precise total of 5,978,000 victims of the Holocaust, or 72 percent of the Jewish population of Europe. However, in a later statistical summary of war losses—which includes such detailed statistics as losses from the bombing of Dresden, the expulsion of Germans from Eastern Europe, and the deaths of the Russian, German, Polish, and Yugoslav civil population—there is no column which includes the Jews.[467]

Kampmann and Michel use figures of the Anglo-American Committee published in 1946 presenting detailed estimates country by country, with high and low estimates for each. The aggregate totals are 4,194,200 (low) and 6,029,500 (high).[468] Although the figures are based on investigations which have been overtaken by more recent and thorough research,[469] this is one of the more conscientious attempts to fulfill Schickel's admonition to be precise with these figures representing Jewish martyrdom to Nazi racial hatred.

Frank includes a detailed breakdown of Nazi victims adapted from Sabastian Haffner, a well-known German journalist and author on the Third Reich. It includes victims of the euthanasia program, wherein is mentioned "all Jewish patients in nerve clinics, and about 3,000 children"; the Polish leadership and intellectual class; Soviet intellectuals "among others (also Jews) by means of execution *kommandos*"; approximately 3 million Russian prisoners of war, the gypsies, and "the European Jews, 4–6 million, among them about 200,000 German Jews." Frank includes also (in a later section) the civilian victims of the SS: "The opposition and retaliation activities (*Vergeltungsaktionen*) of the Occupation forces cost many people their lives (30,000 alone in France). The cruelty of German Occupation policies will always be connected with the villages of Lidice (Czechoslovakia) and Oradour-sur-Glane (France)."[470] It should be noted that the innocence of the populace of these two massacred villages has not been mentioned by Frank. Indeed, the passage obscures this critical point.

Only one upper-level history examines the difficulty of establishing precise figures for the victims of the Holocaust. Grütter makes the significant point that:

The number of murdered Jews cannot be determined exactly. The sometimes hefty strife over 5 or 6 million [victims] is absurd. Even the murder of a few Jews would have sufficed to brand the National Socialist regime as criminal.[471]

Elsewhere, however, he overstates this point:

Himmler had ordered the burning of the bodies; one was not to be able to draw any conclusions about the number of murdered Jews.[472]

Only a few texts emphasize the magnitude of the killings apart from what the figures themselves show. Grütter notes that at the Wannsee Conference all European lands were included in Heydrich's plan, including England, Ireland, Turkey, and Sweden. Heydrich carefully recited the numbers of Jewish inhabitants in those countries, as Grütter writes, giving "proof of the powerful political *hubris* at the beginning of 1942."[473] Baumann refers to "the murder of 5 to 6 million Jews from all parts of Europe; the magnitude of their suffering," he concludes, "exceeds the capacity of human imagination."[474] Gallmeister cites 4.5 to 6 million victims, or "the murder of approximately a third of all Jews on earth."[475]

The Significance of the Event

It is the fate of some epochal events that their significance is not seen in the generation in which they took place. It will be reserved for a future century to pass final judgment on the meaning of the two world wars which have made this century the bloodiest in human history, and on two epochal events of the last global war—Hiroshima and Auschwitz—which deeply call into question the optimism about human progress prevalent since the Enlightenment.

The four decades since the Third Reich are a long enough period, however, for tentative historical, political, and philosophic assessments to have appeared in textbooks about the significance of the Holocaust and for authors to have begun to place this extraordinary event in perspective. As inadequate as any effort may be to comment and pass judgment on such events, it is surely far worse—and unacceptable—to treat the Holocaust as history-as-usual. If that is not quite true of West German textbooks—for there are authors who realize that this event is not to be harmonized with the usual conduct of nations—many authors do stand before the Holocaust as if *Fassungslos*—stunned. As Romano Guardini wrote, "The conscience stands aghast before the fearfulness of the event."[476] Many authors appear awed by the subject, at a loss to account for it or to place it within the mainstream of German history. Perhaps it is from bewilderment and helplessness before these events that so many authors end the subject with a document, making no attempt to draw a perspective or evaluation.

Faced with the challenge, the majority of textbook authors treat the subject as if it had been a historical accident of the most improbable kind: unique, unrepeatable, underivable from prior German culture or history, and certainly a closed event. Thus, for example, Lachner's textbook draws no conclusion whatever about the significance of the Holocaust, nor does Steinbügl's, which, like many others, concludes with a document.

No textbook mentions the challenge which the Holocaust poses to Enlightenment assumptions of human progress; the threat posed to the liberal humanist assumptions of Western civilization; nor, after Auschwitz, Christianity's crisis of credibility created by its historic role in transmitting religious anti-Semitism. On the contrary, the Duisburg scholar Heinz Kremers, citing Elite Wiesel's contention that the Holocaust constitutes a watershed event in religion, that "For theologians in Germany, it is . . . difficult to see in the Holocaust 'a watershed event in Religion,' a turning point in Christian religion."[477]

But, if the Holocaust has not been perceived as a watershed event for Christianity, it certainly was for Judaism in Europe. It brought to an end two millennia of Jewish life in Europe, and constitutes the greatest catastrophe for Judaism in two thousand years. For Europe it has meant the loss of the spiritual, cultural, scientific, and economic contribution of the Jews. The international and cosmopolitan influences of the European Jews, so feared and resented by anti-Semites and which contributed so much to the economic, cultural, and scientific modernization of Europe, will no longer be carried forward by the Jews of Europe. Gone is the cultural milieu which produced, in a single century, Marx, Freud, and Einstein. The six million murdered Jews took with them their whole future—a Jewish spiritual and intellectual power and a Judaic culture which leavened the thought and the society of Europe for centuries.

The loss to Europe or to the Jews is dimly reflected in some textbooks; the majority, however, cannot be said to acknowledge the historic loss at all. Menzel and Textor, for example, in a section treating "The Legacy of World War II" include the numbers of war dead, the German refugees driven from Eastern Europe, prisoners of war, lost housing, destroyed cities and the loss of economic wealth— but nothing about the loss of the Jewish people to Germany or Europe.[478] Similarly, Heinloth presents a summary of the "Consequences of the National Socialist Dictatorship" in which he assesses losses to Europe. Along with figures on refugees, expellees, destroyed buildings and cities, he includes civilian losses to bombing, to combat actions "or killed by extermination activities,"[479] a mention which may scarcely be interpreted as giving recognition or commemoration of the Jewish dead of the Holocaust.

Boeck has a section entitled "The Second World War Caused Horrible Wounds," in which he describes the "pain, distress and misery suffered by the people as never before." There he describes the numbers of dead, the homeless, German losses of life, the destruction of buildings, the loss in property and other valuables, the financial costs of the war, changes in political geography, the legacy of poverty, mistrust, fear, and hostility from the war, and the advent of the atomic bomb[480]—but he makes no mention of the destruction of the European Jews as a "wound" of the Second World War.

Instead, the textbooks often discuss the loss to Germany of world-famous Jews due to emigration. This appreciation of the Jewish contribution to world culture is placed, however, in the section of the persecutions of the late 1930s, and not with the legacy of World War II or Nazi Germany. The emphasis is on the loss to German science, art, literature, and economic life. The texts mention famous emigrés—almost all Jewish—such as Albert Einstein, Max Born, Fritz Haber, Sigmund Freud, Lise Meitner, Martin Buber, Franz Werfel, Arnold and Stefan Zweig, Max Reinhardt, Ernst Deutsch, Elisabeth Bergner, Bruno Walter, Paul Ehrlich and Kurt Tucholsky. Tenbrock includes a half page of pictures of Einstein and Walter, a reduction from the full page in earlier editions which included Max Reinhardt and Lise Meitner.[481] Pelzer, Lachner, Tenbrock, Burkhardt (in the Baden-Württemberg edition), and others mention the loss of scientists, poets, artists, musicians, writers, actors, lawyers, doctors, and professors to Germany. Frequently they list the many German Jewish Nobel prize winners in the arts, literature and the sciences. Lachner asks the typical study question: "What losses did Germany suffer in the areas of science and culture because of the emigration of the Jews?"[482]

Only a few authors appear to comprehend the more tragic meaning of these losses. Grassmann (though he carries the usual list of Jewish scientists, artists, and Nobel prize winners) writes that "the contribution of Jewish academics and artists to German culture cannot begin to be described in a few lines. Germany suffered an irreparable loss through the expulsion and destruction of these fellow citizens."[483] And Steinbügl perhaps vaguely senses the larger issue as he asks his students, "What consequences did the emigration of numerous Jewish intellectuals have on the spiritual life of Germany?"[484]

Such expressions of appreciation for Jewish contributions to European culture may be taken as sincere and well-intentioned. However, the impression left by most textbooks (whatever the state guidelines sought) is that the murder of the Jews of Germany and Europe is condemned more as an economic and cultural loss than as the tragic end of a cherished—or even valued—part of the family of Europe. One can ponder what impression is made on young people when they read lists of famous German Jews representing the "scientific" and "cultural" losses to their country by Jewish emigration. Young persons have little sense of people in terms of their professional skills or cultural value. Instead, they sympathize with human suffering on a more direct and intuitive level. One can only wonder what the pedagogical intention could be when the loss of the Jews—culminating in the Holocaust—is portrayed as a matter of economic and cultural loss. In a sense, it is reminiscent of the pragmatic arguments noted in Hug's text, deploring the murder of innocent Jews because it was militarily and strategically counterproductive.[485]

The expression of appreciation of the Jewish people in economic, scientific, and cultural terms is obviously grossly misplaced in this context. The fundamental loss is a human one—the loss of fellow beings sacrificed because not enough people dared or cared to oppose the persecution and murder of the Jews. What occurred is a deep spiritual loss to the German people—and many other Europeans— as well. The fundamental question posed by the Holocaust is a moral one: Indeed, the Holocaust raises important questions about the behavior of people and societies throughout Western culture.

Some German educators, while not textbook authors, in fact do have a strong sense of the dimensions of the catastrophe which occurred in German history as a result of the Holocaust. The renowned educator Georg Picht saw the Holocaust as signalling the snapping of traditional ties of conscience, as manifesting the loosening of a moral order which previously had set limits on human behavior. In 1946 he wrote:

> The situation in which we find ourselves is the same for young and old alike. We are all swimming in the whirlpool of a dark current, fighting for the plank in the wreckage which may yet save us, which may carry us further—though where, no one knows. Not only has the structure of our former lives been physically wrecked, not only has the social order collapsed, but each of us gradually has come to realize that for some time the spiritual order within which we developed has

been set in motion, is sliding incomprehensibly and incalculably beneath us—and we are all sliding with it.[486]

Picht was painfully aware of the educational task before Germany. In 1965, after the physical rubble had been largely cleared away, he wrote of the scarcely begun task of moral reconstruction.

> We are on the threshhold of an educational task so unprecedented that we do not yet have the ability to visualize its dimensions. The inherited tradition of pedagogic experience is insufficient to show us even the horizon within which we may be able to work successfully. The assumptions which previous pedagogues could take for granted are denied us. Today when all morals are loosened, all values outdated, when all systems of order have been called into question, it is up to us to teach fundamentals which earlier generations could inherit unconsciously and uncritically from the resources of the ancient past. But, in this moment in which we are challenged to teach what we really believe ourselves to possess, we must acknowledge that the rudiments of human existence are unknown to us. Our ancestors taught us only how people inherited morals, traditional knowledge, and existing order. But in order to awaken morals, knowledge and order out of nothing one must know and be able to teach what makes morals, knowledge and order possible—and how they are called into existence.[487]

Some authors have found the means of expressing the significance of the Holocaust, at least in terms of the enormity of the event. Ebeling and Birkenfeld are struck by the magnitude of the horror and the unprecedented perversion of the use of technology by the state to carry out the Holocaust. They cite the work of the historian Helmut Krausnick:

> There had often been persecutions of the Jews in the course of history, but never one like *the* persecution—ordered by the state and carried out with such diabolical consequence of planning, and cold, systematic execution, with such horrifying magnitude and results by the National Socialist regime within its sphere of influence and using all its administrative and machine-technical means.[488]

But clearly the emphasis on the awesomeness of the destruction through the increased power of modern technology is only a beginning in coming to grips with the Holocaust. No recognition in spiritual terms is expressed about the meaning of the smoking chimneys of Auschwitz. The Holocaust marked to an unprecedented degree the breaking of the moral tether limiting what human beings were permitted to do to one another. The triumph of the Nazi world view was accompanied by the utter collapse of traditional moral inhibitions—the end of moral limits on human behavior. Herein lay the genesis of the smoking chimneys of Auschwitz; herein lay the task of moral reconstruction described by Georg Picht.

In treating the Holocaust, scarcely any authors relate the martyrdom of the Jews to the defeat of Germany: the fear and resentment of Germany's allies and enemies because of the brutal policies and racial arrogance of Germany, the increased determination of the Allied Powers that Germany surrender unconditionally were significant consequences of Hitler's War and Nazi brutality.

A generation ago, Eberhard Quester urged German authors to make connections between the Nazi hatred of the Jews and the German catastrophe of World War II. "This is necessary," he wrote, "because the catastrophe of the German people is so unmistakably connected with the blame [*Verschuldung*] in regard to the Jewish people."[489] Berndt Engelmann, in his pioneer work, *Deutschland ohne Juden. Eine Bilanz* (Germany without Jews. An Accounting), asks if the hoped-for advantages to be gained by the destruction of the Jews was limited to the Nazi persecutors, for "We know all too little till now, about whether [the Holocaust policy] brought—or could have brought—the Germans some kinds of advantages, and whether these advantages were no more than those . . . which the persecutors of the Jews themselves hoped to gain by their actions."[490]

Whatever advantage the Germans may have hoped for by the spoliation of the Jews, Engelmann concludes that the persecutions ultimately cost the Nazis the war.[491] While this kind of thesis needs careful examination, it is the type of larger perspective worth considering in textbooks. It bears mention also that no connection is made in texts between the Holocaust and the state of Israel. The complex relationship between the end of the two-thousand-year history of Jewish life in Europe, Zionism, and the beginning of the state of Israel is passed over in silence.

The loss of the German Jews is sometimes recalled by followup questions in texts intended to encourage students to learn more about Jews once living in their locale, and to find out their fate during the Holocaust. Hoffmann and Hug, for instance, ask students to "seek to obtain information about the fate of former Jewish fellow-citizens of your hometown."[492] Tenbrock instructs students to "Find out whether a synagogue and a Jewish cemetary exists in your area or in the nearest large city. Is there anything still to be seen of these places?; are there plaques or other memorials?"[493] In his review, Pelzer suggests that students ask contemporaries of the Third Reich about the Nazi era: "In your neighborhood surely you can still find out how people got along with each other and how they discussed political questions."[494] Grassmann, in his assignment, asks the students more directly to "Ask contemporaries about their memories of the persecution of the Jews." He tells students to find out more about Jews, synagogues, the Star of David, anti-Semites, the persecution of Jews, pogroms, the Nuremberg Racial Laws, the 1938 pogrom, and the Holocaust by looking up these words in an encyclopedia.[495]

However valuable and necessary the memorialization of the Jews, the reconstruction of their local contributions, and the trace they left in the memories of contemporary German villagers and townspeople, these efforts are no substitute for the establishment of Jewish history in the texts. In light of the rich Judaic heritage bequeathed to historical Christianity, this is especially necessary. Bishop Faulhaber of Munich in speaking of the German Christian resistance once said that he would not understand his own religion if he did not understand Judaism. This is even truer in the modern era, when Jewish contributions have been stimulating in virtually every area of life in vast disproportion to Jewish numbers or recognition. When one considers that the Jews of Germany were a repressed, ostracized, tiny minority suffering disabilities over centuries, their influence and effect is even more remarkable.

Many textbooks report the percentage of Jews in the German population—less than 1 percent in 1933—but they rarely place it in a meaningful context. Such figures belong with the contributions of Jews proportionate to their small numbers, or, as Muggenthaler places it,[496] in the section on anti-Semitism in counterpoise to the Nazi myth making Jews responsible for the problems of Germany. In either case, students should realize what a small percentage of Germans were Jews, and their contribution to history in proportion to their numbers—or in proportion to the ills which anti-Semites ascribed to them.

At present, only a small fraction of textbooks include even a condensed Jewish history. The reporting of Jewish history in textbooks is still overwhelmingly connected with depiction of the Holocaust. But, as Martin Broszat has written, "If scientific historical writing seeks first and foremost to be organized memory, it dare not limit itself to the reconstruction of the activity of destruction but must, above all, maintain *what* was destroyed and lost."[497]

Because *what* was destroyed and lost was the people of a tiny religious minority whose imposing contributions to culture, economics, and intellectual leadership have been as much resented as admired, their remarkable history is still accorded little space in the modern

European texts of West Germany. In an age of nationalism, it is thought that history is the story of national majorities, not that of social, ethnic or religious minorities. Only Lucas warns against the arrogance of majorities tyrannizing over minorities, employing such suggestive questions as: "What are the possibilities of any person belonging to a minority or getting into one?—within one's own group?—or as a member of a group?" Before students have fully reflected on this question—or recovered their complacency—he concludes the section with this striking sample of seeking to educate for tolerance: "Something not many people think about: Presently only about 30 percent of all people—the Europeans, North Americans, Australians, and some other peoples—are white. In the year 2000, it is predicted that only about 20 percent of human beings will be white."[498]

In a number of textbooks, the meaning of the Holocaust has long been expressed as a gigantic warning system against the danger of anti-Semitism in Germany and of general social intolerance. Lucas alludes to rising anti-Semitism in contemporary Germany, and criticises "those people in Germany today who deny or ignore the scientific truth regarding prejudice, and who forget the crimes to which National Socialism led. They seek to blame economic and political difficulties on others—on minorities." Lucas expresses cautious optimism about lessons learned by the Germans, emphasizing Christian postwar documents in solidarity with the Judaic faith, the amending of former attitudes, and especially Catholic and Protestant declarations which condemn religious anti-Semitism. He reports a nationwide charity drive for German Jews found living in poverty in postwar France, and afraid to return to Germany. When their situation was known, more than one million Deutschmarks were collected for the Jewish refugees.[499] Lucas concludes by assigning students the task of "repeatedly examining" themselves for prejudice against other groups of peoples and religions. To enable students to conduct this examination, he lists a series of 18 human characteristics and qualities to be compared against a second list of nationalities, religions, and other groups. He explains that people who are prone to intolerance of minority and other groups "always ascribe good characteristics only to their own group and bad or questionable ones to alien groups."[500]

Lucas's tone expresses prudent hopefulness that from this terrible catastrophe to the Jews and Germans, historical progress has been made in the postwar years. For such textbooks, the meaning of the Holocaust lies in the hope that from this terrible tragedy a lesson may be learned. Many Germans welcomed Eugen Kogon's article, *"Befreit durch Niederlage. Dreißig Jahre deutscher Wiederaufstieg"* (Freed by Defeat. Thirty Years of German Resurgence), which appeared in the *Frankfurter Hefte* in 1975. Kogon, a highly respected Catholic political scientist and a concentration camp survivor, saw in Germany the beginnings of progress emerging from total defeat:

> When one views the road behind us from the distance of the thirty years since May 8/9, 1945, it is not to be ignored or denied that the total German defeat of that time has proven to be the beginning of historical progress for Germany: From a center of unparalleled trouble-making, from which emanated a gigantic political upheaval of world proportions, has emerged a factor of the highest order of stability.[501]

Many German texts interpret the *Wiedergutmachung* treaty with Israel signed in September 1952, as evidence that Germany has learned from the past, and that the Israeli government's willingness in 1965 to resume normal diplomatic relations with Germany suggests that Germany has made substantial progress in overcoming the stigma of its Nazi past. Some texts print a portion of the Restitution Treaty, with an ideal self-image of Germany codified in the text:

> In their overwhelming majority, the German people detested and did not participate in the crimes committed against the Jews. There were many Germans, during the era of National Socialism who, endangering themselves, and for reasons of religion, conscience, and shame over the disgracing of the name of Germany, showed helpfulness to their Jewish fellow citizens. In the name of the German people, however, indescribable crimes were carried out which require moral and material reparation of us as a duty.[502]

Though the treaty is a postwar political document, many texts interpret the historical German relationship to Jews during the Nazi era in a similar manner.

While the accompanying commentary in Ebeling and Birkenfeld is tastefully handled, some texts, such as Heumann (Bavarian edition) state the monetary amount of the restitution, and Schmid stresses the economic importance of the treaty for Israel.[503]

The sense of optimism, found in so many texts, suggesting that the past has been overcome, that Germans have learned the lessons of Auschwitz, is offset by the references by a few authors to the upsurge in neo-Nazi groups and anti-Semitic terror activities in the Federal Republic during the 1970s and 1980s. In these texts, cautious optimism gives way to increasing apprehension that the past has not been so easily mastered and learned from as had been hoped. Ebeling and Birkenfeld mark the period of change: "Not until the attack on the Israeli participants in the 1972 Olympics in Munich and the TV program 'Holocaust' in 1979 did many Germans allow themslves to think about the relations of Germans and Jews again."[504]

Ebeling and Birkenfeld cite the cover story in *Der Spiegel* (The Mirror)—the national news weekly of Germany—about the Holocaust TV series, "which started a lively discussion between the generations."[505] Grassmann also notes the revival of interest in the subject by Germans. "Holocaust," he reports, "severely disturbed 20 million Germans. This U.S. TV series . . . became a subject of conversation in the U.S.A. and many European countries."[506]

Grassmann reflects the increasing interest in Third Reich German-Jewish relations by including a special section entitled "We are Writing a Chapter of our History: National Socialism in Our Area—a Project." The text contains a detailed discussion of how students may reconstruct aspects of their local history. Sample questions: How did relatives and acquaintances experience the Nazi seizure of power?—the persecution of the Jews?—the outbreak of the war?—capitulation?[507]

Heinloth also notes a growing debate about the Third Reich and its deeds: "Today, in Germany and abroad, more lively discussions are carried out on Hitler, National Socialism and the Third Reich than on any other aspect of German history."[508] Heinloth points out that many West Germans would like to put an end finally—*Schlusstrich* (draw a line under)—to these discussions, while others see it as a warning system to future generations. He thinks that the German international reputation will be measured in terms of its ability to come to grips with this past. He concedes that there are Germans now, as there were during the Third Reich, who "secretly or publicly cultivate a certain admiration for Hitler's 'achievements' "—but notes, too, that "others utterly condemn Hitler and view all acts of the Third Reich entirely in negative terms."[509]

Although the vast majority of texts treat the Holocaust as an unrepeatable event, and make no mention of neo-Nazi activity in postwar Germany—thereby strongly suggesting that Germany has overcome its past—Grassmann's recent text breaks entirely new ground. A section entitled *"Is It Possible Again?"* contains a dialectical discussion about the possibility of a Fascist revival. Grassmann notes that some specialists consider National Socialism and Fascism as belonging to the dead past, but that

> Others argue that the political, economic and social prerequisites have
> not changed so decisively since the Second World War that the genesis
> of Fascism and National Socialism have become impossible. Naturally,
> no one denies that neo-Fascist and neo-Nazi movements, parties and

attitudes exist. But there is disunity about how seriously one must take these manifestations. Is it a matter of a few unteachables, or the beginning of a new disaster?[510]

Grassmann includes color illustrations of Swastika-smeared Jewish gravestones and marching neo-Nazi youth groups. He follows this presentation with a full chapter analysis of the characteristics of Fascism and National Socialism and the circumstances which brought these ideologies into being. He also alludes, in an assignment, to the Holocaust deniers: "For what reasons do the neo-Nazi youths of 1978 contest the mass extermination of the Jews?"[511]

No other text has such intelligent and balanced coverage of the significance of the Holocaust for postwar Germany as Grassmann's. His text is a hopeful sign. Only a few other authors appear to recognize that the Holocaust has relevance for the present and future. Burkhardt, in his Baden-Württemburg edition, asks the question, "What does it mean if sometimes even today gravestones in Jewish cemeteries are overturned or painted with Swastikas?"[512] and Hug in his teacher manual asks "What can be done to prevent a repetition of the Holocaust?"[513]

More often, however, the texts portray the danger of prejudice and the persecution of groups outside Germany. Heumann in the Bavarian edition of his text asks, "Where are people persecuted today because of their political or religious convictions? What can we do against this? Inform yourself about the work of 'Amnesty International,' the 'Society for Human Rights' and other aid organizations."[514] In Heumann's teacher manual is found the answer: The denial of human rights in the Soviet Union.[515] In like manner, Binder and Burkhardt ask "Where were—and are—there still racial laws similar to the National Socialist laws?"[516] The answer in the teacher manual is that Uganda under Idi Amin persecuted Indians because of their race; Indonesia opposes the Chinese living there; and South Africa has atrocious *Apartheid* policies.[517]

Hug compares the lack of response to the persecution and murder of the Jews to today's response to world hunger and outcast groups, in a strident manner:

Have we learned from history? Does today's youth possess more courage, sensitivity to justice and helpfulness than their parents? The wielders of power of the Third Reich murdered approximately 6 million Jews. Today, about 25 million human beings die annually of hunger. . . . None of us can later say: "We didn't know about that." What groups in our present society are on the outside? Discuss these problems in your class.[518]

As shown above, insofar as the Holocaust has historic meaning or significance in the textbooks, it is primarily for what *other* countries may learn from the experience. The texts convey little concern about the problems observed in contemporary German society: neo-Nazi activity, the persistance of anti-Semitic attitudes, and the reproduction of traditional attitudes from the National Socialist and pre-National Socialist era. The texts generally do not base Holocaust presentations on the assumption that such events could ever again take place in Germany. Even the few texts which treat it as a *Warnsystem* are more likely to warn against potential persecutions and mass-killings of defenseless people in other parts of the world. In downplaying the importance of the "few unteachables" who perpetuate the thought models once dominant in the Nazi era, the texts reflect the social and political confidence in the strength and orderliness of the present democratic state of Germany.

4
Conclusions

The study has attempted to shed light on how a nation which is proud of its history and culture is attempting to come to terms with a powerfully negative event in that history, and how it integrates such a dark, admonitory event into its national past. The Holocaust is the most disastrous occurrence in Germany's national history, has caused a darkening of Germany's historical reputation, lasting suspicion abroad and considerable soul-searching at home. The study of German textbooks documents the struggle within Germany to fashion a negative historical experience into a "usable past" so that something may be learned from it without causing psychic traumatization of the young in the socialization process of becoming German citizens.

The experience has obvious lessons for other countries, including the United States, which has drawn only awkwardly into its history such negative chapters as the treatment of the American Indian, slavery, the incarceration of Japanese-Americans during World War II, Vietnam, and Watergate, to name a few traumatic historical experiences generally passed over lightly in U.S. history texts.

All West German textbooks treat at least three broad themes: the anti-Semitic roots of Nazism, the Nazi persecution of the Jews during the 1930s, and the Holocaust. In treating these themes the texts share a largely common perspective and emphasize many of the same aspects of the Holocaust and related subjects, so that it is possible to draw a composite analysis.

Most texts, having evolved through many editions, no longer suffer from significant factual inaccuracies. However, many texts omit various facts and aspects, and no single text may be said to present a detailed treatment. In quantitative coverage, the German texts compare favorably with other nations' textbook depictions of the subject, although the treatment is often little more than a narrative presentation of the major aspects of the subject and related events.

There is no doubt that German educators at the government and school level perceive a special obligation to treat the National Socialist persecutions and Holocaust in the texts and in the classroom curriculum. They make it clear that the genocide was an unprecedented catastrophe. Although other groups of victims are named, it is pointed out that the Jews were the primary victims of Nazi barbarity, and that they were unique in being singled out for genocide.

There is virtually no trace of anti-Semitism in the 50 works examined, although there are cases of awkward phrasing, and many cases of texts needlessly presenting vicious anti-Semitic source materials of Nazi and pre-Nazi racial anti-Semites to portray Nazi racial ideology, a practice which can only perpetuate negative stereotypes in the minds of students. All texts universally condemn the persecution and murder of the Jews as well as every other aspect of Third Reich theory and practice, a condemnation which has brought about the unintended result that many students find it incomprehensible that their grandparents' generation could have ever given loyalty and devotion to such a regime.

In treating the roots of the Holocaust, the description of the various manifestations of anti-Semitism is inadequate to teach the student how the persecutions and the Holocaust could have come about. The treatment of racial anti-Semitism is lengthy, but often merely perpetuates negative stereotypes. The religious roots of anti-Semitism to be found in Christianity are only briefly mentioned in most textbooks. Economic factors of competition, greed, and envy are also only partially analyzed in the majority of texts. Only a few textbooks analyze the functions which prejudice serves in the psychic economy of human beings, and only a handful of texts make use of psychological or sociological explanations to help clarify anti-Semitism. In fact, however, large-scale historical events motivated by irrationality and social pathology—as, for instance, the Crusades, the Inquisition, witch trials and burnings, the nineteenth-century Russian pogroms, the twentieth century Armenian massacres and the Holocaust itself—require examination using an interdisciplinary approach, something which German texts scarcely undertake.

While the presentation of religious, economic, racial, and political motives of anti-Semitism is clearly necessary to historically accurate explanation, these factors do not in themselves convey the important psychological roots of anti-Semitism. Prejudices are rooted in insecurities, causing guilt-projection, scapegoating, resentments, frustrations, envy, and greed, which may culminate in lethal behavior. Some textbooks show signs of a growing awareness of the progress of psychology and sociology in explaining prejudice, and a few texts, indeed, do present partial functional analyses of anti-Semitism. None, however, interpret anti-Semitic prejudice as a psychological disorder, as a pathological social aberration. No text provides a coherent explanation of the Holocaust based on the analysis of anti-Semitism as a serious mental disorder which reached murderous proportions in the Nazi Era. In short, they still skate the surface of the phenomenon.

All texts offer a factually accurate treatment of the persecution of the Jews during the 1930s, and include the major stages of the persecutions from 1933 to 1941. These presentations are largely uniform and appear to follow state guidelines. All such accounts correctly describe the major persecutions, but only a few describe the suffering of the victims. A few texts, it may be said, focus on Jewish children as a means of evoking empathy among young readers, but no text emphasizes the deprivations, disabilities, or confiscations suffered by German Jews. Such an approach would make it easier for young people to identify with the victims' plight. In particular, the deprivations and humiliations which made Jewish daily life so cruel should be given greater recognition in the texts. In the same manner, the tragedy of Jewish expulsions from Germany and the looting of Jewish property require greater attention, and the economic motives for anti-Semitism a more thoroughgoing assessment.

The student learns remarkably little about the Jewish people or their history from the texts. The result is a shadowy depiction of the Jewish victims of the Nazi regime. Despite the sympathy expressed by many textbook authors and a special emphasis in some texts on the sufferings of Jewish children, the young student learns little about the German Jews.

This deficiency is due perhaps to postwar German repression of the subject, to the neglect of German scholarship to examine German popular attitudes toward Jews—i.e., German-Jewish social history—during the Third Reich, and to continuing postwar anti-Semitism. The detailed examination of German relations with Jews will have to await further research. The results of this new search will add fresh pain as well as some additional cases of unsung German civic courage. The present depiction of German-Jewish relations during the 1930s minimizes the existence of German anti-Semitism and over-emphasizes German fear of the Nazi regime and the distorting of propaganda. In the social history of the era, the Germans are portrayed as passive. The texts make little criticism of the conduct or attitudes of Germans during the Third Reich, and many texts characterize the German response to the Nazi persecutions solely in terms of horror and private condemnation.

All textbooks depict the mass murders of the Holocaust, but they are frequently brief regarding the immediate antecedents to the killings. Only a small minority of texts, for example, raise the issue of the Führer order or the Wannsee Conference for planning the genocide. On the other hand, the texts which do treat these aspects leave no doubt that Hitler gave the order for genocide and some texts include evidence of Himmler's, Göring's and Goebbels' additional complicity in the genocide.

The textbooks cannot be said to downplay even the most gruesome aspects of the Holocaust, but the underrepresentation of Jewish survivor accounts gives the depictions an air of detachment, almost of remoteness, and are inadequate in their evocation of the historical magnitude of this tragedy. The choice of German instead of Jewish eyewitness documents for every stage of persecution—from ghettoization, transportation, SS *Einsatzgruppen* massacres, concentration camp life, to killing centers—leaves the reader with a stronger sense of alienation from the victims than of empathy. The killing process itself—the gassings and cremation—is not omitted from any text, but the depiction is entirely devoid of comment or evaluation. Many authors close the subject by the use of a quotation from an original document which describes the killing process, then proceed, with shocking abruptness, to another subject—usually the German resistance. One might imagine the surprise of a young student who has just read Hoess's or Gerstein's terrifying account of mass gassings and cremation, to find the subject dropped entirely without evaluation.

While all texts mention by name some of the killing centers and describe the gassings and cremation, the murders are portrayed almost as if they took place by automatic processes. The texts barely indicate the identities of the perpetrators. Typically, Hitler, Nazi leaders, or the SS are cited as the prime culprits responsible for all horrors. Most texts exhibit scant interest in the broader circles of complicity involved in murdering millions of men, women and children. The German people are conspicuously disassociated from mention in any connection with the perpetration of the Holocaust. The texts do not examine the personnel requirements of an operation involving the murder of six million people. In the same fashion, the role of business, bureaucracy, or economic and industrial practice in connection with the killings is not discussed in most texts, and treated only incidentally in the rest.

The texts also exhibit little agreement on the number of Jews killed in the Holocaust. The figures range from a minimum of 3.6 million to more than 6 million. Despite recommendations by specialists that the source of figures be documented, few texts do so, and only a small proportion of books place the figures in a meaningful perspective or comment on the significance of these figures for Jewish and European history.

A common weakness of textbooks is the absence of conclusions about the meaning of the Holocaust or its accompanying events. It is not uncommon for German historical writing—and especially in the area of the Holocaust—to present the relevant factual data, but pass over any inferences which may be drawn. The absence of any conclusions, so apparent to the non-German reader, does not seem to have been a matter of concern to German observers. Perhaps they are more aware of progress made over decades in getting the factual elements of this subject in the textbooks than of the absence of a discussion of the historical significance of these events. Whatever the case, little attention has been directed toward seeking agreement on meanings and inferences to be drawn from the events depicted in the factual narrative. In this regard, other countries, particularly the United States, have forged ahead in interpreting the meaning of the Holocaust in works of history, political science, philosophy, psychology, sociology, and theology. German scholarship in general, it may be said, has been cautious and reserved in drawing major conclusions about this event. Especially difficult for German scholars has been the formulation of conclusions which may appear to condemn the social, mental, or political attitudes of Germans of the Third Reich, particularly if the cultural traditions which sustained these attitudes are still latent in the society.

The function of textbooks is generally accepted as the socialization of the nation's youth into the mainstream of contemporary society, and not the attempt to reform or revolutionize basic mental attitudes of the society, an aim which possibly could lead young people out of the traditional socioeconomic and political framework of the nation. Thus, while a few innovative textbook authors cite major German scholarly works criticizing the authoritarian personality, the bureau-cratic mind, and the economic practices of capitalism, such analyses are not integrated into a discussion of the Holocaust. Provocative textbook interpretations risk public censure and pressure on state education authorities to ban their use. Textbooks for educating the young in history and politics are viewed as having the purpose of socializing young people to be self-respecting, loyal, and proud members of the national community. To facilitate this, the search for a "usable past" continues. Should a large block of materials be seen as unserviceable for this purpose—as with the Holocaust—it will be dutifully reported as long as this is required by state guidelines, but left as an "erratic bloc," undigested, shocking, and only superficially assimilated, as, for example, a warning against totalitarianism and a basis for support of democratic government.

There are signs in the 1980s that West German scholarship may be on the threshold of coming to grips with some of the suppressions of the past. There is a renaissance of Third Reich and Holocaust research in Germany which complements the worldwide explosion of Holocaust and related research which began in the 1970s. As a new generation of scholars comes of age in Germany, increasing numbers of researchers have sufficient distance to examine the generation of their grandparents. Since the nationwide broadcast in West Germany of the NBC television series "Holocaust" in 1979, there has been a phenomenal growth in the number of books, articles, films, television programs, conferences, commemorations, university courses, and local history projects, all of which signal a different kind of interest than the "Hitler Wave" of the early 1970s.

In addition to a natural curiosity of the young, the "Hitler Wave" included a great deal of nostalgia and furtive admiration of Nazism. The new interest is more firmly determined to ask difficult questions about Germans, Nazis, Jews, and genocide without the inhibitions and rationalizations which characterized earlier generations. Moreover, the disquieting reemergence of neo-Nazism and neoracism in some Germans' attitudes toward foreign laborers living in Germany and the highly ambiguous message conveyed by the Bitburg cemetery visit of 1985 adds further urgency to the question of what is taught in the German schools about the Holocaust, racial bigotry, and pluralistic values in texts of the Federal Republic of Germany.

Notes

1. Among the best recent examinations of the subject are Chaim Schatzker, *Die Juden in dem deutschen Geschichtsbüchern,* Bonn: A. Bernecker, 1981; Heinz Kremers, "Die Darstellung der Juden in neuen Schulbüchern in der Bundesrepublik Deutschland," *In: Schulbuchanalyzse und Schulbuchkritik, Im Brennpunkt: Juden, Judentum und Staat Israel,* eds. Gerd Stein, Horst Schallenberger, Duisburg, 1976; Dieter Schmidt-Sinns, Gernot Dallinger, Hellmut Wettlauffer, eds., *Der Nationalsozialismus als didaktisches Problem. Beiträge zur Behandling des NS-Systems und des deutschen Widerstands im Unterricht,* Bonn: A. Bernecker, 1980; Günter van Norden, *Das Dritte Reich im Unterricht,* Frankfurt am Main: Hirschgraben, 1977; E. Horst Schallenberger, Gerd Stein, "Juden, Judentum und Staat Israel in Deutschen Schulbüchern," *In: Lebendiges Zeugnis,* 32, 21/ 1977. Band: *Judentum und Christentum;* Bundeszentrale für politische Bildung, *Beiträge zur Auseinandersetzung mit dem Nationalsozialismus,* Bonn, 1983; Peter Meyers and Dieter Riesenberger, *Der Nationalsozialismus in der historisch-politischen Bildung,* Göttingen: Vandenhoeck und Ruprecht, 1980.

2. Karl-Ernst Jeismann, "Internationale Schulbuchforschung, Aufgaben, Arbeitsweise und Probleme," *Aus Politik und Zeitgeschichte,* Bonn, B36/82, Sept. 11, 1982, p. 29.

3. Wilhelm Schreckenberg, "Das jüdische problem im Geschichtsunterricht. Historikertagung der Gesellschaft für christlich-jüdische Zusammenarbeit," *Geschichte in Wissenschaft und Unterricht,* Stuttgart, 1954, p. 440.

4. Alfred Dauch, "Das Schulbuch aus der Sicht des Verlegers," *Zur Sache Schulbuch,* Düsseldorf, no. 1, 1973, p. 46.

5. *Ibid.*

6. *Ibid.,* p. 60.

7. Arbeitsgemeinschaft Buchproduktion, *Schulbuch-Produktion und Profit.* pad extra, no. 3/4, 1973, p. 15.

8. Harold Kastner, "Zur Behandlung des Nationalsozialismus im Unterricht," *Aus politik und Zeitgeschichte,* Bonn, vol. 22, June 2, 1979, p. 20.

9. Dauch, p. 47, p. 51.

10. *Arbeitsgemeinschaft Buchproduktion,* p. 15.

11. "German Debate on How to Teach the Holocaust Story," *Patterns of Prejudice,* London, vol. 13, no. 4, July/Aug., 1979, p. 20.

12. Konrad Schilling, "Beitrag zur Behandling von Judentum und Anti-semitismus im Oberstufenunterricht," *Geschichte in Wissenschaft und Unterricht* Stuttgart, 1960, p. 134. The Germans have only begun to adopt the word "Holocaust" in the 1980s.

13. Schreckenberg, p. 438.

14. Schilling, pp. 135 and 138.

15. *Ibid.*, p. 135.

16. *Ibid.*

17. *Ibid.*, p. 134.

18. Ekkehart Krippendorff, "The Presentation of Jewry in Teachers Training and in the Classroom," *In: Education for Democracy in West Germany, Achievements—Shortcomings—Prospects,* ed. Walter Stahl, New York: Praeger, 1960, p. 125.

19. "Erklärung des Deutschen Ausschusses für das Erziehungs- und Bildungswesen aus Anlaß der antisemitischen Ausschreitungen," *Geschichte in Wissenschaft und Unterricht,* Stuttgart, vol. 3, no. 60, 1960, pp. 129–131.

20. *Amtsblatt des Hessische Kultusministers,* 1960, p. 70ff.

21. *Ibid.*, 1962.

22. Wolfgang Bobke, "Jews in West German History Textbooks," unpublished study for the *American Jewish Committee,* New York, 1979/80, p. 12.

23. Heinz Kremers, "Judentum und Holocaust im deutschen Schulunterricht," *Aus Politik und Zeitgeschichte,* Bonn, B4/79, Jan. 27, 1979, p. 40.

24. Kastner, p. 22; Bobke, p. 17.

25. Marhild Hoffmann, "Der Nationalsozialismus in Richtlinien und Lehrplänen. Kritische Anmerkungen zu Beispielen aus fünf Bundesländern," *In: Der Nationalsozialismus als didaktisches Problem. Beiträge zur Behandlung des NS-Systems und des deutschen Widerstands im Unterricht,* ed. Dieter Schmidt-Sinns, *Schriftenreihe der Bundeszentrale für politische Bildung,* 156, Bonn: A. Bernecker, 1980, p. 36.

26. *Ibid.*

27. The section which follows is based largely on Hoffmann's study, pp. 23–29.

28. *Ibid.*, p. 26. The Nazi-Soviet Non-Aggression Pact of August, 1939, did not constitute alliance with Germany; nor did its trade agreement or Secret Protocol to the Non-Aggression Pact, which led to the fourth partition of Poland.

29. *Ibid.* This is not to be confused with the Lower Saxony guidelines for the *Gymnasium* level.

30. *Ibid.*, p. 30.

31. *Ibid.*, p. 31.

32. See especially the Bavarian Curriculum Guidelines for Social Science at the intermediate level (7–9 grade); the Hessian Plan for Social Studies (Section I, Social Science); and the Guidelines for the *Gymnasium* of Lower Saxony, where the threat of totalitarianism arising within a democratic society is described, referring to the defeat of the Weimar Republic by the National Socialists.

33. Hoffmann, p. 23.

34. Schilling, p. 151.

35. Frank Hennecke, *Staat und Unterricht. Die Festlegung didaktischer Inhalte durch den staat im öffentlichen Schulwesen*, Schriften zum öffentliche Recht, 179, Berlin: Duncker und Humblot, 1972, pp. 48–51.

36. *Ibid.*, p. 48.

37. Eckehardt Stein, *Das Recht des Kindes auf Selbst Entfaltung in der Schule. Verfassungsrechtliche Überlegungen zur freiheitlichen Ordnung des Schulwesens*, Neuwied am Rhein/Berlin: Leuchterhand, 1967, p. 45.

38. *Ibid.*

39. Oskar Anweiler, "Das Schulbuch als Spiegel Gesellschaftlich-politiker Entwicklung," In: *Das Schulbuch. Produkt und Faktor gesellschaftlicher Prozesse*, ed. E. Horst Schallenberger, Ratingen: Aloys Henn, 1973, p. 77.

40. Horst Gies, "Schwierigkeiten und Probleme, den National-Sozialismus in einem Schulbuch darzustellen, das sich als Arbeitsbuch versteht." Berlin, 1979. Address presented at the *Tagung der Konferenz für Geschichtsdidaktik*, Berlin, Sept., 1979, unpublished paper, p. 3.

41. Margarete Dörr, "Das Schulbuch im Geschichtsunterricht—Kriterien für seine Beurteilung," In: *Die Funktion der Geschichte in unserer Zeit*, ed. Fackel und Weymar, Stuttgart, 1975, p. 295.

42. Alfred Baumgartner, "Schulbücher sind heute anders. Alte Vorurteile—neue Inhalte," *Blickpunkt Schulbuch*, 19, Frankfurt a.M. November, 1976, p. 35.

43. Peter Kalb, "Die Angst des Verlegers beim Schulbuchzulassen," *betrifft: erziehung*, 6, Sept. 3, 1973, p. 16.

44. *Ibid.*

45. Dauch, p. 53.

46. Robert Multhoff, "Beispiele der Schulbuchverbesserung," *Internationales Jahrbuch für Geschichts- und geographie- Unterricht*, 13, Braunschweig: Albert Limbach, 1970/71, p. 32.

47. Dauch, p. 50.

48. *Ibid.*, p. 47.

49. Berger, p. 23.

50. Kastner, pp. 19–20.

51. Helmut Meier, "Der westdeutsche Geschichtslehrerverband. Seine Rolle im System der geschichtsideologischen Manipulation in Westdeutschland," *Geschichtsunterricht und Staatsburgerkunde*, 12:9, Berlin, D.D.R., 1970, p. 784.

52. Herbert Stein, "Juden in Deutschland 1983," *Tribüne." Zeitschrift zum Verständnis des Judentums*, Frankfurt a/M., 86, 1983, pp. 40–43.

53. Jeismann, "Internationale Schulbuchforschung," p. 28.

54. Gerhard Weise, "Erziehung zur Toleranz. Vorurteile in Geschichts-büchern," *Europäische Begegnung*, Essen, 8:2, 1968, p. 87.

55. Jeismann, "Internationale Schulbuchforschung," p. 27.

56. E. Horst Schallenberger and Gerd Stein, "Juden, Judentum und Staat Israel in deutschen Schulbüchern," In: *Lebendiges Zeugnis* Band: *Judentum und Christentum*, 32:1/2, Feb. 1977, p. 51.

57. Karl-Ernst Jeismann, "Forum. Holocaust—einmaliges oder exemplarisches Ereignis?," *Internationale Schulbuchforschung,* vol. I, 1979, p. 46, citing E. Weisel, "Then and Now: The Experiences of a Teacher," *Social Education,* Apr. 1978, p. 266.

58. Jeismann, "Internationale Schulbuchforschung," p. 47.

59. *Ibid.,* p. 31.

60. Rolf Wernstedt, "Schulbuchrevision ist Filigranarbeit," *Eriziehung und Wissenschaft Niedersachsen,* vol. 20, 1975, p. 5.

61. Bobke, p. 17.

62. Christoph Klessmann, "Zur Methodik vergleichender Schulbuchanalyse," *Internationales Jahrbuch für Geschichts- und Geographie-Unterricht,* XVII, Braunschweig: Georg-Eckert-Institut für Internationale Schulbuchforschung, 1976, pp. 63–64.

63. Jeismann, "Internationale Schulbuchforschung," p. 34.

64. Multhoff, p. 35; Edward H. Dance, *History the Betrayer,* London: Hutchinson, 1960, p. 150.

65. Jeismann, "Internationale Schulbuchforschung," p. 34.

66. Kremers in G. Stein and E. Horst Schallenberger, p. 148, citing Phina Levinsohn.

67. Alfred Schickel, "Sind unsere Geschichtsbücher noch zeitgemäss?," *Die neue Ordnung,* Vienna, 31:1, 1977, p. 47.

68. Alfred Schickel, "Die Darstellung der nationalsozialistischen Judenverfolgung in neueren Geschichtsbüchern der Bundesrepublik Deutschland," *Emuna Israel Forum,* Rothenburg, vol. 4, 1976, p. 21.

69. Romano Guardini, "Verantwortung. Gedanken zur jüdischen Frage," *Geschichte in Wissenschaft und Unterricht,* vol. 8, 1952, p. 458.

70. Dietrich Goldschmidt, "Zur Soziologie des Antisemitismus," *Geschichte in Wissenschaft und Unterricht,* Stuttgart, 1960, pp. 295–296.

71. Walter Hoffmann, "Ein Beitrag zur Widerlegung des Antisemitismus," *Die pädagogische Provinz,* Frankfurt a/M, vol. 3, 1949, p. 678.

72. Kremers in G. Stein and E. Horst Schallenberger, p. 149.

73. Heinz Kremers, "Israel und das Judentum," *Emuna Israel Forum,* Rothenburg, vol. 5/6, 1978, p. ix.

74. Martin Broszat, "Holocaust und die Geschichtswissenschaft," *Vierteljahreshefte für Zeitgeschichte,* Stuttgart, Apr., 1979, p. 295.

75. *Ibid.,* p. 296.

76. Wolfgang Hug, Joachim Hoffmann, Elmar Krautkrämer, *Lernimpulse 3, Begleitheft zum Arbeitsbuch "Geschichtliche Weltkunde,"* vol. 3, Frankfurt am Main: Moritz Diesterweg, 1980, p. 47.

77. Helmut Kistler and Werner Stroppe, *Harms Arbeitsmappen Geschichte,* vol. 4, Von 1848 bis zur Gegenwart, München: List, 1980, p. 14; Heinz Dieter Schmid, ed., *Fragen an die Geschichte. Geschichtliches Arbeitsbuch für Sekundarstufe I.,* vol. 4, *Die Welt im 20. Jahrhundert,* Frankfurt am Main: Hirschgraben, 1979, p. 61; Hans Heumann, H. J. Blödorn, W. Freund *et. al., Geschichte für morgen, Arbeitsbuch für den Geschichtsunterricht in der Sekundarstufe I,* vol. 4, *Zeitgeschichte,* Frankfurt am Main: Hirschgraben, 1980, p. 70.

78. Otto Boeck, Artur Dumke, Robert Hubner, Fritz Klenk, Otto Kratzert, Eugen Sohns, *Damals und heute* 4, *Geschichte für Hauptschulen,* Stuttgart: Ernst Klett, 1976, p. 29.

79. Hans Döhn, Fritz Sandmann, *Geschichte 3. Erkunden und erkennen,* Hannover: Hermann Schroedel, 1977, p. 98.

80. Hans Muggenthaler, Wolfgang and Hannah Marks, *Geschichte für Realschulen,* vol. 4., *Neueste Zeit,* München: Kösel-Verlag, p. 113.

81. Schmid, p. 61.

82. Kistler and Stroppe, p. L14.

83. Friedrich J. Lucas, Heinrich Bodensieck, Erhard Rumpf, Günter Thiele, *Menschen in ihrer Zeit,* 4, *In unserer Zeit,* Stuttgart: Ernst Klett, 1981, p. 227.

84. Eduard Steinbügl, Anton Schreiegg, *Geschichte,* vol. 4: *Neueste Zeit,* München: R. Oldenbourg, 1973, p. 85.

85. Friedrich Deuschle, *Du und die Politik, Lehr- und Arbeitsbuch für die politische Bildung,* Homburg: Max Gehlen, 1977, p. 77.

86. Friedrich Deuschle, *Du und die Politik, Lehrbuch für die poltische Bildung. Lehrerheft,* Homburg: Max Gehlen, 1977, p. 48.

87. Hans-Georg Fernis and Andreas Hillgruber, *Grundzüge der Geschichte. Sekundarstufe II Historisch-politisches Arbeitsbuch.* vol. 2. *Vom Zeitalter der Aufklärung bis zur Gegenwart,* Frankfurt am Main: Diesterweg, 1972, p. 164.

88. Muggenthaler, p. 113.

89. R.H. Tenbrock, K. Kluxen, *Didaktischer Grundiß für der Geschichtsunterricht,* vol. 4: *Zeiten und Menschen,* Paderborn: Schöningh, Schroedel, 1981, p. 71.

90. Gerhart Binder, Hermann Burkhardt, Helmut Christmann, Alfred Jung, Fritz Klenk, *Damals und heute* 5, *Geschichte für Hauptschulen. Vom Ersten Weltkrieg bis heute,* Stuttgart: Ernst Klett, 1977, p. 94.

91. Schmid, p. 61.

92. Hans Ebeling, Wolfgang Birkenfeld, *Die Reise in die Vergangenheit. Ein Geschichtliches Arbeitsbuch,* Braunschweig: Westermann, 1982, p. 164.

93. Lucas, p. 226.

94. Eugen Kaier, Herbert Deißler, Herbert Krieger, *Grundzüge der Geschichte.* (Sekundarstufe I), Gymnasium. vol. 4: *Von 1890 bis zur Gegenwart,* Frankfurt am Main: Moritz Diesterweg, 1977, p. 32.

95. *Ibid.*

96. R. H. Tenbrock, K. Kluxen, *Zeiten und Menschen,* vol. 4, *Europa und die Welt. Das 20. Jahrhundert,* Paderborn: Schoningh, Schroedel, 1966, p. 137. Unfortunately, this statement has been dropped from Tenbrock's latest edition.

97. Robert-Hermann Tenbrock, Kurt Kluxen, Erich Goerlitz, Erich Meier, Helmut Mejcher, Kerrin Gräfin Scherwin, *Zeiten und Menschen,* K edition, vol. 4, *Geschichte für Kollegstufe und Grundstudium Politik, Gesellschaft, Wirtschaft im 20. Jahrhundert.* Part I: *Vom 1919 bis 1945,* Paderborn: Schöningh, Schroedel, 1982, p. 116.

98. Hermann Meyer, Wilhelm Langenbeck, *Vom Zeitalter der Aufklärung bis zur Gegenwart. Grundzüge der Geschichte. Sekundarstufe II. Historisch-politisches Arbeitsbuch,* Quellenband II, Frankfurt am Main: Diesterweg, 1975, p. 233.

99. Hans-Georg Fernis, Heinrich Haverkamp, *Grundzüge der Geschichte,* Sekundarstufe II, *Von der Urzeit bis zur Gegenwart,* Frankfurt am Main: Diesterweg, 1975, p. 311.

100. Altrichter and Glaser, *Geschichtliches Werden,* Oberstufe IV, *Vom Zeitalter des Imperialismus bis zur Gegenwart,* Bamburg: C. C. Buchners, 1971, p. 28.

101. *Ibid.* Emphasis in original.

102. Kaier, p. 33.

103. Ebeling and Birkenfeld, *Arbeitsbuch,* p. 164.

104. Joachim Hoffmann, *Spiegel der Zeiten,* vol. 4: *Von der russischen Revolution bis zur Gegenwart,* Frankfurt am Main: Moritz Diesterweg, 1978, p. 81.

105. S. Grassmann, ed., *Zeitaufnahme, Geschichte für die Sekundarstufe I,* vol. 3: *Vom Ersten zum Zweiten Weltkrieg,* Braunschweig: Westermann, 1981, p. 71.

106. Kistler and Stroppe, p. L14.

107. Wolfgang Hug, ed., *Geschichtliche Weltkunde.* Vol. 3: *Schülerarbeitsheft 1. Von der Zeit des Imperialismus bis zur nationalsozialistischen Diktatur in Deutschland,* Frankfurt am Main: Diesterweg, 1979, p. 68.

108. Wolfgang Hug, Joachim Hoffmann, Elmar Krautkrämer, *Geschichtliche Weltkunde,* vol. 3: *Von der Zeit des Imperialismus bis zur Gegenwart,* Frankfurt am Main: Diesterweg, 1979, p. 114.

109. Hoffmann, *Von der russische Revolution,* p. 82.

110. Joachim Hoffmann, *Spiegel der Zeiten, Lehr- und Arbeitsbuch für den Geschichtesunterricht. Handreichung für den Lehrer.* Vol. 4: *Von der russischen Revolution bis zur Gegenwart,* Frankfurt am Main: Diesterweg, 1979, p. 42.

111. Grassmann, p. 56.

112. Muggenthaler, p. 114.

113. Heumann, *Sekundarstufe I, Zeitgeschichte,* p. 70.

114. *Ibid.*

115. Hug, *Imperialismus bis zur Gegenwart,* p. 114.

116. *Ibid.*

117. Steinbügl, p. 86.

118. Grassmann, p. 84.

119. Tenbrock and Kluxen, *Didaktischer Grundriß,* p. 71.

120. Hans Heumann, Johannes Hampel, Max Rieder, *Geschichte für morgen. Arbeitsbuch für bayerische Hauptschulen.* Vol. 5: *Zeitgeschichte,* 9. Schuljahr, Frankfurt am Main: Hirschgraben, 1982, p. 21.

121. Döhn, p. 98.

122. Steinbügl, p. 85.

123. *Ibid.,* p. 7.

124. Grassmann, p. 56. Italics in original.

125. Binder and Burkhardt, p. 81.

126. Hermann Burkhardt, Helmut Christmann, Gerhard Jaacks, Fritz Klenk, *Damals und heute 5, Geschichte für Hauptschulen. Vom Ersten Weltkrieg bis heute. Lehrerbegleitheft,* Stuttgart: Ernst Klett, 1976, p. 117.

127. Hoffmann, *Von der russische Revolution*, p. 82.

128. Hans-Hermann Hartwich, *ed., Politik im 20. Jahrhundert*, Braunschweig: Westermann, 1980, p. 130.

129. Tenbrock and Kluxen, *Zeiten und Menschen, Geschichte für Kollegstufe*, p. 116.

130. Altrichter and Glaser, p. 28.

131. Tenbrock and Kluxen, *Zeiten und Menschen, Geschichte für Kollegstufe*, p. 116.

132. Fernis and Hillgruber, p. 163.

133. Deuschle, *Lehr- und Arbeitsbuch*, pp. 77–78.

134. Hermann Meyer, *Probleme des Totalitarismus. Materialien für die Sekundarstufe II*, Hannover: Schroedel, 1980.

135. Herbert Baumann, *Politische Gemeinschaftskunde*, 19. Auflage, Koln-Porz: H. Stam GmbH, 1983, p. 238. Emphasis in original.

136. Hartwich, p. 129.

137. Tenbrock and Kluxen, *Zeiten und Menschen, Geschichte für Kollegstufe*, p. 115.

138. Altrichter and Glaser, p. 120.

139. Ebeling and Birkenfeld, *Arbeitsbuch*, p. 164.

140. Heumann, *Sekundarstufe I, Zeitgeschichte*, p. 71. Emphasis added.

141. Lucas, pp. 120, 227. See below, p. 75.

142. R. H. Tenbrock, *Didaktischer Grundriß*, p. 123.

143. Mommsen cited in Binder and Burkhardt, p. 96.

144. Peter Furth, Joist Grolle, Wolfgang Hilligen, Friedrich J. Lucas, *et. al., Menschen in ihrer Zeit*. Vol. 5. *Handreichungen für den Lehrer*, Stuttgart: Klett, 1980, p. 71.

145. *Ibid.*

146. Hoffmann, *Handreichung für den Lehrer*, p. 43.

147. Furth, p. 71.

148. Goldschmidt, p. 292.

149. Bodo von Borries, "Geschichte lernen—mit heutigen Schulbüchern?," *Geschichte in Wissenschaft und Unterricht*, 1983/9, p. 556.

150. Hoffmann, *Handreichung für den Lehrer*, p. 45.

151. Hoffmann, *Von der russische Revolution*, pp. 81–83.

152. Hug, *Imperialismus bis zur Gegenwart*, p. 26.

153. *Ibid.*, p. 115.

154. Lucas, pp. 229–230. Emphasis in original.

155. Theo Fruhmann, "Überwindung des Antisemitismus," *Die pädagogische Provinz* 3, 1949, p. 48.

156. Ebeling and Birkenfeld, *Arbeitsbuch*, p. 164.

157. Burkhardt, *Lehrerbegleitheft*, pp. 94–95.

158. Schmid, p. 61.

159. Kistler and Stroppe, p. L14.

160. Burkhardt, *Lehrerbegleitheft*, p. 96. The authors do not always escape the negative symbolism associated with the presentation of the Jews, as seen

by their selection of Karl Marx's attacks on the Jews as part of their source material.

161. Muggenthaler, p. 114.

162. Gerhard Jaacks, Artur Dumke, *Damals und heute 4. Geschichte für Hauptschulen.* Lehrerbegleitheft, Stuttgart: Klett, 1980, p. 31.

163. Burkhardt, *Lehrerbegleitheft*, p. 97.

164. Heumann, *Sekundarstufe I, Zeitgeschichte*, p. 71.

165. Schmid, p. 61.

166. Hans Heumann, Johannes Hampel, Max Rieder, *Geschichte für morgen. Arbeitsbuch für bayerische Hauptschulen*, vol. 5: *Zeitgeschichte*, 9. Schuljahr, *Lehrerbegleitheft*, Frankfurt am Main: Hirschgraben, 1982, p. 3. Grassmann adds to this list: the Versailles Treaty, unemployment, inflation and capitalism. Grassmann, p. 72.

167. Schmid, p. 59.

168. Jaacks, p. 31.

169. Hermann Burkhardt, Helmut Christmann, Gerd Noetzel, *Damals und heute. Geschichte 9*, Baden-Württemberg, *Von der Zeit des Imperialismus bis heute*, Stuttgart: Ernst Klett, 1981, p. 97.

170. Binder and Burkhardt, pp. 70, 72.

171. Hug, *Schülerarbeitsheft 1*, p. 68. Unfortunately, it is reproduced in the Workbook in such small size that nothing may be read except the headlines.

172. Hoffmann, *Von der russischen Revolution*, pp. 82–83.

173. Binder and Burkhardt, p. 70.

174. Burkhardt, *Lehrerbegleitheft*, p. 118.

175. Hoffmann, *Handreichung für den Lehrer*, p. 93.

176. Altrichter and Glaser, p. 27.

177. Tenbrock and Kluxen, *Zeiten und Menschen, Geschichte für Kollegstufe*, p. 116.

178. *Ibid.*

179. Meyer and Langenbeck, pp. 233–234.

180. *Ibid.*

181. Tenbrock and Kluxen, *Zeiten und Menschen, Geschichte für Kollegstufe*, p. 116, p. 127.

182. Hartwich, p. 130. Italics in original.

183. *Ibid.*

184. Fernis and Hillgruber, p. 163, p. 172.

185. Werner Ripper, *Welfgeschichte im Aufriß, Die nationalsozialistische Außenpolitik und der Zweite Weltkrieg*, Frankfurt am Main: Diesterweg, 1977, pp. 55–56.

186. *Ibid.*, p. 56.

187. Bernd Hey, Joachim Radkau, *Politische Weltkunde II, Themen zur Geschichte, Geographie und Politik, Nationalsozialismus und Faschismus*, Stuttgart: Ernst Klett, 1983, p. 105.

188. Hartwich, p. 129.

189. E. D. Gallmeister, *Grundriss der Geschichte für die Oberstufe der Höheren Schulen*, Vol. III, *Von 1850 bis zur Gegenwart*, Stuttgart: Ernst Klett, 1978, p. 105.

190. Henning Eichberg, *Minderheit und Mehrheit*, Braunschweig: Westermann, 1979, p. 24, p. 37, p. 28.

191. Heumann, *Sekundarstufe I, Zeitgeschichte*, p. 50.

192. *Ibid.*, p. 50, pp. 70–71.

193. Kaier, p. 32.

194. *Ibid.*, pp. 125–126.

195. Kistler and Stroppe, p. L14.

196. Karlheinz Pelzer, *Geschichte für die Hauptschule. Arbeitsbuch für das 8. und 9. Schuljahr*, Donauwörth: Auer, 1974, p. 67; Hug, *Imperialismus bis zur Gegenwart*, p. 115, p. 158; Schmid, p. 59.

197. Kaier, p. 220.

198. *Ibid.*, p. 151.

199. Grassmann, p. 56.

200. Schmid, p. 72.

201. Burkhardt, *Imperialismus bis heute*, p. 103.

202. Tenbrock and Kluxen, *Zeiten und Menschen*, p. 72.

203. Hartwich, p. 129.

204. Wolfgang Hug (ed.), *Geschichtliche Weltkunde, Quellenlesebuch*, vol. 3: *Von der Zeit des Imperialism bis zur Gegenwart*, Frankfurt am Main: Diesterweg, 1983, pp. 143–144.

205. Burkhardt, *Imperialismus bis heute*, pp. 97–98.

206. Schmid, p. 46.

207. K. H. Menzel, F. Textor, *Staatensystem und Weltpolitik*, Stuttgart: Ernst Klett, 1980, p. 108.

208. Grassmann, pp. 72–73.

209. R. H. Tenbrock, *Europa und die Welt. Das 20. Jahrhundert*, p. 137.

210. Heumann, *Sekundarstufe I, Zeitgeschichte*, p. 71.

211. Hug, *Quellenlesebuch*, p. 144.

212. Erich Kosthorst, *Das nationalsozialistische Regime. Geschichte, Politik, Unterrichtseinheiten für ein Curriculum, Materialheft*, Paderborn: Schroedel, 1980, p. 82.

213. Tenbrock and Kluxen, *Didaktischer Grundriß*, p. 72.

214. Grassmann, pp. 72–73.

215. Kaier, p. 178.

216. Though in Nazi hands after 1940, he was found to be still alive in 1957 and living quietly in Paris. See *Aufbau*, May 10, 1957, "Herschel Gruenspan lebt!," p. 1, pp. 5–6.

217. Boeck, p. 30; Heinloth, p. 131.

218. Menzel and Textor, *Staatensystem*, p. 108.

219. Binder and Burkhardt, p. 71.

220. Kistler and Stroppe, p. L15.

221. Hans Ebeling, Wolfgang Birkenfeld, *Die Reise in die Vergangenheit. Ein geschichtliches Arbeitsbuch, Lehrerband*, Braunschweig: Westermann, 1983, p. 165.

222. Pelzer, p. 68.

223. Hannelore Lachner, *Geschichte für Realschulen*, vol. 4: *Neueste Zeit*, Bamburg: Buchners, 1981, p. 140.

224. Hug, *Imperialismus bis zur Gegenwart*, p. 113.

225. Hoffmann, *Von der russischen Revolution*, p. 108. Italics in original.

226. Josef Schwandner, *Geschichte 9. Jahrgangsstufe*, München: R. Oldenbourg, 1973, p. 86.

227. Schmid, p. 61.

228. Hug, *Imperialismus bis zur Gegenwart*, p. 113.

229. Binder and Burkhardt, p. 71.

230. Boeck, p. 30.

231. Burkhardt, *Vom Ersten Weltkrieg bis heute, Lehrerbegleitheft*, p. 115.

232. Grassmann, pp. 72–73.

233. Binder and Burkhardt, p. 71.

234. Lucas, p. 90.

235. Hug, *Imperialismus bis zur Gegenwart*, p. 113.

236. Kistler and Stroppe, p. L15.

237. Grassmann, p. 73.

238. Binder and Burkhardt, p. 71.

239. Heumann, *Sekundarstufe I, Zeitgeschichte*, p. 72.

240. Wanda Kampmann, Berthold Wiegand, Wolfgang W. Mickel, *Politik und Gesellschaft, Grundlagen und Probleme der modernen Welt. Lehr- und Arbeitsbuch für den historisch-politischen Lernbereich*, Sekundarstufe II, Frankfurt am Main: Hirschgraben, 1981, p. 175.

241. Tenbrock and Kluxen, *Zeiten und Menschen, Geschichte für Kollegstufe*, p. 141.

242. Hartwich, p. 129. Emphasis in original.

243. Tenbrock and Kluxen, *Zeiten und Menschen, Geschichte für Kollegstufe*, p. 141.

244. Eichberg, p. 35.

245. Altrichter and Glaser, p. 121.

246. Werner Grütter, *Hinweise und Interpretationen*, vol. 2, *Zeiten und Menschen*, Paderborn: Schöningh, Schroedel, 1976, p. 379.

247. *Ibid.*

248. Werner Ripper, *Weltgeschichte im Aufriß, Der europäische Faschismus und das Dritte Reich*, Frankfurt am Main: Diesterweg, 1977, p. 108.

249. Hans Ritscher, Alfred Krink, *Welt der Politik II: Lehrbuch der Zeitgeschichte*, Frankfurt am Main: Diesterweg, 1975, p. 80.

250. Gallmeister, p. 105.

251. Deuschle, p. 78; Tenbrock and Kluxen, *Zeiten und Menschen*, p. 141; Altrichter and Glaser, p. 121.

252. Ripper, *Der europäische Faschismus*, p. 93.

253. Grütter, p. 379.

254. Elmar Krautkrämer, Eberhard Radbruch, *Wandel der Welt*, Bad Homburg vor der Höhe: Max Gehlen, 1975, p. 190.

255. Fernis and Hillgruber, p. 173.

256. Kampmann and Mickel, p. 175.

257. Ripper, *Der europäische Faschismus*, p. 93, p. 109.

258. *Ibid.*, p. 110.

259. Willi and Margret Frank, *Politik heute*, Darmstadt: Winklers, 1981, p. 356.

260. Kurt Gönner, Rolf Krug, Heinz-Theo Niephaus, Eugen Weiß, *Politik in unseren Tagen*, Bad Homburg vor der Höhe: Max Gehlen, 1980, p. 193.

261. *Ibid.*, pp. 193–194.

262. Fernis and Haverkamp, p. 311.

263. Baumann, p. 250.

264. Altrichter and Glaser, p. 121.

265. Ritscher and Krink, p. 80.

266. Gallmeister, p. 105.

267. Ripper, *Der europäische Faschismus*, p. 109.

268. Albrecht Thiemann, "The Holocaust in German Schools: Personal Experiences and a Report," unpublished paper delivered at *Duquesne History Forum*, October, 1979, in possession of author, p. 4; H. Kremers, "Judentum und Holocaust im deutschen Schulunterricht," p. 42.

269. R. H. Tenbrock, *Europa und die Welt. Das 20. Jahrhundert*, p. 136.

270. Karl Heinz Menzel, Fritz Textor and others, *Kletts Geschichtliches Unterrichtswerk*, vol. 4, edition C, *Lehrerheft*, Stuttgart: Klett, 1982, p. 109.

271. Ebeling and Birkenfeld, *Lehrerband*, p. 164.

272. Hoffmann, *Von der russischen Revolution*, p. 108.

273. Hug, *Imperialismus bis zur Gegenwart*, p. 113.

274. Lachner, p. 140.

275. Kaier, p. 178.

276. Kistler and Stroppe, p. L15.

277. Kaier, pp. 178–179.

278. Bernhardt Heinloth, Helmut Kistler, *Geschichte*, Munich: R. Oldenbourg, 1982, p. 131.

279. Burkhardt, *Imperialismus bis heute*, p. 98; Boeck, p. 30.

280. Heumann, *Sekundarstufe I, Zeitgeschichte*, p. 72.

281. Eichberg, p. 35.

282. *Ibid.*

283. Tenbrock and Kluxen, *Zeiten und Menschen, Geschichte für Kollegstufe*, p. 142.

284. Ritscher and Krink, p. 80.

285. Kistler and Stroppe, p. L15; Pelzer, pp. 68–69.

286. Ebeling and Birkenfeld, p. 164.

287. Kaier, p. 221.

288. Schmid, p. 61.

289. Baumann, p. 251.

290. *Ibid.*

291. Ripper, *Der europäische Faschismus*, p. 92.

292. Martin and Eva Kolinsky, "The Treatment of the Holocaust in West German Textbooks," *Yad Vashem Studies*, Vol. X. Jerusalem, 1974, p. 177.

293. Kaier, p. 177.
294. Kistler and Stroppe, p. L15.
295. Tenbrock and Kluxen, *Zeiten und Menschen*, p. 106.
296. Menzel and Textor, *Staatensystem*, p. 109.
297. Binder and Burkhardt, p. 71, p. 91.
298. Grassmann, p. 142.
299. Lachner, p. 140.
300. Heumann, *Arbeitsbuch für bayerische Hauptschulen*, p. 21.
301. Burkhardt, *Imperialismus bis heute*, p. 100.
302. Tenbrock and Kluxen, *Zeiten und Menschen*, p. 105.
303. *Ibid.*, pp. 106–107.
304. Heinloth, p. 131.
305. Using Gerald Reitlinger's figures, the number of emigrés amounts to about 285,000; however, Reitlinger advises that the figures are problematic and only a starting point. See Gerald Reitlinger, *The Final Solution. The Attempt to Exterminate the Jews of Europe, 1939–1945*, New York: A. S. Barnes, 1961, p. 491.
306. Heinloth, p. 153.
307. Boeck, p. 30.
308. Krautkrämer, p. 189.
309. Fernis and Hillgruber, p. 172.
310. Mickel and Kampmann, p. 175.
311. Kurt Gönner, Rolf Krug, Heinz-Theo Niephaus, Eugen Weib, *Politik, informationen, Probleme, Erkenntnisse. Lehr- und Arbeitsbuch für Gemeinschaftskunde*, Bad Hamburg vor der Höhe: Max Gehlen, 1981, p. 168.
312. Ritscher and Krink, p. 80.
313. *Ibid.*
314. Hey, *Nationalsozialismus und Faschismus*, p. 66.
315. Bernd Hey, Joachim Radkau, *Politische Weltkunde II, Nationalsozialismus und Faschismus, Handreichung für den Lehrer*, Stuttgart: Ernst Klett, 1982, p. 37.
316. Gallmeister, p. 187.
317. Ritscher and Krink, p. 79.
318. Frank, p. 197.
319. Hoffmann, p. 83.
320. Boeck, p. 26.
321. Burkhardt, *Imperialismus bis heute*, 103; Binder and Burkhardt, p. 91; Heumann, *Zeitgeschichte*, p. 73.
322. Heumann, *Sekundarstufe I, Zeitgeschichte*, p. 73.
323. Binder and Burkhardt, p. 91.
324. Döhn, *"wie Ungeziefer vertilgen,"* p. 98.
325. Jaacks, p. 31.
326. Kistler and Stroppe, p. L15.
327. Kaier, p. 160.
328. Grassmann, p. 72.
329. Fernis and Haverkamp, pp. 307–308.

330. *Ibid.*

331. Fernis and Hillgruber, p. 173, p. 164.

332. Baumann, p. 239.

333. Tenbrock and Kluxen, *Zeiten und Menschen, Geschichte für Kollegstufe,* p. 126.

334. *Ibid.,* p. 142.

335. Gönner and Krug, *Politik in unseren Tagen,* p. 168; Gallmeister, p. 105; Ritscher and Krink, p. 80; Altrichter and Glaser, p. 121.

336. Ritscher and Krink, p. 79.

337. Eichberg, p. 35.

338. Ripper, *Der europäische Faschismus,* pp. 108–109.

339. Kistler and Strope, p. 24; Hug, *Imperialismus bis zur Gegenwart,* p. 160.

340. Binder and Burkhardt, p. 91.

341. Burkhardt, *Imperialismus bis heute,* p. 101.

342. Boeck, p. 30, p. 42. Italics in original.

343. Döhn, p. 130.

344. Lucas, p. 120.

345. Grassmann, p. 130.

346. *Ibid.,* p. 130.

347. Binder and Burkhardt, p. 91.

348. *Ibid.*

349. Grassmann, p. 73.

350. *Ibid.*

351. David Irving is the most prominent among them. See his *Hitler's War,* New York: Viking Press, 1977, pp. 12–16, pp. 329–332.

352. *Der Tagespiegel,* May 6, 1984, "Annihilation the Jews: How the Decisions were made," cited in the *German Tribune,* Hamburg, May 20, 1984. The conference was organized by the Stuttgart *Bibliothek für Zeitgeschichte,* the University of Stuttgart's Historical Institute and Committee of the Federal Republic of Germany for the History of the Second World War. For a summary of the proceedings, see John P. Fox, "The Final Solution: Intended or Contingent? The Stuttgart Conference of May 1984 and the Historical Debate," *Patterns of Prejudice,* London, vol. 18, no. 3, 1984, pp. 27–39.

353. For detailed accounts of the scholarship on Hitler and the Holocaust, see Gerald Fleming, *Hitler und die Endlösung. "Es ist des Führers wunsch . . .",* Munchen: Limes Verlag, 1982, English edition: *Hitler and the Final Solution,* Berkeley: U. of California, Press, 1984, and John P. Fox, *Hitler and the Jewish Question,* Macmillan, forthcoming.

354. Kosthorst, 80.

355. *Ibid.,* p. 84. See also Joseph Goebbels, *The Goebbels Diary,* New York: Doubleday, 1948, p. 86. *Ibid.; Goebbels Diary,* p. 138. *Ibid.; Goebbels Diary,* pp. 147–148. *Ibid.; Goebbels Diary,* p. 241. *Ibid.; Goebbels Diary,* p. 266.

356. Burkhardt, *Lehrerbegleitheft,* p. 138, citing K. D. Erdmann.

357. Binder and Burkhardt, p. 91.

358. Heumann, *Zeitgeschichte,* p. 73.

359. Jaacks, p. 31.
360. Grassmann, p. 73.
361. *Ibid.*
362. Kosthorst, p. 81.
363. Hug, *Imperialismus bis zur Gegenwart,* p. 47.
364. Tenbrock and Kluxen, *Zeiten und Menschen,* p. 141.
365. Hey, *Handreichung für den Lehrer,* p. 37.
366. Altrichter and Glaser, p. 122.
367. Frank, p. 193, p. 196. Parentheses in original.
368. Gönner and Krug, *Politik in unseren Tagen,* p. 170.
369. Fernis and Hillgruber, p. 320.
370. Gallmeister, p. 187. Emphasis in original.
371. Krautkrämer, p. 190.
372. Fernis and Hillgruber, p. 187.
373. Ritscher and Krink, p. 80.
374. Mickel and Kampmann, p. 176, citing Krausnick.
375. Grütter, pp. 399–400.
376. Eichberg, p. 35.
377. Baumann, p. 252.
378. Kampmann and Mickel, p. 176.
379. Grütter, p. 405.
380. *Ibid.*
381. *Ibid.*
382. *Ibid.,* pp. 405–406.
383. *Ibid.,* p. 406.
384. Hey, *Nationalsozialismus und Faschismus,* p. 66.
385. Ritscher and Krink, 81; Ripper, *Die nationalsozialistische Aussenpolitik,* p. 63.
386. Schmid, p. 60. Klepper and his wife committed suicide shortly thereafter.
387. Heinloth, *Geschichte 4.,* p. 153.
388. Lachner, p. 170.
389. Burkhardt, *Imperialismus bis heute,* p. 102.
390. Boeck, p. 42.
391. Heumann, *Zeitgeschichte,* p. 73.
392. Ebeling and Birkenfeld, *Arbeitsbuch,* p. 164.
393. Grassmann, p. 73.
394. *Ibid.,* p. 74, citing *Frankfurter Rundschau,* Jan. 25, 1979.
395. Lucas, pp. 88–89. Ellipses in original.
396. Burkhardt, *Imperialismus bis heute,* pp. 100–101.
397. The following books may be recommended for materials by or about Jewish children caught in the maelstrom of the Holocaust: Dorothea Stanic, ed. *Kinder im KZ* (Children in Concentration Camps), Elepanten Press, 1979; *Kinder der Nacht. Schicksale jüdischer Kinder 1939–1945* (Children of the Night. The Fate of Jewish Children, 1939–1945), Hirschgraben Verlag, 1963; Roman Hrabar, Zofia Tokarz, Jacek E. Wilcqur, *Kriegsschicksale pölnische Kinder* (The

Fate of Polish Children in the War), especially "*Das Schicksal der jüdischen Kinder*" (The Fate of Jewish Children), pp. 157–169, Polska Agencja Interpress, 1981, English edition, 1981; Azriel Eisenberg, *The Lost Generation. Children in the Holocaust,* 1984; Eli Pfefferkorn, *The Untold Tale,* forthcoming.

398. Hug, *Quellenlesebuch,* pp. 196–197, pp. 202–204.

399. Hug, *Imperialismus bis zur Gegenwart,* p. 160; Hoffmann, *Von der russischen Revolution,* p. 118.

400. Kistler and Stroppe, p. L24.

401. Döhn, p. 130.

402. Schmid, p. 61.

403. Heinloth, p. 152.

404. Burkhardt, *Imperialismus bis heute,* p. 101.

405. Grassmann, p. 73.

406. Gönner and Krug, *Politik in unseren Tagen,* p. 197.

407. *Ibid.,* p. 200.

408. Ritscher and Krink, p. 80; Kampmann and Mickel, p. 176.

409. Grütter, p. 399.

410. *Ibid.,* p. 400.

411. Baumann, p. 251.

412. Fernis and Hillgruber, p. 187.

413. Burkhardt, *Imperialismus bis heute,* p. 101.

414. Kistler and Stroppe, p. L23.

415. Schmid, pp. 58–59, p. 195.

416. Heumann, *Sekundarstufe I, Zeitgeschichte,* p. 73.

417. Boeck, p. 42.

418. Menzel and Textor, *Staatensystem,* p. 130.

419. Binder and Burkhardt, p. 93.

420. Steinbügl, p. 104.

421. Schmid, p. 60.

422. Döhn, p. 130.

423. Kosthorst, pp. 89–92.

424. Lucas, p. 89.

425. Grassmann, p. 71.

426. Kaier, pp. 221–222.

427. Deuschle, *Lehr- und Arbeitsbuch,* p. 79.

428. Fernis and Haverkamp, p. 320.

429. Fernis and Hillgruber, p. 87.

430. Gallmeister, p. 187.

431. Grütter, p. 401, p. 403.

432. Ritscher and Krink, p. 81.

433. Tenbrock and Kluxen, *Zeiten und Menschen,* p. 152.

434. Kampmann and Mickel, p. 176.

435. Baumann, p. 252.

436. Gönner and Krug, *Politik in unseren Tagen,* p. 198.

437. Altrichter and Glaser, p. 122.

438. Hey, *Nationalsozialismus und Faschismus,* pp. 156–157.

439. Eichberg, pp. 49–50.

440. Gallmeister, p. 188.

441. Grütter, p. 403.

442. Baumann, p. 251.

443. Martin Broszat, *Studien zur Geschichte der Konzentrationslager*, Stuttgart: Deutsche-Verlags Anstalt, 1970, p. 8. See also Broszat's introduction to the subject in "*Nationalsozialistiche Konzentrationslager, 1933–1945,*" In: *Anatomy des SS-Staates*, vol. 2, p. 9ff.

444. Wolfgang Scheffler, "Anmerkungen zum Fernsehfilm 'Holocaust' und zu Fragen zeithistorischer Forschung," *Geschichte und Gesellschaft*, Göttingen, 5:4, 1979, *Antisemitismus und Judentum*, ed. Reinhard Rürup, p. 577.

445. Martin and Eva Kolinsky, p. 177.

446. Schickel, p. 22. Ironically, Schickel, a co-author of H. Lachner's *Geschichte für Realschulen*, cites no source reference for the conservative figure of 4.5 million Jewish victims used in this text.

447. *Ibid.*, p. 27.

448. Menzel and Textor, *Staatensystem*, p. 131.

449. Ebeling and Birkenfeld, *Arbeitsbuch*, p. 168.

450. Kosthorst, p. 88.

451. Hug, *Imperialismus bis zur Gegenwart*, p. 162.

452. Heinloth, p. 153.

453. Lucas, p. 122.

454. Burkhardt, *Geschichte für Hauptschulen, Lehrerbegleitheft*, p. 138.

455. Schmid, p. 61.

456. Heumann, *Sekundarstufe I, Zeitgeschichte*, pp. 94–95.

457. *Ibid.*, pp. 74–75.

458. Quester, p. 337.

459. Schickel, pp. 27–28.

460. Ebeling and Birkenfeld, *Lehrerband*, p. 168, citing Helmut Krausnick.

461. Boeck, p. 42.

462. Binder and Burkhardt, *Arbeitsbuch*, p. 93.

463. Eichberg, p. 36.

464. Fernis and Hillgruber, p. 187.

465. Kurt Gönner and others, *Geschichte und Politik I, Lehr -und Arbeitsbuch für den Unterricht in Geschichte mit Gemeinschaftskunde*, Homburg: Max Gehlen, 1978, p. 170.

466. Gönner and Krug, *Lehr- und Arbeitsbuch*, p. 237.

467. Hey, *Nationalsozialismus und Faschismus*, p. 69, pp. 106–107.

468. Kampmann and Mickel, p. 177.

469. See Helen Fein, *Accounting for Genocide*, New York: Macmillan, 1979.

470. Frank, p. 194, p. 196.

471. Grütter, p. 406.

472. *Ibid.*, p. 403.

473. *Ibid.*, p. 405.

474. Baumann, p. 252.

475. Gallmeister, p. 188.

476. Guardini, p. 457.

477. H. Kremers, "Judentum und Holocaust in Deutschen Schulunterricht," p. 39.

478. Menzel and Textor, *Staatensystem*, p. 137.

479. Heinloth, p. 162. The total figure is 26.4 million dead.

480. Boeck, p. 51.

481. Tenbrock and Kluxen, *Zeiten und Menschen*, p. 105.

482. Lachner, p. 140.

483. Grassmann, p. 72.

484. Steinbügl, p. 86.

485. Hug, *Imperialismus bis zur Gegenwart*, p. 162.

486. Picht, p. 14.

487. *Ibid.*, p. 20.

488. Ebeling and Birkenfeld, *Lehrerband*, p. 168, citing Krausnick. Emphasis in original.

489. Quester, "Die Darstellung des Judentums im Geschichtsunterricht," *Die Realschule*, Hannover, Nov., 1963, p. 342.

490. Berndt Engelmann, *Deutschland ohne Juden. Eine Bilanz*, München, 1970, pp. 8–9.

491. *Ibid.*, p. 248ff.

492. Hoffmann, *Von der russischen Revolution*, p. 121; Hug, *Imperialismus bis zur Gegenwart*, p. 163.

493. Tenbrock and Kluxen, *Zeiten und Menschen*, p. 107.

494. Pelzer, p. 66.

495. Grassmann, p. 75.

496. Muggenthaler, p. 113.

497. Broszat, "Holocaust und die Geschichtswissenschaft," p. 297. Emphasis in original.

498. Lucas, p. 230.

499. *Ibid.*, pp. 229–230.

500. *Ibid.*, p. 230.

501. Kogon, "Befreit durch Niederlage," p. 13.

502. Ebeling and Birkenfeld, *Arbeitsbuch*, p. 251.

503. Heumann, *Arbeitsbuch für bayerische Hauptschulen*, p. 70; Schmid, p. 60.

504. Ebeling and Birkenfeld, *Arbeitsbuch*, p. 251.

505. *Ibid.*

506. Grassmann, p. 82.

507. *Ibid.*

508. Heinloth, p. 163.

509. *Ibid.*

510. Grassmann, p. 80.

511. *Ibid.*, p. 81.

512. Burkhardt, *Imperialismus bis heute*, p. 96.

513. Hug, *Begleitheft*, p. 47.

514. Heumann, *Arbeitsbuch für bayerische Hauptschulen*, p. 21.
515. Heumann, *Lehrerbegleitheft*, p. 10.
516. Binder and Burkhardt, p. 82.
517. Burkhardt, *Lehrerbegleitheft*, p. 118.
518. Hug, *Schülerarbeitsheft*, p. 67.

APPENDIX I:
List of Textbooks, Workbooks
and Teacher-Aid Books Consulted

Altrichter, Helmut and Hermann Glaser. *Geschichtliches Werden*, Oberstufe. vol. 4. *Vom Zeitalter des Imperialismus bis zur Gegenwart*, Bamberg: C.C. Buchners, 1971.

Baumann, Herbert. *Politische Gemeinschaftskunde*, 19. Auflage. Koln-Porz: H. Stam GmbH, 1983.

Binder, Gerhart, Hermann Burkhardt, Helmut Christmann, Alfred Jung, and Fritz Klenk. *Damals und heute* 5. *Geschichte für Hauptschulen. Vom Ersten Weltkrieg bis heute*. Stuttgart: Ernst Klett, 1977.

Boeck, Otto, Artur Dumke, Robert Hubner, Fritz Klenk, Otto Kratzert, and Eugen Sohns. *Damals und heute* 4. *Geschichte für Hauptschulen*. Stuttgart: Ernst Klett, 1976.

Burkhardt, Hermann, Helmut Christmann, Gerhard Jaacks, Fritz Klenk, *Damals und heute* 5. *Geschichte für Hauptschulen. Vom Ersten Weltkrieg bis heute, Lehrerbegleitheft*. Stuttgart: Ernst Klett, 1976.

Burkhardt, Hermann, Helmut Christmann, Gerd Noetzel, *Damals und heute. Geschichte 9* (Baden-Württemberg) *Von der Zeit des Imperialismus bis heute*. Stuttgart: Ernst Klett, 1981.

Deuschle, Friedrich. *Du und die Politik, Lehrbuch für die politische Bildung. Lehrerheft*, Homburg: Max Gehlen, 1977.

———. *Du und die Politik, Lehr- und Arbeitsbuch für die politische Bildung*. Homburg: Max Gehlen, 1977.

Döhn, Hans and Fritz Sandmann. *Geschichte 3. Erkunden und erkennen*. Hannover: Hermann Schroedel, 1977.

Ebeling, Hans, and Wolfgang Birkenfeld. *Die Reise in die Vergangenheit. Ein Geschichtliches Arbeitsbuch*. Braunschweig: Westermann, 1982.

———. *Die Reise in die Vergangenheit. Ein geschichtliches Arbeitsbuch. Lehrerband*. Braunschweig: Westermann, 1983.

Eichberg, Henning. *Minderheit und Mehrheit*. Braunschweig: Westermann, 1979.

Fernis, Hans-Georg and Heinrich Haverkamp. *Grundzüge der Geschichte*. (Sekundarstufe II.) *Von der Urzeit bis zur Gegenwart*. Frankfurt am Main: Diesterweg 1975.

Fernis, Hans-Georg and Andreas Hillgruber. *Grundzüge der Geschichte. Sekundarstufe II. Historisch-politisches Arbeitsbuch.* Vol. 2. *Vom Zeitalter der Aufklärung bis zur Gegenwart.* Frankfurt am Main: Diesterweg, 1972.

Frank, Willi and Margret. *Politik heute.* Darmstadt: Winklers, 1981.

Furth, Peter, Joist Grolle, Wolfgang Hilligen, Friedrich J. Lucas, and others. *Menschen in ihrer Zeit.* Vol. 5. *Handreichungen für den Lehrer.* Stuttgart: Klett, 1980.

Gallmeister, E.D. and others. *Grundriss der Geschichte für die Oberstufe der Höheren Schulen.* Vol. 3. *Von 1850 bis zur Gegenwart.* Stuttgart: Ernst Klett, 1978.

Gönner, Kurt, Rolf Krug, Heinz-Theo Niephaus, and Eugen Weiß. *Politik in unseren Tagen.* Bad Homburg vor der Höhe: Max Gehen, 1980.

———. *Politik, Informationen, Probleme, Erkenntnisse. Lehr- und Arbeitsbuch für Gemeinschaftskunde an beruflichen Schulen.* Bad Homburg vor der Höhe, Max Gehlen, 1981.

Gönner, Kurt, and others. *Geschichte und Politik I, Lehr- und Arbeitsbuch für den Unterricht in Geschichte mit Gemeinschaftskunde.* Homburg: Max Gehlen, 1978.

Graßmann, S. ed. *Zeitaufnahme. Geschichte für die Sekundarstufe I.* Vol. 3. *Vom Ersten zum Zweiten Weltkrieg.* Braunschweig: Westermann, 1981.

Grütter, Werner. *Hinweise und Interpretationen.* Vol. 2, *Zeiten und Menschen.* Schöningh: Schroedel, 1976.

Hartwich, Hans-Hermann, ed. *Politik im 20. Jahrhundert,* Braunschweig: Westermann, 1980.

Heinloth, Bernhardt and Helmut Kistler. *Geschichte 4.* München: R. Oldenbourg, 1982.

Heumann, Hans, Georg Droege, and others. *Unser Weg durch die Geschichte,* (Ausgabe für Realschulen). Vol. 4. *Die Welt gestern und heute.* Frankfurt am Main: Hirschgraben, 1975.

Heumann, Hans, H.J. Blödorn, W. Freund, and Others. *Geschichte für morgen, Arbeitsbuch für den Geschichtsunterricht in der Sekundarstufe I.* Vol. 4. *Zeitgeschichte.* Frankfurt am Main: Hirschgraben, 1980.

Heumann, Hans, Johannes Hampel, and Max Rieder. *Geschichte für morgen. Arbeitsbuch für bayerische Hauptschulen.* Vol. 5. *Zeitgeschichte* (9. Schuljahr). Frankfurt am Main, Hirschgraben, 1982.

———. *Geschichte für morgen. Arbeitsbuch für bayerische Hauptschulen.* Vol. 5. *Zeitgeschichte* (9. Schuljahr). *Lehrerbegleitheft.* Frankfurt am Main: Hirschgraben, 1982.

Hey, Bernd and Joachim Radkau. *Politische Weltkunde II. Themen zur Geschichte, Geographie und Politik. Nationalsozialismus und Faschismus.* Stuttgart: Ernst Klett, 1983.

———. *Politische Weltkunde II. Nationalsozialismus und Faschismus. Handreichungen für den Lehrer.* Stuttgart: Ernst Klett, 1982.

Hoffmann, Joachim. *Spiegel der Zeiten,* Vol. 4. *Von der russischen Revolution bis zur Gegenwart.* Frankfurt am Main, Moritz Diesterweg, 1978.

———. *Spiegel der Zeiten, Lehr- und Arbeitsbuch für den Geschichtsunterricht. Lernziele und Lernschritte Handreichung für den Lehrer.* Vol. 4. *Von der russischen Revolution bis zur Gegenwart.* Frankfurt am Main: Diesterweg, 1979.

Hug, Wolfgang, ed. *Geschichtliche Weltkunde, Quellenlesebuch.* Vol. 3. *Von der Zeit des Imperialism bis zur Gegenwart.* Frankfurt am Main; Diesterweg, 1983.

———. *Geschichtliche Weltkunde.* Vol. 3. *Schülerarbeitsheft 1. Von der Zeit des Imperialismus bis zur nationalsozialistischen Diktatur in Deutschland.* Frankfurt am Main: Diesterweg, 1979.

Hug, Wolfgang, Joachim Hoffmann, and Elmar Krautkrämer. *Geschichtliche Weltkunde,* Vol. 3. *Von der Zeit des Imperialismus bis zur Gegenwart.* Frankfurt am Main: Diesterweg, 1979.

———. *Lernimpulse 3, Begleitheft zum Arbeitsbuch "Geschichtliche Weltkunde,"* (Vol. 3). Frankfurt am Main: Diesterweg, 1980.

Jaacks, Gerhard, and Artur Dumke, *Damals und heute 4. Geschichte für Hauptschulen, Lehrerbegleitheft.* Stuttgart: Ernst Klett, 1980.

Kaier, Eugen, Herbert Deißler, and Herbert Krieger. *Grundzüge der Geschichte.* (Sekundarstufe I, Gymnasium.) Vol. 4. *Von 1890 bis zur Gegenwart.* Frankfurt am Main: Moritz Diesterweg, 1977.

Kampmann, Wanda, Berthold Wiegand, and Wolfgang W. Mickel. *Politik und Gesellschaft. Grundlagen und Probleme der modernen Welt. Lehr- und Arbeitsbuch für den historisch-politischen Lernbereich* (Sekundarstufe II). Frankfurt am Main: Hirschgraben, 1981.

Kistler, Helmut, and Werner Stroppe. *Harms Arbeitsmappen Geschichte.* Vol. 4. *Von 1848 bis zur Gegenwart.* München: List, 1980.

Kosthorst, Erich. *Das nationalsozialistische Regime. Geschichte, Politik, Unterrichtseinheiten für ein Curriculum. Materialheft.* Paderborn: Schöningh, 1980.

Krautkrämer, Elmar and Eberhard Radbruch. *Wandel der Welt.* Bad Homburg vor der Höhe: Max Gehlen, 1975.

Lachner, Hannelore. *Geschichte für Realschulen.* Vol. 4. *Neueste Zeit.* Bamberg: Buchners, 1981.

Lucas, Friedrich J., Heinrich Bodensieck, Erhard Rumpf, and Gunter Thiele. *Menschen in ihrer Zeit, 4. In unserer Zeit.* Stuttgart: Ernst Klett, 1981.

Menzel, Karl-Heinz and Fritz Textor. *Staatensystem und Weltpolitik.* Stuttgart: Ernst Klett, 1980.

———. *Kletts Geschichtliches Unterrichtswerk, Lehrerheft* to vol. 4 (edition C). Stuttgart: Ernst Klett, 1982.

Meyer, Hermann. *Probleme des Totalitarismus. Materialien für die Sekundarstufe II.* Hannover: Schroedel, 1980.

Meyer, Hermann and Wilhelm Langenbeck. *Grundzüge der Geschichte. Sekundarstufe II. Historisch-politisches Arbeitsbuch.* (Quellenband II.) *Vom Zeitalter der Aufklärung bis zur Gegenwart.* Frankfurt am Main: Diesterweg, 1975.

Muggenthaler, Hans, Wolfgang Marks, and Hannah Marks. *Geschichte für Realschulen.* Vol. 4. *Neueste Zeit.* München: Kösel-Verlag.

Pelzer, Karlheinz, *Geschichte für die Hauptschule. Arbeitsbuch fur das 8. und 9. Schuljahr.* Donauwörth: Auer, 1974.

Ripper, Werner, ed., *Weltgeschichte im Aufriß. Die nationalsozialistische Außenpolitik und der Zweite Weltkrieg.* Frankfurt am Main: Diesterweg, 1977.

————. *Weltgeschichte im Aufriß. Der europäische Faschismus und das Dritte Reich.* Frankfurt am Main: Diesterweg, 1977.

Ripper, Werner and Eugen Kaier. *Weltgeschichte im Aufriß.* (Neubearbeitung für den historische-gesellschaftlichen Lernbereich der Sekundarstufe II.) Vol. 3, Part I. *Vom Ersten Weltkrieg bis 1945.* Frankfurt am Main: Diesterweg, 1979.

Ritscher, Hans and Alfred Krink. *Welt der Politik II: Lehrbuch der Zeitgeschichte.* Frankfurt am Main: Diesterweg, 1975.

Schmid, Heinz Dieter, ed. *Fragen an die Geschichte. Geschichtliches Arbeitsbuch für Sekundarstufe I.* Vol. 4. *Die Welt im 20. Jahrhundert.* Frankfurt am Main: Hirschgraben, 1979.

Schwandner, Josef. *Geschichte 9. Jahrgangsstufe.* München: R. Oldenbourg, 1973.

Steinbügl, Eduard and Anton Schreiegg. *Geschichte,* Vol. 4. *Neueste Zeit.* München: R. Oldenbourg, 1973.

Tenbrock, R. H., Kurt Kluxen, Erich Goerlitz, Erich Meier, Helmut Mejcher, and Kerrin Gräfin Schwerin. *Zeiten und Menschen* (K edition, Vol. 4.) *Geschichte für Kollegstufe und Grundstudium. Politik, Gesellschaft, Wirtschaft im 20. Jahrhundert.* Part I: *Vom 1919 bis 1945.* Paderhorn: Schöningh, Schroedel, 1982.

Tenbrock, R. H. and K. Kluxen. *Zeiten und Menschen, Zeitgeschichte: 1917 bis zur Gegenwart.* Paderhorn: Schöningh, Schroedel, 1983.

————. *Didaktischer Grundriß für den Geschichtsunterricht,* Vol. 4. *Zeiten und Menschen.* Paderborn: Schöningh; Schroedel, 1981.

PART II

ISRAEL

Ruth Firer

5
Introduction

They came upon me as a wide breaking in of waters: in the desolation (Sho'ah) they rolled themselves upon me.

Job, 30, 14.

Sho'ah is the Hebrew name given to the mass murder of the Jewish people by the Nazis. Etymologically, this means: "destruction," "catastrophe," "cataclysm," and "abyss." All these elements were connected with the Jewish fate during the Second World War.

"Holocaustus" means: "Whole-burnt offering," or a "Wholesale sacrifice," which is completely different in its source and meaning from the Hebrew term.

The Holocaust has been accepted in the English usage, quite often in order to describe all the atrocities committed by the Nazi regime, or even to symbolize every existing, or expected, evil in the world. But the *Sho'ah* is unique, because it refers to the planned mass-murder of a whole people for one reason only: *They were Jews.*

The nearest term to Holocaust is genocide, defined by its originator, Raphael Lemkin, as an attempt to denationalize the victims in economic, political, religious, and cultural spheres, accompanied by brutalities and systematic murder of *selected* groups out of the attacked nations.[1] But the Nazis planned to destroy the entire Jewish people. Therefore, the Holocaust is more than genocide; it is unique, it is the *Sho'ah.*

The Holocaust is one of the most terrible disasters in all of Jewish history, and the central one in the modern epoch. Many Jews who did not suffer personally from the Nazis have made the Holocaust a part of their national and individual identification. This process

I would like to thank the pupils, teachers, headmasters, members of the Ministry of Education, of the Universities, Seminars and friends, who have contributed to the present essay. Special thanks are also due to Mr. P. Krieger for many helpful linguistic remarks.

developed in Eretz-Israel before the establishment of the Jewish State and has continued.

Even when, in the fifties, the Israelis detached themselves from the Holocaust, the pains of the memory were repressed into the collectiove subconsciousness, waiting for an opportunity to explode openly, as happened when the Eichmann trial took place in Jerusalem in 1961.

Similar to the evolution of mourning after the death of a close relative, at first came the shock, mingled with self-accusation (because of not having saved the European Jews), and anger against the murdered (for going "like sheep to the slaughter"), resulting in a silence taboo about discussing the Holocaust. The second phase of the mourning led the Israeli society to an open confrontation with the past, when each Israeli war sharpened the necessity of it.

The educational system, and its curricula and textbooks, reflect the political and cultural processes within the society, quite often delayed by about 5 to 10 years from their origin. Then, post factum, the system justifies itself by pedagogical, moral, and national arguments. The educational estblishment is an agency by which the adult society transfers to their youngsters the heritage of the past, the lifestyles and values of the present, and the expectations of the future. Therefore, the textbooks have become a valuable source for inspecting cultural processes in society, and their research has been developed in national and international organizations.

Scientific revision of textbooks and curricula grew in the period between the two world wars, side by side with the development of historical research. Organizations like The International Federation of Teachers, The International Institute for Textbooks in Brunswick, Germany, and—after World War II—UNESCO continued the revision of textbooks with the hope of strengthening international understanding, human tolerance, and peace and love.[2]

In this trend of research, the attitude of Gentiles toward Jews, and the Holocaust, in textbooks have been researched by few historians and educationalists, most of them represented in the framework of this anthology.

Most of the institutes devote themselves to the improvement of the methods of teaching the Holocaust in schools, among them The American Association for Jewish Education, The National Curriculum Research Institute in New York, the National Institute on the Holocaust in Philadelphia, and Yad Vashem in Israel.

In Israel, very little research has been done on how the Holocaust is presented in textbooks and teaching programs. Although many articles about methods of teaching the Holocaust have been published, none have been about the development of this theme in history textbooks in large scale—as the present research does.

The only comprehensive research on this subject undertaken in Israel is the Ph.D. thesis of this writer.[3] The thesis was based upon 85 textbooks on the history of the Jewish people, which were used in Israel from 1900 to 1980. It also deals with the development of description and explanation of anti-Semitism and the Holocaust in these textbooks, and is the basis of this essay.

The Holocaust is taught in Israel with the help of three different kinds of textbooks:

Mikra'ot: Similar to the English "readers," these are a collection of texts, chosen for linguistic and literary reasons, and adjusted to the different grades in the elementary schools. The books are usually written by teachers who do not necessarily specialize in history. The Holocaust is either spread over different subjects or has a chapter of its own.

History Textbooks: Based on historical research, elaborated and simplified for educational needs, they describe, explain, and evaluate historical processes, either in chronological or thematical order. They are meant for pupils in upper elementary grades and high schools. The books are usually written by history teachers, who are not necessarily experts in the research of the Holocaust. Until the seventies, the Holocaust had its special chapters within the textbooks, and later on it became the topic of complete books.

Research Textbooks. Used by college students, they contain general, basic information. They are meant for basic courses. They appear in the "required reading" sections of syllabi. These research textbooks have been written by historians who specialize in research on the Holocaust.

Beside these texts, there are geography and literature textbooks for high schools and colleges which refer to the subject in different ways. In addition, there are some books designed "for further reading" which enlarge and deepen the knowledge, understanding, and emotional experience of students.

All these educational institutions use literature texts of various sorts, as well as history and research textbooks actually meant for higher levels—e.g., eighth-graders may use high school textbooks.

In this essay, only the three kinds of textbooks defined above will be examined and evaluated. The differentiation of textbooks is based on the levels of the Israeli educational system: the *Mikra'ot* are meant for ages 6 to 13, the history textbooks for ages 13 to 18, and the research textbooks for those over 18.

Another outstanding classification is based on a distinction between the Zionist-Religious trend and the nonreligious one, which divides the whole Israeli education system.

Besides the abovementioned differentiation, there are others: textbooks may be designed to conform to the professional specialization of the school, or its ultra-religious or instructional attitudes. The non-Zionist textbooks, for Jews or non-Jews in Israel, are not included in this research. Only the Zionist textbooks, as divided into age groups, used in different kinds of schools, are included here. The schools of the nonreligious and the religious Zionists are under the supervision of the Ministry of Education, while the academic institutes are autonomous.

Only after 1948, when the Israeli state was established, did the textbooks start to include the Holocaust, although the information about the Final Solution had already reached the *Yishuv* (Jewish Community of Palestine) in 1942. It took such a long time because of the situation in the country during and after the war, when 650,000 Jews had to face the restricted immigration policy of the British Mandate, fighting it directly and indirectly, and later the struggle against 2 million Arabs from five states, which led to independence.

In addition, there was the psychological gap between learning about the Holocaust and understanding the consequences.

The textbooks from 1948 will be examined and evaluated according to the development of the historio-philosophical angles, which have influenced the description and evaluation of the Holocaust in the books, while all other classifications will be subordinated to this central category.

What will be the criteria by which these changing attitudes are isolated and defined?

The national and the international textbook-revision organizations have established various means to reveal bias, values and attitudes in textbooks. Most of the methods used by the researchers are based on textual analyses, while the minority prefer quantitative means, like the E.C.O (Evaluation Coefficient Analysis) system developed by Pratt.[4] Similar criteria, and in similar proportions, are used here. Textual analysis is thus dominant here, because that method reveals the various direct and subtle meanings of the texts and their organization. In order to understand the intentions of the authors or the editors, there is no need to mention hundreds of examples, while very often one sentence, or one single word, can be sufficient.[5]

The quantitative measurement supports the textual analysis, with the purpose of characterizing the textbooks according to the development of the writer's attitudes. The frequency of the characteristics in many textbooks indicates dominant historio-philosophical or educational trends within a definite period.

Among Boden's criteria for revision of textbooks, are the following:[6]

1. Oversimplified presentation of situations, nations and problems.
2. Partial descriptions and evaluations of situations, issues, and people.
3. Unfitting emphasis of situations, people, and issues.
4. Biased translations of opinions and explanations.
5. Usage of emotional language, or emotional associations, with the purpose of influencing the pupils.
6. Presenting facts, processes, and evaluations from only one point of view.
7. Use of general remarks containing value judgments without any evidence or explanation.

The Israeli Ministry of Education accepts this kind of criteria, adding to them Zionist, democratic, religious, or nonreligious values and educational standards.[7]

The suggested means are here subordinated to the type of research required by the evaluated text. This study therefore simply evaluates the material at hand, and makes no attempt to discuss errors within the evaluated text.

To explain and evaluate the changing characteristics of the subject under discussion, the research will be helped by the history and the historiography of the Holocaust, and by the history of the State of Israel during the period 1948–1984. Attitudes of Israeli society concerning the Holocaust will be referred to, including the way they are reflected in the policy of the Israeli Ministry of Education. Educational and psychological evaluation will be integrated into the research.

Evaluated here are 22 *Mikra'ot*, 21 history textbooks, and 11 research textbooks. All have been used in Israel during the 36-year period of the study.

The explanatory elements cannot regard the personal intentions of the textbooks' authors, if they are not expressed in their books. Sometimes, when a distinction based on the students' point of view is needed, I have been helped by my 17 years of experience teaching in high school, and by many conversations with other teachers and students at different levels.

All the methods are subordinate to these central questions:

What are the messages contained in the description and evaluation of the Holocaust in the textbooks?

When, how, and why, have these been changed?

In this way the present essay may contribute to the research of the historiography of the textbooks as well as the development of Israeli educational attitudes regarding the teaching of the Holocaust.

6
The Mikra'ot

Every Israeli child is born as if already crucified by the burden of the Jewish historical experience. From infancy he is faced with the siren that pierces every home in the country on the morning of the Day of Remembrance. Embraced by his parents, the toddler experiences the first collective terror while standing at the memorial to six million Jews who were massacred during World War II.

In the following years the child gets explanations from his parents, and later on from his kindergarten teacher. Each year brings new details, as the story is told again and again.

The small child thus acquires emotional attitudes toward the Holocaust before he starts school. And, until the fourth grade, he is taught mainly to master reading and writing by textbooks designed for this purpose. They contain stories, poems, and language exercises, usually named *Mikra'ot*. These pieces are divided into various subjects and aspects of life, like "Nature," "Family Life," "Friendship," and subjects of national interest. (Since the late sixties, the *Mikra'ot* have been slowly replaced by a series of booklets, each dealing with a different subject, composed by the Ministry of Education. The Holocaust has not yet been the subject of such a booklet.) The first-grade textbooks usually do not contain literature about the Holocaust, and whenever they do, it is within other chapters;[8] for example, in the one devoted to "Ingathering the Exiles."[9]

In most of the Zionist-Israeli *Mikra'ot* meant for the fifth grade and beyond, a specific chapter is devoted to the Holocaust. In accordance with the maturation of the pupil, this chapter grows in size. The fourth-grader is presented with four pages in a 300-page book. His eighth-grade counterpart will find 25 such pages, in a book of the same size. This is the average amount of space set aside for every topic except Independence Day—almost always the largest chapter.

From the sixth grade onward the children start to study history as a separate subject, not included in the general lessons. Until the

eighth grade they learn about world and Jewish history from ancient
times until World War II, which together with the Holocaust is taught
by historical methods when the child is about 13 or 14 years old.
Until this age the *Mikra'ot* are the main source for teaching the
Holocaust, and from then on, they become supplementary.

Described and evaluated below is the Holocaust-theme in 22 *Mikra'ot*
which have been used in Israel during the period 1948–1984 by
Zionist-Jewish pupils of the ages 9 to 14.

The chapter about the Holocaust is usually found after the Passover
Chapter, and before the Independence Day section, in coordination
with the calendar. The memorial day is on the 27th of Nissan, (in
honor of the Warsaw Ghetto Uprising of 1943), between the abovementioned feast days. A few of the religious textbooks consider the
subject twice, on the 27th of Nissan, and in connection with the
10th of Tevet, which is the date of the beginning of Nebuchadnezzar's
siege of Jerusalem in 587 B.C., and is a prayer day, when the Jewish
nation says "Kaddish" for its victims who did not have relatives to
pray for their souls. Thus the massacred Jews of the Holocaust are
included.[10]

In the *Mikra'ot* are, in decreasing order of frequency, as follows:
reminiscences, diaries,[11] short stories, poems and prayers (usually
translated into easier language), and quotations from the Bible and
the Yad Vashem Law of 1953. Rarely is a historical explanation added,
and whenever it does appear, it is meant for the seventh and eighth
grade, and has a declarative nature; like Ben-Zion Dinur's speech in
the Knesset on May 12, 1953.

In this way, in spite of the child's knowledge of reading, the teacher
is the focal point. He or she must explain the literary pieces, and
provide the historical background. Because the Holocaust is subordinated to the memorial day, it has more of a ritual nature than a
historical one. The editors do not speak directly in the book, but
prefer to reveal their message through their choice of passages. Thus,
the Holocaust in the *Mikra'ot* both improves the child's reading and
textual understanding, and deepens the collective national grief.

As presented in the *Mikra'ot*, the child is the protagonist of the
Holocaust. He gets most of the space in the chapter, and through
him the different angles of the Jewish *Sho'ah* (Holocaust) are emphasized.

The Maintenance of the Human Image

The description of the suffering and extermination of abandoned
orphans is virtually omitted from the textbooks, and tends to appear
in poems rather than in prose.[12]

Usually the prose passages describe the child, even when very young, struggling for his survival; this fight is detailed, while the inevitable end is hinted at—or mentioned briefly at the end of the story. Most of the stories describe the child in connection with other persons who tend to be loving or sympathetic, and only through them is the child confronted with the cruel and the hostile environment. The motif of a child left in the ghetto with his mother is repeated in the textbooks. In these stories, the whole lifestyle and human relationshps are turned upside down; instead of the normal dependency of the child on his mother, in the Holocaust they change roles, and the young one takes responsibility for the adult.

He smuggles food for his mother, supports her physically and spiritually, and by his inward power of life, love, and childish optimism, helps her to survive the horrors.[13] Likewise, he rescues the remnants of his family, by his courage and innocence, which borders on misunderstanding the situation.[14] The story of Janush Korczak is an exception to this trend, when the great educator, being like a father to his orphans, continued to fulfill the adult role, supporting the children through their last voyage.[15]

The groups of the children, who live together by themselves, turn out to be the alternative to the destroyed family; they are united by an existential need for human warmth against the cold of the outside world, and by the physical struggle to survive. These groups smuggle food into the ghetto, or live outside its walls, among the Gentiles. They succeed in bringing out the human side of the non-Jewish individuals, who cannot resist their charm, and therefore help them. Sharing food, fears, and affections, being supporters and supported by their fellows, they have created something like a new kind of "family" for themselves.[16] In many ways, their story resembles typical child's adventure stories.

Another aspect of the struggle to maintain the human image in the Holocaust was the religious one. The traditional Jewish meaning of Sanctification of the Holy Name (*Kidush Ha'Shem*) refers to the situation in which the Jew was faced with two alternatives: Being converted to Christianity and staying alive, or dying in honor of His Name; and the Jew very often preferred the second choice. The Nazis did not offer the Jews any escape, and therefore, the meaning of the Sanctification received a new relevance during the Holocaust. According to the Holy Book, every human being was created in God's image, and therefore, any perversion of him by torture and humiliation is a direct abuse of God's will—and still more is killing His creatures, whom He had endowed with life. This general implication is sharpened in the destiny of the Jews who believed themselves to be God's chosen people.

The Jews in the Holocaust had two alternatives: to give up the struggle and accept degradation and eventual death, or to struggle for physical and spiritual existence, dying with their heads high and thus fulfilling the Sanctification of Life, and of His Name.

This notion is embodied in stories about adults and children,[17] who endangered themselves by keeping God's commandments, and by doing so retained their inner freedom.[18]

For the Germans the Jews were not human beings, but when the Jews practiced God's precepts, they were reassured of the contrary, feeling that they had been chosen by God to keep his image in man, in life and death, as the Rabbi of Grudeziski said:[19]

Our 'Aquedah' is in honor
of his Name—be He blessed.*

The same Jew who a moment ago had humbly accepted the Nazis' oppression was so changed by the power of his prayer that even the Germans were astonished, and respectful.[20]

Whenever an adult or a child was troubled by the question of why had God allowed the Holocaust to happen? the answer pacified the Jews:[21]

God have mercy and pity
because I want only you;
My Will—is your Will,
My Wish—is your Wish,
God, God, God
listen to my prayer.

The described attitude toward the religious issues, is the same in the religious and the nonreligious *Mikra'ot*.

The Armed Resistance

The resistance in Warsaw is described almost in every textbook; the stories usually recite the final phase of the rebellion, concluding with the escape of the few survivors through the sewers. In this manner the stories answer the pupil's question "What was the end

---

*"Aquedah"—the sacrifice of Isaac. All the translations from Hebrew are the author's.

of the fighters?" with reassuring information.[22] The centrality of the Warsaw Ghetto may impress the pupils in two different, and misleading, ways: The child may conclude that the only Jewish armed resistance was in Warsaw, or else that it symbolizes many similar fights,[23] thus balancing the destruction and the extermination.

Until the seventies, very few books tried to avoid giving such an impression by including descriptions of different types of resistance in places other than Warsaw. The tendency to do so was increased in later textbooks,[24] which reflect the change in attitude in the Israeli society toward the subject.

The imaginative tales based on the Warsaw Ghetto resistance are full of such military expressions:[25] "military positions," "fort," and "fighting troops." Another editor chose an original way to emphasize this characterization, when he located the Warsaw Ghetto resistance in a chapter called "The War of Independence," next to the description of breaking into the old part of Jerusalem.[26]

In the *Mikra'ot* for the high school grades, Ben Zion Dinur's speech in the Knesset in 1953 supplies the historical background. This quotation clearly connects the armed resistance during the Holocaust, the fighting Jews in World War II, and the Israelis in the War of Independence. Together they constitute "one chapter of Jewish Heroism."[27]

The protagonist of the Resistance stories is the Jewish youngster, while the child takes the role of a messenger and helper. Sometimes the personal story of the child becomes a literary means to emphasize the historical background of the resistance.[28]

The two other manifestations of armed heroism—the Jewish partisans and the Israeli volunteers in Europe—get quite a small place within the chapter on the Holocaust. The partisans are usually presented by several lines from the following quotation:[29]

Do not say: It is my last way,
the clouded sky covered the lightened day—
The day we yearned for, shall rise and come,
and our marching will thunder: Here We are!

The Israeli parachutists, sent by the British army to Europe, hoping to help European Jewry, are given even less space in the *Mikra'ot* than the partisans. Hannah Senesh represents the 32 parachutists, and is often included in other chapters than the one about the Holocaust. According to the *Mikra'ot*, the armed resistance and the struggle to maintain the human image are different aspects of the same Jewish heroic fight against the Nazis. This war is the central theme of the chapter, which is usually called: "The Day of the Holocaust and Heroism," or just "The Holocaust and Heroism."

The description of the physical suffering, and the detailed extermination, is shunted off to the background.

The Ritual Angle

Side by side with the texts meant for teaching, there is a ritualistic part, which clearly summarizes the moral lessons that emerge from the teaching material. This part, which usually opens and closes the Holocaust chapter, includes quotations from the Bible, from the Law which established Yad Vashem in 1953, as well as poems and short commandments.

The Vengeance Issue

Assuming that the wish to take revenge is human and natural, Jews who know about the Holocaust may experience this feeling. The *Mikra'ot* never offer the Israeli child any direct revenge on the Germans. As already mentioned, the Jews took a sort of revenge by refusing to be dehumanizied by the Nazis, and by their armed resistance. The obvious and direct wish for revenge is expressed by a prayer to God to pay the murderers their due:

> Let them be confounded and troubled
> for ever, yea, let them be put to shame, and perish.[30]

This sort of prayer appears often in the ritual part of the Holocaust chapters, both in the religious and the nonreligious textbooks. Young Israelis are taught that direct vengeance for the Holocaust is not and cannot be put into human hands, and that only God can avenge his chosen people. The *Mikra'ot* prefer to offer an alternative of revenge, urging the Jews to revive themselves as a proud independent nation, and thus take historical and moral revenge on the Nazis. By a process of transfer, the hatred toward the Nazis is directed into creative national salvation. Some *Mikra'ot* prefer a poem to carry this message, like Guri's "From That Fire," which describes Israeli soldiers in the Independence War of 1948, who had taken a torch out of the Holocaust fire to light the future in Israel, and a burnt brick out of the ruins to build the homeland—doing so, they felt that:

> We revenge your bitter and lonely death
> With our heavy and hot fist

We erect here a monument for the burnt ghetto
living memorial, which will last forever.[31]

The Commandment to Remember

As Guri's poem pointed out, part of the revenge was to remember what had happened in the Holocaust. The German plan was to uproot the Jews from human history and human consciousness; and later on, some of them tried to wipe the Holocaust from the memory of mankind.

Thus, the Jews are committed to remember and to remind others of the six million murdered. The commandment to remember, instilled in the Israeli child's first experience of the siren on the Day of Remembrance, is deepened through the passing years, when he learns more about the subject, and keeps attending the ritual every year. Through Shlonski's poem "The Vow," the child is sworn in to remember the Holocaust:

I took a VOW to remember all
to remember—and not to forget anything.[32]

The Commandment to Implement the Zionist Vision

The vengeance and the vow to remember are both an individual and a collective obligation of spiritual and practical nature, which can be realized only by creative activity. The child is directed to fulfill his vow by taking part in the building and in the defense of his homeland, as justified by the following argument:

The Jews are: "A Nation with only one way left
Only one way: In this country
In its only homeland: Eretz-Israel."[33]

The Consolation

The motif of consolation dominates the chapter about the Holocaust, as presented by the Israeli Mikra'ot. This stands out particularly in two items: The Passover Seder and the Zionist salvation in Eretz-Israel. These two frequently mingle between themselves and with others. The Passover feast crowns God's will to free his people from slavery; for two thousand years, the Jews in the Diaspora, under the yoke of the Gentiles, prayed every Passover Seder, "Next year in Jerusalem," thus demonstrating their lasting hope to get free, return to Israel, and never give up their inner freedom. Tragically, the Seder night became a traditional pogrom time, when the Gentiles, accusing

the Jews of the use of Christian blood to bake the Matzot, massacred
Jewish men, women, and children. The Nazis, who did not kill Jews
because of their religion, but because of their ethnic Semitic origin,
had forbidden the Jews to practice their religion as a part of their
wish to dehumanize them. The "traditional" connection between the
Passover night and the Jewish death escalated into the unbelievable
horrors of the Holocaust. Wishing to spoil the Nazis' plan, by
maintaining their hope for freedom, the Jews tried their best to perform
the Seder in spite of the death penalty. Through the imaginative
stories, the *Mikra'ot* transfer this message to the young pupils.

There is a story about a Seder in a hut for sick people in Bergen-
Belsen. The Jews, although their fate was sealed and they knew it,
secretly celebrated the Passover-night, hoping that:

> We shall celebrate the Seder for
> endless years more, and also when
> their language shall die in their mouth,
> our sons shall recite the story of the
> exodus from Egypt, in the *Hagada*
> language, and without any translation.
> Because our language shall live in
> the mouth of all our offspring.[34]

This text also carries a nuance of revenge, well known by the famous
Yiddish tagline, heard throughout the Holocaust era: *"Überleben"*—
"We shall outlive them."

The Seder is also connected with the armed resistance in the
Warsaw Ghetto, which started on the eve of the feast. In one of the
stories, a child smuggles flour to bake the Matzot from the Aryan
side into the ghetto. On his way back, he is severely wounded by a
German guard, and during the night, while his grandfather performs
the traditional ritual, he dies. Watching him the grandfather understands:

> Why his grandson sent to bring flour for baking the Matzot. . . . Yes,
> Yes, the free man stands against his enemy, as the Jews confronted
> their enemies in Egypt.[35]

The small child dies after having asked the traditional four questions.
The story offers the following answer to why this night is different
from all other nights: "The day after, the resistance in the ghetto
broke out against the Germans."[36]

Through the thoughts of the old man (a consolatory figure), the young Israeli pupils learn about the eternal Jewish commitment to freedom, as fulfilled by the dying child, and by the fighting youngsters in the ghetto.

The significance of the Passover Seder reaches the borders of the past, spreading to the present and the future by the power of the Zionist vision, which fulfills the ancient prayer for freedom in Eretz-Israel.

Stories about a Seder which is celebrated in a Kibbutz fuse the different meanings of the Passover feast, and intensify the importance of the past in the new epoch of the Zionist Renaissance.[37] In the midst of the celebration in the Kibbutz, the protagonist of the story remembers the Exodus, and his own experience, as a child at the Seder night in the Warsaw Ghetto in 1943. The flashbacks in his mind stand in contrast to the joyous feast in the Kibbutz, and function as a means of consolation, by telling how the Jewish child has emerged from the ashes of the burnt-out ghetto, and has become an Israeli pioneer in a Kibbutz. The Kibbutz in itself carries a consoling message, symbolizing the renovation of the Jewish people, rooted again in their natural setting, living justly and in equality in a commune.

Because in the majority of the *Mikra'ot* the chapter about the Holocaust comes directly after the one about Passover, the Seder element turns out to be a carrier of a consoling message. In addition, because the chapter concerning the establishment of the Jewish state in Israel is usually located after the chapter about the Holocaust, it also becomes a source of consolation.

As already mentioned, the Eretz-Israel element appears in connection with various subjects, but it is especially emphasized in three motifs concerning Jews who escaped from the Holocaust, and immigrated to Eretz-Israel.

The Imaginative Escape to Israel

The child's imaginative interpretation of reality dominates the stories in the textbooks and softens the horrors of the Holocaust. In addition to this general tendency, the editors of the *Mikra'ot* have chosen stories in which the child succeeds in escaping from the reality on the wings of his imagination.

In these stories the children's dream carries them to Israel, where they enjoy the landscape, and freely breathe the air. Other children imagine themselves rescuing family and friends in miraculous ways from Europe, and bringing them safely to Israel.[38] Every child's dream echos the pain and the prayer:

Already several times I have asked
myself, if I still shall be worthy, in
my lifetime, to put my foot on the
holy land. If God will yet let
me stand and walk on it? HO!
how much my soul yearns for Ye,
my homeland, How much my eyes
long to see thee, my country—
Eretz-Israel.[39]

On the Way to Eretz-Israel

Whenever the stories deal with this issue, they tend to describe
Jewish children who came to Israel *after* the Holocaust, saved by
relatives or by Jewish agents;[40] often the survivors had to be relieved
from their gentile savers who had tried to convert them to Christianity.

In Eretz-Israel

The description of children rescued from the Holocaust, and already
living in Israel, is parallel to the story of children who had imagined
Israel in the midst of the Holocaust; In Israel the children experience
their fulfilled dream, but continue to remember the Holocaust.[41]

Thus, the Eretz-Israel motif, which has a consoling power, is
restricted by the recollections of the survivors, and by the vow to
remember the Holocaust, as sworn by the whole Jewish nation.

Thus, it may be stated that almost every subject included in the
chapter about the Holocaust contains some elements of consolation:
the children who struggled for food, shelter, and human warmth;
their insistence on keeping their religion; their dreams of Israel, which
were sometimes fulfilled; the armed Jewish rebels; and even the
vengeance.

It is impossible to measure quantitatively the impact of the discussed
motifs. Therefore, a textual evaluation has to sufffice, concluding that
the Holocaust in the Israeli *Mikra'ot* tends to lean heavily on a motif
that satisfies a certain need for comforts.

Conclusion

It is difficult to state whether the children deeply absorb the poems
and the stories; probably part of the evaluation suggested here does
not reach them. The level of understanding achieved by the pupils
depends mainly on the teacher's ability to direct the discussion in
the classroom. Another factor which affects the process of learning
emerges from the origin of the pupils. It may be assumed that a

child of a survivor family and a child from a family who did not suffer respond differently to the subject. The reaction eventually changes with the passing years, when the Holocaust becomes rather a historical occurrence for the two groups.

The issue concerning the process of teaching the Holocaust in Israel has not yet been researched quantitatively, and therefore any accurate data cannot be offered here. Nor has any research been published about the presentation of the Holocaust in the *Mikra'ot*, by educators, teachers, or the textbook editors. As a result, the present essay is the first of its kind, and derives its conclusions from the *Mikra'ot* themselves. Although the textbooks are different in structure and in choice of texts, they share two common and central messages:

1. Universal human values, combined with the Jewish interpretation: as expressed by the struggle to maintain the human and the Jewish image.
2. The Zionist assumption: the existential necessity of which was proved by the Holocaust as reflected in the consolation motif, and others.

These two aspects complement each other in the Zionist vision which contains, and depends upon humanistic and nationalistic values. As such they may present, at one and the same time, two different points of view: According to the first one, the Holocaust is used as a means to form a sensitive, democratic citizen, who will build and defend Israel. This conception grasps the Holocaust as an indirect tool, and the child as a direct means to achieve the Zionist goal.

The second approach is based on the notion that the child is the center of the educational process. According to this point of view, the values serve the benefit of the child, answering his needs for supporting meanings, in the sense of Frank's (1955) logotherapy.

The literary texts in the *Mikra'ot* may evoke deep feelings in the children, and contribute to their personal identification with the values. (It seems to me that the two concepts mingle by identifying the Zionist goal as benefiting the child.)

The Israeli child is invited by the *Mikra'ot* to identify himself with the protagonists of the literary texts, who very often are Jewish children in the time of the Holocaust. The heroes of the stories are brave, resourceful, and loyal to their families and friends. They are moral and conscientious toward their kin. The horrid circumstances are filtered through their optimism and fantasy. They strive to remain children, maintaining the charm and the innocence of youth, but at the same time, they function like adults, and often give shelter to their seniors. They play the game of survival against the Germans, and frequently win the game. Thus, the child during the Holocaust, as described by the *Mikra'ot*, is always good, and successful in the fight against evil.

The stories prefer to blot out the death of the protagonists by literary devices, and as a result the pupil gets the impression that all the Jewish children survived. This ideal child is never treacherous toward his friends and family, never spiritually weak or a defeatist. The *Mikra'ot* very seldom present the child's feelings of shame, insult, and self-hatred when confronted with the fact that Jews were destroyed by the Nazis without armed resistance. Such feelings, if aroused, always conclude with something on the order of the following example: The Germans "should be ashamed" at having forced Jews to wear the Yellow Star. "These shall be like a burning scar for every German with a conscience, who tries to think about the future of his people."[42]

According to this example, whenever questions are asked, or self-hatred and self-shame are expressed in the textbooks, they are answered appeasingly. It may be difficult for the Israeli pupil to identify with those one-sided, overpositive, fictional protagonists, because of the special conditions in Israel; the Israeli child lives constantly under the threat of war, experiences stress and anxiety over possible harm or death to himself and his family; he sometimes has guilt feelings for having enjoyed the "benefits" derived from the state of war (like release from everyday duties) and thus develops anxieties and horror fantasies, some on an unconscious level.[43] To these specific Israeli objects of stress and anxiety, all the normal emotions of the kind of everyday life can be added.

A kind of high-quality children's literature strives to be relevant by presenting protagonists who are genuine in emotions and in behavior: This sort of literature invites the young reader to grasp the emotional processes within the fictional characters, and thus to improve his self-awareness. The certain natural detachment of fiction helps the child to understand the interpersonal situation involved on a broader and more objective as well as on a personal subjective level.

It is doubtful if the protagonists in the *Mikra'ot* answer to the mentioned criteria. If they do not, they may only enlarge the gap between the Israeli child and the Jewry during the Holocaust, as represented by the literature. Not being able to identify himself with the "good" fictional heroes, the Israeli child may feel morally inferior, and because of this unpleasant feeling he may come to reject the whole subject.

In addition to the "figures" issue, the editors of the *Mikra'ot* also have a problem with the Holocaust itself. They have seldom chosen texts which describe detailed physical suffering or death, and whenever they do so they prefer the framework of the ritual texts, which allow for a more general and detached approach. In the stories the Holocaust becomes the background for many other topics, as we have seen. It seems that these conditions are the result of the following conceptions:

1. The belief that a child cannot grasp the meaning of death and severe physical suffering.
2. The wish to spare him the traumatic experience, which may harm his proper mental development.
3. The apprehension that the pupil will create for himself a psychological self-defense mechanism, which will reject the whole subject, because of the disturbing feelings it arouses.

Although all these calculations are legitimate when they concern the choice of what shall be included in the textbooks, it seems that the editors of the *Mikra'ot* are overly cautious, which reflects their own difficulties in dealing with the morbid issues. The young pupil with whom they are concerned is Jewish and Israeli at the same time. Being a Jew, he knows—albeit vaguely—about anti-Semitism and the Holocaust from his early childhood. Being an Israeli he hears from his infancy about the daily casualties caused by wars and Arab terrorism.

In the Israeli society which is small in size, and close in relationship, the pain for the wounded and killed is an intimate experience for everyone. The truth is that the issues of death and physical suffering are not properly handled by the Israeli educational system, which tends to ignore the need to approach them with psychotherapeutic methods.[44] Psychological research indicates that the child's age, intelligence, and lifestyle determine his capacity of understanding the meaning of death. From the age of nine, the child can grasp the finality of death, and this is preceded by earlier stages, in which comprehension is partial and vague.[45] Therefore, there is neither justification to include the Holocaust in only textbooks meant for the fifth grade and above, nor to minimize the description of death and physical suffering in the books for older children.

There is an internal dependency between the description of The Final Solution and the other elements; only with the help of the complete details can the Jews' struggle to maintain their human image, and their armed resistance, be fully appreciated. By the same rule, the motif of consolation has a proper impact only as an answer to the real tragedy. Therefore, the claim for more details in the *Mikra'ot* about the process of extermination is justified on historical, psycho-

logical, and educational grounds, as well as by the human and Zionist
values the chapter about the Holocaust imparts. The Israeli child
learns about the Holocaust, from the *Mikra'ot* until he reaches the
eighth grade; only then he is confronted by the subject with the help
of the history textbook.

The *Mikra'ot* are completely literary, and ignore any historiographical
methods, such as a preface, linking themes, or chronological arrange-
ment. In Israel children start learning history as a specific subject
from the age of 9 or 10, on the assumption that at this age they are
able to understand historical processes. Therefore, an argument on
this ground cannot excuse the absence of the historical framework
for the literature texts in the *Mikra'ot*. Apparently, the historical
explanations are usually given by the teacher in the classroom. This
probability cannot free the textbooks from the obligation to include
basic facts, and elementary historical explanations in the textbooks.
If offered, such historical elements might deepen the child's understanding of the literature, and vice versa.

The psychological approach is another element almost entirely
absent in the textbooks. The psychohygienical approach, in which
emotional problems are considered without moral judgments, might
be adjusted to the educational and teaching processes, thus striving
to enable the child to become aware of his emotional difficulties, and
helping him to confront them. The child's benefit is the sole goal of
this philosophy. I believe that any editors or authors of texts about
the Holocaust have to take the abovementioned considerations into
account—especially when Jewish-Israeli children are the object.

But the dominating trend of the *Mikra'ot* is didactic. Its discussion
of the Holocaust conforms to the humanistic-Zionist values, using the
subject as a means to form the child's character. Its goal is an Israeli-
Jewish adult, who is sensitive to human values and a keen Zionist
as well. Only through such citizens can the Zionist vision be realized.
Belief that this is the only way for a Jew to achieve personal fulfillment
turns the child into a means to achieve the national goal in addition
to developing him as an individual.

Basically, I agree with these conceptions; nevertheless, I have doubts
about the efficiency of the ways chosen to achieve them. I would
prefer a less direct, less didactic approach—one that employs a more
historical approach, combined with a psycho-hygienic attitude. This
might well lead to better results.

However, the humanistic-Zionist values have been the consistent
framework of the texts about the Holocaust, in the Israeli *Mikra'ot*.
The development of the subject in the *Mikra'ot* at all grade levels has
known only one turning point; until the seventies, approximately 15

percent of the *Mikra'ot* meant for children between 9 and 13 hardly included the Holocaust, and many of those which did preferred to spread the issue over different subjects. This situation can be explained by the general desire of the Israeli society to spare the young children the horrors of the past, and to compensate them with the present and the future of the new life in Israel.

The turning point of the Israeli attitude toward the Holocaust occurred during the Eichmann trial in 1961. The public was deeply involved in it. At last the silence-taboo concerning the Holocaust had been broken for adults as well as for children. The television broadcast that started in Israel in 1967, and which presented programs on the Holocaust, helped to spread this new approach. Thus, from the sixties the Israeli adult society confronted the children with the Holocaust on a larger scale, and more directly than the textbooks in the classroom.

This general change of attitude resulted in a new, or readapted, *Mikra'ot* in the seventies, most of which include the Holocaust in separate chapters, and very often from the early school grades onward.[46] While the editors accepted the change in attitude, as reflected in their textbooks, the Ministry of Education has been slow to react. Although it started to publish booklets on various subjects in the late sixties, it has not yet prepared a special one on the Holocaust. It seems that its overprofessional team system has prolonged the decision-making process, especially concerning the problematic issue of presenting the Holocaust to very young pupils.

As a result, from the seventies the schools have tended to exchange the *Mikra'ot* for the booklets of the Ministry of Education, especially for the early grades. Thus, the turning point which presented the Holocaust as a separate "Teaching-Subject" in most of the *Mikra'ot*, has been weakened by the hesitation of the Ministry of Education. In the early eighties, as in the fifties, the Holocaust tended to be a matter for ceremonies of Memorial Day, and was often subordinated to other subjects. The Ministry of Education has not succeeded in editing sufficient booklets for the sixth grade and above; therefore, the pupils from the age of 11 continue to use the *Mikra'ot*.

There are no accurate data about the use of the new booklets and, assuming that teachers tend to be conservative, it can be presumed that Israeli schools, in all grades, use old and new textbooks simultaneously, tending to prefer the new for the earlier grades, and the old in the senior ones.[47]

The Ministry of Education, having an advantage over the private textbook editors, through their financial sources, professional staff, and the power of official recommendation, have sharpened this problematic situation. The spread of the state-published booklets is therefore probable, and the resulting postponement of specific booklets on the Holocaust may cause an educational vacuum in this field.

The need for new booklets about the Holocaust, composed and edited according to the suggestions which have been detailed here, is strengthened by the competition of television, which presents high-quality programs on the Holocaust, meant for both adults and children. The new *Mikra'ot* must contain historical and literary texts which will offer the pupils and the teachers the opportunity to discuss processes, emotions, and controversial issues.

I believe that this kind of *Mikra'ot*, used by techers who have been trained accordingly, may prepare the child for the next stage of studying the Holocaust on the level of history textbooks.

7
The Holocaust in History Textbooks

The textbooks on the history of the Jewish People which deal with the Holocaust, and are used in different Zionist schools, are divided into two groups:

1. Books published from 1948 until the seventies—approximately 16, written by authors with the help of various organizations, and not under the guidance of the Ministry of Education.
2. Five books that were published from the seventies through 1984, and written with the help, and under the guidance of, the Ministry of Education.

In addition to these technical differences, there are also other meaningful distinctions between these two groups.

The Holocaust—A Proof of Zionist Truth (Israel 1948–1977)

The textbooks which include the Holocaust were published in Israel from the early fifties. Until then, the *Yishuv* was occupied with its own struggle for existence, and was unable to collect the bits of information into a comprehensive historical description.

The arrival of the Holocaust survivors after 1948 had a strong influence on the writing of textbooks during this first period. This becomes obvious when one compares the attitudes and explanations of modern anti-Semitism and of traditional hatred of Jews in these books with those in textbooks that were published in Israel in the years 1930–1948.[48]

While in the books of the pre-state period, the physical injuries caused by "hooligans" are detailed (e.g., Chmielnitzky, in the seventeenth century, and the pogroms of the late nineteenth and early twentieth century Russia), the books from the fifties go into very few details about the physical injuries involved.[49]

One may get the impression that the authors of the textbooks considered these injuries negligible in comparison with the horrors of the Holocaust. Possibly they also thought that a repetition of these descriptions might create defensive attitudes in the minds of the students which could diminish, or block completely, the power of the emotional impact caused by studying the Holocaust in the classroom.[50]

The history textbooks published in Israel before World War II did not clearly differentiate between the hatred of the Jews based on religious, cultural, and sociological reasons and modern anti-Semitism, which is based on genetic-racial arguments.

Only after the Final Solution was the differentiation between these two kinds formulated by historians, especially be Professor S. Ettinger of the Hebrew University in Jerusalem. However, textbooks are usually late in absorbing new historical approaches, by at least ten years, because of the time which is necessary for the new concepts to get through to the public, and because of the time needed to compile the textbooks. Ettinger's textbook is exceptional when compared with other books of the first period, and most of his influence can be traced in textbooks of the second period (during the middle seventies).

The authors of the "Zionist" period (1948–1977) tried to explain these phenomena by using historical methods, combined with personal emotions. These emotions are expressed in an extreme, heavily emotionally charged terminology. Their technical tools are stereotypic, deprecatory terms, and persuasive definitions.[51]

For early teenagers, the haters of the Jews are described, for example, in the following ways:

- "Horrible demons," "Wild animals" (from a description of the Spanish Inquisition).[52]
- "Horrible plague, like an infectious disease" (describing modern anti-Semitism in the same book).[53]

Another textbook meant for the same age group uses these explanatory definitions:

- "The Nazi devilish evilness," and:
- "The crazy Nazi animal at the peak of its fit of madness."[54]

For the late teenagers, the authors use the following definitions in their explanations:

- "Murderous instincts," "Diseased imagination."

- "Savage boorishness and the German characteristic technical perfection."[55]
- "Evil animal," "Dark powers," "Savage brute."[56]
- "Adventurers, cheaters, simple thieves, and psychopathic characters."[57]

This kind of expression is charged with hatred (the author's) and diminishes the possibility that the student will be able to cope with these subjects on a rational level.

Even in those paragraphs which are properly formulated, the general direction is toward demonic mysticism, or the pathology of anti-Semitism, which abolishes the justification of an analytic study.[58] These tendencies may lead to pessimistic fatalism in the students' response, and to minimize the moral responsibility of the anti-Semites throughout history: because they are chronically ill, or are possessed by demonic powers, they cannot be held guilty.

The shock of the Holocaust caused the textbook writers to describe the historic persecutions of the Jews as a portent of the genocide to come, which had not been properly understood by the nation in the past.

This type of explanation is emphasized, in the textbooks of modern Jewish history, in such phrases as "When Zionism warned and was not listened to. . . ." The echoes of these accusations can be traced in textbooks published between the years 1930 and 1948, especially in descriptions of the Diaspora Jews who were characterized by passivity, and evoked pity and contempt; they were shown as the antithesis of the pioneer Jews in Israel. This contrast was based on the prevailing negative attitude toward the Diaspora among the *Halutzim* (Pioneers), in Israel in those years.[59]

After the Holocaust, having to face the catastrophe and the need to absorb the refugees, it was hard to continue to denigrate the Diaspora and thus to do injustice to the memory of those who had been exterminated. Besides, the creation of Israel made new attitudes possible, regarding Jews who "for the time being" remained in the Diaspora (in accordance with the concept of "National Centre and Periphery"—influenced by Ahad Ha'am's Zionist theory). At the same time, it is possible that the heroism of the War of Independence deepened the feeling of shame in the minds of the students for those Jews who were annihilated without armed resistance.

The question "Why were they slaughtered like sheep?" is asked also in connection with descriptions of pre-Holocaust pogroms. The passivity of the Jews is regarded as "shameful behavior," while instances of "religious self-sacrifice," or of armed resistance, are considered honorable.

This conception reaches its peak in descriptions of the suffering and the annihilation of the Holocaust. Although the textbooks from 1948 to 1977 mentioned more details of the physical suffering of the Jews killed by the Nazis, compared with descriptions of pre-Holocaust pogroms, they do prefer to shorten them. This becomes obvious when comparing them with descriptions of armed resistance, or even to other historical chapters, such as in Spivak/Avidor's book[60] (meant for nonreligious pupils, aged 12–14) where out, of 220 pages, 10 are devoted to Napoleon and only one to the Holocaust.

The writers add long lists of facts and figures about how many and where Jews were killed, but sensing that this cannot bring the historical reality closer to the students' minds, they emphasize the suffering of elderly people, women, and children. Probably they feel that the supposedly passive state of such people is less shameful than that of young men who die without fighting—especially for Israelis who know that, in Israel, almost every man is also a soldier.

Even so, the authors cannot free themselves from the issue of "shame-honor," and therefore they explain Jewish passivity in various ways. Several of them mention the Nazi lies which fooled many Jews until the last moments before their actual deaths, or the isolation of the Jews facing the Nazis and those who cooperated with them, or the silence of the free world. Others explain the psychological state of those sent to their deaths, which prevented them from defending themselves. Very often explanations use all these motifs together.

Against the Nazis' genocide program, the Jews reacted with armed resistance and by fighting to preserve their humanity under inhuman circumstances. Doubtlessly, most of the historical expressions of the struggle against the Nazis were of the second kind, but in the textbooks of the first ("Zionist") period (1948–1977), less space is devoted to this subject than to descriptions of the suffering and destruction of Jews.

Out of 14 textbooks: nine devote six to seven lines to the fighting to preserve their humanity; two do it on a large scale; while three do not mention it at all. There exist quantitative and qualitative correlations between the tendency to detail the suffering and destruction of the Jewish people, and to describe their heroism in maintaining their humanity; for only under such horrible conditions can the greatness of the human struggle be appreciated.

There is no such dependency between the theme of suffering and the theme of armed resistance; the latter possesses a heroic quality in its own right. Instead of reciting in detail the affirmations of life in the midst of death, the authors prefer to evaluate in their own language (which is often pathetically exaggerated), the struggle of Jews to assert their humanity during the Holocaust. They consider it as miraculous—a symbol of the potential greatness of which human beings are capable.

Presumably the average Israeli student, whose knowledge of the suffering and the mass killing of Jewry is poor, and remote from his personal experience, has difficulties in understanding and identifying with the acts of heroism involved in founding kindergartens and schools in the midst of the Holocaust. It is more difficult to clarify and explain this sort of greatness than it is to depict the process of fighting back—especially with the background of the military activity in Israel.

Human existence under inhuman conditions may be understood by the students as just another expression of the ability of the Jews to adapt themselves to any circumstances, while the Zionist ideology calls for rebellion against them. This is the reason why many of these chapters are concluded in the following way: "In the heroic position of the ghetto Jews, there was a compensation for the *shameful surrender* of the Jews who were transported to death camps"[61] (italics supplied).

This conception states that the historical honor of the Jews was restored by their armed resistance, and indeed out of 14 textbooks (1948–1977) that recite the story of the Holocaust, nine devote at least twice as much space to the description of the armed resistance than to "Suffering and Destruction," and "Maintenance of Humanity."

The resistance of the Warsaw Ghetto is used in the books as a typical example of the various Jewish attempts against the Nazis, and thus may leave the false impression with the student that similar attempts were made elsewhere.

Fighters who are called "Hebrews," or "Israeli youngsters," and who are presented as members of pioneer-youth organizations, emphasize the contrast between themselves and "the Jews who were slaughtered like sheep."[62] The connections between the fighters in the Warsaw Ghetto and the young Hebrew pioneers may create an impression that Zionism fought against the Nazi regime, and won by building the Jewish State of Israel out of the ashes of the war. This simplified way of presenting "The blood-soaked epoch,"[63] concludes with a "happy ending" in the style of "from apocalyptical destruction to national renaissance," and the powerful impact of this kind of presentation can prevent the development of a rational attitude toward the Holocaust.

Instead, such writing tends to regard the Holocaust as the war of the children of light against the children of darkness—one which ends with the victory of Zionism in 1948 by the creation of the State of Israel—which may also justify the "war" and its horrible human "price."

The religious history textbooks in that period were few in number, and therefore—in the religious schools—teachers often used the "secular" textbooks.

Although the few religious books are not different in essence from the others, they tend to shorten the description of the *Sho'ah*, and do not touch the problematic religious angle in the evaluation of the Holocaust. There is a strong contrast between the pedagogical publications of the teachers and educators and the sterile religious textbooks. Perhaps the problem was considered too complicated to be expressed in a textbook, which can be read even without the help of a teacher.

There are two possible explanations for that situation; either the religious trend was in those years not ready to mold its opinions in its textbooks, or it preferred this problematic issue to be kept completely under the control of the teacher in the classroom.

The Holocaust as a Stimulus of Humanistic-Education 1977–1983

From the late fifties, textbooks and curricula were revised on a large scale in the U.S. and in Europe.[64] In Israel many articles were published by education-researchers, teachers, and public figures about the alienated attitude of the Israeli students toward Zionism and the Holocaust. The cynicism and revulsion of the pupils concerning the Holocaust, as it was taught in schools, evoked criticism and suggestions for improvement in these publications.[65]

Eichmann's trial in Jerusalem in 1961 aroused profound interest in thousands of Israelis and proved that this subject was not, in itself, repulsive, but that the methods of teaching it in schools caused these negative reactions.

Then the Ministry of Education started to compose new textbooks and curricula. Its new approach abolished the previous system, in which teachers were obliged to teach modern Jewish history in its entirety; instead, it now offered a choice from among a list of compulsory and optional subjects. The Holocaust was not obligatory for secondary schools, while for the upper grades in the elementary schools, three to four hours a year were considered appropriate. It was not until 1980 that the Holocaust became a mandatory subject in secondary schools.[66] Since 1982, teachers have been obliged to devote 30 hours a year to the Holocaust, and the topic appears on the final examination.[67]

Usually, the Ministry of Education has published one textbook for each subject. The Holocaust, however, was represented in two special textbooks (Schatzker's and Carmon's—both meant for secular high schools, although they were also used by religious students).

In these books a new attitude toward the Holocaust appears, which also influences other books which deal with anti-Semitism and descriptions of the physical suffering of Jews throughout their history. They accord with Ettinger's concept that whenever one wants to understand anti-Semitism in any period, one has to take into account the growth of anti-Semitism throughout history, layer by layer, each layer built on the previous one, and adding on those special expressions of anti-Semitism that are peculiar to that period.[68] By this approach, one develops different methods of teaching the Holocaust.[69]

These influences can be identified in the:

1. Combination of sociological and psychological aspects with historical descriptions and explanations.
2. Concrete terminology which is clear of abusive terms and persuasive definitions.
3. Tendency to include many sources and articles from different realms of knowledge.
4. Guidance for students to study according to historical research methods.

All these characteristics are new, compared with the textbooks of the Zionist period.

Perhaps the textbook authors in the former period were personally too close to the Holocaust, and therefore did not believe that these phenomena could be approached rationally, while more recent writers have learned that the emotional attitude in teaching this special period has deepened the unwillingness of the pupils to study and face the dilemmas of the Holocaust. The tendency to shorten the story of the physical suffering of the Jews in the new books is the result of this approach.

But one has to keep in mind the technically qualitative difference between the textbooks written before 1977, and those written after. The former were composed by private writers and are descriptive— standard textbooks. The books of the Ministry of Education were written by teams of specialists of various sorts, and their frame is a combination of a textbook and (usually) two booklets: a guidebook for the teacher, and one for the student.

Therefore, when comparing the textbooks of the two periods, it is necessary to consider these booklets. The team-writers after 1977 could be content with the booklets' guidance on how the material was to be presented. The pre-1977 private authors had to use their textbooks also as a means of educational guidance. Indeed, in two history books (for young children in nonreligious schools),[70] the booklet asks the instructor to teach the pogroms of the ancient times by means of simulation. In the textbooks themselves, there were no details of the physical suffering—perhaps on the assumption that the child could imagine the horrors from his own personal world.

Probably, most of the authors, who, like the students, did not themselves suffer from anti-Semitic persecution, think that only by simulation can the Israeli pupil identify himself, to some degree, with the self-sacrificing Jews. This can also be the reason why the writers prefer to emphasize the spiritual and social suffering of the Jews rather than the physical tortures. Personal and national discriminations and limitations are closer to the personal experience of the student, and therefore more understandable, and thus make it possible for him to identify with Jewish nation in the Diaspora.

But the main shift in attitude becomes apparent in the textbooks about the Holocaust; in the presentation of the issues: physical suffering and annihilation, armed resistance, and the struggle to maintain their humanity under inhuman conditions.

In Carmon's textbook, *Ha'shoah* (The Holocaust), there is no separate chapter describing the physical suffering and the mass killing. This is the background on which Jewish human vitality is emphasized, while in Schatzker's *The Roots of Modern Antisemitism and the Holocaust*, a chapter on Auschwitz concludes the book.[71]

Probably Carmon hesitated to confront the students directly with the theme of suffering and preferred to present it by indirect means. Schatzker was more likely of the opinion that it is necessary and possible to make adolescents face the details of the extermination camps.

That the Auschwitz chapter is at the end of Schatzker's book may indicate the author's intention to prepare the student by analytic means to deal with the emotional shock of the last chapter of the book.[72]

This theme is not subordinate to the Zionist attitude toward the question of "Honor and Shame" (as it is in the textbooks of 1948–1977). Likewise, the descriptions of armed self-defense have become shorter. (In Schatzker's book, 20 pages out of 353; in Carmon's, 33 pages out of 293.) For both of them the fight of the Warsaw Ghetto is no longer the sole or main example of armed resistance, and they mention other places without putting stress particularly on anyone of them.

In this manner, the Warsaw resistance is not presented as atonement for the guilt of being slaughtered, caused by a failure to heed the Zionist warning, but takes its place in the textbook in proportion to its part in history.

The central issue in the new textbooks is the dilemma of preserving the human image. The textbooks deal with the two aspects of this issue: the process of *losing* one's human nature; the struggle for *preserving* one's humanity.

The question at the beginning of both books is: "How is it possible to turn civilized man into a murderous animal?" By historical and sociological explanations, the authors try to clarify this process within the German nation. (Carmon includes many articles written by psychologists and sociologists.)

But the main part of the books is dedicated to the description of the struggle of the Jews (as human beings) against the Nazis' efforts to turn them into animals that fight only for their physical existence. The authors do not praise this struggle, but instead describe (through historical sources) its defeats and its victories, so that the student can appreciate the meaning, for example, of continuing educational concepts such as youth-movements or of keeping religious *mitzvot* under the Nazis.

By their presentations, the authors hope that the students will face the two human issues that are relevant for them in their adolescence, and in their future as members of a democratic society.[73]

With the help of the textbooks of the second period, adolescents are supposed to recognize the dangers of being in a strong political and physical position: personal judgment of what is right and what is wrong may be weakened, turning the individual into a predator. On the other hand, they have to learn that under inhuman conditions humans may become prey. It is important for the students to understand these two processes of dehumanization in the hope that they can help to prevent a future Holocaust.[74]

The universal human lesson of these books is well presented by the lines which Carmon chose to finish his textbook:

> There is only one answer to this horrible tragedy: Reconfirmation of the meaningfulness and value of life by deeds of love . . .[75]

From 1983 On—a New Period?

In 1983 two new high school textbooks about the Holocaust were published in Israel. One had a religious orientation and tends to be (like books in the 1970s) based on historical sources. The latter is a classical textbook. Both of them describe the physical agony and the annihilation of Jews on a scale larger than ever before. They emphasize that the Final Solution was meant for the whole Jewish nation, and include historical sources and references regarding the Sephardic and Oriental Jewry during the years 1939–1945.[76]

This attitude is based on a belief, which Gutman and Schatzker[77] have put into the following phrase:

> The Holocaust was not a concern only of this part or another of the whole Jewish Nation, in the same way as the War of Independence and all Israel's wars were not only the concern of those who were killed in them.

On the background of the suffering and the mass murder of the Jewish people by the Nazis, the abovementioned authors describe the everyday Jewish heroism in maintaining their human image; represented by children, youth movements, and Ghetto life. The Zionist lesson is taught by chapters devoted to the period after the Holocaust, which led to the creation of Israel. In comparison to these subjects and to others (Raoul Wallenberg is described in 74 lines), the struggle of Jews to perform religious rituals is condensed into a mere 28 lines.[78]

The first religious textbook for pupils in their late teens which considers the religious problems connected with the Holocaust was published in Israel in 1983. Its authors declare that they aim to present the *Sho'ah* from

> Problems and points of view—unique to the religious education, which were not expressed in the existing books on the Holocaust.[79]

Thus, the issues of sanctification of the Holy Name, and sanctification of life are dealt with at length. It is suggested to the pupils that they consider the Holocaust as an atonement for the sins of the Jewish nation.[80] The religious student is openly directed by the textbook to identify himself with Joseph Rakover's prayer:

> I believe in Him—The God of Israel
> Although He did everything that
> We shall not believe in Him"
> Hear, O Israel; The Lord our
> God, The Lord is one.

Into thine hand I commit my
Spirit.[81]

The armed fight against the Nazis is second in importance in these
textbooks, but relative to the other textbooks from previous periods
they emphasize again the Warsaw-Ghetto Resistance, without ne-
glecting other cases of armed rebellion which took place during the
Holocaust, nor do they submit it to the shame-honor issue, as was
done in the Zionist period.

Evaluation of the Treatment of the Holocaust
in History Textbooks (1948–1984): An Overview

The events of the Holocaust became known to the Israelis as early
as 1942, and certainly after the arrival of the survivors to Israel in
the late 1940s, but a discussion of those events would not appear in
textbooks until the 1950s, after they had absorbed the popular attitudes
of the adult society. During that time the Israelis were occupied with
the question: "Why were they slaughtered like sheep?" It was repeated
in public forums, and often replaced the teaching of the Holocaust
in classrooms. Textbooks were obliged to provide answers to the
abovementioned question, and they could not satisfy themselves with
such an answer:

> Did millions die for the sanctification of God? As it appears to me,
> they found a meaningless death, in their endless numbers in this
> outbreak of the brutalities of man, and nothing more.[82]

This bitterness and shame is somehow balanced by the emphasis
put on the heroic armed resistance of the Warsaw-Ghetto. This
"balanced" attitude is also reflected in the 1953 law, "Remembrance
of the Holocaust and the Heroism," which announced the foundation
of the Yad Vashem institute. In this law, 17 words are connected with
the suffering and extermination, 32 with armed resistance, and only
six words are related to the Jewish struggle to maintain their human
image.

The tendency to stress Jewish heroism in the Holocaust was also
the result of the self-image of the young and active state during the
1950s. The Wars of 1948 and 1956, and the constant defense against
Arab terrorists formed the image of a new Jew who fought for his
freedom and life successfully. This sort of Israeli had difficulties when
faced with the six million murdered Jews, especially, when for a long
period he had disassociated himself from the Diaspora Jew, who was

represented as the opposite of the Zionist.[83] Ambivalent feelings developed from the *yishuv* sense of guilt that a maximum effort was not made to rescue the European Jewry during the Holocaust. This consciousness is in the textbooks which avoided or shortened any controversial issues concerning such topics as Joel Brand's mission or Kastner's negotiations with the Nazis. Instead, the textbooks preferred to stress the great efforts made by volunteers from the Yishuv in order to help Jews doomed by the Nazis. All these elements mingled into a "Zionist-model" which directed the description, and the evaluation of the Holocaust in the history textbooks from 1948 to 1977:

1. A great part of the Jewish nation did not understand, or refused to accept the truth of Zionism, because of their illusions concerning Jewish Emancipation in the Diaspora.
2. The Final Solution destroyed these illusions and punished the stubborn Jews.
3. The conclusions and the results of that "lesson" were realized by the Jews who returned to "Eretz-Israel."
4. The catastrophe ended with the miracle of the State of Israel.

During the 1950s and the 1960s, many critical articles were published decrying such teaching-methods, which led youngsters to reject the Holocaust. The critics differ widely in their suggestions of how to make improvements:[84]

1. What is to be recommended: to shorten, or to specialize the description of physical suffering and the process of extermination? Shortening may cause ignorance and help to create aggressiveness, resulting from self-identification with the "Jewish Warrior" during the Holocaust (as emphasized in textbooks). On the other hand, detailing agony and death may create alienation or even unconscious empathy with the murderous Nazis.
2. Should the teacher, or the textbook mention the numbers killed and the names of the Jewish communities destroyed? Doing this may be meaningless because of the large numbers, and strange names, while omission of these facts is also impossible because of the obligation toward the memory of the massacred, and because it may minimize the historical evidence of the horrors.
3. Has a teacher, or a textbook, a chance of changing—through improved methods—the rooted attitude of the Israeli pupil? Or

can this be achieved only by a cultural process within the Israeli nation?

While the educators were debating these and other issues, the youngsters continued to use terms like "musselman" (a term used in the camps for those who gave up on life) or "soap," which the Nazis would manufacture out of the flesh of the slain. These terms meant cowardice. No wonder that in such an atmosphere, the Holocaust survivors preferred to keep silent.

The educators, and the public leaders were aware of what the pupils were saying, and demanded a revision of textbooks and teaching methods.

But it is not easy to change public opinion. The turning point did not come until David Ben Gurion's 1961 announcement in the Knesset of the capture of Adolf Eichmann. His subsequent trial and execution was followed by ten years of ambivalent and ambiguous attitudes toward the Holocaust, which brought forth the new textbooks of the "Humanistic Period."

Eichmann's trial provided an impetus for the transition into the second epoch. On one hand it provided the Holocaust survivors with a chance to testify and to reveal their everyday struggle just to survive as human beings. On the other hand, Eichmann's presence demystified the Nazi regime, and its servants. The oversimplified picture of the six million victims who were slaughtered "like sheep" by "demonic powers of evil" was shattered, and openly disputed by the Israeli public.

The Six-Day-War of 1967, evoked two main reactions which had an indirect influence on this present topic. In the long weeks preceding the war, Israel was surrounded by hostile Arab states, and Prime Minister Levi Eshkol was indecisive and apparently weak. The possibility of being physically exterminated by the Arabs became a reality for everyone. The experience of fear, and even of helplessness, enabled the Israelis to identify themselves with the Jews of the Holocaust. It was obvious that the "New Israeli" was not immune to "Jewish fear," when faced with the threat of destruction. The miraculous Israeli victory lifted the nation from the depth of anxiety into the height of euphoria.

In spite of the general high spirits during the years 1967–1973, there were public voices who pointed out the moral dangers of power. They turned out to be true when the "Yom Kippur War" of 1973 demonstrated that feelings of power were temporary illusions. Again the Israelis felt the historical Jewish fear of being condemned to destruction.

Those shifting attitudes put question marks to many of the Zionist tenets, such as the belief in the heroic image of the Zionist pioneer and in security of the State of Israel when contrasted with the lack of security in the Diaspora.

During those years, two nonreligious textbooks for high school students appeared[85] which were completely different from the previous ones.

The new books are wholly devoted to the Holocaust, while the others included it only within their large-scale history books. The "old" ones are narrative, while the "new" ones are based on selections from historical sources.

The authors of the new textbooks were influenced by the criticism of the previous "Zionist" approach and by the events of what might be called the "intermediate incubation" years between 1961 and 1977. Instead of presenting the Holocaust as an apocalyptic war between Zionism and Nazism which ended with the establishment of the State of Israel, they now told a different story: that of the crisis of the individual in the modern totalitarian state—the crushing of freedom of choice by political and cultural indoctrination processes.

This struggle between the individual and the state is presented as resulting in the "failure of man," who becomes an SS executioner. Parallel to this narrative line there is the story of the war (mainly spiritual) of man (the Jew) against the totalitarian system. In spite of the heavy sacrifices in that war, the human spirit prevailed. Because of these characteristics, the second period (1977–1983) may be called the "humanistic epoch," in which the teaching of the Holocaust is used as a means by which these specific educational aims are achieved.[86]

The result of the criticism of "the Zionist use" of the Holocaust in the textbooks of the first period, and the attitudes emanating from the Eichmann trial and the wars of 1967 and 1973, is that the national-Israeli-Zionist meaning of the Holocaust was almost completely omitted in the new textbooks.

Probably the authors of the second period tried to turn from the Zionist way of teaching the Holocaust to a universal democratic approach, because they believed that after Zionism had realized its goal in creating Israel in 1948, the dramatic historical phase was completed and that Israel, as a modern state, had to change its educational purposes accordingly, in order to prepare students for life in a democratic, humanistic society.

The textbooks of the "humanistic period" are not used on a large scale in the Israeli high schools today, because of methodological and attitudinal reasons.

The Methodological Reason. Teachers and pupils need a textbook which condenses the vast information into a clear narrative that describes the thematical as well as the chronological historical developments. Such a book enables them to prepare for the final examination within the allotted classroom hours. The history sources collected by Schatzker and Carmon[87] did not answer these needs.

The Attitudinal Reason. The teachers who looked carefully at these books, which are rather complicated, found that they lacked the national-Zionist angle and that the humanistic-universal message could not in itself be relevant for the Israeli pupil.

As happens very often, textbooks written with great effort and skill become out of date shortly after they are published.

The political elections to the Knesset in 1977, and 1981, which brought to, and maintained in power, the Likud Government were the result of sociocultural processes that had continued from the sixties. The Labor regime had failed to absorb the new immigrants from Arab countries, who regarded the old pioneer ethos as a means by which the European Jewish elite was trying to keep wealth and power to itself. Since they could not join the perceived "pioneer elite club," they rejected it. They alienated themselves from the Jewish history of the Holocaust, and occasionally some of them expressed their frustration by painting Swastikas on public walls, calling for the death of the "Nazi-European Jews."

The oriental Israelis, together with many natives of European origin, who were disappointed with the Labor government, especially after the Yom Kippur War, put into power a new government.

The conviction of many historians and educational researchers that the history of the Sephardic and Oriental Jews had to be part of the description of the Holocaust was realized in the textbooks of the early 1980s.

The prior liberal period, which encouraged the asking of many questions, evoked also an urgent need for answers, which were supplied by radical parties and ideological movements. Textbooks, by definition, tend to satisfy general needs of the majority in the society, and so did the textbooks of 1983—which by subtle and direct means draw lessons from the Holocaust.

The Holocaust and its Meaning by Gutman and Schatzker[88] carries three main messages:

1. The universal-humanistic meaning, which concerns the problem of the German individual who lost his human values, in contrast with the Jew who most often succeeded in maintaining them, in spite of the dehumanized circumstances. The lesson drawn

emphasizes the importance of freedom, and self-responsibility of the individual.

2. The national-Jewish meaning, which stresses that the Final Solution was meant for the whole Jewish nation, and actually was practiced on different levels, and at different stages, against the European, the Sephardic, and the Oriental Jews.

3. The Zionist lesson, which connects the Holocaust and the birth of the Jewish State in 1948.

The first religious textbook on the Holocaust for high school students was published in Israel in 1983.[89] It is a collection of historical topics and sources, emphasizing both humanistic and religious attitudes.

The quantitative proportions and the qualitative content of this book, instruct the student to view the Holocaust with *pride* (on account of the religious Jews who fought for their rights to practise religion), *acceptance* (to believe in God, after the Holocaust without doubting God's ways), and *understanding* (to comprehend that the Holocaust was a confrontation between Judaism and Nazism that, according to the religious textbook, was won by Judaism).

While the abovementioned book does not stress the Zionist lesson, the nonreligious one devotes little space to the description of the religious Jews in the Holocaust.

And so these questions arise:

Does the religious editor not believe in stressing the importance of the Zionist lesson, drawn from the Holocaust?

Do the nonreligious authors not consider the struggle of the believers to practice their religion an important part of the universal human meaning of the Holocaust?

Without having ready answers, I may assume that the books reflect the authors' opinions, and perhaps the tendencies within the religious and the nonreligious groups in Israeli society today.

Could this be an indication of the growing gap of difference between these two groups?

8
The Research Textbooks

Most Israeli university professors would deny they use "textbooks." They insist instead on using research works and primary historical sources. Thus, Israeli students are prepared to study the Holocaust on a high academic level when they reach the university. Believing that textbooks tend to narrow the academic sphere of the students, the Israeli professors prefer to supply reading lists of various kinds.[90]

A definition of textbook is based both on its instructional purpose and its usage. The only textbook in Israel, and it is meant for American universities, is Yehuda Bauer's *A History of the Holocaust*.[91] Assuming that this book includes the characteristics of college textbooks, the following elements define it:

1. Basic chronological information about German and Jewish aspects.
2. Clear, well defined structure, detailed in topics and arranged either thematically or chronologically.

Another possible way to define the term textbook is by its usage, even when it does not include the above elements. Such an approach states that as long as *any* book fulfils the functions of a textbook, it may be regarded as such. In the Israeli universities the students use general history books for introductory lessons. While these books are used as textbooks, other specific research work and collections of documents are meant for a higher academic level. The general history books are based on methodical research, and therefore will here be refered to as "research-textbooks."

Several of these books are German, translated into English; others are put together by Israelis in Hebrew.[92] They have been used by students for 30 years, first in the Hebrew University in Jerusalem, and later on in other universities throughout the country.

Teachers in teacher-training institutes also use these research-textbooks, side by side with *Mikra'ot* and history-textbooks, as the curriculum of the Ministry of Education requires, and according to their professional needs. The universities have complete autonomy in selecting subjects and methods of research and teaching.[93] On the other hand, instructors in teachers colleges are directed by the needs of society, and therefore have to consider the needs of the public, including, if necessary, the state regulations. A diagnosis of the changes in the research textbooks during the years 1948–1984, has to consider the time lag between the conceiving of the research work and its publication, which often results in books that reflect old-fashioned historiographical trends. By the same rule, every periodical differentiation offered here, takes into account a preliminary epoch in which the new attitudes developed.

The German-Centered Research-Textbooks

Five prominent descriptive research-textbooks have been used by the Israeli students during the first decades after the Holocaust.[94]

Hilberg opens his book with the following statement: "Let it be pointed out that this is not a book about the Jews. It is a book about the people who destroyed the Jews."[95] Does a similar attitude dominate all these textbooks? Using the enormous quantity of official German documents, historians, until the late 1960s, tended to be divided into two main groups: those who advocated the ideologically oriented approach, centered around Hitler. Tim Mason called them "intentionalists." Others stressed the development of the political structure as the catalyst of the Final Solution, and Mason called them "functionalists."[96] The "intentionalists" emphasize Hitler's fear and hatred of the Jews, which were apparently justified by social, cultural, racial, and territorial reasons.[97]

Thus, the basic driving force behind the Nazi policy toward the Jews, was the anti-Semitism of Hitler.[98] Accordingly: "The Nazi policies with regard to the Jews were consistent from the start: elimination commercially, professionally, and physically of all Jews under German power." "Only the methods changed—from migration through deportation to murder."[99]

The emphasis of Hitler's role in planning and performing The Final Solution, encourages an analysis of the Führer and his assistants, which tends to be of psychological nature.[100]

While the German historians were satisfied with a "scientific" approach the Israelis added another angle to it. Frager, who is ideologically centered, uses a demonic and pathological terminology when he explains the sources and the elements of anti-Semitism.[101] Tenenbaum details Hitler's characteristics, concluding with the remark:

"Hitler was a poor lover, but an insatiable hater."[102] In the Hebrew edition of his book, there are the following metaphors about Nazi anti-Semitism: "It was more than this—[it was] a kind of burning obsession of a bloodsucker upon his prey, or of witchcraft—conduct of man-eaters. Hitler's anti-Semitic screamings were like the curses coming out of the mouth of the fiend."[103] He mentions Hitler's "witchcraft power," or his "devilish-demonic personality."[104]

The functionalists opposed the overimportance given to Hitler by the intentionalists,[105] and they prefered to emphasize the power of the structure and the political processes of the Third Reich. According to this attitude the Final Solution was the end product of the developing Nazi system, rather than the result of a preliminary program.[106]

This differentiation does not imply that any one trend avoids the aspects of the other; rather, it clarifies the different emphasis in description and evaluation concerning the powers behind the Final Solution.

All of them describe in an anonymous way the annihilation of the Jews; they detail the machinery of destruction. While the historians in general prefer a neutral detached terminology, the Israelis are emotionally involved.

Nevertheless, all historians of this period regard the Jews as passive, who obeyed the Nazis' decrees, and were led to death. The Jews are virtually absent in accounts of their own destruction—especially in the German books. The *death* of the Jews is described. The authors express at length their opinions regarding the question "How did millions die, how did millions accept the verdict?"[107] But almost nothing is said about the Jewish life: their organizations, their struggle to survive, their efforts to resist.

The historians of the first period regard the Jews as passive objects of the destructive Nazi machinery. But their styles differ. Among the Germans, Reitlinger, for example, does not reveal his point of view by direct means; it can be concluded from the emphasis upon the German aspects of his book.

Usually his approach toward the catastrophe of the Jews is neutral and detached. He discloses his opinion when he evaluates the resistance in the Warsaw Ghetto, stating that its "symbolic angle must determine the verdict of history. From this angle, the ghetto rebellion (is a continuation) of Bar Kochba in the reign of Hadrian. It was the precursor of the defence of Jerusalem's 'Old City' and the three invasions of Sinai." He continues: "Accordingly, the ghetto rebellion has become a Jewish epic in its own right, and it must forever remain so."[108] Reitlinger's attitude toward the millions who did not fight like

Bar Kochba may be concluded from this rare piece of emotional confession.

Hilberg bluntly reveals his opinions, saying that he does not intend to dwell on the Jewish suffering, nor to explore the ghetto life: "Insofar as we may examine Jewish institutions, we will do so primarily through the eyes of the Germans: as tools which were used in the destruction process."[109] In order to do so, he specifies the historical patterns of the behavior of the Diaspora Jewry. According to him, there have been four stages of Jewish reaction toward the expressions of anti-Semitism, each stage occurring whenever the previous one had failed them. From "alleviation," the Jews pass through "reaction of evasion, and of flight" and to paralysis; and when all "attempts have been unsuccessful, automatic compliance has been the normal course of action."[110]

The Jewish leadership has been guilty of encouraging these behavior patterns, and thus played its part in hastening the destruction of the Jewish communities.[111] Along with the above described line, Hilberg's attitude toward the Germans in seemingly justified. "The German destruction of the European Jews was a tour de force, the Jewish collapse under the German assault was a manifestation of failure."[112]

The Israeli research-textbooks take different attitudes. Frager tends to present the Holocaust as a historical and ideological conflict between Nazism and Judaism.[113] He expresses pain and agony describing the suffering and the annihilation of the Jews.[114] The passivity of the Jews is explained by the Nazi policy of deceiving and isolating the Jews, helped by the anti-Semites of the occupied countries.[115] To these reasons the historian adds the Jewish adaptability which had been developed during the years in the Diaspora. History encouraged the Jewish tendency to believe that every threat to destroy the Hebrew people has more of a spiritual, social, and economic meaning than a physical one. Therefore, the Jews' reaction to the Nazi plan was unrealistic.[116] Thus their fight was "pseudo-war," "in vain," "worthless conflict." The mistaken reaction prevented the necessary preparation for the real fight against the Final Solution. These opinions are sharpened by the following conclusion: "With all the enormous sorrow involved, we should be cruel to ourselves and say clearly: Those millions who marched in procession into the arms of ruin, if they really were misled by various kinds of illusions, they did it out of a *moral collapse*" (Emphasis mine), because "The commandment to confront the murderer, and to defend oneself—'He who comes to kill you—rise up before and kill him'—is a moral, sublime, and holy commandment."[117]

Tenenbaum also presents the Jews as a passive object, and hardly mentions any internal expression of Jewish life; but unlike the others, he does not reveal his attitude toward these issues—although by reading between the lines we may find a hint of it. In comparison to the others, Eck's book (1976), includes details about the Jewish struggle for life during the Holocaust, and their resistance in ghettos and death camps.[118] This information is spread throughout the central theme of the book, which describes the Nazi machinery of destruction in action.

Finally, it may be stated that all the historians cited are German-centered. They regard the Jews as "objects" rather than as a living and active population. This approach always carries resentment toward the Jews, and sometimes even alienation. It reaches its peak when the Jews are blamed, by several historians, of cooperation with the Nazis in their own destruction.

Eck's book ushers in a new period of Holocaust research. He reflects the opposition of the Israeli historians of the 1960s to the previous historiography. He expresses the changes that were underway in that decade, and probably this is the reason for Eck's ambivalent and hesitant attitude, which is ill defined and lacking in thematic structure.

Though it may have been impossible to grasp the meaning of what happened on "the other planet,"[119] the five historians convey their viewpoint by direct and indirect means. The "intentionalists" warn the post-Holocaust generations of the hypnotizing influence of an ideology which is based on racism and hatred, when inflamed by nationalistic enthusiasm. Those of them who focus on Hitler either state clearly or hint that charisma may turn out to be a mortal danger.[120] They are concerned with the cultural and psychological processes in society, which are beyond the individual's control, and turn him into a murderous robot. The "functionalists" confront the overmechanized state system, which may break loose of its confines and sweep its human operators into madness. This mechanistic approach is clearly recognized by Hilberg: "The bureaucrat of tomorrow is better equipped for mass-murder, than the German Nazis were. The ever-growing capacity for destruction cannot be stopped."[121]

The negativism toward the total power of the German leader, and his ideology and system, turns into rejection of the Jewish passivity and weakness. Reitlinger praises the Warsaw Ghetto resistance, and compares it with ancient and present-day Israeli wars.[122] Hilberg also resents the Jewish passivity, and is of the opinion that it helped the Nazis to annihilate the Jews. He describes ironically the Diaspora Jews who, even after the lesson of the Holocaust, "seek to perfect

their position in society by perfecting the society in which they live,"
but nevertheless established for themselves a place of refuge in Israel.
In his opinion, both methods are bound to fail.[123] According to the
German historians the only realisitc answer to the threat of future
Jewish genocide is by armed force. Like these authors, the Israeli
historians warn against the corrupting power of a racist ideology,
charismatic leaders, and totalitarian systems. They reject Jewish pas-
sivility, while Eck mentions the present active Jewish life.

While Tenenbaum avoids a direct Zionist lesson, Frager surveys
the development of the Jewish self-illusion throughout history, based
on the belief that the existence in the Diapora is possible. This delusion
was shattered by the Holocaust. The lesson of the Holocaust is Zionist,
calling for national ingathering and survival in Eretz-Israel.[124] Eck
expresses his Zionist message through the chapters which describe
the Holocaust survivors striving to reach Eretz-Israel. He states that
the Holocaust was one of the important reasons for establishing the
State of Israel.[125] Thus, while the German historians suggest the
creation of Jewish forces against the power of anti-Semitism, the
Israelis prefer the Zionist option, which includes Jewish military
strength as one characteristic of a normal nation.

The characterization of the discussed research-textbooks can be
concluded with these two questions: Why are these books German-
centered? What are the sociopsychological motives of the authors?
Each question can be subdivided. Friedman[126] named the first decade
of research after the Holocaust as "*Nazi*-centered," because the general
research books were based on the Nazi aspect. However, it seems
preferable to refer to them as *German*-centered. In addition to Nazism,
the German cultural and historical processes are considered in these
books. The German-centered orientation is the result of many factors,
among them the plethora of documents left by the Third Reich. The
German sources were multiplied during the Nuremberg trials, as the
defendants had been collecting and encouraging the publication of
memoirs.[127] The historians' efforts to relate to the vast historical
information, and their closeness in time to the Holocaust resulted in
monographs which sometimes tended to be vague about the historical
process and to have a journalistic nature. The numerous German
sources somehow "supplied" the means of confronting the question
of how a European cultural nation could have committed the Holocaust.

Nolte, Krausnick, Hillgruber, Jaeckel, and Bracher constituted the
"intentionalist" trend in the German historiography which blamed
Hitler and his anti-Semitism for the Final Solution.[128] This trend is
also apparent in the research textbooks of Frager, Tenenbaum, Reitlinger, and Eck. The attack upon the intentionalist school was developed

during the late 1960s, led by the functionalists Broszat and Mommsen. They criticized the narrow, one-sided historical consideration of their seniors, and emphasized the structure and the political processes within the Nazi Reich and movement. Accordingly, Broszat sees Hitler merely as someone around whom the existing forces within the system could coalesce. Mommsen, indeed, states that Hitler actually lost control of the system.[129]

The Hitler-centered orientation of Reitlinger and Hilberg and of the Israeli monographs may have the following moral implication: The Führer cannot be blamed for his corrupt psychopathological demonic personality or mental state, nor can the Germans, who were hypnotized by the leader and his ideology and dutifully obeyed their "betters." The mechanistic-structural approach of the functionalists, explains how the system abolished every moral judgment of the individual—who was robotized by it, and therefore irresponsible for his deeds. The two German research-textbooks do not detail the Jewish suffering, perhaps because of the resentment of disciplined historians toward emotional testimonies, as most of the Jewish sources were in the 1950s, or perhaps because of their complex attitude toward the Jews. In any case, by avoiding the description of human suffering, and the human efforts to live through the Holocaust, they turned the Jews into objects of the German plan, who even helped it by their passivity. While a general warning against another Holocaust, and a lesson for the Jews exist in these books, a specific direct moral point-of-view regarding the Nazis is missing.

The Israeli research-textbooks of the first decade after the Holocaust are influenced by the German historiography and by the Jewish self-experience. This mixture resulted in a dichotomic approach. The German influence tends to clear the Germans of moral responsibility, as opposed to the Jewish suffering and death, which is described with empathy by the authors, and puts the blame on the murderers. The absence of the description of internal Jewish life in the Israeli textbooks can be explained by the technical shortage of documents on this issue, while the shock of the Holocaust released itself in the "outcry-literature." Friedman calls this the Martyrlogical School.[130]

But a martyr knows and justifies his self-sacrifice, while the Jews massacred in the Holocaust did not do so. Neither were they so described in the research-textbooks. They are rather described as a community, misled by its own illusions and by the Nazi policy, which took advantage of their self-delusion, and by the leadership, which practiced self-delusion. Thus, in spite of the pain, the Israeli research-textbooks admit the Jewish complicity in their own destruction. Their basic Zionist belief fits into these historiographical patterns, as Zionism, although it had not foreseen the Holocaust, rebelled against the Diaspora, warning in vain against its possible destruction. This attitude that only Zionism can avoid a future Holocaust may partially explain the absence of a description of Jewish life in the Israeli research-textbooks. Its lack may be considered as manifesting a typical Jewish capacity to adjust to all circumstances, instead of fighting and changing them, as Zionism decrees. It appears that the authors of the research-textbooks used in Israel felt that the conventional discipline of historical research cannot suffice to describe and evaluate the uniqueness of the Holocaust. The ambivalence, the emotionally charged style, or the confused moral attitudes of the research-textbooks expressed their difficulties regarding this theme.

The Judeo-Centered Research-Textbooks

By 1959, Friedman was already calling for a rejection of the Nazi-centered approach in favor of a Judeo-centered one, which would regard the Holocaust merely as one chapter in the whole of Jewish history. The Jews would be seen not as passive victims, but as a living community.[131] After the Eichmann trial of 1961, more and more textbooks began to adopt this approach. The earlier books were general histories for the most part; the newer ones, in addition to these traditional texts (of which Davidowicz and Levin are good examples),[132] also included books in which one aspect of the Holocaust was taken as representative of the whole. Trunk's *Judenrat* is of this kind.[133] In addition, universities in Israel have been recommending collections of prominent historical documents, accompanied by short historical outlines compiled by the editors and there have also been collections of historical essays on various aspects of the day-to-day Jewish struggle to survive.[134]

In some cases, the essays of one historian, as for example those of Bauer, are published. Bauer also has written a more traditional textbook. Although written in English, and meant for non-Israeli students, it has, because of its historical quality, recently been included in a few Israeli reading lists.

The newer books share several characteristics: their authors have broken free of chronological description, and have instead structured their books thematically. This trend is justified by current opinion, which considers that "the vastness of the Holocaust has to be illuminated from various angles, rather than unfolding one story—therefore the frame of the collection of essays is preferred."[135] Perhaps this is the reason why no traditional texts have been published since 1970.

Today's textbooks continue to use German documents when describing and evaluating the German aspects, but unlike their older counterparts, they seriously regard Jewish historical sources of various kinds. Dawidowicz and Levin even include in their works poems, jokes, and reminiscences, to which they impart sociopsychological meaning, helping them to revive the atmosphere of the everyday life.[136]

This multidisciplinary approach rehabilitates the literary sources, and turns them into legitimate tools of the historian's research. The richness and the vividness of the description reflects the historians' concept, which rejects the stereotype of the Jews as passive objects.

The Judeo-centered approach is also seen in the amount of space devoted to the German and Jewish material. Unlike earlier historians, the later ones devote most, if not all, of their works to Jewish aspects. Levin's book is exceptional, not only in the amount of space she devotes to Jewish life, but also in the quality of her work.

The chapters which deal with the Germans still reflect the division beteen the intentionalists and the functionalists, which Kulka, when referring to German historiography, prefers to call "ideological" and "structural."[137]

Although the books are obliged to demonstrate "the mutual influences and interplay of ideology and action, belief and program, national character, political behavior," they have their preferred approaches. When Dawidowicz details Hitler's life, in order to clarify his obsession with the Jews, she tends to the intentionalist point of view.[138]

Gutman, who states in his introduction that the racist Nazi ideology had inevitably to result in the brutal Nazi policy against the Jews, prefers the ideological approach.[139] In Gutman and Rothkirchen, the same angle is presented by four essays about the development of anti-Semitism.[140] Bein, in his essay in this book, makes connections between Hitler's "paranoic fantasies," his "pathological make-up," and the "neurotic age," in which Hitler's distorted beliefs were nurtured.[141] The editors' choice of articles reflects their ideological-intentionalist orientation.

Levin's work tends to be functionalist. More than any other post-1970 author, she details German history. Without declaring so openly, she describes the development of the Final Solution as a process decreed by the chainging situation, when every more extreme step was taken after the former one had failed to get the Jews out.[142] Unlike the other books of recent years, Levin is exceptional in maintaining the German-centered approach; and aside from the Jewish resistance and the rescue efforts, she does not deal with Jewish community life. (Perhaps this is the reason for the relatively rare recommendation of the book in Israeli academic institutions.)

Although Bauer explains Nazi anti-Semitism at length, he avoids the intentionalist approach, and when, for example, he recites Heydrich's order of 1939, or the Nisko plan, or the Madagascar plan, he prefers the functionalist historical evaluation.[143]

All the historians share, however, the recognition that anti-Semitism was fundamental to German history before and during the Third Reich.[144] Sometimes the reader of these books gets the impression that German history is as if subordinated to the Jewish problem, and may wonder if such a description does not unintentionally absorb some degree of anti-Semitic propaganda.

This tendency is strengthened by the post-Holocaust German historians, who certainly have their own reasons for emphasizing the Jewish issue in their national historiography. Perhaps further researches in the history of the Holocaust and the German people will provide some answers to these doubts.[145]

While Friedman demanded a Judeo-centered consideration of the Holocaust, Esh emphasized the goal and the conclusion of this orientation: "the spark of life" was "a glowing blaze, *Kiddush-ha-hayyim*, the sanctification of survival, was more than a phrase; it was reality."[146] Esh relies on Rabbi Nisenbaum, who stated in Warsaw in the years 1940–1941: "This is the hour of *Kiddush-ha-hayyim*, and of the sanctification of God through death. In the past the enemies wanted the soul, and the Jew sacrificed his body in sanctification of His Name (that is to say, he kept precisely what the enemies wished to take from him), now, when the oppressor demands the Jewish body, it is the obligation of the Jew to protect himself, and to keep his life—'I shall not die, but live.'"[147] This interpretation dominates the description and evaluation of the day to day life of the Jews and their reaction to the Nazi policy in all the research textbooks of recent years.[148]

While most of the social, economic, and cultural aspects of Jewish life are covered by the books, the religious one is quite neglected. Michman has, however, explored this area of research.[149] Instead of describing the religious activities during the Holocaust, the textbooks frequently refer to problems of "Faith after the Holocaust" which confronts the question of the existence of God, and the theological meanings of the Jewish catastrophe.[150] The armed resistance was only one of the Jewish reactions and activities during the Holocaust, and is regarded as such in the research-textbooks (only Levin enlarges the description of this issue).

The books of the first decade after the Holocaust referred to the *Judenrat* (Jewish Council) all the stereotypic "Jewish defects." Friedman resented this generalization, and demanded a distinction among the different Jewish councils and a careful consideration of the moral problems involved in the issues. Trunk dedicates his book to these dilemmas, and rejects the previous attitude which blamed the *Judenrat* for their collaboration with the Nazis. He explores the theme from the traditional Jewish *Kehila* (community) structure and development, following the different *Judenrat* in various ghettos, in the changing environments. He concludes with a differentiation between *Judenräte* which were devoted to the needs of their community, and those which exercised their authority for personal needs.

The research into the *Judenrat* opened new areas of Jewish life for the historians, and catalyzed the Judeo-centered trend in the historiography of the Holocaust. This is the reason why Trunk's book, in spite of its limited theme, is used by a large number of Israeli students.

All the historians included in the present essay have accepted the new attitudes toward the *Judenrat* and the Jewish life, while many of them try to explain the sociopsychological and historical patterns of Jewish collective behavior. While the previous textbooks used these "behavior-models" to explain Jewish passivity, the latter ones enlighten the special kind of Jewish activity which originated from the historical and cultural Jewish past. According to them, the *Kiddush-ha-hayyim* (sanctification of life) was the indispensable result of this complex, and the only possible way to fight against the Final Solution. The optimism of the Jews, which was based on their belief in God, or on philosophies and ideologies which believed in the triumph of justice and human rationality, blocked their perception of evil, especially when the Nazis did their utmost to delude them, while everybody else kept silent.

Every research-textbook tries to explain Jewish behavior, most of them directly, as implied here, and some indirectly, as Bauer does. In his textbook[151] he preferred to devote the first chapter to the question of "Who are the Jews?" All these explanations echo the author's respect toward the Jewish standing during the Holocaust. In many ways the attitudes and the opinions of the historians, as apparent in these textbooks, carry also a moral message. The warning against another Holocaust calls for human values and individual responsibility, as realized in a democratic system. Levin's book and the Israeli textbooks add a Zionist angle to the general moral orientation, which connects the Holocaust and the Jewish survival in Eretz-Israel, without necessarily conditioning the establishment of a Jewish State by the outcome of the Holocaust.[152] It is only appropriate to mention that despite the newer textbooks, the old ones remain in use.[153] Thus, it is up to the instructors to make students aware of the newer trends.

The later textbooks reject the dominant tendency in the description of the Germans before and during the Holocaust; they oppose the centrality of the German aspects; they negate a generalization of any kind, contradicting the "passivity" of the Jews and the antipathy toward them.

The new research-textbooks adopt the Judeo-centered attitude, as well as analytic disciplinary methods of research. They prefer to emphasize the complexity of the situation and process, and to reject simplified generalizations.[154]

Some Reasons for Changes in Approach

According to Kulka, from the 1960s onward, the German historians (Nolte, Jäckel, Hillgraber) have developed a growing awareness of the centrality of the Jewish issue in the Nazi movement. The opposing trend has stressed the irrelevance or marginality of ideology as reflected in the political decisionmaking process, but nevertheless has recognized the important place of the Jewish problem within the internal dynamics which led, by their own rule of development, to the Final Solution (Mommsen, Höhne, Adam).

Broszat adheres to the same approach by striving to synthesize the two methodologically and conceptually opposed approaches.[155] In contrast to the described developing schools, no progress has been made by the German historians regarding the internal Jewish life during the Holocaust.[156] Furthermore, in various countries the "revisionist trend" has appeared, which denies the Holocaust and its historical significance. Writers like Rassinier, Butz, and App have supplied a pseudo-thesis to many anonymous pamphlets of the same spirit, published in France, England, Germany and the U.S.A.[157]

The German historians' attitude toward the European Jewry during the Holocaust, the lack of information about the internal life of this population, and the revisionists' efforts to deny the Holocaust were the motivating force behind the changes in approach. Only a well-proven historical description of Jews living, suffering, and dying may contradict the anti-Semitic-revisionist plot. This mission has been carried out by the Judeo-centered historians. Probably the growing distance in time from the Holocaust has blurred the pain and made the composition of memories of historical value possible. By the same rule, it has helped the historians to explore these fields.

The Eichmann trial revived worldwide interest in the history of the Holocaust, and encouraged and supported research work on the subject. Bauer (1984) rejects any direct connection between the history of the State of Israel and the tendencies within the Holocaust historiography, apart from the correlation between crises and the increasing amount of research work on the subject.[158] But it seems to me that historians have to some degree been influenced by their time and place. The public reactions of the Holocaust historians on social, cultural, and political Israeli issues may support this assumption.[159] As it appears, the emphasis on the Jewish struggle for an everyday human life is a manifesto against militaristic tendencies, which reflect more than historiographical opinions. The present analysis cannot include all the possible reasons for the newer Judeo-centered trend, nor the meaningful correlative connections among them. These issues, and many others, concerning the neglect of the religious life during the Holocaust, are proper themes for other researchers. The present essay has to be content with exploring the development of Israeli textbooks during the years 1948 to 1984.

Although the Israeli academic teachers reject the usage of regular textbooks in the universities, stating that their students are more prepared to study the Holocaust than the students outside Israel because of their highschool background. Israeli students nevertheless receive very few hours of general modern history in high school, and even their knowledge of Jewish history is quite fragmentary and superficial, thanks to the vastness of information they are obliged to absorb by the State matriculation system. The years of army service remove Israeli youngsters from books, and confront them with existential problems of life and death. To return from such experiences to academic studies is rather difficult. Therefore, an ordinary textbook, which includes basic information about the general, German, and Jewish history, and well structured descriptions of the Holocaust, can be of great help in the introductory phase of study.[160]

All the research-textbooks used in Israel deal in different ways with moral issues. More than any other historical chapter, the Holocaust embodies fundamental existential human problems. Although the newer textbooks reject demonization of Hitler and the Nazis, they cannot avoid it completely while describing the horrors or analyzing its machinery. The explanation of the ultimate evil is beyond human capacity, and therefore they turn to metaphysical terms, when referring to it.

Future textbooks have to include chapters about the religious life during the Holocaust, and the reactions of the Jews in Palestine and the U.S.A. toward European Jewry. Although these issues are emotionally loaded, they will in time find their way into the textbooks, just as the subject of the *Judenrat* did. Modern historiography tends to synthesize various academic fields into a rich multidisciplinary historical description and evaluation. While Dawidowicz and Levin use these symbiotic tools in their books, the Israeli historians are more conservative. But even the criteria of qualitative evaluation of historiography change with time.

9
Conclusion

The present essay covers the Holocaust as dealt with in 54 textbooks which were used in Israel during the years 1948–1984. Twenty-two of them are *Mikra'ot*, 21 are history-textbooks, and 11 are research-textbooks. Many articles about the teaching of the Holocaust were published in Israel, and for a long time few, if any, dealt with the subject as they appear in different textbooks; therefore, the present work is the first of its kind in Israel. The textbooks included in this framework are different in structure and in quality, which changed during the period under study.

The *Mikra'ot* are literary collections, which have changed comparatively slightly with time. Seldom do they integrate the Holocaust in various other topics, and frequently they devote a whole chapter to it. Until the late 1970s, the Holocaust was just one epoch among others in modern Jewish history, as described in standard-history textbooks, and since then special books were dedicated to it. These are of two kinds. Most of them are of narrative character, while others are collections of historical sources and excerpts from essays. Each of the research-textbooks is entirely centered on this subject, including many kinds of forms; from monographs to collections of primary sources and essays to specific research-work, and even one academic textbook.

Besides their variety, the research-textbooks are the only ones which include non-Hebrew and non-Israeli textbooks.

The Holocaust in all these textbooks is presented in accordance with the conception shown in Table 1.

The educational system is cyclic. It assumes that the same subject will be repeated, with each cycle introducing material for a higher educational level. But at the same time, note that there is an inverse variation between the emotional and the cognitive levels, shown in Table 2.

In spite of the *Mikra'ot* authors' efforts to minimize the description of death and physical suffering, they aspire emotionally to impress

Table 1

Structural characterizations of the Holocaust in textbooks	Age of reader
Usually the subject does not appear in books meant for the three first grades, or appears in other topics. The orientation is ritual.	6-9
The separate chapter about the Holocaust includes stories about children, in addition to the ritual part.	9-12
The stories about children and the ritual parts have sometimes a general historical explanation as their background.	12-14
The history of the Holocaust is described chronologically, using literary sources or elaborated historical sources. The subject is integrated in modern Jewish history.	14-17
The subject is presented on a chronological thematic level, including pieces of primarily historical sources. The Holocaust is studied as a part of Jewish history, even when a special book is being used.	17-18
The Holocaust is described, analyzed and evaluated on an academic level. Presented as part of Jewish history, open to professional specialization of historians.	Adult

Table 2

Emotional Level	Cognitive Level	Readers
A high level of emotional pressure	A low level of rational analysis	children
A gradual lowering of the emotional impact	The rational analytic level becomes higher with the age of the students	adolescents and adults

the pupils by describing the lives of children during the Holocaust. All the other textbooks deal by analytic means with the larger aspects of collective Jewish catastrophe, which by definition is less emotionally involving.

This model is probably based on a belief that attitudes instilled in young children will last for life, and that children are not capable of historical analysis. But how can the authors and/or editors be sure that the chosen stories arouse the children's empathy?

Furthermore, childhood is not solely an age of "emotions," nor should the Holocaust be studied by adolescents and adults only on an "analytic" level. The Holocaust belongs to history, but at the same time it involves great human moral issues. Therefore, it has to be considered emotionally and cognitively, at every age and in appropriate proportions. The conception outlined above emerged from the textbooks and teaching methods in classrooms, rather than from a well-planned centralistic state policy. The authors of the Mikra'ot and the textbooks were until recent years privately paid individuals usually senior teachers. The Israeli Minister of Education has adjusted itself to the situation, or responded to public criticism concerning the teaching of the Holocaust.

The archives of the Ministry of Education are loaded with private and public demands to enlarge the studies of the Holocaust. These demands have even reached the Knesset.[161] But only a few months before Eichmann's capture, senior officials of Yad Vashem and the Ministry of Education started to consider the issue.[162] Even then it took another eleven years until the Ministry of Education required instructors to teach the subject according to required curricula.

To this day, there is no official textbook about the Holocaust for elementary schools, and the four history textbooks for high schools were supported and approved by the Ministry of Education, but had been written outside its auspices. Only one intermediate, nonreligious textbook has been written by officials of the Ministry of Education (From War to War). All the textbooks in Israel are under the control of the Ministry of Education, which provides every year an official list of required and supplementary books. The lately growing centralization and supervision of the Ministry of Education, its financial help for approved authors, and its subsidized prices have actually served to abolish any possibility that a private author can compete with the state system. As a result, the choice of textbooks may be narrowed.

In contrast to the situation in the state schools, Israeli universities are completely free from any governmental interference.

The comparison of the different textbooks reveals a division between the books of the immediate postwar and more recent years, with the period of the Eichmann trial serving as a transition. The changes in the *Mikra'ot* are less prominent than in other books, but the history textbooks had their "Zionist period" (1948–1977), and their "humanistic period" (1977–1983). Since 1983 they have expressed a symbiotic tendency. The research textbooks have exchanged their German-centered orientation (1947–1970), for a Judeo-centered approach (1970–1984).

It is quite astonishing that the *Mikra'ot* were the first to express the Jewish heroism of everyday life, while the history textbooks were obsessed with the honor-shame issue, and the research textbooks presented the Jews as passive victims. The authors and/or editors of the *Mikra'ot*, who were also directed by pedagogical needs, presented the Holocaust through the eyes of children, necessarily emphasizing the heroism of human survival. Therefore, the *Mikra'ot* represent a more balanced approach to the armed resistance than early history textbooks, and they adopted a Judeo-centered orientation far earlier than did academic books. Perhaps this is one of the reasons for the stability of the *Mikra'ot*.

Another reason may be the Israeli attitude to educational issues of the young children; since they are far from the age of political voting, service in the army, and paying taxes, they are not in the first priority of public interest. The few articles written about the problems of teaching the Holocaust in elementary schools, the near absence of public criticism about this subject, and the postponing of publishing state-sponsored books prove this assumption. On the other hand, Israeli adolescents are taken more seriously. Their opinions and criticisms are listened to, and very often published. Almost all the activities of persons and institutions have been in connection with adolescents, because the Israeli youngster is supposed to carry on the Zionist vision, often endangering his own life through the process. Therefore, the Holocaust in history textbooks also functions as a means of Zionist socialization, reflecting the changes which have taken place in the Israeli society concerning this goal.

In the first period, the history textbooks stressed the armed resistance and the Zionist lesson; in the second period they preferred to stress democratic human values, even at the expense of the Zionist lesson. Today, they try to integrate and balance different angles. Thus, the history textbooks, more than any other kind, reflect the changing attitudes of the Israeli society toward the Holocaust.

While the *Mikra'ot* have been directed by pedagogical needs, and subordinated to the national goals, and while the history textbooks have reflected the changing Israeli attitudes toward the Holocaust, the research-textbooks have been least influenced by the needs of the students and society. They derive their inspiration from the research, starting with the German historiography, and concluding with the creation of an autonomous Jewish school, which turned Israel into the world center of the Holocaust research. Although the first obligation of the historians has been toward the discipline of historiography, it is doubtful if the Judeo-centered orientation would have developed without the personal, as well as the professional, needs of the historians to explore this field. Thus, while the high school textbooks originate from Israeli-Jewish roots, the research-textbooks had to free themselves from the outside German influence. This is the reason why the earlier ones contain no expression of the day to day Jewish heroism nor of the centrality of the Warsaw Ghetto resistance.

It seems that until 1983 the three sorts of textbooks were developing along almost different paths, without any mutual enrichment. The historians did not direct the composition and the teaching methods of the Holocaust in schools, because when they started to develop their own research in the 1960s, there were already many textbooks which had a fixed orientation toward the subject. Later on, the historians satisfied themselves with occasional criticism about the schools' failure to teach the subject. Only in recent years have a few historians, with pedagogical backgrounds, started to compose history textbooks about the Holocaust. These historians have had to make a compromise between the needs of the Israeli society and of academic disciplines. Very often educational goals have been sacrificed to national goals. Therefore, even today's textbooks cannot guarantee an open attitude toward the Holocaust: open to controversial issues, open to "unpleasant" phenomena, and open to different evaluations. The academic historians may in their textbooks strengthen the dichotomy between the "emotional" approach meant for young children, and the cognitive approach meant for adolescents. By doing so they may block a multidisciplinary attitude toward the Holocaust.

I would suggest a "dis-harmonic *Gestalt*" approach toward the Holocaust in future Israeli textbooks. Gestalt psychology considers the human being as one unit, physically and psychologically, emotionally and rationally. It rejects any theory which believes in an arithmetic combination of different human functions and needs, or any priority of one characteristic over the functioning of all the others. The Gestalt aims to free the individual from inward blocks, widening his self-awareness and functioning. On its behalf, I call upon textbook authors to face courageously the dis-harmony of the failure and the triumph of human beings, as revealed during the Holocaust. Human wholeness does not lie within aspired harmony, but in its opposite. Paradoxically, the tension, the ambiguity, and the unanswered questions, which are seldom enlightened by moments of understanding, are the real harmonic essence of humanity.

An open, multidisciplinary description of the Holocaust will not need indoctrinary lessons. Such content will, by its own merits, encourage Zionist-humanistic-Jewish attitudes. They will emerge from the emotional and the cognitive autonomic personality of students, loaded with their constant inward lifetime conflicts and moral sensitivity—as the human Gestalt determines.

Thus, the present work should be read not only as an analysis of the development of textbooks, but as an illuminator of the processes of socialization and culturization within the Isreali society. The Holocaust cannot be left to the historians. It has to stay alive in the consciousness of the population, and therefore it is important that future textbooks will be improved. I hope that the modest present research may contribute to this end.

Notes

1. Yehuda Bauer, *The Holocaust in Historical Perspective.* Seattle: University of Washington Press, 1978, 181 p.

2. Philip K. Boden, *Promoting International Understanding Through School Textbooks.* N.p.: George Eckert Institute for International Textbook Research, 1977, 54 p.; Walter Mertineit, "Strategies, Concepts and Methods of International History Textbook Revision." *International Journal of Political Education,* Amsterdam, vol. 2, no. 2, Apr. 1979, pp. 101–115; O. Ernest Schuddekopf, *History Teaching and History Textbook Revision.* Strasbourg: Council for Cultural Cooperation of Council of Europe, 1967, 235 p.; UNESCO, "Better History Textbooks." *In: UNESCO and Its Program.* Paris, 1950, 29 p.

3. Ruth Firer, *Todaah ve'Yedia* (Formation and Information). Dissertation, The Hebrew University of Jerusalem, 1980, 385 p.

4. David Pratt, *How to Find and Measure Bias in Textbooks.* New Jersey: 1972, 50 p.

5. Bernard Berelson, *Content Analysis in Communication Research.* Glencoe, Ill.: Free Press, 1952, p. 210.

6. P. Boden, pp. 17–26.

7. The Israeli Ministry of Education has published three kinds of instructions, concerning textbooks: A. General instructions and criteria for the confirmation of textbooks and auxiliary books. B. Questionnaires handed to the specialists for the evaluation of the books. C. Annual publications of the approved and recommended list of textbooks and auxiliary books.

8. The Holocaust is covered in different chapters: S. Zalman Ariel, Moshe Blich *and* Natan Perski, *Mikra'ot Israel* (Israeli Reader). Jerusalem: Massada, 1960, 2d ed. 1958, pp. 158–163; Bezalel Veksler *and* Abraham Rosen, *Arugot* (Garden Beds). Tel Aviv: Amichy, 1961, pp. 56–61; 132–137; Yitzhak Piter, *Mikra's Hadasha* (New Reader). Jerusalem: Kiriat Sefer, 1962, p. 92; Ministry of Education, *Leket Hemed LaYamim Hanorim.* (Lovely Collection—For the High Days). Jerusalem: T'al, 1978, pp. 6–10.

9. S. Zalman Ariel, Moshe Blich *and* Natan Perski, *Mikra'ot Israel* (Israeli Reader). Jerusalem: Massada, 1959, pp. 239–240.

10. Jeshua Teberski *and* Alexander Malkiel, *Halichot Israel* (Manners of Israel). Tel Aviv: Amichy, 1961, p. 192.

11. The often used diaries are those by Yitzchak Rodashavsky, Moshe Flinker, Eva Heiman, and Anna Frank.

12. See the poems cited in Arieh Buchner, Yehuda Levynton *and* Levin Kippnis, *Sefer Hakita Zaien* (Book for the Seventh Grade). Tel Aviv: Drir, 1965, pp. 260–262, Z. Moshe Efrati *and* Naftali Melumad, *Psiot* (Steps). Tel Aviv: Yavneh, 1953 (2d ed. 1958), pp. 374–376.

13. On the issue of children supporting adults, see S. Zalman Ariel, Moshe Blich *and* Natan Perski, *Mikra'ot Israel* (Israeli Reader). Jerusalem: Massada, 1963, p. 335; A. Buchner, Y. Levynton *and* L. Kippnis, *Sefer Hakita Zaien*, pp. 275–278; S. Z. Ariel, M. Blich *and* N. Perski, *Mikra'ot Israel*, 1960, pp. 161–162.

14. *Ibid.*

15. For example: Perski, 1978 (III) 278–280.

16. On children in bands, see Natan Perski, *Mikra'ot Israel Hadashot* (New Israeli Readers). Ramat Gan: Massada, 1978 pp. 278–280, A. Buchner, Y. Levynton *and* L. Kippnis, *Sefer Hakita Zaien*, pp. 265–267, and N. Perski, *Mikra'ot Israel Hadashot* (New Israeli Readers). Ramat Gan: Massada, 1978, pp. 286–289.

17. On the sanctification of life, and of God's name, see Z. Moshe Efrati *and* Naftali Melumad, *Psiot Hadashot* (New Steps). Tel Aviv: Yaveneh, 1963, pp. 169–171; Z. Efrati and N. Melumad, *Psiot* (Steps). Tel Aviv: Yavneh, 1956, p. 229; S. Ariel, M. Blich *and* N. Perski, 1956, pp. 429, 432, 442–446; Dvorah Bergman, *Neta'im* (Plants). Tel Aviv: Karni, 1969, p. 160.

18. On the issue of self-endangerment for the sake of religion, see S. Z. Ariel, M. Blich and N. Perski, *Mikra'ot Israel*, 1960, pp. 161–162, 427–430; S. Z. Ariel, M. Blich and N. Perski, *Mikra'ot Israel*, 1958, p. 432; Levin Kippnis, Arieh Buchner *and* Yehuda Levynton, *Sefer ha'Kita Vave*. Tel Aviv: Drir, 1964 (2d ed. 1967), pp. 286–290; Ministry of Education, "H'emed," 1980, p. 20; Ministry of Education, "H'emed," 1978, p. 7.

19. Z. Moshe Efrati *and* Naftali Melumad, *Psiot* (Steps). Tel Aviv: Yavneh, 1956, p. 229.

20. S. Zalman Ariel, Moshe Blich *and* Natan Perski, *Mikra'ot Israel* (Israeli Reader). Jerusalem: Massada, 1956, pp. 429, 432.

21. Dvorah Bergman, *Neta'im*, p. 160.

22. On the end of resistance in the Warsaw Ghetto, see S. Z. Ariel, M. Blich *and* N. Perski, *Mikra'ot Israel*, 1960, pp. 471–474; Bezalel Veksler *and* Abraham Rosen, *Arugot* (Garden Beds). Tel Aviv: Amichy, 1966, pp. 56–58; Z. Moshe Efrati *and* Naftali Melumad, *Psiot*, 1953, pp. 378–380; S. Zalman Ariel, Moshe Blich *and* Natan Perski, *Mikra'ot Israel*, 1958, pp. 471–474.

23. On the symbolic meaning of the Warsaw Ghetto Uprising, see footnote 22. See also Z. M. Efrati *and* N. Melumad, *Psiot*, 1956, p. 222.

24. The expressions of open resistance appear frequently in Perski's books. See, for example, his *Mikra'ot Israel Hadashot*, 1978, pp. 289–292, which includes references to resistance in Treblinka and Sobibor. The textbook is designed for children in the 9–10 age groups.

25. S. Z. Ariel, M. Blich *and* N. Perski, *Mikra'ot Israel*, 1960, pp. 282–283.

26. Y. Piter, pp. 92, 99–100.

27. Z. M. Efrati *and* N. Melumad, *Psiot*, 1956, p. 222.

28. On children during the Warsaw Ghetto Uprising, see Arieh Buchner, Yehuda Levynton *and* Levin Kippnis, *Sefer ha'Kita Zalen*, 1965, pp. 269–274; Raphael Balgor, *Yesodoth* (Foundations). Tel Aviv: A Karni, 1966, pp. 20–23; S. Z. Ariel, M. Blich *and* N. Perski, *Mikra'ot Israel*, 1960, pp. 284–289.

29. Levin Kippnis, Arieh Buchner *and* Yehuda Levynton, *Sefer ha'Kita Gimel* (The Book for the Third Grade). Tel Aviv: Drir and Sefer, 1962, p. 205.

30. Psalm 83:17.

31. S. Z. Ariel, M. Blich *and* N. Perski, *Mikra'ot Israel*, 1956, p. 446.

32. A. Buchner, Y. Levynton *and* L. Kippnis, *Sefer ha'Kita Zaien*, p. 280. See also M. Efrati *and* N. Melumad, *Psiot Hadashot*, pp. 166–167, 174; Z. M. Efrati *and* N. Melumad, *Psiot*, 1953, p. 381; A. Buchner, Y. Levynton *and* L. Kippnis, *Sefer Hakita Zaien*, p. 278; and Natan Perski, *Mikra'ot Israel Hadashot*, p. 280.

33. Ytzhak Feler, *Netivot* (Pathways). Jerusalem: Kiriat Sefer, 1953, p. 285.

34. Paris De Binjamin *and* Jeshua Teberski, *Halichot* (Manners). Tel Aviv: Teberski, p. 253.

35. R. Balgor, p. 23.

36. *Ibid.*

37. On stories about the "Seder" in the Kibbutz, see L. Kippnis, A. Buchner *and* Y. Levynton, *Sefer ha'Kita Vave*, 1967 (1964), pp. 286–290; A. Buchner, Yehuda Levynton *and* L. Kippnis, *Sefer ha'Kita Zaien*, pp. 269–274.

38. On the theme of children dreaming about Eretz-Israel, see S. Z. Ariel, M. Blich *and* N. Perski, *Mikra'ot Israel*, 1963, p. 332; D. Bergman, p. 160; N. Perski, *Mikra'ot Israel Hadashot*, 1978, pp. 284–285.

39. D. Bergman, p. 160.

40. On the theme of children saved after the Holocaust, see S. Z. Ariel, M. Blich *and* N. Perski, *Mikra'ot Israel*, 1963, pp. 328–329; N. Perski, *Mikra'ot Israel Hadashot*, 1978, pp. 294–295; S. M. Efrati *and* N. Melumad, *Psiot*, 1953, pp. 350–353; L Kippnis, A. Buchner and Y. Levynton, *Sefer ha'Kita Vave*, pp. 279–283.

41. On the theme of children in Israel remembering their experience during the Holocaust, see M. Efrati *and* N. Melumad, *Psiot*, 1958 (1953), pp. 350–358; M. Efrati *and* N. Melumad, *Psiot Hadashot*, pp. 283–289; Arieh Buchner, Yehuda Levynton *and* Levin Kippnis, *Sefer ha'Kita Dalet* (Book For the Fourth Grade). Tel Aviv: Drir, 1954, pp. 286–290. See also ft. 37.

42. Natan Perski, *Mikra'ot Israel Hadashot* (New Israeli Readers). Ramat Gan: Massada, 1977, p. 259.

43. Dvora Koubovi, "Therapeutic Teaching of Literature During the War and Its Aftermath." *In: Stress and Anxiety.* Edited by D. Charles Spiedberger *and* G. Irwin Sarason. New York: Hemisphere Publishing Corporation, 1982, vol. 8, p. 347.

44. Sara Smilanski, *Tfisat Ha'maret Beainai Yaladim* (Conception of Death by Children). Haifa: "Ahe," 1981, p. 103.

45. *Ibid.*, p. 110.

46. The change in attitude is apparent in Perski's textbooks, which emphasize the deaths of the children at the end of the stories. N. Perski, 1977, pp. 272–277; N. Perski, 1978, pp. 273–276. For details of the resistance in Treblinka and Sobibor for children aged 9–10, see N. Perski, 1978, pp. 289–292.

47. This paragraph is based on conversations with people working in the Curriculum Department of the Ministry of Education and with teachers and headmasters in Jerusalem, 1984.

48. For further details on various issues in textbooks from 1900–1980, see R. Firer, *Todaah ve'Yedia.*

49. Based on quantitative checking.

50. Very few authors mention their intentions or explain their way of writing; thus all the evaluation in this article came from this writer.

51. See D. Pratt.

52. All the translations from Hebrew are mine. Baruch Avivi *and* Natan Perski, *Toldot Amenu* (History of Our Nation). Vol. IV. Jerusalem: Zionist Organization, 1975, pp. 53–63, 68.

53. *Ibid.,* vol. V, p. 245.

54. Yitshak Spivak *and* Moshe Avidor, *Am Israel Be'artzo u'Banechar* (Jewish Nation in Its Country and in the Diaspora). Vol. IV. Tel Aviv: Massada, 1948, pp. 4, 185.

55. L. Shimshon Kirshenbaum, *Toldot Am Israel Bedorem* (History of the Israeli Nation in Our Generation). Tel Aviv: Omanut, 1965, Vol. I, pp. 127, 189.

56. Effraim Shemuali, *Toldot Amenu Bazman Hahadash* (History of Our Nation in the Modern Period). Tel Aviv: Yavneh, 1970, vol. V. pp. 11–12.

57. Shlomo Horovitz, *Kiztur Toldot Yisrael Baet H'Hadach'a* (Summary of the History of Israel in the Modern Period). Haifa: Beit Hasefer Ha'reali, 1961, Vol. 1, p. 127.

58. Chaim Schatzker, "Bayot Didactiot Behora'at Hasho'a" (Didactical Considerations in Teaching the Holocaust). Ramat Gan, no. 2, 1961; Arieh Carmon, "Teaching the Holocaust as a Means of Fostering Values." *Curriculum Inquiry,* Jerusalem, vol. 9, no. 3, Fall 1979.

59. For more details, see, R. Firer, *Todaah ve'Yedia,* pp. 167–171.

60. Y. Spivak *and* M. Avidor, vol. II.

61. L. Kirshenbaum, *Toldot Am Israel Bedorem,* Vol. 2, p. 278.

62. Although many articles were published in Israel on methods of teaching the Holocaust to religious students, religious textbooks are quite similar to the secular ones.

63. Moshe Katan, *Toldot Ha'Yehudim Mimihemet Ha'olam Harishona ve'Ad Yamenu* (The History of the Jews From the First World War to Our Time). Jerusalem: Kiryat Sepher, 1958, p. 178.

64. See P. Boden; W. Mertineit; R. Multhoff, "The Experience of Brunswik International Textbook Institute, in the Field of History Textbook Revision During the Last 20 Years" (Synopsis); O. E. Schuddekopf; UNESCO.

65. Most of them are in Hebrew; for references in English, see Yehuda Bauer, *The Holocaust in Historical Perspective.* Seattle: University of Washington

Press, 1978; A. Carmon, "Teaching the Holocaust as a Means of Fostering Values"; Chaim Shatzker, "The Holocaust in Israeli Education." *International Journal of Political Education*, vol. 5, no. 1, Apr. 1982.

66. It is interesting to note the connection between the official announcement and the film "The Holocaust" on Israeli TV. About its impact, see Hannah Levinsonn, "The Television Series 'Holocaust' in Israel." *International Journal of Political Education*, Amsterdam, vol. 4, no. 1/2, May 1981, pp. 151–161.

67. In accordance with the Israeli system, by which various subjects entitled the student to a certain number of points in the matriculation examinations.

68. Shmuel Ettinger, *Ha'Anti Shemiut Baet Ha'Hadasha* (Anti-Semitism in Modern Times). Tel Aviv: Sifriat Hapoalim, 1978.

69. In Israel—see footnote 64 and Herman J. Blumberg, "Some Problems in Teaching the Holocaust." *The Reconstructionist*, New York, vol. 34, no. 16, Dec. 1968, pp. 13–20; Hillel Klein *and* Uriel Last, "Cognitive and Emotional Aspects of Attitudes of American and Jewish Youth Toward the Victims of the Holocaust." *Israeli Annual of Psychiatry and Related Disciplines*, Jerusalem, vol. 12, no. 2, June 1974, pp. 111–131; Alan Rosenberg *and* Jack Zerin, Teaching About the Holocaust as Part of a Genocidal Universe." *Social Studies*, vol. 72, no. 3, May-June 1981, pp. 107–110; and K. Dianne Roskins, *Teaching the Holocaust to Children*. New York: Ktav, 1975.

70. Like in the booklet enclosed in the textbook: "From Rome til the Beginning of the New Period," p. 51.

71. Descriptions of physical suffering appear in almost every chapter in this textbook.

72. As long as there is no research on the cognitive attitudes of the students toward these two books, we cannot offer any explanation about the nature of the psychological transition from a logical attitude to an emotional one.

73. For more about the author's intentions and purposes see A. Carmon, "Teaching the Holocaust as a Means of Fostering Values," and Chaim Schatzker, "The Teaching of the Holocaust: Dilemmas and Considerations." *The Annals of the American Academy of Political and Social Science*, Philadelphia, vol. 450, July 1980, pp. 218–226; and C. Schatzker, "The Holocaust in Israeli Education."

74. A. Carmon, "Teaching the Holocaust as a Means of Fostering Values," and C. Schatzker, "The Teaching of the Holocaust: Dilemmas and Considerations." This aspect is strongly emphasized by researchers outside Israel, like M. George Krene *and* Leo Rapport, *The Holocaust and the Crisis of Human Behavior*. New York: Holmes & Meier, 1980; and A. Rosenberg *and* J. Zerin.

75. A. Carmon, *Ha'Shoa* (The Holocaust). Jerusalem: Ministry of Education, 1980, vol. 2, p. 290.

76. A. Carmon, *Ha'Shoa*, already included the issue in his textbook, but he did not emphasize it, as the latter textbooks do.

77. Yisrael Gutman *and* Chaim Shtazker, *Ha'Shoa u'Mashmauta* (The Holocaust and Its Meaning). Jerusalem: Merkaz Shazar, 1983. See teacher's guidebook, 1983, p. 17.

78. *Ibid.*, pp. 74, 123, 150–152.

79. Arieh Morgenstern, *ed.*, *Mekorot ve'Mechkarim al Ha'shoah.* (Sources and Researches About the Holocaust). Tel Aviv: Ministry of Education, 1983, p. 3.

80. *Ibid.*, p. 221.

81. *Ibid.*, pp. 321–325.

82. Jacob Talman, "Ha'historia Ha'Eropeit Kereka la'sho'ah" (The European History as the Background of the Holocaust). *In: Ha'shoah ve' Hatkuma* (The Holocaust and the Revival). Jerusalem: Yad Vashem, 1974, p. 22.

83. R. Firer, *Todaah ve'Yedia.*

84. See M. Alexander Dushkin, "Ma Ne'asa Lehanchlat Lekeh ha'Sho'a" (What Is Done to Transfer the Lesson of the Holocaust?) *In: Hora'at ha'Sho'a Bebeit ha'Sefer* (Teaching the Holocaust in School). Jerusalem: Ministry of Education, 1961, pp. 7–10; Meir Dvorzetski, "Hataluma shel ei Yediat ha'sho'a" (The Mystery of the Absence of Knowledge About the Holocaust). *In: Hora'at ha'sho'a Bebeit Hasefer* (Teaching the Holocaust in School). Jerusalem: Ministery of Education, 1961, pp. 11–15; Sara Neshamit, *Letoldot ha'sho'ah ve'Hameri* (History of Holocaust and Resistance). Beit Lohamei Haghetta'ot, 1961, pp. 61–65.

85. Chaim Shatzker, *ed.*, *Antishemiut ve'Shoah* (Anti-Semitism and Holocaust). Jerusalem: Hebrew University, Ministry of Education, 1977; Arieh Carmon, *Ha'Shoa* (The Holocaust). Jerusalem: Ministry of Education, 1980, 2 vols.

86. C. Shatzker, "The Holocaust in Israeli Education," p. 80, uses the term "Instrumental Function."

87. C. Shatzker, ed., *Antishemiut ve'Shoah;* A. Carmon, *Ha'Shoa.*

88. Y. Gutman *and* C. Shatzker, *Ha'Shoa u'Mashmauta.*

89. A. Morgenstern, *ed.*

90. Based on conversations with Prof. Yehuda Bauer (April 11, 1984), and Prof. Yisrael Gutman (May 2, 1984) in Jerusalem.

91. Yehuda Bauer, *A History of the Holocaust.* New York: Franklin, Watts, 1982.

92. English is the first foreign language required in the Israeli educational system. Other languages are needed for high-level specialization in the universities.

93. Conversation with Prof. Gutman (May 2, 1984), in Jerusalem.

94. Moshe Frager, *Hurban Israel Be'Eropa* (The Destruction of Jews in Europe). Tel Aviv: Ha'kibbutz Ha'Meuhad, 1947; Joseph Tenenbaum, *Race and Reich.* New York: Wayne, 1956, Raul Hilberg, *The Destruction of the European Jews.* Chicago: Quadrangle, 1961; Gerald Reitlinger, *The Final Solution.* New York: A. S. Barnes, 1968; Natan Eck, *Shoat ha'am ha'Yehudi be'Airopa.* (The Holocaust of the Jewish People in Europe). Jerusalem: Yad Vashem, 1976.

95. R. Hilberg.

96. Tim Mason's suggestions for grouping, in R. Christopher Browning, Approaches to the Final Solution in German Historiography of the Last Two

Decades. *The Fifth International Historical Conference on the Historiography of the Holocaust.* Jerusalem: Yad Vashem, Apr. 1983.

97. Andreas Hillgruber, *Hitlers Strategie: Politik und Kriegsfuehrung 1940–41.* Frankfurt, 1965, pp. 519, 524–25. See also Hillgruber's "Die Endloesung und das deutsche Ostimperium als Kernstueck des rassenideologischen Programms des Nationalsozialismus," *Vierteljahrshefte fuer Zeitgeschichte,* Munich, vol. XX, no. 2, 1972, pp. 133–53.

98. G. Reitlinger, p. 5; N. Eck, pp. 17, 207; M. Frager, p. 67;

99. J. Tenenbaum, p. 212.

100. G. Reitlinger, pp. 3, 6.

101. M. Frager, pp. 18–22.

102. J. Tenenbaum, p. 13.

103. *Ibid.,* p. 2.

104. *Ibid.,* p. 4.

105. See the references to Broszat and Mommsen in R. C. Browning, p. 6.

106. R. Hilberg, p. v.

107. M. Frager, p. 238.

108. G. Reitlinger, p. 203.

109. R. Hilberg, p. v.

110. *Ibid.,* pp. 14, 16.

111. *Ibid.,* p. 17.

112. *Ibid.,* p. v.

113. M. Frager, p. 17.

114. *Ibid.,* pp. 188–191.

115. *Ibid.,* p. 240.

116. *Ibid.,* p. 246.

117. *Ibid.,* pp. 247–249.

118. N. Eck, pp. 60, 74, 136–137, 246–250, 253–254, 255, 269–272, 333.

119. Term used by Yehiel Dinu ("Katzetnik") in his references to Auschwitz. See his testimony at the Eichmann trial in *Eduyot Ha'yoetz Ha'mishpati; Ha'memshalah neged Adolf Eichmann.* Jerusalem, 1963, pp. 122–123.

120. M. Frager, pp. 17, 18; G. Reitlinger, pp. 3, 6; J. Tenenbaum, p. 5.

121. R. Hilberg, p. 760.

122. G. Reitlinger, p. 293.

123. R. Hilberg, pp. 763, 765.

124. M. Frager, pp. 242–246, 256.

125. N. Eck, pp. 342, 349.

126. Philip Friedman, "Preliminary and Methodological Problems of the Research on the Jewish Catastrophe in the Nazi Period." *In: Yad Vashem Studies,* vol. 2, Jerusalem: Yad Vashem, 1958, pp. 95–131.

127. Saul Esh, *Teunim Be'Heker Ha'shoa Yahadut Zmanenu* (Considerations on the Research of the Holocaust and Jewry in Our Time). Jerusalem: The Hebrew University, 1973.

128. R. C. Browning, p. 5.

129. *Ibid.,* pp. 6–7.

130. P. Friedman, p. 28.

131. *Ibid.*, p. 30.

132. Lucy S. Dawidowicz, *The War Against the Jews, 1938–1945*. New York: Holt, Rinehart and Winston, 1975; Nora Levin, *The Holocaust: The Destruction of European Jewry, 1933–1945*. New York: Schocken Books, 1975.

133. Isaiah Trunk, *Judenrat: The Jewish Councils in Eastern Europe Under Nazi Occupation*. New York: Macmillan, 1974.

134. Yitzhak Arad, Yisrael Gutman *and* Abraham Margaliot, *eds., Hashoa Betiud* (The Holocaust in Documents). Jerusalem: Yad Vashem, 1978; Yisrael Gutman *and* Livia Rothkirchen, *eds., Shoat Yehudai Eropa* (The Catastrophe of European Jewry). Jerusalem: Yad Vashem, 1976.

135. Yehuda Bauer, "Right and Wrong Teaching of the Holocaust." *In: The Lesson of the Holocaust.* Philadelphia: National Institute on the Holocaust, Oct. 1978, p. 6.

136. L. Dawidowicz, p. 212; N. Levin, pp. 79, 84, 213–214.

137. O. Dov Kulka, "Major Trends and Tendencies in German Historiography on National Socialism and the 'Jewish Question' (1924–1982)." *The Fifth International Historical Conference on the Historiography of the Holocaust.* Jerusalem: Yad Vashem, Apr. 1983, p. 12.

138. L. Dawidowicz, pp. xv, 4.

139. Yisrael Gutman, Chaim Schatzker *and* Dov Kulka, "ha'Sho'a Bemehkar u'behoraa be'batai ha'Sefer" (The Holocaust in Research and Teaching in Schools). *In: Siach Lamoreh le'Historia* (Conversation with the History Teacher). Jerusalem: Mercaz Shazar, no. 3, Nissan, 1979, p. 19.

140. Y. Gutman *and* L. Rothkirchen.

141. *Ibid.*, p. 45.

142. N. Levin, pp. 11, 112.

143. Y. Bauer, *A History of the Holocaust*, pp. 151, 152, 194.

144. O. D. Kulka, p. 16.

145. Zimerman does not agree with Kulka's conclusion about the prominent place of the Jewish issue in German historiography, and emphasizes the opposite. (His views were expressed in a lecture at the Congress of Israeli historians, Mercaz Shazar, Jerusalem, July, 1984.)

146. Y. Gutman *and* L. Rothkirchen, p. 361.

147. Psalm 118:17.

148. Bauer in a conversation (April 11, 1984), stressed Esh's influence on the second generation of Holocaust researchers in Israel.

149. Dan Michman, "Research of the Life of Religious Jews During the Holocaust." *The Fifth International Historical Conference on the Historiography of the Holocaust.* Jerusalem: Yad Vashem, Apr. 1983.

150. Y. Gutman *and* L. Rothkirchen, pp. 671–684, and Y. Bauer, *A History of the Holocaust*, p. 348.

151. Bauer, *A History of the Holocaust*.

152. *Ibid.*, p. 348; Y. Gutman *and* L. Rothkirchen, pp. 671–684; N. Levin, pp. 712–713.

153. Based on conversations at Yad Vashem and at the Hebrew University.

154. Leni Yahil, "Mekoma shel hasho'ah be'Historiographia ha'yehudit" (The Holocaust in Jewish Historiography). *Yad Vashem Studies.* Vol. VII. Jerusalem, 1968, p. 62.

155. O. D. Kulka, pp. 15–16.

156. *Ibid.*, p. 17.

157. Yehuda Bauer, The Phenomenon of the 'Revisionists'—The Denial of the Holocaust and its Historical Significance. *The Fifth International Historical Conference on the Historiography of the Holocaust.* Yad Vashem, Apr. 1983. (Synopsis.)

158. Based on a conversation with Bauer (April 11, 1984) in Jerusalem.

159. See, for example, "Historians Rape Begin." *The Southern Israelite,* Atlanta, Georgia, Aug. 20, 1982. (Prof. S. Ettinger and Prof. Y. Gutman criticize Prime Minister Menachem Begin for what they called his excessive use of the term "Holocaust" for political purposes.); J. Waitz, "Unfortunate Accident." *Ma'ariv,* Tel Aviv, Jan. 14, 1983. (About the Israeli public dispute concerning his explanation of the Holocaust to soldiers.); and J. Bauer, "Here We Are Responsible." *Ma'ariv,* Apr. 10, 1983. (General social and moral implications of the Holocaust for the Israelis.)

160. Bauer's *A History of the Holocaust* is appropriate for this purpose, but because it is in English it may be difficult for Israeli students in their first years in the academic institutes.

161. On December 29, 1978, for example, Mr. Hammer, the Minister of Education, answered Shilanki's question in the Knesset, declaring that the Ministry of Education would make the teaching of the Holocaust compulsory in the higher grades. See also Mrs. Shtern-Kattan's amendment to the State-Education Law (No. 3, 1979), providing for the teaching of the Holocaust in schools. On March 23, 1981, the teaching of the Holocaust in schools was debated in the Committee on Education and Culture of the Knesset.

162. Jaacob Shelhav, "Mifneh Behora'at Tkufat Hasha'a ve'Hagvuva" (Turning Points in Teaching the Period of the Holocaust and Heroism." *Yediot Yad Vashem* (Yad Vashem News), Jerusalem, no. 29, July 1962, pp. 41–44.

Bibliography

B. Ahia and M. Harpaz, *Toldot Am Israel* (The History of Israel). Vol. 5. Tel Aviv: Shershevski, 1964, 250 p. (H.T.N.R.)

Yitzhak Arad, Yisrael Gutman *and* Abraham Margaliot, eds., *Hasho'a Betiud* (The Holocaust in Documents). Jerusalem: Yad Vashem, 1978, 403 p. (R.T.)

S. Zalman Ariel, Moshe Blich *and* Natan Perski, *Mikra'ot Israel* (Israeli Reader). Jerusalem: Massada, 1959, 470 p. (Mik. N.R. III.)

S. Zalman Ariel, Moshe Blich *and* Natan Perski, *Mikra'ot Israel* (Israeli Reader). Jerusalem: Massada, 1963, 456 p. (Mik. N.R. IV.)

S. Zalman Ariel, Moshe Blich *and* Natan Perski, *Mikra'ot Israel* (Israeli Reader). Jerusalem: Massada, 1958, 374 p. (Mik. N.R. V.)

S. Zalman Ariel, Moshe Blich *and* Natan Perski, *Mikra'ot Israel* (Israeli Reader). Jerusalem: Massada, 1956, 469 p. (Mik. N.R. VI.)

S. Zalman Ariel, Moshe Blich *and* Natan Perski, *Mikra'ot Israel* (Israeli Reader). Jerusalem: Massada, 1960, 521 p. (Mik. N.R. VII.)

S. Zalman Ariel, Moshe Blich *and* Natan Perski, *Mikra'ot Israel* (Israeli Reader). Jerusalem: Massada, 1956, 527 p. (Mik. N.R. VII.)

Baruch Avivi *and* Natan Perski, *Toldot Israel* (History of Israel). Vol. 6. Tel Aviv: Yavneh, 1957, 460 p. (H.T.N.R.)

Baruch Avivi *and* Natan Perski, *Toldot Amenu* (History of Our Nation). Vol. III. Jerusalem: Zionist Organization, 1970, 218 p. (H.T.N.R.)

Raphael Balgor, *Yesodoth* (Foundations). Tel Aviv: A. Karni, 1966, 110 p. (Mik. N.R. IV.)

J. Richard Bates, "Politics, Ideology and Education: The Possibility of New Sociology of Education." *International Journal of Political Education.* Amsterdam, vol. 1, no. 4, Nov. 1978, pp. 315–325.

Yehuda Bauer, *A History of the Holocaust.* New York: Franklin, Watts, 1982. 398 p. (R.T.)

List of Abbreviations:

Mik	Mikra'ot
R.T.	Research Textbook
N.R.	Non-Religious
H.T.	History Textbook
R.	Religious
I, II, III, etc.	Grades

Yehuda Bauer, *The Holocaust in Historical Perspective.* Seattle: University of Washington Press, 1978, 181 p. (R.T.)

Yehuda Bauer, The Phenomenon of the 'Revisionists'—The Denial of the Holocaust and its Historical Significance. *The Fifth International Historical Conference on the Historiography of the Holocaust.* Yad Vashem. Apr. 1983, 4 p. (Synopsis.)

Yehuda Bauer, "Right and Wrong Teaching of the Holocaust." *In: The Lesson of the Holocaust.* Philadelphia: National Institute on the Holocaust, Oct. 1978, pp. 3–13.

Yehuda Bauer, "Megamot be'heker ha'shoa" (Trends in Holocaust Research). *In: Yad Vashem Studies.* Vol. XII, Jerusalem: Yad Vashem, 1977, pp. 7–36.

Arieh Bauminger, "Horaat Ha'Shoa Bebiet Ha'Shepher" (Teaching the Holocaust in School). *In: Hora'at Ha'Shoa Bebeit HaShepher* (Teaching the Holocaust in School). Jerusalem: Ministry of Education, 1961, pp. 19–21.

Bernard Berelson, *Content Analysis in Communication Research.* Glencoe, Ill.: Free Press, 1952, 220 p.

Dvorah Bergman, *Neta'im* (Plants). Tel Aviv: Karni, 1969, 356 p. (Mik. R. VI)

Gershon Bergson, "Ha'Shir Vehasipur al ha'Shoam" (The Poem and the Story About the Holocaust). *In: Shifrut Yeladim vaNoar* (Children and Youngsters Literature). Vol. 8, Jan. 1981, pp. 17–22.

Herman J. Blumberg, "Some Problems in Teaching the Holocaust." *The Reconstructionist,* New York, vol. 34, no. 16, Dec. 1968, pp. 13–20.

K. Philip Boden, *Promoting International Understanding Through School Textbooks.* N.p.: George Eckert Institute for International Textbook Research, 1977, 54 p.

R. Christopher Browning, "Approaches to the Final Solution in German Historiography of the Last Two Decades." *The Fifth International Historical Conference on the Historiography of the Holocaust.* Jerusalem: Yad Vashem, Apr. 1983, 22 p.

Arieh Buchner, Yehuda Levynton *and* Levin Kippnis, *Sefer Ha'Kita Dalet* (Book For the Fourth Grade). Tel Aviv: Dvir, 1954, 370 p. (Mik. N.R. IV.)

Arieh Buchner, Yehuda Levynton *and* Levin Kippnis, *Sefer Hakita Zaien* (Book for the Seventh Grade). Tel Aviv: Dvir, 1965, 427 p. (Mik. N.R. VII.)

Arieh Carmon, *Ha'Shoa* (The Holocaust). Jerusalem: Ministry of Education, 1980, 2 vols. (320 and 292 p.) (H.T.N.R.)

Arieh Carmon, "Teaching the Holocaust as a Means of Fostering Values." *Curriculum Inquiry,* New York, vol. 9, no. 3, Fall 1979, pp. 209–229.

Lucy S. Dawidowicz, *The War Against the Jews, 1938–1945.* New York: Holt, Rinehart and Winston, 1975, 460 p. (R.T.)

M. Alexander Dushkin, "Ma Ne'asa Lehanchlat Lekeh Ha'Sho'a" (What is done to transfer the lesson of the Holocaust?) *In: Hora'at ha'Shoa Bebeit Ha Sefer* (Teaching the Holocaust in School). Jerusalem: Ministry of Education, 1961, pp. 7–10.

Meir Dvorozetski, "Hataalum shel ie Yediat ha'Shoa" (The Mystery of the Absence of Knowledge about the Holocaust). *In: Hora'at ha'Shoa Bebiet Hasefer* (Teaching the Holocaust in School). Jerusalem: Ministry of Education, 1961, pp. 11–15.

Natan Eck, *Shoat Ha'am Ha'Yehudi Be'Airopa.* (The Holocaust of the Jewish People in Europe). Jerusalem: Yad Vashem, 1976, 451 p. (R.T.)

Moshe Efrati *and* Naftali Melumad, *Psiot Hadashot* (New Steps). Tel Aviv: Yaveneh, 1963, 384 p. (Mik.R.VI.)

Z. Moshe Efrati *and* Naftali Melumad, *Psiot* (Steps). Tel Aviv: Yavneh, 1953, 360 p. (2d ed. 1958; Mik. R. VII.)

Z. Moshe Efrati *and* Naftali Melumad, *Psiot* (Steps). Tel Aviv: Yavneh, 1956, 368 p. (Mik. R. VIII.)

Saul Esh, *Teunim BeHeker ha'shoa ve'Yahadut Zmanenu* (Consideration in the Research of the Shoa and Jewry of Our Time). Jerusalem: The Hebrew University, 1973, 427 p.

Shmuel Ettinger, *Ha'Anti Shemiut Baet Ha'Hadasha* (Anti-Semitism in Modern Times). Tel Aviv: Sifriat Hapoalim, 1978, 285 p.

L. Emil Fackenheim, *God's Presence in History.* New York: Harper, 1972, 104 p.

Ytzhak Feler, *Netivot* (Pathways). Jerusalem: Kiriat Sefer, 1953, 305 p. (Mik. N.R. VII-IX.)

Ruth Firer, *Sochnim Shel Ha'Hinuch Ha'Zioni* (Agents of the Zionist Education) Tel Aviv: Ha'Kibbutz Ha'Meuhad, 1985, 228 p.

Ruth Firer, "Al Ha'Sefer HaShoa UmaShmauta"' (Concerning the Book "The Holocaust and its Meaning"). *In: Si'ach Lamoreh Lehistoria* (Conversation with the History Teacher). Jerusalem: Mercaz Shazar, no. 21, 1983, pp. 13–20.

Ruth Firer, *Todaah ve'Yedia* (Formation and Information). Dissertation, The Hebrew University of Jerusalem, 1980, 385 p.

Ruth Firer, *Ha'Shoa* (The Holocaust). Tel Aviv: Taga, 1984, 15 &15 p.

Moshe Frager, *Hurban Israel Be'Eropa* (The Destruction of Jews in Europe). Tel Aviv: Ha'kibbutz Ha'Meuhad, 1947, 372 p. (R.T.)

E. Victor Frankl, *Man's Search For Meaning.* Boston: Beacon Press, 1970, 150 p.

Philip Friedman, "Preliminary and Methodological Problems of the Research on the Jewish Catastrophe in the Nazi Period." *In: Yad Vashem Studies,* vol. 2. Jerusalem: Yad Vashem, 1958, pp. 95–131.

Shmuel Gadon, *Alumot* (Shafts). Tel Aviv: Messilot, 1960, 493 p. (Mik. N.R. VII.)

Shmuel Gadon, *Alumot* (Shafts). Tel Aviv: Tarbut ve'Hinuch, 1965, 529 p. (Mik. N.R. VIII.)

Yisrael Gutman, "Jewish Resistance—Views and Evaluations in Historical Writings." *The Fifth International Historical Conference on the Historiography of the Holocaust.* Jerusalem: Yad Vashem, Apr. 1983, 3 p. (Synopsis.)

Yisrael Gutman *and* Livia Rothkirchen, eds., *Shoat Yehudai Eropa* (The Catastrophe of European Jewry). Jerusalem: Yad Vashem, 1976, 757 p. (R.T.)

Yisrael Gutman *and* Chaim Shatzker, *Ha'Shoa U'Mashmauta* (The Holocaust and Its Meaning). Jerusalem: Merkaz Shazar, 1983, 191 p. (H.T.N.R.)

Yisrael Gutman, Chaim Schatzker *and* Dov Kulka, "Ha'Shoa Bemehkar Ubehoraa Bebatai Ha'Sefer" (The Holocaust in Research and Teaching in

Schools). *In: Siach Lamoreh Le'Historia* (Conversation with the History Teacher). Jerusalem: Mercaz Shazar, no. 3, Nissan. 1979, pp. 3–22.

Raul Hilberg, *The Destruction of the European Jews.* Chicago: Quadrangle, 1961, 788 p. (R.T.)

Shlomo Horovitz, *Kiztur Toldot Yisrael Baet H'Hadach'a* (Summary of the History of Israel in the Modern Period). Haifa: Beit Hashefer Ha'reali, 1961, 1973, vol. 3, 231 p. (H.T.N.R.)

Moshe Katan, *Toldot Ha'Yehudim Mimilhemet Ha'olam Harishona ve'ad Yamenu* (The History of the Jews From the First World War Till Our Times). Jerusalem: Kiryat Sepher, 1958, 1966, 264 p. (H.T.N.R.)

Jacob Katz *and* Moshe Hershko, *Israel ve'Ha'amim* (Israel and the Nations). Tel Aviv: Dvir, 1962, vol. III, 276 p. (H.T.R.)

Levin Kippnis, Arieh Buchner *and* Yehuda Levynton, *Sefer Ha'Kita Gimel* (The Book for the Third Grade). Tel Aviv: Dvir and Sefer, 1962, 335 p. (Mik. N.R. III.)

Levin Kippnis, Arieh Buchner *and* Yehuda Levynton, *Sefer Ha'Kita Vave* (Book for the Sixth Grade). Tel Aviv: Dvir, 1964, 1967, 380 p. (Mik. N.R. VI.)

L. Shimshon Kirshenbaum, *Toldot Israel Badorot Ha'achronim* (The History of Israel in Recent Generations). Tel Aviv: Mishlav, 1969, 339 p. (H.T.N.R.)

L. Shimshon Kirshenbaum, *Toldot Am Israel Bedorenu* (History of the Israeli Nation in Our Generation). Tel Aviv: Omanut, 1965, vol. 1, 377 p. (H.T.N.R.)

Hillel Klein *and* Uriel Last, "Cognitive and Emotional Aspects of Attitudes of American and Jewish Youth Toward the Victims of the Holocaust." *Israeli Annual of Psychiatry and Related Disciplines,* Jerusalem, vol. 12, no. 2, June 1974, pp. 111–131.

Dvora Koubovi, "Therapeutic Teaching of Literature During the War and Its Aftermath." *In: Stress and Anxiety.* Edited by D. Charles Spiedberger *and* G. Irwin Sarason. New York: Hemisphere Publishing Corporation, 1982, vol. 8, pp. 345–349.

M. George Kren *and* Leo Rapport. *The Holocaust and the Crisis of Human Behavior.* New York: Holmes & Meier, 1980, 176 p.

O. Dov Kulka, "Major Trends and Tendencies in German Historiography on National Socialism and the 'Jewish Question' (1924–1982)." *The Fifth International Historical Conference on the Historiography of the Holocaust.* Jerusalem: Yad Vashem, Apr. 1983, 17 p. (Synopsis.)

Nora Levin, *The Holocaust: The Destruction of European Jewry, 1933–1945.* New York: Schocken Books, 1975, 768 p. (R.T.)

Hannah Levinsohn, "The Television Series 'Holocaust' in Israel." *International Journal of Political Education,* Amsterdam, vol. 4, no. 1/2, May 1981, pp. 151–167.

Walter Mertineit, "Strategies, Concepts, and Methods of International History Textbook Revision." *International Journal of Political Education,* Amsterdam, vol. 2, no. 2, Apr. 1979, pp. 101–115.

Dan Michman, "Research of the Life of Religious Jews During the Holocaust." *The Fifth International Historical Conference on the Historiography of the Holocaust.* Jerusalem: Yad Vashem, Apr. 1983, 2 p. (Synopsis.)

Ministry of Education, *She'elon Leha'archat Sfarim le'Talmidim* (Questionnaire for the Evaluation of Textbooks and Auxiliary Books for Pupils). Jerusalem: Department of Confirmation of Textbooks, 1981, 4 p.

Ministry of Education, *Sifrai Limud ve Sifrai Ezer Latalmidim Leshnat Halim udim* (Textbooks and Auxiliary Books for Pupils for the Year.) Jerusalem, 1957–1958.

Ministry of Education, "Ishur Sefrai-Limud Vesfrai Ezer Letalmidim—Horat—Keva." (Confirmation of Textbooks and Auxiliary Books for Pupils—Permanent Instruction). *In: The General Manager's Circular.* Jersualem, Oct. 5, 1977. (Item 45, Lamed-Hait 2.)

Ministry of Education, *Historia Ba'hativa Ha'eliona bebiet HaSefer Hamamlachti* (History for the Non-Religious High School). Jerusalem: Hamerkaz Letochniot Limudim, 1977, 56 p.

Ministry of Education, "Hasbara Hinuchit Shel Tkufat Ha'Shoa Ve Hagvura" (Educational Explanation of the Period of the Holocaust and Heroism). *In: Hora'at HaShoa Bebiet HaSefer* (Teaching the Holocaust in School). Jerusalem: The General Manager Circular, Apr. 25, 1961, pp. 83–87, (Item 141, 11/21.)

Ministry of Education, *Meymai Habaiet Harishon veAd Yemai Hamalka Shlomzion* (From the Days of the First Temple to the Queen Shlom-Zion). Jerusalem: Mercaz Letochniot Limudin, 1973, (H.T.N.R.)

Ministry of Education, *Tochnit Limudim Behistoria la'hativa ha'eliona Bebiet Hasefer Hadati* (History Curriculum for the Religious High School). Jerusalem: Hamerkaz Letchniot Limudim, 1979, 17 p.

Ministry of Education, *Leket Hemed laYamim Hanorim.* (Lovely Collection—For the High Days). Jerusalem: T'al, 1978. (Mik. R. IV) (Experimental edition)

Ministry of Education. *Leket Hemed leShalosh Regalim* (Lovely Collection for the Three Feasts). Jerusalem: T'al, 1980, 71 p. (Grade is not mentioned; experimental edition.)

Arieh Morgenstern, *ed., Mekorot ve'Mechkarim al ha'shoah.* (Sources and Researches about the Holocaust). Tel Aviv: Ministry of Education, 1983, 368 p. (H.T.R.)

R. Multhoff, "The Experience of Brunswik International Textbook Institute, in the Field of History Textbook Revision During the Last 20 Years" (Synopsis.)

Sara Neshamit, *Letoldot ha'Shoah Ve'Hameri* (History of Holocaust and Resistance). Beit Lohamei Haghetta'ot, 1961, 105 p.

Binjamin de Paris *and* Jeshua Teberski, *Halichot* (Manners). Tel Aviv: Teberski, 1950, 254 p. (Mik. R. VI.).

Natan Perski, *Mikra'ot Israel Hadashot* (New Israeli Readers). Ramat Gan: Massada, 1978, 472 p. (Mik. N.R. III.)

Natan Perski, *Mikra'ot Israel Hadashot* (New Israeli Readers). Ramat Gan: Massada, 1978, 482 p. (Mik. N.R. IV.)

Natan Perski, *Mikra'ot Israel Hadashot* (New Israeli Readers). Ramat Gan: Massada, 1977, 512 p. (Mik. N.R. VI.)

Natan Perski, *Mikra'ot Israel Hadashot* (New Israeli Readers). Ramat Gan: Massada, 1979, 560 p. (Mik. N.R. VIII.)

Yitzhak Piter, *Mikra'a Hadasha* (New Reader). Jerusalem: Kiriat Sefer, 1962, 304 p. (Mik. N.R. V.)

David Pratt, *How to Find and Measure Bias in Textbooks.* New Jersey, 1972, 50 p.

Amiram Raviv, Avigdor Klingman *and* Moshe Horovitz, *eds.*, *Yeladim beMatzavai Lahatz* (Children in Condition of Stress and Crisis). Tel Aviv: Otzar Hamoreh, 1980, 311 p.

Gerald Reitlinger, *The Final Solution.* New York: A. S. Barnes, 1968, 667 p. (R.T.)

Eliezer Riger, *Toldot Israel Bazman Ha'hadash* (History of Israel in Modern Period). Vol. 3. Tel Aviv: Dvir, 1957, 316 p. (H.T.N.R.)

Alan Rosenberg *and* Jack Zerin, "Teaching About the Holocaust as Part of a Genocidal Universe." *Social Studies,* vol. 72, no. 3, May-June 1981, pp. 107–110.

K. Dianne Roskies, *Teaching the Holocaust to Children.* New York: Ktav, 1975, 65 p.

Chaim Shatzker, *ed.*, *Antishemiut ve'Shoah* (Anti-Semitism and Holocaust). Jerusalem: Hebrew University, Ministry of Education, 1977, 353 p. (H.T.N.R.)

Chaim Shatzker, "The Holocaust in Israeli Education." *International Journal of Political Education,* Amsterdam, vol. 5, no. 1, Apr. 1982, pp. 75–82.

Chaim Schatzker, "The Teaching of the Holocaust: Dilemmas and Considerations." *The Annals of the American Academy of Political and Social Science,* Philadelphia, vol. 450, July 1980, pp. 218–226.

Chaim Schatzker, "Bayot Didactiot Behora'at Hasho'a" (Didactical Considerations in Teaching the Holocaust). *Modi'in Lamoreh Le Historia* (Information for History Teacher), Ramat Gan, no. 2, 1961, pp. 11–15.

O. Ernest Schüddekopf, *History Teaching and History Textbook Revision.* Strasbourg: Council for Cultural Cooperation of Council of Europe, 1967, 235 p.

Jaacob Shelhav, "Mifneh Behora'at Tkufat ha'Shoa ve' Hagvuva" (Turning Points in Teaching the Period of the Holocaust and Heroism." *Yediot Yad Vashem* (Yad Vashem Information), Jerusalem, no. 29, July 1962, pp. 41–44.

Effraim Shemuali, *Toldot Amenu Bazman Hahadash* (History of Our Nation in the Modern Period). Tel Aviv: Yavneh, 1970, vol. vii, p. 441 (H.T.N.R.)

Phishel Shneurson, *Psichologia Pdeogagit Ivrit* (Hebrew Pedagogical Psychology). Tel Aviv: Massada, 1951, 277 p.

Sara Smilanski, "Musag Hamavet Ezel Yeladim Israelim" (The Death Term Within Israeli Children). *In:* *Yeladim be'Matzavai Lahatz Vmasber* (Children in Situations of Stress and Crisis). Tel Aviv: Otzar Hamorch, 1970, pp. 102–141.

Sara Smilanski, *Tfisat Ha'mavet Beainai Yaladim* (Conception of Death by Children). Haifa: "Ahe," 1981, 310 p.

D. Charles Spielberger *and* G. Irwin Sarason, *eds.*, *Stress and Anxiety.* Vol. 8. New York: McGraw-Hill, 1973, 456 p.

Yitshak Spivak *and* Moshe Avidor, *Am Israel Be'artzo U'Banechar* (Jewish Nation in Its Country and in the Diaspora). Vol. IV. Tel Aviv: Massada, 1948, 248 p. (H.T.N.R.)

Jacob Talmon, "Ha'historia Ha'Eropeit Kereka la'Shoa" (The European History as the Background of the Holocaust). *In: Ha'shoa ve'Hatkuma* (The Holocaust and the Revival). Jerusalem: Yad Vashem, 1974, pp. 11–35.

Jeshua Teberski *and* Alexander Malkiel, *Halichot Israel* (Manners of Israel). Tel Aviv: Amichy, 1961, 327 p. (Mik. R. III.)

Jeshua Teberski *and* Alexander Malkiel, *Halichot Israel* (Manners of Israel). Tel Aviv: Amichy, 1958, 255 p. (Mik. R. V.)

Joseph Tenenbaum, *Race and Reich.* New York: Wayne, 1956, 554 p. (R.T.)

Isaiah Trunk, *Judenrat: The Jewish Councils in Eastern Europe Under Nazi Occupation.* New York: Macmillan, 1972, 664 p. (R.T.)

UNESCO, "Better History Textbooks." *In: UNESCO and Its Program.* Paris, 1950, 29 p.

Bezalel Veksler *and* Abraham Rosen, *Arugot* (Garden Beds). Tel Aviv: Amichy, 1961, 378 p. (Mik. N.R.V.)

Bezalel Veksler *and* Abraham Rosen, *Arugot* (Garden Beds). Tel Aviv: Amichy, 1966, 69 p. (Mik. N.R. VI.)

Yad Vashem, *Jewish Resistance During the Holocaust. Proceedings of the Conference on Manifestations of Jewish Resistance.* Jerusalem: Yad Vashem, 1968, 562 p.

Leni Yahil, "Mekoma shel ha'Shoa BeHistoriographia Ha'yehudit" (The Holocaust in Jewish Historiography). *Yad Vashem Studies,* Jerusalem, vol. vii, 1968, pp. 53–67.

Leni Yahil, "Historians of the Holocaust, a Plea for a New Approach." *The Wiener Library Bulletin,* London, vol. xxii, no. 1, 1967/1968, pp. 2–5.

Meir Weil, HaShoah BeSfarim LeYeladim" (The Holocaust in Children's Books). *Hed Ha'Hinuch* (Echo of Education), Nissan 1968, no. 3, pp. 12–13.

Moshe Zimmerman, *ed., Mi'Milhamah LeMilhamah* (From War to War, 1918–1945). Jerusalem: Ministry of Education, 1981, 218 p.

Michael Ziv *and* Jacob Tori, *Divrai Hayamim Bazman Ha'hadash* (History of the New Period). Vol. II. Tel Aviv: Yavneh, 1958, 1966, 293 p. (H.T.N.R.)

Michael Ziv, Shmuel Ettinger *and* Jacob Landau, *Divrai Hayamim* (The History). Vol. IV, Part II. Haifa: Yuval, 1966, 596 p. (H.T.N.R.)

PART III

The United States of America

Glenn S. Pate

10
The Selection of Textbooks

Since there is no national textbook selection system, there is no simple, single answer to the question of how textbooks are selected. The procedures vary with educational level and with states. The only common thread is the function of an open, free enterprise system with a large number of publishers, each with a profit motive, competing for the huge markets. As the procedures for the selection of textbooks at the college level is simple, most of this report is concerned with the elementary and secondary levels.

Elementary and Secondary Levels

At this educational level there are two basic textbook selection approaches: state adoption systems and local school district option systems. Twenty-two of the 50 states, primarily located in the South, Southwest, and Far West, have a state adoption system. In this system a local school district may not purchase or use a textbook that has not been approved by that state's Department of Education. In the local option system, a school district has the complete choice of textbooks.

The publishing companies give a great deal of attention to the adoptive states because some of the more populous states, such as California and Texas, are adoptive states. If their textbooks are not approved or selected by these states, the companies suffer severe economic consequences.

The state adoptive systems vary considerably. In some states the adoption is simply a list of titles approved or recommended for local school use. In other states a particular title is selected for use throughout the state. A few states make adoptions for the elementary level only. Some states allow for the use of textbooks and materials that are not on the approved list with certain restrictions and conditions. States also vary in the procedures used, in the size of the selection committee, and in the proportion of lay citizens participating. Persons serving on a state selection committee are usually appointed by the chief school official. The majority of committee members are teachers with some university personnel and some lay citizens. The influence of lay people appears to be increasing in recent years.

The following excerpt describes the adoption procedures in a sample adoption state, California:

> The biennial adoption cycle is initiated, usually in July, by the Education Department's publication of a call for bids and for submission of materials in a particular subject area. The call will state the governing legal and qualitative criteria developed by the commission and its advisory committees and approved by the Board of Education. Within two weeks of the call, producers must notify the Education Department of their intent to submit. Samples must be delivered to the department by the beginning of September, and price bids by the end of December. Although producers may have access to draft criteria before their formal adoption, this close timing indicates that the commission and its advisory committees generally frame their criteria to reflect the nature of materials already being used in California and elsewhere.
>
> In the first stages of the selection process, a Legal and Factual Committee appointed by the commission reviews the submitted materials for compliance with the legal criteria (such as balanced portrayal of minority contributions) and for their factual accuracy. For these purposes, commissioners may also appoint their own Legal and Factual Analysis Committees from among teachers, school officials, and minority group representatives residing within the geographical area that the commissioner represents.
>
> At the next stage, scheduled to take four to five months, materials are screened for instructional quality. Committees formed by individual commissioners conduct the review at this stage and are often aided by subcommittees and even sub-subcommittees. Each sub-subcommittee or subcommittee is expected to report back to its governing committee, which in turn provides its commissioner with reports and tabulated short answer forms for presentation to the entire commission. Hundreds, even thousands, of local teachers, school officials, and special interest group representatives become involved in the work of these evaluation teams, some on their own initiative and others by invitation.
>
> Samples of submitted materials are circulated among the evaluation teams, with round-robin procedures devised for the dissemination of more bulky or costly nontext materials. In some cases, publishers will be invited to demonstrate the use of their materials, while in others the commissioner or the evaluating team may insist that publishers have no contact with the evaluators. Evaluators may ask publishers to provide the results of preuse pilot tests conducted by the publishers; publishers may in turn seek permission from local districts to test their materials in selected district classrooms.

The commission reviews these reports and within a month selects a final list of instructional materials to present to the Board of Education for adoption. The board then completes its review over a three-month period. At its first monthly meeting during this period it receives the recommendation of the commission and approves the commencement of a thirty-day public display period mandated by statute as a prerequisite to final adoption. At its next monthly meeting the board holds a public hearing, at which anyone may speak on the materials proposed for adoption. At its third monthly meeting, the board is expected to vote on the commission's recommendations for the adoption.[1]

Textbook selection in those states that do not have a state adoption system operates in a similar, though vastly simplified, procedure. In these states, each district, in some cases each school, makes the selection. A textbook selection committee is appointed for the district or school, usually consisting of interested teachers. At times volunteer lay citizens or school administrators also serve on the committee. Teachers clearly play the central role in determining what materials are used in the classroom through their involvement on the selection committee and their control of classroom activities.

Similar to the state adoption system, the local option system follows a prescribed procedure. Guidelines of criteria for selection are established (in most cases) and are available for public review. The appointed committee receives sample copies from publishers, establishes subcommittees as needed, and proceeds to review the materials. The committee's selections are still subject to review and approval, although in most cases the recommendations are accepted. Others who may be involved in the chain of adoption are principals, department chairmen, subject matter supervisors, curriculum councils, and superintendents' offices. In some districts a title may be selected for all schools within the district; in other districts each school may use a different textbook. Thus there is a great range in local option, varying from those schools where each department has the basic determination in the textbook used to those states which select, at the state level, the titles to be used throughout the state.

Although criticism and challenges have been directed at textbooks for many years, these attacks have sharply increased in recent times. The attacks have been focused on both the content of particular books and on the selection of textbooks. In addition to attacks, numerous groups have been attempting to influence the content of textbooks for generations. These special interest groups have ranged from chambers of commerce to oil companies to racial minorities to religious groups. In the last few years some groups, especially religious fundamentalists and the political/religious New Right, have become much more aggressive—and have achieved substantial success—in influencing the selection of textbooks. These influences, at both the state adoption level and the local option level, are generally well-organized and are consistent with the general "back to basics" school of thought. Textbooks which are challenged for selection are challenged for the following aspects: secular humanism, Darwinism and evolution, scientific theories, criticism of American history, values clarification, undermining of the traditional family, atheistic or agnostic views, anti-traditional views, negative or pessimistic views, moral relativism, and situational ethics. From all indications thus far, the most active textbook selection pressure groups are not interested in promoting the study of the Holocaust. In fact, they would probably be opposed to any criticism of the United States for the action not taken relevant to the Holocaust.

Criticism is also directed toward publishers for various aspects of their textbooks. They frequently feel pressure from many groups but must satisfy everyone in order to sell their books. Reacting to criticism in an earlier study of textbook treatment of the Holocaust, one spokesman, the president of a medium-sized publishing company, said: "Every kind of pressure group wants space from us." The spokesman went on to note that,

> he hears regularly from labor unions, the consulate of a Mideastern nation, the U.S. Chamber of Commerce, a manufacturers' trade association and outraged citizens who claim his books aren't teaching Americanism. "We have to evaluate each demand and ask, 'Is this a good use of our space?' In selecting content," he continued, "authors have to consider the historical context. The Holocaust is a sensitive issue and one that can easily be taken out of context. This is an event that occurred only 30 years ago. It's hardly in perspective yet. In many other cultures there have been similar instances, just as traumatic, of whole tribes being wiped out—the American Indians, for example. And we are accused of not giving them adequate coverage."[2]

Speaking a little less defensively, and perhaps revealing the philosophy of publishers toward textbook content is another spokesman.

> Robert T. Rasmussen, vice-president of the school division of the Association of American Publishers, observed that textbook publishers may not take note of particular issues or events until their significance is brought before the public consciousness. "Books reflect the thinking and views of people in a given time," he said. "The Holocaust was not uppermost in people's minds until there was a TV show about

it—just the way women and minorities were given limited coverage until they also became part of the public consciousness."[3]

College Level

The selection of textbooks at the college level is infinitely more simple. College instructors may select whatever textbook they choose—especially if a particular instructor is the only person teaching a particular course. No one nor group challenges the selection. Academic freedom is certainly seen in the selection of textbooks at the college level. The only exceptions to this pattern are instances where multiple sections of the same course are offered. These courses are virtually always at the lower level of college requirements, such as a basic United States history course. In these cases the department or the instructors involved may agree to use a particular book for all sections of the course. It may be that one instructor does not like the choice, but the selection, and influence for the selection, resides within the department. Outside influence, or influence beyond the departmental level, is exceedingly rare for college textbook selection.

11

The Holocaust in American Textbooks

This study represents an extensive effort to determine how American textbooks treat the Holocaust. The approach is basically an analytical and descriptive one, although the author's opinions and judgments do surface at times. Three educational levels are included within the scope of the study: elementary (through grade six), secondary (through grade twelve), and the university level. The textbooks of the elementary and secondary levels are books used throughout the country; most are currently in use although a few older books were examined for comparison purposes. No attempt was made to select particular texts or representative samples, but rather to examine all available texts.

For the college level, a decision had to be made as to what constitutes a textbook. There are many books on the market, but they cannot all be considered textbooks. For the purposes of this study, a book was considered to be a textbook if it was assigned for student use in a particular course. A large, public institution of higher learning, the University of Arizona, was used as the sample college from which to select textbooks. The catalogue of courses was examined to determine all possible courses that may include topics relevant to the Holocaust. A total of 36 such courses was identified. Then a list was made of all textbooks used by these courses. This list then formed the bases of the college level textbooks for the study. While this approach identified textbooks in a more representative fashion than for the elementary and secondary levels, there is every reason to believe that the conclusions drawn from a study of these textbooks would be representative of college textbooks in general.

In order to present an objective, analytical, and categorical study, 15 separate topics and questions were considered for the elementary and secondary textbooks. This approach was not appropriate for the college textbooks. The 15 topic/questions are:

1. What was the total amount of coverage given to the Holocaust?

2. Did the Holocaust coverage receive at least one separate paragraph?
3. What was the coverage of non-Jewish victims?
4. Who caused the Holocaust? Why?
5. What was the coverage of the pre-war period of oppression?
6. Were pictures included?
7. Were particular camps identified?
8. Were the terms genocide or Holocaust used?
9. What was the coverage of resistance to the Holocaust?
10. What was the coverage of Holocaust survivors?
11. Were questions to students or suggested activities given?
12. Were the Nuremberg Trials discussed?
13. Were suggested readings given?
14. Was the tone of the author critical of the events or simple, objective reporting?
15. What was included about the role of the United States relative to the Holocaust?

The textbooks are categorized by educational level, with the secondary and college levels having several subdivisions. The secondary level subdivisions are:

Social Studies
United States History
World History/Western Civilization
Government/Civics
Area Studies/Geography
Psychology
Sociology

The college level subdivisions are:

History
Sociology
Political Science
Religious Studies
Humanities

Elementary Social Studies Textbooks

Nine textbooks were examined, and some do make slight reference to the Holocaust. None of the texts comes close to providing a lucid, complete description or explanation of the events.

Four of the nine texts do say that Jews were killed. Two texts approach the idea of scapegoat as a cause; the other two books give no reason for the persecution. King has, "Hitler blamed the Jewish people for things that had gone wrong. His easy answers were lies, but they set the Germans to ridding themselves of their 'problems'— the Jewish people."[4] Two pages later in discussing Israel we find this: "The Jews had suffered more than 6,000,000 deaths during the years when Hitler held power."[5] Notice that the book does not say they were killed, only that they died. These two references are the book's total coverage of the Holocaust. The only other book that includes the scapegoat idea and the only one which mentions the pre-war oppression is Berg's.

> Hitler knew that one way to get people to follow him was to blame someone else for everything that was going wrong. Hitler blamed the country's troubles on certain groups of people. He said that German Jews, Slavs, and Germans who wanted a more democratic government were to blame. He said Jews should not be allowed to do business with other Germans. He said that criticism of his government should not be allowed. The German legislature passed laws he asked for. Laws took away homes and businesses from Jews and gave them to other Germans. They put Jews in prison camps. Laws put other limits on freedom.[6]

The above excerpt is the book's only reference to the Holocaust and does not include the fact that Jews were killed.

One of the more direct and brief accounts is given by King: "And the world learned of the terrible happenings in concentration camps throughout Central and Eastern Europe. More than six million people, mostly Jews, had died horrible deaths in such camps."[7] While this account does have descriptive words as terrible and horrible, there is absolutely no explanation of why people had died. The above quote is the text's total treatment of the Holocaust.

Three textbooks make reference to survivors, in a somewhat distorted manner. In a section on Israel, Servey has a short history of Jews.

> Then, in Europe during World War II, six million Jews were killed under the rule of the German dictator, Adolf Hitler. After World War II, the Jews who survived the Holocaust, as Hitler's mass murders are called, wanted to live in the country they had once ruled. In 1948, the United Nations created the country of Israel as a homeland for the Jews.[8]

Again, there is no explanation of why people were killed. This is the only elementary textbook that uses the term Holocaust.

In discussing immigration in the United States, Stanek notes, "Immigration increased again during World War II. At that time thousands of Jewish refugees came to the United States. They wanted a safer and better place in which to live and raise their families."[9] The implication is that those who wanted to come to the United States were free to do so and that the gates of the United States were open to all. This is the only elementary textbook that includes a question to students: "Why were the Jewish people anxious to escape from Germany when the Nazis were in power?"[10] The book does not provide an answer to this question.

The only other elementary text that makes reference to the Holocaust is Berry's. In a section on Israel he states, "Ruth was a recent immigrant from England. Her parents had fled from Germany to England in 1939." In the margin of the page there is this notation, "During World War II millions of Jews were killed by the German dictator, Hitler, and his followers, the Nazis. Many Jews, such as Ruth's parents, fled to other countries."[11] The book has another reference to survivors,[12] in a discussion of Jerusalem: "Then after the war, many European Jews were displaced persons. They had lost their land and possessions in Europe. Jerusalem seemed a logical place for them to go. They came in great numbers." There is no reference to the British policies on immigration to Israel, and as do the other texts which mention survivors, this one gives the impression that people were free to go wherever they chose and that host countries welcomed all who came. The other three elementary textbooks examined contain no reference of any sort to the Holocaust.

The excerpts included above are not representative excerpts, they are the total coverage of the Holocaust. While there is some disagreement about the appropriateness of studying the Holocaust in elementary schools, no textbook attempts a reasonable or complete explanation of the events. Perhaps it is better for a text to omit the Holocaust than to give distorted facts and false impressions.

The following statements give a summary of elementary textbook treatment of the Holocaust. Of the nine texts examined:

- There is a total of nine sentences dealing directly with the Holocaust.
- Only one book gives a separate paragraph to the topic.
- No book includes any reference to non-Jewish victims.
- Two books make reference to Jews as scapegoats, but no books explain why Jews were killed.

- One book refers to the pre-war period of oppression.
- One book[13] includes a picture.
- No book names or describes the camps.
- One book uses the term Holocaust, and no book uses the term genocide.
- No books refer to resistance, although one book[14] mentions Polish freedom fighters.
- Three books mention survivors, although in a misleading manner.
- One book has a question for students, although the answer to the question is not in the book.
- No book refers to the Nuremberg Trials.
- No book has suggested reading for students.
- No book refers to any role the United States may have played before and during the Holocaust, and one book implies our immigration policies were much more relaxed than they were.

Secondary Level Textbooks

Most of the seventh through twelfth grade books examined here are currently on the market, although a few older ones are included for comparison purposes. The intent of the reviewer was to be all-inclusive and examine all texts available rather than to examine representative samples. It is assumed that the most likely place to find references to the Holocaust is in the various disciplines of the social studies, especially history. Because of the type of category system, it is more appropriate to discuss the books by discipline, with the topics as subcategories.

United States History Textbooks

Total Coverage. For this section of the study, 65 secondary United States history textbooks were examined.

In order to determine the relative amount of text space devoted to the Holocaust, lines of text were counted. Most textbooks are printed with two columns per page with two to four lines making one sentence. The approximate number of sentences on the topic may be calculated by dividing the total lines by three. Coverage given to the pre-war period of oppression during the 1930s and coverage given to the persecution of non-Jews are included in the figure for total coverage.

One indication of the amount and type of coverage given to the Holocaust is seen in the structure of the writing. If at least one separate paragraph is devoted to the topic, students are more likely

Table 1
Secondary United States History Textbooks

Total Coverage of the Holocaust

Number of Lines	Number of Textbooks
75–83	2
70–74	0
65–69	1
60–64	2
55–59	2
50–54	2
45–49	1
40–44	1
35–39	2
30–34	5
25–29	4
20–24	3
15–19	4
10–14	5
5–9	9
1–4	13
0	9

Median coverage = 10 lines, about 3 sentences

to take notice than if phrases or sentences are in different locations in the text. Of the 65 texts examined, 35 do not have a separate paragraph on the Holocaust. Since nine textbooks do not include any coverage, 26 books have some coverage, but not as a separate paragraph.

Table 1 displays an overview of the total coverage on the Holocaust. About one-third of the texts devoted fewer than two sentences to the topic. The book with the greatest amount of coverage,[15] has 83 lines, roughly one page. Much of that coverage is a personal account by a survivor. While this account provides invaluable insights to the student reader, we should remember that space given to the personal account is not space of explanatory text.

As table 1 indicates, the median coverage is three lines. The following excerpt is from a book which is close to median coverage and is presented to illustrate typical coverage.

Few of them [Americans] knew all that had been going on in Germany under Hitler's rule. The dictator had a violent hatred for people of the Jewish faith. In Germany and elsewhere, these people were taken from their homes and placed in special prisons known as "concentration camps." There several million Jews died or were put to death in gas chambers.[16]

We are critical of the above sample coverage for all the topics, descriptions, and explanation not included, but consider that half the textbooks have less coverage.

Most texts that make slight reference to the Holocaust simply state that Jews died or were killed without any explanation. A sample of this type coverage is Brown.

Of course there was joy at the news of victory in Europe. For three reasons however the celebrations were dimmed by sorrow. For one, the conquest of Germany revealed that millions of Jews had been put to death in concentration camps located in central and eastern Europe.[17]

This is the book's total coverage of the Holocaust.

Another book which gives slight attention to the Holocaust is Garraty's. In discussing changes in the United States during World War II, the textbook gives an unique connection to the Holocaust.

The war affected blacks in many ways. Several factors operated to improve their lot. One was the reaction of Americans to Hitler's senseless murder of millions of Jews, an outgrowth of his doctrine of "Aryan" superiority, which compelled many Americans to re-examine their own views about race.[18]

Any discussion of textbook treatment of the Holocaust includes the concern of coverage of more recent texts compared with the coverage of earlier texts. A comparison of the amount of coverage by publication date of the 65 secondary United States history textbooks is displayed in table 2.

Care should be taken to avoid overinterpreting the data from this table. The average number of lines for the years with very few texts published can be misleading. Nevertheless, there appears to be no pattern to the amount of coverage. It is somewhat encouraging to observe that the most recent book examined,[19] has three times the coverage as the average of the total group. Still the book with the greatest amount of coverage was published in 1971.

Table 2
Secondary United States History Textbooks

Total Coverage by Years of Publication

Year of Publication	Number of Textbooks	Average Number of Lines
1982	1	32
1980	1	3
1979	7	27
1978	7	31
1977	16	14
1976	5	9
1975	9	18
1974	6	17
1973	2	25
1972	4	22
1971	4	34
1970	2	10
1967	1	29

Another way to get a sense of changes over time is to compare books that have undergone revision. The revision of Abramowitz's *American History* is a good example of real revision.[20] The 1979 edition has 55 lines while the 1971 version had only eight. Not all revisions are actual revisions, however, at least on the sections dealing with the Holocaust. Risjord's *People and Our Country* (1978) was reprinted under the title, *A History of the United States From 1877* (1979).[21] Not a word on the Holocaust was changed. Similar conclusions are found when comparing Wood's *America: Its People and Values* (1979)[22] with the previous edition of 1975. Again, no changes are found with Brown's *Let Freedom Ring: A United States History* (1977).[23] It appears to be the same book published in 1974 with the title, *Man in America.*

Much of the emphasis and attention to studying the Holocaust was sparked by NBC TV's series *The Holocaust* (1978). Much time does elapse between a textbook's conception and actual publication. Perhaps it is still too soon to tell if the recent attention to the Holocaust will be reflected in textbooks. Thus far there are glimmers of hope and cause for optimism, but nothing truly substantial.

Causes of the Holocaust. Once we have seen that the United States history texts do not devote much coverage to the Holocaust, it is hardly surprising to learn that effective explanations of the events are scarce. Of the books surveyed, 9 do not mention the Holocaust; 11 mention it but do not say who caused it; 17 put the blame on the Nazis; 16 identify Hitler as the cause; 8 include both Hitler and the Nazis; one book identifies Germans and the Nazis, and one book the Germans.

Of the books that address the issue at all, the most common comment is that Hitler hated the Jews. It is an incredible jump from that simple statement to the assertion—without any explanation—that six million people died as a consequence of his hatred, but only a few books attempt such an explanation. Similarly, while a few books refer to Hitler's use of the Jews as scapegoats, only one book explains this concept in some detail.

> Once in power, the Nazis set up concentration camps for political opponents. Soon the camps were being used mostly for persons who belonged to groups Hitler hated. The group he hated most was the Jews. The Nazis blamed the Jews for the economic troubles of the 1920's. The Germans were suffering from harsh times and the Nazis knew it was easier to gain and keep power by creating widespread hatred of identifiable individuals, such as Jews, rather than to talk about complicated economic facts relating to gold prices, production-consumption gaps, etc. Furthermore, because Jews had a different religion from their neighbors, who were mainly Christians, it was easy to point to the Jews and say that they were not like other Germans and, therefore, "un-German."[24]

Three books refer to racism and the master race concept as a cause. VerSteeg has, "the racism of the Nazis reached a particularly maddened climax with a campaign against the Jews."[25] Smith has, "Acting on this belief [master race] the Nazis systematically imprisoned, enslaved, tortured, and killed millions of people—Poles, Russians, Ukrainians, Gypsies, as well as Jews—because they were not included in his master race."[26] Also, "This was part of Hitler's plan to kill off all of the people he considered 'unacceptable.'"[27]

While many books mention that Hitler hated the Jews without explanation, only one book attempts to face the reason for the hatred. Banks says, "It is not clear why Hitler hated the Jews so much."[28] Three books refer to anti-Semitism. "Even before embarking on a career of conquest, Hitler had revealed his irrational cruelty by his treatment of the Jews. As soon as the Nazi regime came into power in 1933, it undertook anti-Semitic measures."[29] Bragdon also has, "Hitler's virulent anti-Semitism strongly aroused public opinion in

America against Germany."[30] Risjord writes, "Hitler eventually un-
leashed the anti-Jewish hysteria by ordering the extermination of all
Jews in Germany, and ultimately, Europe."[31] Only Okum refers to
the antecedent prejudice. "For Germany, along with much of Europe,
had a long record of anti-Jewish prejudice."[32]

The above excerpts are not samples. They are all the explanations
of the causes of the Holocaust in the 65 United States history texts
examined. Collectively, they do not offer much explanation. A student
reading the textbooks, however carefully, will likely develop the
impression that the Holocaust just happened.

The Period of Pre-War Oppression. As we have seen, the secondary
United States history textbooks do not adequately treat the causes
of the Holocaust. They also do not adequately deal with the events
leading up to the actual extermination. If students are to learn anything
from their study of history, they should learn that events of the
magnitude of the Holocaust do not simply just happen. They should
also learn from their study of the Holocaust, lessons which would
help safeguard their future. To understand the sequence of events—
how each repressive action was slightly more repressive than the
preceeding ones, which helped lull people, both the oppressors and
the victims, into inaction—would help students be more alert, more
perceptive citizens. The textbooks do not present these lessons. Two-
thirds of the textbooks do not devote a single line to this period.
Nine books do not have anything on the Holocaust, therefore nothing
on the pre-war oppression period. Of the textbooks that do have
something on the Holocaust, 24 have nothing on the pre-war oppression, and 32 do include at least one line.

Thus only 57 percent of the books that mention the Holocaust
also include some attention to the events leading up to the exterminations. At least half of these texts devote two sentences or fewer
to the period. We are then left with only 12 of the 65 books that
give more than two sentences to the period. When we consider these
facts, it is no wonder that most of our students are ignorant of this
part of history. An example of one of the more complete treatments
of the period (17 lines) is given below by Bragdon.

As soon as the Nazi regime came to power in 1933, it undertook
anti-Semitic measures with the dismissal of "non-Aryan" officials,
teachers, and army officers from their posts through legislation and
"spontaneous" vigilante action, and the Jews of Germany were subjected
to ever-increasing persecution. They were denied citizenship, kept out
of schools and professions, forbidden to marry any but their own kind,

Table 3

Secondary United States History Textbooks

Coverage of the Period of Prewar Oppression

Number of Lines	Number of Textbooks
21–27	2
16–20	3
11–15	1
6–10	6
1–5	12
0	41

subjected to humiliating penalties, and systematically robbed by the state. Tens of thousands were placed in "protective custody" in concentration camps, from which very few would ever return.[33]

While we may disagree with the author's omission of many details and explanations or with the use of the phrase "their own kind," we note that this excerpt is one of the most complete on this period. Madgic also gives some details of the oppressive decrees and concludes the paragraph with, "and forced eventually into internment and slave-labor camps where they were grossly mistreated."[34] To put the total coverage of the pre-war period of oppression in another perspective, if we total all the lines of the 65 books, we have a space equivalent to 63 sentences, or about 2.5 pages. If a student were to read all 65 texts, he would still not receive an adequate explanation of the period. An interesting observation is made when we look more closely at some of the textbooks with the greatest amount of coverage on this period. It appears that books that give more than slight coverage of the pre-war period run out of space, or for some reason, do not give proportionate coverage to the Holocaust in general.

Non-Jewish Victims. We have seen that the textbooks give scant attention to the Holocaust in general and to the period of pre-war oppression. They almost do not recognize the five to six million non-Jewish victims at all. Of the 65 books reviewed, 39 (60 percent) have absolutely nothing on this group of victims. Of the 26 books that have something on this topic, only nine have more than one sentence. Some sample excerpts of token coverage are given below.

Glenn S. Pate

Table 4
Secondary United States History Textbooks

Comparison of Selected Textbooks'
Coverage of Pre-War Oppression
With Total Coverage of the Holocaust

| | Lines of Coverage | |
Textbook	Other Than Pre-War Period	Pre-War Period
Bragdon (1970)	4	17
Heller	10	27
Magdic	16	15
Shenton	32	26

"Several million non-Jews had also been killed."[35]

"The weapons Hitler used to persecute the Jews (and other minorities such as the Catholics) were name-calling, fear and ignorance."[36]

"Thousands of other people whom the Nazis considered enemies were also murdered."[37]

Two books with the greatest amount of coverage on this topic are Banks and Wiltz. Their complete descriptions of these several million victims are given.

> The Germans also enslaved great numbers of non-Jews from occupied countries, particularly Russia. A high percentage of them—victims of malnutrition, disease, overwork and abuse—did not survive.[38]
>   Hitler's Nazis did not only kill Jews. They murdered millions of other people with whom they did not agree or of whom they were afraid. Among these were people who wrote or spoke out against the Nazis and people of other political beliefs, such as communists. Victory in Europe came too late for the millions of Europeans who were put to death by the Nazis.[39]

In reading the above excerpts, you have just read one-fourth of the total coverage of the non-Jewish victims of the Holocaust as presented in the 65 books examined.

The Tone of the Textbooks. There may be some disagreement over the proper language of a history textbook. In general, writers present the facts of what happened without converting the text into an essay. On the other hand, it is usually easy to determine what an author thinks are good or bad events or movements. In describing the Holocaust the facts do speak for themselves and strong language is not needed. Still, it would seem that a writer would feel compelled to express outrage at the events of the Holocaust.

This researcher attempted to categorize each textbook, based on the language used, as being either critical of the events or simply reporting them in an objective manner. Of the 65 secondary United States history textbooks examined, eleven do not have enough on the Holocaust to make a judgment, 39 are critical in tone, and 15 are objective in tone.

Sample language of those characterized as critical in tone are:

"This senseless slaughter in Germany . . . ."[40]

"Such massive and senseless brutality was new in the history of mankind."[41]

"the horrors of Hitler's inhuman Nazis."[42]

"systematically and diabolically killed in specially built extermination camps."[43]

Two samples of writing characterized as objective are:

Hitler said that the Jews were not part of the master race. He encouraged people to blame the Jews for Germany's troubles and to hate the Jews. Some Jews escaped from Germany. The others were sent to prison camps. There, over a period of 10 years, more than 6 million Jews were killed on Hitler's orders.[44]

Hitler believed that the Germans were a master race. The Nazi party blamed bad times in Germany on the Jews. Six million Jews were killed by the Nazis. Soon Hitler and the Nazi party totally controlled the lives of the German people.[45]

The above two examples of objective writing both say that the Jews were blamed for Germany's troubles. Notice that neither text adds that the Jews, in fact, were not to blame. A student reading without great care could easily leave with the impression that the Jews were to blame.

The Camps. To a great many people, thoughts about the Holocaust conjure images of life and death in the concentration and extermination camps. Certainly the most detailed and revealing descriptions of the camps will be found in personal accounts by survivors, but it would seem that the history textbooks would have some space for these incredible experiences. With very few exceptions, the textbooks examined omit the camps. A few books use adjectives such as terrible and horrible to describe the camps—most books do not.

A few texts give some details. Reich, for example, has, "After the Allied troops conquered Germany, they discovered the terrible German concentration camps. These were special prison camps where prisoners were tortured and killed."[46] Gardner gives a more detailed description.

> Jews, Communists, and non-Germans who were considered a threat to the Nazis were sentenced to concentration camps. Families were separated: fathers sent to one camp, mothers and children to another. There they were forced to work on labor gangs and to live on mere scraps of food.[47]

Wiltz adds some details by referring to the use of hair, gold teeth, bones, and ashes. The Social Science Curriculum Center gives a three-paragraph account of an extermination scene. The eyewitness may have been an Ukrainian prisoner/guard, although his identity is not clear. The most complete description is by Cuban, who has a five-page personal account.

In addition to details of the camps, the books have the option of adding some specificity by giving the names of some of the camps. Of the 56 secondary United States history texts which give some attention to the Holocaust, only 11 identify a camp by name. Okum gives an impressive statement without naming any camps. "As Allied troops passed through Nazi-occupied Europe, they saw eighty-five concentration camps."[48] One fault with references to the camps, and to the coverage of the Holocaust in general, is that most books give the impression that most, or all, of the people killed were Germans, and that the camps were all in Germany. It is interesting to note that Treblinka, which ranks second on the total deaths scale, is not identified by any textbook (see table 5).

Resistance. While many victims of the Holocaust seemingly went willingly, or at least passively, one of the great myths of the Holocaust is the absence of resistance. Some observers of the Holocaust may have recorded victimization without resistance, although they may have not recognized passive resistance when they saw it. Other observers may not have recognized resistance by those who left when they could, or those who joined partisan forces to fight with military weapons, or those who died while resisting in their various own

Table 5
Secondary United States History Textbooks

Concentration and Extermination Camps

Number of Camps Named	Number of Textbooks
4	2
3	2
2	2
1	5
0	54

Name of Camp	Number of Textbooks Naming
Auschwitz	6
Bergen-Belsen	6
Buchenwald	5
Dachau	5
Terezin	1

ways, or those who survived due to their resistance. The myth is that none of the six million Jewish victims and the several million non-Jewish resisted. This myth does great disservice to large numbers of individuals and to a whole people.

The secondary United States history textbooks help perpetrate this myth. Of the 65 texts surveyed, not one, repeat, not one, indicates that there was resistance to the Holocaust. Gardner comes closest: "The Nazis forced the Jews into one section of . . . [Warsaw]. They also executed thousands of Poles. But a resistance movement grew stronger, despite Nazi terror."[49] This book does mention some form of resistance, but it is not clear as to who the resisters were. No book makes reference to the rebellion at Bialystok, to the destruction of the crematoriums at Auschwitz, or to one of the most incredible and superhuman epochs of resistance ever, the Warsaw Ghetto uprising. Small wonder that students do not understand this period and that the myth continues.

"Genocide" and "Holocaust". The events of the Holocaust could be described and explained without using these two terms, but students

should be aware of them. It is difficult to imagine writing on the topic without using both terms. Surely students need to know the concept of genocide and of the prime example, the Holocaust.

Of the 65 texts examined, 56 include some attention to the Holocaust. Of these 56 texts, 44 do not use either term. Only six books have the term genocide and another six texts have the term Holocaust. No book uses both terms; neither does any book have either term in the index. One book[50] has Holocaust as a heading of a section. A text which uses one of the terms usually includes a brief definition. Weisberger calls genocide, "the deliberate, planned destruction of an entire people."[51] Madgic says it is, "racial extermination."[52] The Holocaust is defined by Social Science Staff as "the Nazi extermination of the Jews of Europe"[53] and by Graff as, "the terrible destruction."[54]

Since the term Holocaust is much better known by the general public now than it was several years ago, it may seem that the more recent textbooks would more likely include it. This is not the case, however. Of the 12 books examined which have been published since 1979, only three use Holocaust. None uses genocide. The percentage of the more recent books using the terms is virtually the same as the total collection.

The Survivors. A unique opportunity exists for the study of history. Usually, the accounts of events are written by the victors, not the victims. With the Holocaust, the survivors represent a group of educated, articulate participants in this most bizarre and incredible series of events. They have become important citizens in several countries, yet the textbooks ignore them.

Of the 56 books which have anything on the Holocaust, only seven mention them, and none of these books gives more than three lines to the survivors. They are mentioned only in passing with no book giving a full paragraph.

Abramowitz has, "The survivors of the death camps told of their fight for survival to a shocked world."[55] Bass gives a different perspective. "For more than thirty years, survivors of the experience would continue to hunt for these people [Nazi leaders] to bring them to trial."[56] Two textbooks note that some survivors came to the United States. "Fortunately, more than three hundred fifty thousands Jews were able to escape from Europe. Many came to the United States."[57] This reference is not clear whether they left Europe before, during, or after the war, although the use of escape implies before or during the war. Pitt's book has the greatest amount of coverage on the survivors. "Over 150,000 European Jews migrated to America after the war. Many were survivors of Nazi concentration camps who had spent time in displaced persons camps after the fall of Germany. They became a living reminder of the Holocaust."[58] Later, the textbook discusses anti-Semitism in America: "Still, any stirring of such prejudices was considered a danger by a people permanently scarred by the Holocaust."[59] Bragdon refers to the survivors in a section on Palestine and includes a hint at immigration restriction. "In the 1920's, many Jewish 'Zionists' had come to settle in this 'homeland,' and more had fled there to escape Hitler's persecutions. After World War II, many such refugees were smuggled into the area by daring volunteers on small ships."[60] Another slight reference, and this one with an unusual angle, is made by Graff, who notes that some of those who had not fled the Nazis in occupied countries "hid Jews and others seeking to escape from German concentration camps."[61]

The above excerpts are the total coverage of the survivors in the 65 secondary United States history texts. It should also be noted that the books which do make some reference to the survivors have more total coverage on the Holocaust than most books. The mean number of lines of these seven books is 31, considerably more than the mean for the total group of texts.

The Role of the United States. Many of the survivors have attributed their will to live to their desire to bear witness to the events. They felt that if the free world knew the facts, intervention and rescue would result.

Nevertheless, although the free world knew of the events in detail, U.S. restrictive immigration rules were not eased. Nor did we attempt to intervene to stop the Holocaust. While most of our military troops and the ordinary citizens back home were unaware of the extermination, our top government officials knew, but chose to do nothing. The textbooks do not include this information, and most give the impression that we were unaware of the Holocaust. Not one book makes reference to the Evian Conference, the voyage of the *St. Louis,* or the implications of each. Hitler used the ineffectiveness of the Evian Conference as a strange rationale for the extermination of the Jews: the Conference demonstrated that the free world really did not care.

Two books approach the topic of intervention. In a question at the end of a chapter is, "Among the tragedies of World War II was the Holocaust—the Nazi extermination of the Jews of Europe. How and why did this happen? Do you think the Allies—Britain, the U.S. and the Soviet Union—were partly to blame?"[62] Bauer also hints at intervention: In discussing the role of the United States, she notes, "The question for the U.S. was how to help the French and British and still keep American troops out of the fighting."[63] Later, he has, "But Americans could not ignore the illegal and immoral acts of Germany and Italy, the Axis Powers."[64] Three pages later he mentions that,

> In the meantime, Jews and opponents of Hitler in Germany were being killed in concentration camps. Some Jews got out of the country before Hitler closed the borders. Most were not that fortunate. Six million Jews would not leave or could not leave. They eventually died in the Holocaust in Germany. What finally brought the United States to declare war? The Japanese attacked the American naval base at Pearl Harbor, Hawaii, on December 7, 1941.[65]

Bauer makes it clear that we went to war to defend ourselves and not to help some friends and innocent civilians in Europe. These are the only two books that even hint at pre-war intervention.

In reference to when we knew about the Holocaust, most of the textbooks which say anything on the topic, give the impression that we had no idea of what was going on until the war was over. Sample excerpts below illustrate this point.

> "At the close of the war American troops had discovered the extent of the systematic murder of Jews and opponents of the Nazi regime in concentration camps."[66]

> "However, victory brought to light the full horror of the Nazi rule."[67]

> "The Allied soldiers, even the hardened combat veterans, were stunned by what they found. Such massive and senseless brutality was new in the history of mankind."[68]

> "Then, in their moment of triumph, the Allies were chilled by [the] discovery of Nazi concentration camps."[69]

> "The resultant reports and pictures stunned people all across the globe."[70]

Three books refer to the discovery of the camps as something less than a total surprise. Cuban has, "Although the rest of the world had heard rumors about the Nazi death camps, many people refused to believe the enormity of the Nazi crime."[71] Clark has, "Rumors of the horrors of Nazi concentration camps became statistical facts following World War II. The people of the world were stunned."[72] Risjord deals more directly with our knowledge of the camps. "Most Americans and Europeans, however, either could not believe the atrocities were occurring or chose to ignore them."[73] A few pages later, Risjord also has, "Hitler's growing persecution of Jews and his increasing appetite for conquest made neutrality seem increasingly immoral."[74]

Allen comes right out and states that we knew of the extermination. "Events in Europe moved swiftly in 1938. News from Germany of the mass extinction of the nation's Jewish population by the horror of Hitler's inhuman Nazis seared the American conscience."[75] The most complete and accurate account of the role of the United States is in Abramowitz.

> During the war, Americans continued to hear stories of terror about the Nazis. In August 1943, the *New York Times* produced evidence of a list of nearly 2.5 million people starved or killed by the Nazis. Many people tried to arrange payment to the German government for release of large numbers of people in Nazi concentration camps. But nothing was done by the Allied governments.
>
> In 1944, a Treasury Department official accused the State Department of neglecting the problem of help for Europe's Jews. President Roosevelt at this point agreed to take limited action. He approved of trying to help Jews in Europe move to Palestine. But British officials who controlled Palestine turned the plan down. They feared it might cause conflicts with Arabs in the region. Once again, nothing was done.[76]

Six books make reference to immigration, either directly or by implication. The excerpts are presented below in a sequence of increasing honesty. The first two imply that our gates were open. "German immigration dropped off in the early twentieth century. In the late 1930's, however, it increased because of the oppression and persecution of Adolf Hitler's government. This persecution was directed mainly at Germany's Jews."[77] This is Brown's only reference to the Holocaust. Ver Steeg has, "the racism of the Nazis reached a particularly maddened climax with a campaign against the Jews, many of whom fled to more friendly countries, including the U.S."[78] Students can be misled by such writing and develop the impression that anyone who wanted to come to the United States would be welcome.

Baldwin does not mention the Holocaust, but does have a section on immigration and admits that we did have quota laws. "There have been exceptions which have permitted additional refugees from war torn countries to enter the United States." No examples or details are given. Continuing on, he notes, "In some cases, people who wanted to escape from an unjust government in another country were not always able to enter the United States."[79]

Three textbooks of the 65 examined deal with the facts in a more complete and honest manner. Risjord has, "Restrictive immigration laws of the early 1920's had stopped millions of Jews from entering the United States after World War I."[80] While this reference is not focused on the Holocaust, it does make a connection between Jews and restrictive immigration laws. Pitt does even better. "Attempts by Jewish leaders to have Roosevelt intervene with Hitler and steer intended victims to the United States met with little success. Immigration policy had frozen in 1924, and no one, not even the President, seemed willing or able to thaw it out in 1942."[81] The only author which includes the difficulties of people leaving Germany and the difficulties of entering the United States is Graff.

> Many of them tried to escape to the free world. But only a small percentage were able to do so. Most countries—including the United States—enforced immigration laws that allowed only a limited number of people to enter each year. In addition, most of these countries required that immigrants have a certain amount of money and papers signed by their local police. Few of those who escaped the Nazis could meet such requirements.[82]

In spite of the frankness of the last three books referred to, most of the textbooks do not give a serious consideration to the role of the United States with regard to the Holocaust. By statement, by implication, or by omission, they give the impression that the Holocaust was something far removed from its concern and its citizens. The overriding implications are that the pre-war period of oppression was irrelevant to us, that we were unaware or helpless during the exterminations, and that we welcomed all those who wanted to come to the United States. Of those that treat the liberation of the camps, the implication is that the U.S. took in all those who wanted to come. These implications are incorrect and misleading. The truth is that we did not do anything before and during the Holocaust that we could have done. The truth is also that our immigration laws were not changed to permit survivors for three years after the end of the war. Our textbooks do not reflect this.

The Nuremberg Trials. Of the textbooks examined which do have some coverage of the Holocaust, 60 percent omit the Nuremberg Trials. In total, only one-third of the books recognize the trials. Most of these do so at the conclusion of the chapter on World War II and give only a sentence or two to the topic.

Shafer's treatment is typical: "The wartime Allies did agree on the punishment of German 'war criminals,' the major Nazi military leaders. Many of them were tried and sentenced to death or long imprisonment by an International Tribunal sitting at Nuremberg from November, 1945, until October, 1946."[83] Notice that this excerpt does not explain why the war criminals were tried, neither do most of the texts that approach the subject. Klose, for example, mentions the trials, but only "for violating international law."[84] Wood gives the greatest amount of coverage to the trials with a six-paragraph discussion. Clearly, our students will not reach an understanding of the Trials by reading these textbooks.

Pedagogical Techniques. Three pedagogical devices common to textbooks are the inclusion of questions to the students, pictures, and suggested additional reading. One way of assessing an author's or publisher's stress on a particular topic is to note the presence or absence of these pedagogical techniques.

Of the 65 books examined, 42 include neither a question nor suggested activity. Twelve books have one question each; two books have a suggested activity; three books have two questions and two activities each; five books have two questions; and one book[85] has three questions. Sample questions and activities are presented below.

"How many Jews perished in Nazi concentration camps?"[86]

"Describe the treatment of Jews in Nazi Germany."[87]

"How and why the world stood silent while Hitler committed his atrocities might be a topic for a group discussion."[88]

"Research the life of Anne Frank. Discuss why her story remains important today to people around the world."[89]

There are 33 pictures in the 65 books examined, but 46 books do not have a single picture. Thirteen books have one picture each; three have two pictures; one has three pictures; one has five; and one[90] has six pictures.

Considering the power and impact that appropriate visuals can have and the insights a student can develop from them, most of the textbooks are missing important educational opportunities. The pictures that are included in the texts range in emotional load from scenes of store windows marked with slogans, to people carrying suitcases, to scenes of mass graves. Some of the pictures are simply inserted into the books without explanatory descriptions. Bragdon,[91] for example, in his discussion of the Nuremberg Trials, supplies a photograph of a mass grave, but without identification of the victims or explanation. There does not appear to be a pattern with number

Summary of Each Textbook's Coverage of the Holocaust

UNITED STATES HISTORY TEXTBOOKS		TOTAL LINES	SEPARATE PARAGRAPHS	NON-JEWS	WHO CAUSED	PRE-WAR	PICTURES	CAMPS	GENOCIDE/HOLOCAUST	ACTIVITIES/QUESTIONS	NUREMBERG	READINGS	TONE
1. Abramowitz	'75	2			NAZI								
2. Abramowitz	'79	55	YES	1	NAZI					3Q	YES		CRIT
3. Allan	'76	0											
4. Allen	'76	4			HIT/NAZI						YES		CRIT
5. Baldwin	'74	3											CRIT
6. Baldwin	'72	0											
7. Banks	'82	32	YES	6	HITLER				H	1A		Anne Frank	CRIT
8. Barlett	'79	17		3	HITLER	2	1			2Q		Anne Frank	OB
9. Barlett	'75	0											
10. Bass	'79	24	YES		NAZI			BUCH/DAC/AUSCH/B-B		1Q	YES		CRIT
11. Bauer	'79	6			HITLER				H			Never Forget	CRIT

#	Name	Year								1Q / 1A			
12.	Bidna	'77	4	YES									OB
13.	Boyle	'70	0										
14.	Brady	'77	2	YES		NAZI							OB
15.	Bragdon	'78	9		1	NAZI	1						CRIT
16.	Bragdon	'70	21	YES		HITLER	17				YES	Shires Bullock	CRIT
17.	Branson	'75	0										
18.	Branson	'77	12	YES			5			1Q	YES		CRIT
19.	Brown	'80	3										OB
20.	Buggey	'77	10	YES	1	GER/NAZI	1	B-B				Anne Frank	CRIT
21.	Chapin	'74	31	YES	1	NAZI	8			2Q			CRIT
22.	Clark	'75	26		1	HITLER	7						CRIT
23.	Cuban	'71	83	YES	4	NAZI	6	BUCH/TER/B-B	G	1Q			CRIT
24.	Current	'74	51	YES	1	NAZI	8	BUCH/B-B/DAC			YES		CRIT
	Eibling	'77	2		1		1				YES		OB
26.	Forcey	'71	8			HITLER					YES		OB
27.	Freidel	'78	27		3	HIT/NAZI	9				YES		CRIT

262

UNITED STATES HISTORY TEXTBOOKS		TOTAL LINES	SEPARATE PARAGRAPHS	NON-JEWS	WHO CAUSED	PRE-WAR	PICTURES	CAMPS	GENOCIDE/ HOLOCAUST	QUESTIONS/ ACTIVITIES	NUREMBERG	READINGS	TONE
28. Gardner	'77	78	YES	1	HIT/NAZI	7	2	AUSCH		2Q			CRIT
29. Garraty	'79	4				1							CRIT
30. Goldshlag	'74	8	YES		HITLER								OB
31. Graff	'67	29	YES	1	NAZI	3				1Q 1A			OB
32. Graff	'78	43	YES	1	NAZI	4	1	DAC	H		YES		CRIT
33. Gross	'77	8			HITLER								CRIT
34. Heller	'71	37	YES	1	HITLER	27				1A			CRIT
35. Hughes	'78	9	YES	1	HIT/NAZI						YES		CRIT
36. Klose	'73	0					2						
37. Leinwand	'75	3			NAZI								OB
38. Linden	'79	16	YES		HITLER			AUS/DAC			YES		CRIT
39. Madgic	'75	31			HITLER	15			G		YES	Last of Just	CRIT

40. Okum	'73	50	YES	2	HITLER							CRIT
41. Pauline	'77	3			HIT/NAZI	1						OB
42. Pitt	'76	28		4					H	1Q		CRIT
43. Pulliam – 1	'77	2										CRIT
44. Pulliam – 2	'77	0										
45. Pulliam – 3	'77	0										
46. Reich	'71	8	YES		GERMAN							CRIT
47. Risjord	'79	67	YES	2	HIT/NAZI	17	1		H	1Q 1A	YES	CRIT
48. Sandler	'75	15			GERMAN		1					CRIT
49. Schwartz	'74	10				4						OB
50. Shafer	'77	11		2	HITLER	2	1			1Q	YES	CRIT
51. Shaftel	'72	8		2	NAZI							CRIT
Shenton	'78	58	YES	1	HITLER	26	1			2Q	YES	CRIT
53. Smith	'77	32	YES	5	HIT/NAZI	9	2	B-B/AUSCH			YES	CRIT
54. Social Science	'77	2			NAZI				H	1Q		OB

264

UNITED STATES HISTORY TEXTBOOKS	TOTAL LINES	SEPARATE PARAGRAPHS	NON-JEWS	WHO CAUSED	PRE-WAR	PICTURES	CAMPS	GENOCIDE/ HOLOCAUST	QUESTIONS/ ACTIVITIES	NUREMBERG	READINGS	TONE
55. Social Studies '75	45	YES		HIT/NAZI	2				1Q			OB
56. Strong '76	0											
57. Todd '77	21	YES	2	NAZI		1	BUC		1Q	YES		CRIT
58. Versteeg '77	30	YES		NAZI	4	3	AUSCH	G	1Q			CRIT
59. Wade '72	61	YES	3	NAZI	20			G				CRIT
60. Weinstein '74	1											
61. Weisberger '76	13	YES		HITLER	1			G	1Q	YES		CRIT
62. Wilder '78	9		2	NAZI								OB
63. Wilson '72	18		5		4						Anne Frank	CRIT
64. Wiltz '78	61	YES		HITLER			AUS/BUC/ DAC/B-B	G	2Q	YES	Anne Frank	CRIT
65. Wood '75	36	YES	4	HITLER					1Q	YES		OB

of pictures and publication date. Of the texts with more than one picture, four were published in 1977, one in 1979, and the book with the most pictures in 1971.

Textbooks frequently include suggested reading for students who wish to pursue a topic of interest or to further their study. Only eight books have titles suggested that are relevant to the Holocaust. Considering the interest students have in the topic (if they are exposed to it) and the large number of excellent books available, most of the books are again missing an educational opportunity.

The Diary of Anne Frank is the most commonly recommended book; it is named by Banks, Barlett, Buggey, Madgic, Wilson, and Wiltz.[92] Madgic also recommends *The Last of the Just*.[93] Bauer suggests *Never to Forget*.[94] Bragdon[95] has, "Study Hitler's organization campaign, particularly the Nuremberg Laws and the Week of the Broken Glass in 1938." Thus 57 books do not recommend a book of Holocaust relevance.

World History/Western Civilization Textbooks

This section considers textbooks used at the secondary level for courses in world history. While some courses and texts focus on the Western world, the term world history is used to include all texts whether or not they are truly world in scope. One of the most amazing aspects of the Holocaust is that it was orchestrated by an educated, technically advanced, Christian people. Perry notes that "the Nazis committed the greatest crime in human history."[96] Surely a textbook describing the history of mankind or of Western civilization would pay great attention to the Holocaust. Many books, however, give only token recognition to the events.

Total Coverage. Twenty-eight textbooks were examined for this section. Half of these books have fewer than 20 lines on the subject, about two paragraphs. The world history texts do have more total coverage than the United States history textbooks.

As table 6 indicates, the median coverage is 20 lines. The excerpt below is from a book which represents the median.

> One of the most frightful discoveries made in the ashes of the Third Reich, as Allied armies raced into Germany, was the shocking brutality and barbarism of the German concentration camps. In these, more than 10 million people, including six million Jews, were exterminated by starvation, poison, shooting, hanging, and burning in crematoria. One of the worst camps was Dachau near Munich. Some 32,000 prisoners were liberated there in April, 1945. The commandant of the camp at

Glenn S. Pate

Table 6
Secondary World History/Western Civilization Textbooks

Total Coverage

Number of Lines of Text[a]	Number of Textbooks
278	1
233	1
123	1
91–100	1
81–90	1
71–80	3
61–70	0
51–60	1
41–50	3
31–40	1
21–30	1
11–20	7
1–10	5
0	2

[a]median = 20 lines   mean = 51 lines

Auschwitz admitted that two and a half million people were exterminated there. Much of the evidence of such Nazi crimes was presented at the 10-month-long Nuremberg trials of major Nazi war criminals in 1945–1946 and at other trials held before military tribunals after 1945.[97]

It is interesting to note that this book mentions five methods of killing and omitted the use of gas. We also note all the ideas, events, explanations, and details not included. Bear in mind that half of the textbooks have less coverage than this example.

Several books give superficial, token coverage to the Holocaust in a sentence or two. In general, they state that Hitler hated the Jews and that during the war, many were killed or died. For example, in an otherwise excellent book, Stavrianos has only token coverage. In discussing the war, and under the heading, "Cost of the War," is "Six million Jews alone were murdered at Hitler's order."[98] Over 400 pages later in a section on Palestine is, "Palestine became more and more a crisis spot during the war years because Hitler carried his anti-Semitic campaign to the point of murdering six million Jews."[99]

Table 7

Secondary World History/Western Civilization Textbooks

Coverage by Year of Publication

Year of Publication	Number of Textbooks	Mean Number of Lines
1981	2	120
1980	2	30
1979	2	140
1977	6	41
1976	2	45
1974	4	23
1973	3	21
1971	1	123
1970	3	24
1969	1	73
1968	1	80
1966	1	20

This is the complete description and explanation of the Holocaust. Furthermore, nine of the 28 books do not devote even one separate paragraph to the topic.

The three books with the greatest amount of coverage were examined in order to determine what they included, which contributed substantially toward the larger coverage. Linder has a total of 278 lines, of which 117 lines are excerpts from Anne Frank's Diary.[100] Kownslar has 233 lines, of which 130 are on the period of pre-war oppression.[101] Perry's 123 lines include a 32-line account by Rudolf Hoess.[102] One book, Thompson's, has a ten-line personal account by Oscar Berger, who is identified only as a survivor of a Nazi concentration camp.[103] There is no reference to the Holocaust nor any explanation as to why he was a prisoner.

Efforts to determine any pattern in the relationship between coverage and date of publication are inconclusive. The relatively small number of books published each year make the mean number of lines less meaningful than if there were more books published.

Causes of the Holocaust. As with the United States history textbooks, many of the world history texts do not adequately explain why the Holocaust occurred. Most of the books which give token coverage simply state that it happened without even attempting an explanation.

Summary of Each Textbook's Coverage of the Holocaust

WORLD HISTORY/ WESTERN CIVILIZATION TEXTBOOKS	TOTAL LINES	SEPARATE PARAGRAPHS	NON-JEWS	WHO CAUSED	PRE-WAR	PICTURES	CAMPS	GENOCIDE/ HOLOCAUST	QUESTIONS/ ACTIVITIES	NUREMBERG	READINGS	TONE
1. Abramowitz '74	21		6	NAZI	5	1	DAC		2Q			FAC
2. Becker '77	98	YES	10	HITLER	29	1	BUC/AUSCH DAC	G	1Q	YES		CRIT
3. Belasco '70	10	YES		HITLER	7							CRIT
4. Cox '81	8		1	HITLER	2				2Q	YES		CRIT
5. Good '68	80	YES	7	HITLER	10		AUSCH/ BUCH/DAC		1Q	YES	Anne Frank	CRIT
6. Hane '73	6		2	HITLER		2			1Q			CRIT
7. Hayes '66	20	YES	4	HIT/NAZI	3				2Q	YES		CRIT
8. Holt '77	37	YES	4	HIT/NAZI	5	1			5Q	YES		CRIT
9. Johnson '76	88	YES	4	HIT/NAZI	5	2	None HAUSEN		3Q			CRIT
10. King '74	19		1	NAZI	6	1						FAC
11. Kownslar '81	233	YES	2		130	1	AUSCH	H	13Q		Dawid.	CRIT
12. Linder '79	278	YES	4	HITLER	10	3	MAP	G/H	15Q	YES	Mischa	CRIT

					HIT/NAZI		1		G/H	1Q			CRIT
13. Marvin	'76	2											CRIT
14. McNeill	'73	16	YES		HITLER	3				1Q			CRIT
15. Perry	'71	123	YES	19	HIT/NAZI	5	2	AUSCH	G/H	6Q	YES		CRIT
16. Petrovich	'70	20	YES	6	NAZI	2		DAC/AUSCH			YES		CRIT
17. Roehm	'70	41	YES		NAZI	23				1Q	YES	Wall	CRIT
18. Rogers	'73	41	YES	3	NAZI	14	2	DAC			YES		CRIT
19. Roselle	'69	73	YES		NAZI	2	1	DAC/AUSCH		1A	YES		CRIT
20. Sankowsky	'74	53	YES	18	HIT/NAZI	9	1	BELSEN		1Q 1A	YES	Mila 18	CRIT
21. Smith	'80	12			HITLER			THEB			YES		CRIT
22. Social Science	'77	19	YES	2	HIT/NAZI	10	2		G		NO		FAC
23. Stavrianos	'79	2			HITLER	1							CRIT
24. Tompson	'77	0											
2. Wallbank	'80	47	YES	8	NAZI	23	2		G	4Q 1A			CRIT
26. Weitzman	'74	0											
27. Welty	'77	16	YES	1	HIT/NAZI		1	AUSCH		1Q	NO	Anne Frank	CRIT
28. Yohe	'77	74	YES	9	HIT/NAZI	3	1			2Q	NO		CRIT

Nine books say that it was due to Hitler, seven identify the Nazis as the cause, and nine mention both Hitler and the Nazis.

The most common explanation given is the use of Jews as scapegoats for the problems that Germany had. Nine books (Becker, Cox, Hayes, Hane, Kownslar, Linder, Marvin, Perry, and Smith) identify the scapegoat theme.[104] Most of these discussions are extremely superficial, such as:

> "He blamed the Jews for the nation's troubles and vowed to avenge Germany's defeat in the war."[105]

> "He intensified his propaganda attacks on the Treaty of Versailles, on the government of the Weimar Republic, on the Communists, and especially on the Jews, on whom he blamed the defeat of Germany in the First World War and the ruinous unemployment of the depression years."[106]

Disturbingly, not all books which refer to the scapegoat concept mention that the Jews were not to blame for Germany's troubles. A reader of some of the texts could get the impression that the Jews were guilty.

Several authors—e.g., Becker, Hane, Kownslar, and McNeill—acknowledge the racial theories as a cause,[107] and most books that include race as a cause do indicate that the racial theories were without foundation. An example is: "all in pursuit of an entirely unscientific ideal of racial purity."[108] The most extensive coverage is given by Kownslar, whose book contains 66 lines, most of which is an interview with Hitler in 1933 and a speech by Goebbels in 1934 in a special section of readings.[109]

Perry and Wallbank both mention the efforts to build a "new order," into which the Jews did not belong. Perry has an eight-paragraph section on reasons why the Jews were victims and scapegoats. The text includes nationalist, economic and social, political, and psychological reasons and concludes with, "Ultimately there may be no rational explanation for Hitler's hatred of the Jews."[110]

Only two of the 28 books examined refer to the historical roots of anti-Semitism in Europe. Linder has, "By building on the anti-Jewish prejudices of many Germans, Hitler was able to get support for his plans to wipe out the Jews of Europe."[111] Abramowitz expresses a similar thought. "There had always been strong anti-Semitism and persecution of the Jewish people in Germany. Now the hatred that many other Germans felt for their Jewish countrymen came to the surface."[112] The books with the most serious attempt at explaining the causes are Linder, Kownslar and Perry.[113] It is difficult to understand

Table 8
Secondary United States and
World History/Western Civilization Textbooks

Total Coverage on the Holocaust

Total Lines[a]	United States History		World History/ Western Civilization	
	n	%	n	%
200–278	0		2	7
100–199	0		1	4
80–99	1	2	2	7
60–79	4	6	3	11
40–59	6	9	4	14
20–39	14	21	2	7
10–19	9	14	7	25
1–9	22	34	5	18
0	9	14	2	7
	65	100	28	100

Median coverage of the Holocaust in U.S. history textbooks—10 lines
Median coverage of the Holocaust in world history/western civilization
textbooks—20 lines

how a student could have a grasp of the Holocaust without a knowledge
of the antecedent anti-Semitism. This knowledge is especially helpful
in understanding the heinous behavior of many people in the occupied
countries, but not one book approaches that aspect. An extremely
rare consideration of the role of the German people is in Perry.

The systematic extermination of European Jewry was the terrible
fulfillment of Nazi racial theories that regarded Germans as a master
race and Jews as sub-human. Nazi executioners convinced themselves
that they were cleansing Europe of a lower and dangerous form of
humanity that threatened the German Fatherland. If they had any
second thoughts about their evil work, they convinced themselves that
they bore no personal responsibility for these deeds, that they were
only following orders, doing their duty like good soldiers. By utilizing
the technology and bureaucracy of a modern state and by relying on
the dedicated service of thousands of "little men" who rounded up the
victims, transported them to the death camps, served as concentration
camp guards, and kept careful records of those destined for execution,
the Nazis committed the greatest crime in human history.[114]

Table 9
Secondary United States and
World History/Western Civilization Textbooks

Total Coverage by Years of Publication

Year of Publication	United States History		World History/ Western Civilization	
	Number of Textbooks	Mean Number of Lines	Number of Textbooks	Mean Number of Lines
1982	1	32	0	—
1981	1	3	2	120
1980	0	—	2	30
1979	7	27	2	140
1978	7	31	0	—
1977	16	14	6	41
1976	5	9	2	45
1975	9	18	0	—
1974	6	17	4	23
1973	2	25	3	21
1972	4	22	0	—
1971	4	34	1	123
1970	2	10	3	24
1969	0	—	1	73
1968	0	—	1	80
1967	1	29	0	—
1966	0	—	1	20

It is unfortunate that more textbooks do not address this crucial aspect of the Holocaust.

In summary, the textbooks, with very few exceptions, either ignore the causes of the Holocaust or else give the topic superficial treatment. The Holocaust is of such magnitude and uniqueness that the textbooks certainly should give an adequate explanation of its causes. Most books do not even attempt an explanation.

The Period of Pre-War Oppression. Just as the world history textbooks do not adequately explain the causes of the Holocaust, they do not explain or describe the oppressive events of the 1930s. Only five of the 28 texts give more than three sentences to this period. Of the 28 books examined, seven have absolutely nothing on the period; 16 have fewer than ten lines; one has between ten and 20 lines; three

Table 10
Secondary United States and
World History/Western Civilization Textbooks

Separate Paragraph

	United States History	World History/ Western Civilization	Total
YES	30–46%	19–68%	53%
NO	35–54%	9–32%	47%

Coverage of Prewar Oppression

Number of Lines[2]	United States History	World History/ Western Civilization
130	0	1
25–30	2	1
20–24	1	2
15–19	3	0
10–14	0	4
5–9	6	6
1–4	12	7
0	41	7
	65	28

[a] 0 lines = median = 5 lines
   3 lines = mean = 11 lines

have between 20 and 30 lines; and one book[115] has 130 lines. Thus only one book gives serious attention to the period.

Some books mention that there was some persecution of the Jews without giving any details. In discussing Arab-Jewish hostility, Stavrianos has, "This was especially true when Hitler started his persecution of the Jews in the 1930's."[116] It is not likely that students can develop a sense of the period by reading such a brief reference. Several books do give a few details. Holt, for example, has "In persecuting the Jewish citizens of Germany, the Nazis destroyed their stores and homes and burned their synagogues. Jews were not allowed to be doctors or lawyers. Nor were they allowed any rights that other citizens had."[117] Good goes somewhat further and quotes some of the Nuremberg Laws.

The textbook with the greatest coverage, by far, is Kownslar. It has a two-paragraph section under the heading of "The Persecution of the Jews." This section describes the scapegoat concept, gives samples of early persecution events, and identifies several of the Nuremberg Laws. The next section, labeled "Kristallnacht," contains a long paragraph describing that event. The book then goes on to describe other oppressive events, the concentration camps, and the resulting destruction. There is also a half-page map of Europe which shows the number of Jews killed in each country. A separate section of readings later in the book devotes a full page to *Kristallnacht*. This book stands out as an example of serious efforts to adequately explain this period, as it does in its attempt to explain the causes of the Holocaust.[118] Most of the books, however, are woefully inadequate in their treatment of this period.

The Non-Jewish Victims. While we know that some five to six million non-Jewish civilians were deliberately killed by the Nazis, most textbooks do not reflect this fact. Only two books have more than ten lines on the subject: Perry has 19 and Sankowsky has 18.[119] The median coverage is two lines, one sentence. Nine texts have no coverage, and 17 have from one to ten lines. Writing which typifies the superficial coverage is usually done by naming groups in addition to Jews which suffered. They also state that those who opposed the Nazis were imprisoned or killed. No book gives a description of the systematic genocide policies against Jehovah's Witnesses, gypsies, homosexuals, and other groups.

The excerpt below is from a book which has more coverage than the average text.

> People who had opposed the Nazis lived in terror from day to day. At any moment the Gestapo might enter their homes and seize them. The Gestapo could arrest anyone at any time and for any reason. Those arrested were given no trial. They were tortured until they gave false confession. Then they were executed or sent to concentration camps. Thousands of innocent Germans—Jews, Protestants, and Catholics— disappeared forever during the Hitler rule. Because its secret police had such great power, Germany became known as a police state.[120]

We notice that the emphasis above is on the terror tactics and the implication that only those who opposed the Nazis were done away with.

Most textbooks are faulty because of the misleading implications and errors of omission. Just as most books imply that only those who opposed the Nazis were killed, they also imply that the civilians killed were Germans. A sample excerpt from a book that recognizes the non-German victims is given by Abramowitz.

> Not all of the dead and wounded were soldiers. Millions of civilians died in bombing attacks. In territories conquered by the Germans, millions of people who did not fit in with Nazi ideas of a "super" race and world conquest were murdered in Nazi death camps. These people included political opponents of the Nazis: Jews, Poles, Ukrainians, and members of the other nationality groups.[121]

The textbook with the greatest coverage on this aspect of the Holocaust is Perry's. The excerpts below illustrate this coverage.

> Over the years many German clergymen, Protestant and Catholic alike, were thrown into concentration camps. Nevertheless, most German clergymen—frightened into silence like their fellow Germans—did not openly protest against Nazi views or policies.[122]

> The Nazis also exploited the conquered peoples as slave labor. Some seven million foreign workers, many of them prisoners of war or recruited by force, were sent to Germany as slave laborers to work in German factories and on German farms. Many never lived to see the end of the war. They died of disease, hunger, and exhaustion.[123]

> Hitler ordered the execution of high Russian government officials, and three million Russian prisoners of war died in German prison camps.[124]

In spite of the above excerpts, the world history textbooks, as a group, grossly overlook the non-Jewish victims. An indication of this inadequate coverage is the fact that the two books with the total greatest coverage on the Holocaust have only four lines and two lines respectively on the non-Jewish victims.

The Tone of the Textbooks. Three of the textbooks are judged to contain factual, objective writing which does not condemn the events of the Holocaust. Three books do not have enough text material on which to make a judgment, and the other 22 books are critical. An example of a book which simply describes events without indicating outrage or at least disapproval is provided by King.

> The Nazis wanted a perfect society. This society should only include people having Germanic ancestors. They believed that all other, especially Jews, were inferior people. As a result millions of Jews were killed by the Nazis.[126]

There is nothing in this example which indicates that the authors/ editors/publishers disapproved of the events or would have disagreed with the Nazi policies. A student reading this excerpt could get the impression that the Jews were not German and that they were indeed inferior.

The majority of the texts are critical of the events. This criticism varies from mild disapproval through the use of terms as murdered or brutal to stronger language. Roehm has, "In their persecution of the Jews the Nazis reached the depths of inhumanity."[127] Johnson is also crystal clear in disapproval. "During World War II the Nazis carried out the most terrible program of mass murder in all of history."[128] On the same page is, "The record of Nazi brutality is more horrible than anything in the course of recorded history."

The Camps. Over half of the textbooks, 15, do not identify any of the camps by name. Aside from the few personal accounts included in the texts, description of life and death in the camps is virtually nonexistent. Many of the books omit any reference to the camps in describing the Holocaust, and several imply that conditions in the camps were most unpleasant. An example of the implication is given by Becker, "evidence that the true situation regarding Nazi treatment of prisoners was far more horrible than the rumors had even hinted."[129] One of the few books that gives any details at all is Perry's. "Concentration camp inmates who were not exterminated in the gas chambers toiled until they dropped in their tracks. Sadistic guards beat, starved, and tortured them to death, and sometimes they were used for cruel medical experiments."[130] When the conditions and functions of the camps are not given, students are deprived of the opportunity to increase their understanding.

Of the camps that are named, Auschwitz is mentioned by seven books, Dachau by six, Buchenwald and Belsen by two each, and Nordhausen and Treblinka by one book each. Good names four camps, and Becker names three camps.[131] Linder views the camps seriously by including a map which identifies six death camps and 20 concentration camps.[132]

Resistance. With a few exceptions, the world history textbooks imply that no civilians resisted the Nazis. To make matters worse, several books include something on resistance, but have no mention of Jewish resistance. For example, Sankowsky notes: "From Norway to the Balkans, sabotage of every kind continued. In every occupied country secret underground organizations fought Hitler's 'New Order.'"[133] Becker has nine lines on resistance with none on Jewish resistance.[134]

Table 11
Secondary United States and
World History/Western Civilization Textbooks

Genocide and Holocaust

	United States History	World History/ Western Civilization
Both Terms	0	2
Genocide	6	3
Holocaust	6	1
Neither Term	53	22

Names of Concentration and Extermination Camps

Number of Camps Named	United States History	World History/ Western Civilization
4	2	1
3	2	1
2	2	2
1	5	8
0	54	52

NOTE: Linder (world history) has a map which identifies 6 death camps and 20 concentration camps.

Perry has a three-paragraph account of resistance in a country-by-country description with no inclusion of Jewish resistance. He mentions the Warsaw underground but not the Warsaw Ghetto.[135]
 Only four books refer to Jewish resistance, all on Warsaw. Thus 22 books include the Holocaust without including Jewish resistance. In reference to a picture, Hane has, "Leveling areas that resisted, such as the Jewish Ghetto, the Nazis destroyed Warsaw, the capital of Poland."[136] A similar reference is given by Welty in discussing the Warsaw Ghetto. "Over 500,000 Jews died there defending themselves against the Nazis."[137] Two textbooks take the story of resistance seriously. Linder has 65 lines on the Warsaw Ghetto, and Johnson devotes a five-page chapter to the Warsaw Ghetto.[138] With the exception of these two notable accounts, the textbooks give the impression that no one resisted the Holocaust and help perpetuate the myth of passive victims.

"Genocide" and "Holocaust". Twenty-two books use neither the term genocide nor Holocaust. Three texts mention genocide, one has Holocaust, and two books use both terms. Usually the terms are followed by a brief definition. An example of this is given by Perry. "A policy of *genocide* (the murder of an entire people) was termed by the Nazis [as] the 'final solution of the Jewish problem.'"[139] In spite of the generally scant coverage of the Holocaust which most books give, they should at least include these two key terms.

The Survivors. As with most aspects of the Holocaust, and as with the United States history textbooks, the world history texts do not include much about the survivors. Of the 28 books, only six make any reference to survivors. Three of these associate the survivors with Israel. Smith and McNeill each have one line in this regard,[140] and Stavrianos has, "Palestine became more and more a crisis spot during the war years because Hitler carried his anti-Semitic campaign to the point of murdering six million Jews. The survivors naturally were anxious to flee to Palestine but the Arabs were strongly opposed."[141]

Two books make reference to the survivors as people who left Germany before the war started. Marvin has a chart showing the chronology of certain events and has, "1930's—many Jewish scholars leave Europe for the United States."[142] Social Science Staff follows a paragraph on pre-war oppression with, "Many Jews got away. Some escaped to England, France, the United States and Canada. Some fled to Palestine. Those who remained during the war were put into concentration camps, where most of them were killed. Today only a few thousand Jews live in Germany."[143]

The only book that gives the survivors more than a passing reference is Yohe. It is the only book that considers the individual characteristics and motives of the survivors. There is an excerpt from *The Survivors* by Terrence Des Pres and 17 lines about the book. "Many survivors had a tremendous will to live. They wanted to stay alive so they could tell the world what happened. Even so, all those who survived had to overcome their desire to die because life seemed too evil to bear."[144] Thus only one book deals directly with the survivors, and no books describe the conditions and welfare of the survivors following the end of the war.

The Role of the United States. The world history texts are even more derelict than the United States history texts in describing any U.S. role relative to the Holocaust. They also give the impression that no one knew of the extermination camps until the Allied armies found them. The following two excerpts illustrate writing which describes the surprise.

> One of the most frightful discoveries made in the ashes of the Third Reich, as Allied armies raced into Germany, was the shocking brutality and barbarism of the German concentration camps.[145]

> Only at the end of the World War II did the rest of the world really learn how cruel the Nazis had been. Allied armies entering Germany reached many of the concentration camps.[146]

Notice that these two excerpts also imply that all the camps were in Germany, ignoring such camps as Auschwitz and Treblinka.

Two books admit that there had been some knowledge of the extermination prior to the end of the war. Becker has, "Persistent reports of Nazi atrocities had been heard, but many people discounted them as propaganda."[147] In a similar vein, Social Science Staff has, "As for Hitler, he had broken his promise again and again. No nation could trust Germany until it was on its knees. Worse still, evidence of ghastly atrocities leaked out of parts of Europe occupied by Germany."[148] These are the only two books that even hint at our prior knowledge. The other 26 books either ignore the topic completely or tell of how surprised we were.

With one exception, the books do not include any discussion of anything the United States could have done before the war. All the other books treat the events as things that happened to other people far away and that thoughts of our possible involvement simply did not arise. Roosevelt even convened a conference to consider what we might be able to do, but the books do not reflect this. Perry has a seven-paragraph discussion of the appeasement and isolation policies of Britain, France, the Soviet Union, and the United States. Regarding the United States there is, "The United States, a powerful ally in World War I, had returned to a policy of isolation. The overwhelming sentiment among the American people was clear: let the Europeans fight their own battles."[149] Not one book refers to the restrictive immigration quotas of the United States before and during the war. Neither do they indicate that the immigration restrictions were just as tight for three years following the end of the war. They imply that anyone who wanted to come to the United States would be welcomed.

The Nuremberg Trials. Never before had legal courts been used to try people for "crimes against humanity." Considering the uniqueness of

Table 12
Secondary United States and
World History/Western Civilization Textbooks

Pictures

Number of Pictures	United States History	World History/ Western Civilization
6	1	0
5	1	0
4	0	0
3	1	1
2	3	5
1	13	10
0	46	12

Questions for Students

Number of Questions	United States History	World History/ Western Civilization
15	0	1
13	0	1
6	0	1
5	0	1
4	0	1
3	1	1
2	5	4
1	15	8
0	44	10

the trials, a textbook of Western civilization or world history would be expected to include a relevant discussion. Of the world history textbooks examined, 13 books do include them and 15 do not. At most the trials are given one paragraph, usually one or two sentences.

Pedagogical Techniques. Nine of the 28 world history textbooks examined do not include any questions or suggested activities for students. Several of these books with no questions have a relatively decent amount of total coverage on the Holocaust. For example, Rogers (41 lines), Petrovich (20 lines), King (19 lines), and Social Science (19 lines), do not have any questions.[150] These nine books contrast sharply with Linder (15 questions) and Kownslar (13 questions).[151] The book with the third greatest coverage, Perry, also is third in number of questions, six.[152] Seven books have one question each; four books have two questions each; one book has three questions; and one book has five questions. In addition, one book has four questions plus a suggested activity; one book has one question and one activity; and one book has a suggested activity. If we total the questions we have 62 questions for the 28 textbooks. However, almost 80 percent of the books have fewer than three.

Undoubtedly authors of textbooks do not have total authority over the textual material of a book, and they almost certainly do not have control of pictures used. Editors of textbooks have a great influence on the final content. Regardless of the location of the influence, 12 books do not contain a picture or illustration relevant to the Holocaust. Ten books have one picture; five books have two pictures; and one book[153] (Linder) has three pictures. The emotional intensity of the pictures ranges from a picture of a Jewish-owned store with anti-Semitic slogans on the windows to crematoria to piles of bodies. The most common type of picture is of concentration camp inmates photographed at the time of liberation. The next most common type of picture shows people being led away, sometimes with the guards shown, sometimes not. In total there are 27 pictures included in the 28 books while only six books have more than one picture. On closer examination there does appear to be a relation between the books with the greatest amount of coverage and the number of pictures included.

Another opportunity for the textbooks to extend students' learning is listing books for suggested reading. Of the 28 world history textbooks, only six take advantage of this opportunity. While the other 22 books may list many titles, none are of relevance to the Holocaust. *The Diary of a Young Girl* is named by Good and by Welty.[154] This is the only book named by more than one text. Kownslar recommends *The War Against the Jews*, a thorough account which may be difficult reading for many secondary-level students. Roehm refers to Hersey's *The Wall*, while Sankowsky names *Mila 18* by Leon Uris.[155] The only textbook which recommends two books is Linder. Ilse Koehn's *Mischling, Second Degree* and Irving Wersten's *The Uprising of the Warsaw Ghetto* are named.[156] While the books named are excellent and informative, many other outstanding books, such as Foreman's *The Survivor* and Meltzer's *Never To Forget* are omitted. Again 22 textbooks do not recommend any book of Holocaust relevance.

Government and Civics Textbooks

Secondary textbooks on government, American government, the Constitution, and civics have been grouped into this section. These textbooks are designed to help students understand the working of the government, political science issues, and their rights and responsibilities as citizens. For this section, ten textbooks were examined.

If the lessons learned from the Holocaust have anything to offer our secondary students of a government/political science/citizenship nature, the textbooks have ample opportunity to display these lessons. One of the paramount reasons why students should study the Holocaust is for them to be better informed, more perceptive citizens. They need to know how Hitler and the Nazis came to power through lawful means and to be aware of the harbingers of potentially dangerous demagogues. Armed with this knowledge, they would be in a better position to identify and combat Hitler-like leadership. This is a very powerful and practical rationale for studying the Holocaust. This rationale is not to study history for history's sake, but to study history for the future's sake. In addition lessons regarding civil liberties, civil rights, governmental functions such as immigration laws, and issues of foreign policy are germane to the Holocaust and study of government and civics. Although textbooks of government and civics are the ideal location for students to learn many of the crucial lessons of the Holocaust, the textbooks examined do not include them. Of the ten textbooks studied, only one touches on the Holocaust. The crucial lessons which our students need to know are not taught in the textbooks of government and civics. In spite of the relevance of the government and citizenship issues, the authors/editors/publishers have chosen to ignore the lessons our students need to learn. The criticism is not with what the texts do contain, but rather with what they omit. For example, Schick has a selection on immigration and does say that the 1924 law had a quota based on national origin. There is no mention of how our immigration restrictions affected thousands of victims who would have otherwise been saved.[157]

One of the lessons from the Holocaust is the need for perceptive citizens and an understanding of the concept of civil disobedience. This is the theme in the passage in the only textbook that draws on lessons from the Holocaust. Kownslar and Smart's *Civics: Citizens and Society* has a chapter entitled, "Our Responsibilities and Duties." In a subsection called, "Thinking about Obeying the Law," they ask:

Is obedience to the law always a mark of good citizenship? Should you obey all laws unquestioningly?

From 1933 to 1945, Germany was ruled by Hitler's Nazis. The Nazis passed a number of laws to eliminate the Jewish people from Germany. The laws set up concentration camps, or prisons, where millions of Jews were confined and murdered. After World War II, some Germans were put on trial for their actions in these camps. Most of them defended their actions. They said that they had only obeyed orders. The orders had been given under laws made by their government. It was not their responsibility to question whether the laws or the orders were right or wrong, they said.

The questions that were raised at these trials are worth thinking about. When would *you* follow an order? When would you question it? No one would deny that we have a responsibility to obey the law. But should we obey *all* laws in *all* cases?[158]

The text continues with a discussion of some historical examples of individuals who refused to obey some laws. It refers to some American colonists who refused to pay taxes imposed by the Stamp Act and of some Americans in the 1840s who refused to pay taxes to support war against Mexico. The discussion continues with a consideration of the concept of civil disobedience, Henry David Thoreau, and Martin Luther King Jr. There is also a picture of the Nuremberg Trials with the caption, "Is there an obligation to obey laws and orders without regard to morality or conscience? This was the central focus of the Nuremberg Trials after World War II."[159]

The above excerpts are the only sections in the text which refers to the Holocaust, and this text is the only one of the ten examined which has anything on the Holocaust.

Sociology Textbooks

In spite of the relevancy of many subtopics of sociology, the textbooks examined for this section do not directly face the issue of the Holocaust. There is ample opportunity for the books to include aspects of the Holocaust, and the texts would probably be more effective instructional materials with such inclusions. The books do include such topics as propaganda, racism, totalitarian regimes, mass behavior, and conditions producing dictatorships. These concepts are obviously related to the Holocaust. Of the three textbooks examined, one has nothing on the Holocaust, and the other two books have only one line each directly on the Holocaust.

Denisoff has a major heading of "Intergroup Relations" and a subheading of "Extermination." Several examples of extermination are given. The text mentions that the United States destroyed two-thirds of the American Indians, that the British destroyed the Tasmanian population, and that the Boers of South Africa hunted Hottentots like animals. Then there is the statement, "Germany between 1933 and 1945 murdered six million Jews."[160] No reasons are given for these examples. This is the only direct statement to the effect that there was a Holocaust.

Two pages earlier under the subheading, "Population Transfer" and in red print is a passage which comes closer to giving an explanation. Notice however, how mild the reference to the Holocaust is and how difficult it would be for a student to understand what happened.

> Many nations and cities drove out Jews in the late medieval period; the United States drove the Indians out of area after area; the British kept the Irish beyond the Pale; the Soviet Union deported millions of her citizens, members of religious and national minorities, during World War II; and Nazi Germany followed a relentless policy, aimed at a homogeneous nation, by forcibly transferring large numbers of persons of many minorities. The *indirect* policy is to make life so unbearable for members of the minority that they "choose" to migrate. Thus czarist Russia drove out millions of Jews. This was also part of Germany's policy.[161]

This is an interesting piece of writing. Notice that the two references to Germany are interrupted by a reference to Czarist Russia. The word Jew and the word Germany are also not in the same sentence. A student may have difficulty in grasping the facts and significance of what occurred by such vague terms as "relentless policy" and "forcibly transferring." The text does not explain to where people were transferred or what happened once they arrived. Nevertheless, there was the one statement cited earlier that declared that Germans killed Jews.

The other textbook that makes reference to the Holocaust is Hunt's. In a section on America's "Other Minority Groups" there is a one-paragraph history of Jews and almost a reference to survivors of the Holocaust. "After World War II some of them returned to the ancient homeland and created the new nation of Israel."[162] Several paragraphs later is a passage which refers to historical anti-Semitism.

> In Europe, prejudice against Jews, or *anti-Semitism*, has existed for centuries and has been very strong in certain countries. [countries not identified] Sometimes it has been tied to religion; sometimes it has been justified by dislike on the part of the majority of the population for certain cultural or "racial" characteristics, largely imaginary, attributed to the Jews as a group. In some parts of Eastern Europe, anti-

Semitism has at times gone to such extremes that thousands of Jews were killed, as in the *pogroms,* or organized massacres, that occurred in czarist Russia. But it was in Nazi Germany that anti-Semitism reached its height, for Jews constituted the great majority of the possibly seven million people who were murdered in Hitler's concentration camps.[163]

While the sociology textbooks examined forego many opportunities to include the Holocaust, and while they do not really describe and explain it, and while they approach the subject in an oblique manner, they do seem to deal with historical anti-Semitism better than do most history textbooks.

Psychology Textbooks

While many secondary students are not able to take a course in psychology, the subject is offered in some schools and has a high relevancy to the Holocaust. The people involved in the Holocaust, victims, oppressors, and bystanders, offer a fertile field for the study of human behavior. Perhaps psychology offers certain intellectual tools which could help us understand the events of the Holocaust better. Not only could the bizarre behavior of the oppressors be better understood through psychology, but also the acquiescent behavior of so many people. Psychology textbooks include a study of prejudice, of which the Holocaust is the extreme example. Perhaps the inclusion of the Holocaust in psychology textbooks is as compelling and as justified as its inclusion in history texts. The authors of the four psychology textbooks examined are not unaware of this, as all four books do include something on the Holocaust. The themes range from power to authoritarianism to prejudice.

The slightest inclusion is in Lugo. There is a discussion of the authoritarian personality and a reference to a study done by K. Levin, "himself a victim of persecution in Nazi Germany."[164] The book could have done much more with the topic than the single, passing reference.

Considering that one school of thought of psychology, Logotherapy, evolved from the Holocaust, it is not surprising to find reference to this in a psychology textbook. Forehand notes:

> Perhaps the most striking examples of individuals with this kind of investment in living are those who survived the horrors of the Nazi concentration camps during World War II. Some even grew psychologically as a result of their experiences. One example is Dr. Viktur Frankl. While Dr. Frankl was in a concentration camp, he wrote a book about the meaning of life. His manuscript was found by guards

and destroyed. When he was later released, he wrote the book all over again.[165]

In a section on prejudice, Forehand also has, "the massive murder of Jews in Europe before and during the war had led many to ask how it could have happened and how it could be prevented in the future."[166] Of course these are the crucial questions for the study of the Holocaust, but the textbook does not present much effort toward answering them.

The role of prejudice is central in understanding the Holocaust, and Ragland gives attention to this, in a discussion of the scapegoat theory of prejudice:

> When Germany was left in an economic shambles after World War I, many Germans were frustrated by the wild inflation that ravaged their country, and at their inability to make a living. Hitler was able to focus their inner feelings of frustration against a minority, the Jews. This group was assigned the blame for almost everything that had gone wrong. Devastating physical aggression against the Jews resulted. Where violence against a target group is prevented, as it is in most countries, more subtle outlets for frustration occurs, such as housing and job discrimination. People who dislike a certain group will, when frustrated, use the group as a scapegoat.[167]

The book also has the famous picture of the young boy with raised hands being led away and the caption, "Jews became scapegoats for German frustrations during the post-World War I Era."[168] While this is a better explanation of why Jews were persecuted than most history textbooks have, the phrase, "devastating physical aggression," is not very complete or illuminating.

McNeil supplies the greatest amount of coverage. In a section entitled "The Power of Authority" there he discusses obedience. "When obedience becomes blind and unquestioning, however, it may conflict with other important values, such as the value of human life. It was obedience to authority that allowed so many Germans to participate in the massive human exterminations that took place during the Nazi era."[169] The text continues with an extensive discussion of Milgram's famous experiments on obedience to authority.

On the same page, in boldface, is a separate section with the heading, "In the Name of Science?"

> In his book *The Rise and Fall of the Third Reich*, William L. Shirer describes experiments conducted by Dr. Sigmund Rascher on human guinea pigs in Germany during World War II. Rascher's inhumane

experiments involved studying the effects of sudden decompression at high altitudes and freezing at subzero temperatures. At the infamous Dachau concentration camp, hundreds of prisoners, mostly Jews, were dumped into a deep tank of ice water until they died. The horror we feel today about this casual torture and slaughter of innocents was evidently not felt by the German scientists of that era. In October 1942, German scientists met in Nuremberg to discuss the results of these death experiments, and not one protest was voiced. Were all these scientists evil men? Could such a thing happen in American society today? Why or why not?[170]

At the end of the chapter there is a series of statements summarizing the important points. "Milgram's experiment with the 'shock generator' showed that orders from a *legitimate authority* can lead people to do things contrary to their deepest values. Such blind *obedience* to authority has led to such atrocities as the Nazi extermination of the Jews and the My Li incident."[171]

The psychology textbooks do take notice of the Holocaust, but none in a complete manner. It seems that different books will focus on different aspects of the Holocaust to the neglect of others. The citations in the psychology textbooks do illustrate, however, that the study of the Holocaust has much to offer in many areas of inquiry.

World Geography/Area Studies Textbooks

While geography textbooks are not the most likely location to find explanations and descriptions of the Holocaust, they usually include history and culture sections. They also usually include discussions of the movements of people, immigration, and the establishment of new nations such as Israel. For these reasons, five secondary level textbooks on world geography were examined.

Of the five books examined, only one includes anything of Holocaust relevance. Beckler, in a discussion of Palestine, has, "Immigration of Jews to Palestine, most of them survivors of the Nazi holocaust [sic] in Europe, became very heavy after World War II."[172] Much later in the book, in a discussion of the concept of migration, he notes, "During World War II, the Nazis were systematically exterminating the Jewish population of countries they were occupying in Europe. Yet few European Jews decided to migrate while they had the chance, despite the growing threat to their lives."[173] The above excerpt can be criticized because of the implications that all Jews were completely aware of the danger and that anyone who chose to do so could leave the home country and be welcomed elsewhere. Nevertheless, it is the only geography text that recognizes the extermination.

Social Studies Textbooks

Although most textbooks are organized by a particular discipline within the social studies, a few books approach the subject in a more generic manner. Scott Foresman has such a series for use in junior high schools, and one text was examined for this study.[174] This text contains nothing relevant to the Holocaust. The book does contain sections on immigrants to America, prejudice, discrimination, and concepts of government.

College Level Textbooks

History—College Level

This section considers textbooks, which were recommended for student purchase by instructors in the history department for courses which may be relevant to the Holocaust. Courses which obviously had no meaning for the Holocaust, such as the Civil War, are omitted from this study. While the courses offered by the department cover a wide range of topics and areas, the textbooks are grouped together in this section because they are all offered under the rubric of history. Because of the wide-ranging concerns of history, these textbooks are subdivided into five topical areas: American history, ethnic American history, Western civilization, political history, and other history concerns. There were 27 college-level history textbooks examined.

United States History. Of the six textbooks examined for this subsection, four of them do contain no references to the Holocaust:[175] Bedford, Blum, Conkin, and Garraty. The other two do.

Morison has a total of 23 lines on the subject.[176] This includes one line which mentions non-Jewish victims—Gypsies and anti-Nazis—and two lines on the pre-war oppression. The text, in a manner out of proportion to its total coverage, names six camps: Buchenwald, Dachau, Belsen, Auschwitz, Linz, and Lublin. The tone is critical of the events and has a very direct reference to the role of the United States.

> The Nazis carried out an appalling pogrom which drove numbers of Germans and Austrian Jews to America, but the United States, in one of its most shameful acts, refused to lower immigration barriers in any substantial way. Many who were denied visas later died in Hitler's gas chambers.[177]

This excerpt can be applauded for its most forthright and direct condemnation of the American immigration program; on the other hand, it does not have much else to offer its college students on the explanation and description of the Holocaust, or of its implications to the United States. Notice that the authors represent the elite of American historians.

The other college text of American history which includes reference to the Holocaust is Sellers and May, well-known to many college students. This text makes reference in three different contexts. One is in the discussion of the end of American neutrality: "These [people who favored support of Britain in 1940] were joined by those who were outraged by atrocity stories, this time true, about Nazi barbarism."[178]

Later, in reference to the conference at Yalta which dealt with the soon-to-be former Nazi Europe: "The incredible Nazi atrocities, increasingly exposed by the reconquest of occupied territory, did not dispose America to be tender of German rights or to think about resurrecting German power."[179]

And last, in a discussion of the immediate postwar period, the authors note that the use of the atomic bomb "was the climax of a period of mounting inhumanity for which all major nations bore some responsibility. The worst atrocity of the period was the systematic German annihilation of six million Jews."[180]

The above excerpts are virtually the total coverage of college textbooks examined which relate to American history. The comparisons with the comparable secondary texts are striking. The college American history texts do not describe or attempt to explain the Holocaust as much as the most complete secondary texts. The college texts do, however, make much more of the American involvement via the immigration program and are much more critical of the American government. The point should be made that only two of the six books studied refer to the Holocaust; thus we must be careful to avoid overgeneralizing about these textbooks.

Ethnic American History. Five books which deal with the subtopic of ethnic Americans within the larger scope of history were examined. One of these texts, Jordan's, deals with black-white relations in the United States and omits any reference to the Holocaust.[181] Each of the other four includes discussions of the Holocaust, all due to lengthy considerations of American Jews. Dinnerstein is perhaps overrepresented in this sample because he is on the faculty at the sample university, however his books are in widespread use.

The only references in Dinnerstein, Nichols, and Reimers are concerned with immigration and are unique among all the textbooks in referring to American immigration following the war.

> American Jews tried to obtain favorable interpretations of immigration legislature as well as new laws to help refugees after World War II.[182]

> After the war the arrival of European immigrants to the United States ostensibly caused less fuss than had the coming of people from those same groups in earlier years. Few people publicly denounced the survivors of World War II who sought admission to the United States outside the quota limits, but at the same time Congress moved slowly before making any special effort to assist those Europeans displaced by the war. When Congress finally did act in 1948, the legislation passed specifically favored individuals of German origin and discriminated against East European Jews.[183]

Passages of this sort are indeed rare among the college texts and almost nonexistent among secondary textbooks. It is therefore understandable why so few citizens are aware of the dilatory and ignoble behavior of the American government before, during, and after the war.

Dinnerstein and Reimers have two and one-half pages on immigration from Germany with the focus on Jews.[184] A description of *Kristallnacht* is included as well as an excellent summary of American immigration restrictions and the diverse views of Jewish immigrants.

Giving a somewhat different perspective on what occurred in Germany is an article by John Garraty in Dinnerstein and Jackson. The editors in their introduction to Garraty's article note that

> Professor Garraty does not discount the suffering that Hitler inflicted on innocent people in Auschwitz, Mawthausen, Buchenwald, and a dozen other death camps, but he argues that the atrocities caused by Hitler should not preclude a scholarly analysis of those areas in which the German dictator acted more reasonably and responsibly.[185]

Garraty's article includes,

> The worse horrors of Nazism were unrelated to Nazi efforts to overcome the depression. Hitler's destruction of German democracy and his ruthless persecution of Jews had little impact on the economy as a whole. Discharging a Jew and giving his job to an "Aryan" did not reduce unemployment. The seizure of Jewish property merely transferred wealth within the country.[186]

Nathan Glazer has a chapter, "The Jews," pages 19–35, in Higham. Sections of this chapter are devoted to a consideration of the role of American Jews relative to the Holocaust. He discusses the dilemma of American Jews, whether their best action would be to remain relatively quiet or create public outcry.

> It was true that every act of Jewish resistance was treated as a provocation by the Nazis and resulted in further restrictions, confiscations, violence visited on German Jews.

> But in view of what we now know of Hitler and his government, we can conclude that even if protest did no good, accommodations would have been even worse.[187]

Glazer concludes this section of his chapter with the poignant statement, "Because six million Jews were killed, American Jews will always ask themselves whether enough was done, whether more could have been done, but whatever answer they give will be unsatisfying simply because of the scale of this numbing event."[188] Glazer also refers to the American immigration laws and the role of England.

> The Jews of Europe were being hunted down and killed in the incredible death factories while the gates of Palestine remained closed, while indeed the gates of the United States remained closed. The immigration laws were enforced with an unbelievable severity, and no mechanism for providing even a temporary refuge for those who could escape was put into effect until near the end of the war.[189]

Glazer also refers the reader to Morse's *While Six Million Died* and Feingold's *The Politics of Rescue: The Roosevelt Administration and the Holocaust*. From these samples, we conclude that the texts on ethnic Americans have more coverage than those texts on United States history in general.

Western Civilization. Five textbooks from the history department which have a Western civilization theme were examined. Four of these include some consideration of the Holocaust. It would seem that a college textbook on Western civilization would be the most likely type of book to find a solid description and explanation of the Holocaust. The textbooks examined do not support this assumption. One book has no coverage at all; one has only six sentences; one includes some speeches but not much expository text; one has only

12 lines on the Jewish extermination; and the best of the group has much less than the best of the high school American texts.

Burns has three sentences on the pre-war period of oppression, two sentences about the Jews as scapegoats, and one slight reference to the impact of the Holocaust on Israel. This last reference is interesting: "Despite her troubles with the Arabs, Israel strengthened her economy, and many new industries were created. Large sums of money flowed into the country as a result of West German restitution for the outrages of Nazism."[190] This is all in a textbook of 928 pages.

Tierney et al. have a textbook entitled *Great Issues in Western Civilization*.[191] Evidently the Holocaust is not considered as one of the great issues, although the book comes close to the topic. There are four lines from a speech by Hitler saying that Jews ruled Germany and one line saying they controlled the money.[192] Later the 25 points of the Party Program of the NSDAP are outlined, one of which states that no Jew can be a member of the German race and another which calls for freedom of religion but which has an anti-Semitic statement.[193] Still later are two anti-Semitic speeches by Hitler with a total of 67 lines. Nowhere in this 63-page chapter, "The Origins of Nazi Germany—German History or Charismatic Leadership?" does it say that Jews, or anyone else, were killed.

A college textbook entitled *The Western Heritage Since 1648*[194] should have something on the Holocaust. It does. It has two pictures with a three-sentence explanation. It also has one paragraph with 12 lines on the Holocaust. In addition there is one of the most extensive treatments of the non-Jewish victims. The 18-line, one-paragraph account is:

> The most horrible aspect of the Nazi rule in Europe arose not from military or economic necessity but from the inhumanity and brutality inherent in Hitler's racial doctrines. He considered the Slavs "Untermenschen," sub-human creatures like beasts who need not be thought of or treated like people. In parts of Poland the upper and professional classes were entirely removed, either jailed, deported, or killed. Schools and churches were closed; marriage was controlled by the Nazis to keep down the Polish birth rate; and harsh living conditions were imposed. In Russia things were even worse. Hitler spoke of his Russian campaign as a war of extermination. Heinrich Himmler, head of Hitler's elite SS guard, planned the elimination of thirty million Slavs to make room for the Germans, and formed extermination squads for the purpose. The number of Russian prisoners of war and deported civilian workers who died under Nazi rule may have reached six million.[195]

The above excerpt is interesting on two counts. For one thing, it illustrates how much text material 18 lines represent and can serve as a guide when other line counts are mentioned. Also, one-third more space was devoted to some of the non-Jewish victims than to the Jewish victims.

Chambers is the Western civilization textbook with the greatest amount of coverage.[196] There are a total of 75 pages on totalitarianism and World War II. On page 988 are 10 lines on Nazi propaganda use of anti-Semitism. Later is one line on the confiscation of Jewish property in order to raise money. Then on page 995 are 25 lines on the oppression of the 1930s which include descriptions of *Kristallnacht* and the Nuremberg laws with their ten specific restrictions. There are four pictures: one of a propaganda effort, one of a Jewish citizen with the Star of David, one of a Jew about to be shot, and one of concentration camp victims. The passage here also makes reference to attacks on churches and to Gypsies and Slavs. Later the chapter has 17 lines on extermination and includes reference to Auschwitz, Buchenwald, and Dachau. "Such horror on such a scale challenges every concept of civilization and raises almost unbearable doubts about Western society and human nature."[197] This section also has 70 lines on resistance, although none on Jewish resistance. Later there is a reference to the Nuremberg Trials, with some strong language. "To signify that their massacres and genocide had gone beyond the limits that a civilized world could endure, even in wartime, an international tribunal tried Hitler's closest associates for war crimes."[198] Even though this text has the most coverage of the college Western civilization textbooks examined, there is a great deal of vital information not included.

In sum, the most ideal forum for a description and explanation of the Holocaust, college textbooks on Western civilization, are weighed in the balance and are found wanting.

History with a Political Science Orientation. Of the textbooks recommended by the history department which have a political science orientation, we find great extremes in coverage of the Holocaust. Of the six books examined, four have nothing on the Holocaust, one has quite a bit on Romania, and one has a tremendous amount on the role of the United States. The four books in this category which have nothing on the Holocaust are Gardner, Heilbroner, Nettl, and Yergin.[199]

Laqueur has approximately 105 lines on the topic, focused on Romania. The excerpts and references given below are presented in the same order as in the textbook.

> In the years immediately following the collapse of Hitler's Reich, as the full horror of Nazi brutality was revealed in all its grisly detail in concentration camps overrun by allied armies [again the surprise], and later in testimony given at the Nuremberg Trials, objective writing on Nazi Germany was virtually impossible.[200]

This writer agrees strongly with Laqueur on the difficulty of writing objectively on the topic even at this late date.

A few pages later Laqueur has 16 lines on Hitler's philosophy and the role of anti-Semitism.[201] Quite a few pages later is a 21-line account of internal disagreement within the Nazi bureaucracy regarding the Jewish question.[202] Some 20 pages later are 13 lines dealing with the role of anti-Semitism in fascism in Romania and Hitler's planned murder of the Jews. Again, some 15 pages later are nine more lines on anti-Semitism in Romania. Then there are seven lines on the use of anti-Semitism by National Socialism as a device to help enroll the working class. Then there are three lines on an anti-Semitic organization in Romania. Later, on page 245, is: "One can read about the most brutal anti-Semitism of the Arrow Cross, which ended up in the atrocities and massacres among Budapest Jewry in the autumn and end of 1944." Much later is the book's last reference. There is a 30-line account on pages 410–411 explaining why anti-Semitism was more effective as a coalescing force in Germany than other Western Europe countries and on the role of labor in the camps in Poland. This section also mentions Auschwitz. Laqueur has much more detail on the events in Eastern Europe than any of the other 207 books.

Paterson has much more on the role of the United States than any other book in the entire survey. There is an extensive, four-page account with 160 lines, including a picture, entitled "Witness to the Holocaust: Americans and the Plight of the European Jews." The opening paragraph of the section explains the American stance.

> Another problem left to the future was that of the refugees, hundreds of thousands of them Jews from Nazi-occupied territories. Many sought asylum in the United States. Although most Americans denounced Hitler's drive to preserve the purity of the "Aryan race" through the persecution and extermination of European Jews, translating moral revulsion into policy proved difficult. United States immigration laws, traditional anti-Semitism, the depression, bureaucratic procedures, wartime fear of spies, and domestic politics shaped the timid American response.[203]

This is followed by an extensive paragraph on the prewar oppression, including the Nuremberg Laws and *Kristallnacht*. The next paragraph gives some statistics and details of the immigration policies. "Openly discriminatory, the National Origins Act of 1924 was designed to limit immigration from eastern and southern Europe." Also, "Potential immigrants had to present as many as 50 pages of documents attesting to their crime-free background, birth, health, and financial status. Many of these papers had to be obtained from Nazi officials."[204]

The next two paragraphs explain the role of certain individuals and groups. Mentioned are labor and patriotic groups, Father Charles E. Coughlin, George Messersmith, Franklin D. Roosevelt and Secretary of State Cordell Hull. Also mentioned is the fact that only 35.8 percent of the German-Austrian quota was used between 1933 and 1945. The last paragraph on the pre-war period describe the Evian Conference and the plight of the ship *St. Louis*. The next paragraph continues to document the ineffectiveness of the United States and refers to what other countries did not do to help. "The record of other countries, in other words, was as bad as that of the United States."[205] A brief overview of the extermination is given which includes reference to Babi Yar, Auschwitz, Zyklon B gas, and the Warsaw Ghetto.

The text includes efforts which were unsuccessful, such as the 1943 conference in Bermuda and efforts by individuals. "Appeals throughout the war years for American planes to bomb the rail lines leading to the death camps and the crematoria went unheeded by the War Department, on the grounds that such diversions would delay victory, itself the best hope for the Jews."[206] The last section gives an overview of the ineffectiveness of the State Department, the role of Hull, Secretary of the Treasury Morgenthau, and Roosevelt, and the creation of the War Refugee Board. The final sentence is telling. "In large measure the Jewish refugees themselves took command of their survival after the war by leading the 'exodus' to Palestine and creating the new nation of Israel in 1948."[207]

History—Other Concerns. This section comprises textbooks from the history department which do not easily fall into one of the above mentioned subdivisions. Of the five books in this section, three do not contain any reference to the Holocaust: Barraclough, Barnet, and Halberstam.[208] The other two books have slight and passing references to the Holocaust.

Jean-Paul Sartre wrote a book in 1948 which has five slight references. These references assume that the reader is familiar with

the Holocaust, do not offer explanations or descriptions, and are used
to illustrate other particular points.

> "Today those Jews whom the Germans did not deport or murder are
> coming back to their homes."[209]

> "During the occupation there was a Jewish doctor who lived shut up
> in his home at Fontainebleau."[210]

> "We have been indignant, and rightly, over the obscene 'yellowstar'
> that the German government forced upon the Jews."[211]

> "Yet the Nazi ordinances only carried to its extreme a situation to
> which we had formerly accommodated ourselves very well."[212]

> "There is not one of us who is not totally guilty and even criminal:
> the Jewish blood that the Nazis shed falls on all our heads."[213]

In a way these excerpts from Sartre are typical of college textbooks
in general. They do make reference to the Holocaust; reference, not
explanation, assuming that the reader already knows the events and
the explanations.

The last history textbook reviewed is Offner's. This book has three
references to the Holocaust with an interesting lack of explanations.

> Although he [Hugh Wilson, minister to Switzerland] did not approve
> of German persecution of the Jews, he thought the "Jewish problem"
> and the American press were the reasons for increasingly bad relations
> between the United States and Germany.[214]

There is no explanation of this statement.

> In November 1938, Germany's brutal pogrom against its Jewish pop-
> ulation further stiffened Roosevelt's attitude, and as a minor protest
> he recalled Ambassador Wilson from Berlin.[218]

There is no explanation of what Roosevelt was protesting. The last
reference deals with Hitler's views of the United States.

> In the bitter aftermath of 1919, Hitler said that two million Jews
> controlled New York's banks, press, and industry and had impelled
> America to war against Germany solely for financial gain.[216]

This passage also quotes Hitler as saying that the United States was
half-Judaized and half-Negrified. The references in this subdivision
do not offer the student reader anything in the way of description

or explanation. The best they can do, of those that have any reference to the Holocaust, is to pique the interest of some curious and interested students.

Political Science—College Level

Courses offered by a department of political science were examined to identify those which may have some relevance to the Holocaust. Fifteen textbooks used by those courses were examined for this study. The textbooks are divided into three subsections: those whose focus is on American foreign policy, on American political concerns, and on international politics.

American Foreign Policy. From the nature of these textbooks, we may expect the Holocaust to be referred to regarding our immigration policies, our isolationist policy, attempts to stop Hitler before the war broke out, the Evian Conference, the establishment of Israel, and so forth. They do not.

Two books, Nathan's and Hughes's, have nothing on the Holocaust.[217] The third book examined, Kegley's, has one very slight reference, in discussing Henry Kissinger: "escape from Nazi persecution in his native Germany . . . culminating in his appointment as the first Jewish secretary of state."[218]

The last text examined for this section, Russett's, has a total of 15 lines on the Holocaust, although not as a separate paragraph. There is one line on non-Jewish victims, and the cause is laid to Hitler on racial grounds. The tone is critical, and the secrecy of the Holocaust is mentioned. "The worst Nazi crimes emerged only in 1943 and later at Nuremberg. German 'medical experiments' and extermination camps were unknown to the world in 1941."[219]

The paucity of Holocaust coverage for this section is a keen disappointment. Surely writers of advanced texts on American foreign policy are aware of the lessons of the Holocaust and their implications for foreign policy. Several high school texts have much more on the foreign policy aspects of our study of the Holocaust than do these college textbooks. Perhaps the sample needs to be expanded.

Political Science—American Focus. Four textbooks whose titles suggest a focus on domestic political science concerns were examined. In these texts there is a total of one sentence referring to the Holocaust. Three books, Abernathy, Cortner, and Crozier, do not include any reference.[220] Sowell's introduction contains the idea that events in human history have not necessarily gotten better with time. "The

Nazis' ruthless campaign of genocide in the middle of the twentieth century exceeded anything ever attempted in the eighteenth or nineteenth centuries."[221] That text, because of the topics included, could have discussed the role of labor in impeding the easing of immigration quotas in the 1930s. Textbooks of political science with a domestic focus are not the place to find the Holocaust discussed.

International Political Science. It would seem that college textbooks with international politics as their thrust would be an ideal place for the Holocaust to be discussed. Such is not the case. For this section, seven textbooks were examined. Three of the books do not include anything on the Holocaust: Beres, Franck, and Sondermann.[222] The other books give only passing reference.

Ziegler has ten pages on World War II and its background. The only Holocaust reference is to the killing of a "large number of civilians."[223] That is certainly an understatement, and without explanation. Speigel, in a reference to Israeli–Arab relations has, "Haj Amin el-Hussein: the Mufti of Jerusalem and latter-day collaborator with the Nazis in the 'Final Solution.'"[224]

Stoessinger (1974) has four slight references. Regarding the invasion of Russia he mentions that "All Russian Jews would perish and the population of Russia would be drastically reduced through starvation and mass execution."[225] Much later he notes that "A large number of Jews, responding to the horror of Hitler's systematic policy of extermination, attempted to save themselves by creating a state of their own."[226] He continues the discussion of Israel: "During the 1930's, when Hitler's persecution of European Jews gathered increasing momentum, Jewish immigration soared dramatically."[227] The last reference is a cutting and poignant one. As one survivor put it, "The Germans killed us, and the British don't let us live."[228] Notice that most of the references are in regard to Israel.

Stoessinger wrote another text, published 13 years earlier. In that one he mentions the Genocide Convention, but does not state that the United States did not sign it.[229] In regard to Israel he writes: "However, the destruction of six million Jews by the Nazis lent new vigor to the Zionist movement."[230] The text later has 48 lines on the Nuremberg Trials, but there is no indication that Jews, or any other specific group, were killed.[231] Still later there is a discussion of the agencies of the United Nations. "The International Refugee Organization was thus the first international humanitarian experiment to approach the refugee problem in its totality. In that sense, the blood, tears, and despair of Buchenwald, Auschwitz, and Bergen-Belsen had perhaps not been entirely in vain."[232] Thus we find that another section of college textbooks does not explain or describe the Holocaust. If a college student will not find these explanations in his history or political science courses, he may not find them at all.

Sociology—College Level

For this section of the study, textbooks used by the department of sociology were examined. Excluded were courses and books whose title implied there was no relevance for the Holocaust. There were 12 texts examined in this section, subdivided into three parts.

Sociology and Protest Movements. Seven books were studied under this rubric. The topics of the texts ranged from protest to collective behavior to violence to revolution. It may be that some of the concepts associated with these topics would also be found in a study of the Holocaust; however, these textbooks do not include any mention of the Holocaust. These textbooks are: Genevie, Gamson, Graham, Piven, Salert, Tilly, and Unseem.[233]

Sociology and Religion. One textbook, Greeley's, was examined which fits this subdivision. It is typical of many college texts in that it refers to the Holocaust in a passing manner which assumes that the reader is familiar with the events. This book has two references, both concerned with the reaction of American Jews. "The disaster of the Second World War to European Judaism produced a reaction in most American Jews that precluded any denial of their Jewishness,"[234] and "The combination of fear of the return of anti-Semitism and a new pride in Jewishness (both, in part at least, influenced by the horrors of the Second World War) reinforced the new Jewish militancy."[235] Considering the concepts included in these texts, such as collective behavior and protest, we should expect more than two sentences from the seven sociology textbooks in this section.

Sociology and Ethnicity. As we saw with history textbooks, most gave only slight, if any, treatment to the Holocaust with the exception of books on ethnicity. Such is also the case with sociology textbooks. Three of the four books in this section do give consideration to the Holocaust. Simmen does not.[236] Thus of the 12 sociology texts which have more than two sentences on the subject, all three are concerned with ethnicity.

Marden has references in three locations in the book, although explicitness is not always present. On pages 121 and 122 is a 21-line account of displaced persons.[237] Specific groups mentioned are Poles,

French-speaking Alsace-Lorrainers, Slovenes, Jews, and non-Jewish political opponents of Nazis. The reasons why these people were displaced are not clearly given.

On pages 122–125 are 122 lines on a thorough treatise of the United States immigration policies of 1945–1965. This is one of the most complete descriptions of the topic of any of the 208 books examined and is quite critical of the United States. It mentions that President Truman thought the 1948 immigration laws were discriminating and anti-Semitic. It also states that during the first year of the International Refugee Organization, 200,000 people were resettled, of whom the United States accepted 16,836.

Marden also has a 22-page chapter on Jews in America. There are two slight references to the Holocaust, after which we find this:

> When the National Socialist Party undid for Germany all the gains made in western European social thought since the Age of Enlightenment and exterminated six million Jews, the bonds of identity of Jews throughout the world which had loosened under two centuries of improved civil status, were re-established and intensified.[238]

This is the only sentence in the book that states that Jews were killed. Ten books for additional reading are listed, none on the Holocaust.

Bahr's is an excellent book on ethnicity. There are four references to the Holocaust, each drawing on lessons from the experience to help explain such concepts as prejudice, racism, and stereotyping.

> Theories of racial superiority have been used to justify human exploitation and genocide, ranging from the treatment of the Indians during the colonization of the Americas, to the institution of slavery, to Nazi Germany's "solution to the Jewish problem."[239]

This is the only reference which uses the Holocaust to help explain pre-World War II American history.

Later, in discussing the idea of denial of ethnicity, there is a two-paragraph excerpt from Bernard Malamud's *The Lady of the Lake.* In this excerpt a woman is showing her tattoo to a gentile friend and makes an extremely powerful and poignant statement. "'Buchenwald,' Isabella said, 'when I was a little girl. The Fascists sent us there. The Nazis did it.'" Later there is, "'I can't marry you. We are Jews. My past is meaningful to me. I treasure what I suffered for.'"[240]

As with the earlier reference to ideas of racial inferiority and superiority, there is "Ideologies of racial inferiority must bear some of the responsibility for the annihilation of over 6 million Jews prior to and during World War II. The 'Final Solution to the Jewish problem' was clearly foreshadowed in the writings of Gobineau and [Houston Stewart] Chamberlain."[241]

The last reference in Bahr touches clearly one of the primary lessons of the Holocaust, in a discussion of cultural explanations of prejudice:

> Hitler's use of stereotypes about Jews, blaming them for many of the problems confronting the German people, is a particularly tragic example of the management of ethnic stereotypes by political elites for their own purposes. In this case the shifting of the blame for the social and economic crises from the government and its policies to an ethnic group helped maintain the Nazis in power.[242]

While the Holocaust should be studied for its own sake, and the sake of victims and survivors, it should also be studied to learn from it in order to understand the present and to safeguard the future. The above examples from Bahr are among the very few in all the textbooks examined which utilize the study of the Holocaust in a constructive, educational manner.

The last of the books studied under sociology is also on ethnicity. Schaefer has several references to the Holocaust from different frames of reference, in considering the history of the Jews:

> Jews have again been used as scapegoats by opportunists who blame them for a nation's problems. The most tragic example of such an opportunist was Adolf Hitler, whose "final solution" to Germany's problems led to what the Jews call the Holocaust, the extermination of 6 million Jewish civilians during World War II. Two-thirds of Europe's Jewish population was killed, and in Poland, Germany, and Austria the proportion of the death toll reached 90 percent.[243]

Identifying the specific percentages is unique and helpful.

A different frame of reference considers the United States.

> When the barbarous treatment of the Jews by Nazi Germany was exposed, most Americans were horrified at such events and individuals like Lindbergh were as puzzled as anyone as to how some Americans were swept up by the pre-World War II wave of anti-Semitism.[244]

Adding a strong statement is: "The atrocities of Nazi Germany have not been forgotten, nor should they be."[245]

In a reference to immigration with an unusual point and to the Jewishness of all Jews, there is:

The immigration acts of the 1920's sharply reduced the influx of Jews as it did other European groups. Beginning in about 1933, the Jews arriving in the United States were not merely immigrants, they were also refugees. The tyranny of the Third Reich began to take its toll well before World War II. German and Austrian Jews fled Europe as the impending doom became more evident. Many of the immigrants tended to be more religiously orthodox and slowly adapted to the ways of earlier Jewish immigrants, if they adapted at all. The concentration camps, the speeches of Hitler, the atrocities, the war trials, and the capture of Nazi leaders undoubtedly made all American Jews—natives and refugees, the secular and orthodox—acutely aware of their Jewishness and the price one is required to pay by virtue of ethnicity alone.[246]

This researcher is unaware that a large portion of those fleeing Europe during the 1930s were religiously orthodox; in fact, most of the writings indicate just the opposite. In the 26-page chapter on Jewish Americans, 14 books are listed for further reading—none focus on the Holocaust. It should also be noted that the book includes Holocaust in the index; has a chapter on extermination[247] which cites four examples; and includes a picture of soldiers arresting Jewish factory leaders.

Religious Studies—College Level

Considering that a great number of people were killed because of their religion, and considering the postulates and humanitarian virtues espoused by the Christian faiths, it would seem that textbooks of a religious studies nature would find the Holocaust a fertile field for examples. They do, but not to a great degree. The religious studies textbooks examined typify many college texts: they make passing reference to the Holocaust, assuming that the reader is conversant with and aware of the meanings of the implications. Of the six textbooks examined in this subsection, two do not include any reference to the Holocaust: Tillich's and Fagan's.[248] The other four are grouped into the three categories of: general religion, Protestantism, and Catholicism.

General Religions. Andrew Greeley, a well known author of popular novels, is in this study for the second time. Although the general intent of his book is for Catholic audiences, the reference to the Holocaust is of a more generic religious interest. In this reference, an extremely important religious concept is approached.

A number of modern writers have insisted that after Auschwitz it is impossible to believe in God, or at least in God's goodness. When six million people could be destroyed in gas chambers because of their religion, God must not be watching, or must not care, or perhaps does not even exist. The problem is serious, although it did not begin with the Nazi concentration camps. Auschwitz, as terrible as it was, was by no means the first mass murder in human history. How could God have permitted any of them?[249]

Then there is: "So we erect concentration camps and gas chambers, commit mass murders and assassinations, manufacture and use Saturday night specials."[250] Although the language is eloquent and the concept cogent and powerful, notice that the text does not say that Jews were killed. This is a good example of reference to the Holocaust by implication, expecting a great deal of inference on the reader's part.

Religious Studies—Protestantism. In spite of the heroism, courage, and true Christian actions of individual churchmen of the Protestant faiths during the Holocaust, the central units of the several Protestant groups can be criticized for the action taken and the action not taken. What does Brown's book *The Spirit of Protestantism* have to say on the subject? There are three separate references. "Lutheranism has historically inclined to an attitude of political quietism, an attitude now being rethought as a result of the church's necessary resistance to nazism."[251] The author seems to assume that the reader is familiar with Nazism and the church's resistance. Later, in a discussion of the sin of idolatry there is:

Christians in Germany were called upon to do just this after Hitler came to power. But the first declaration of the Barmen Conference in 1934, one of the great utterances of modern church history, demonstrated an obedience to the first commandment and showed how an affirmation of the Lordship of Christ meant a denial of all other claimants. Christ is Lord, so Hitler cannot be Lord. "Other events and powers" (Hitler, nazism, anti-Semitism) must be repudiated.[252]

The last reference is in a footnote. "For vivid examples of how this principle has come alive in recent times, see Gollwitzer, Kuhn, Schneider, eds., *Dying We Live*, Fontana, a collection of letters from Christians condemned to death for their opposition to Hitler."[253] This is the only textbook examined which deals directly with Protestantism, and the above excerpts are the total coverage of the Holocaust.

Religious Studies—Catholicism. Two books on the Catholic Church were examined. Considering the influential role of the Catholic Church in Europe and the controversial behavior of Pope Pius XII, it is interesting to see how these books approach the Holocaust.

One of the books, McKenzie, discusses the Pope and the role of the church, although in somewhat circular terms.

> The traditional union of church and state has meant that the established Roman Church, as such, has taken no position on war; its international character does not allow it to take sides. Pius XII was criticized for not rejecting Nazism more explicitly. In individual nations the Roman Church in war teaches the duty of patriotism; it is recognized that this may at times not be enough, but the Roman Church will certainly encounter the civil government in any country in which it teaches anything else.[254]

And a paragraph later, there is:

> No one who has any idea of what a church is, however, will deny that war and racial problems are moral as well as political issues and that a church which remains silent on serious moral issues weakens its claim to be taken seriously.[255]

Just as some sociology and psychology textbooks include a discussion on the problems of obedience, one religious studies text approaches the topic from a very different frame of reference. In a discussion of national law, Hellwig has:

> The point of the natural law theory in the Catholic Church was precisely to guarantee a place for reason and to show the continuity between reason and revelation. It is bad because it makes people passive in their moral responsibilities. It leaves only one obligation, to obey explicit commands. We know that this sort of obedience—morality— leads to situations like that of Nazi Germany, in which a man feels justified in murdering large numbers of men, women, and children if his proper superior commands it.[256]

Later there is one other reference to the Holocaust. "The Nazi holocaust, and the silence of the Christian nations in face of it, proclaimed to the Jews of our century as loud as the blare of trumpets that the Messianic times are not yet."[257] This last excerpt is typical of passages which demand inference by the reader. If a person did not already know of the events of the Holocaust, passages such as this would not instruct him. The above excerpts are the total references to the Holocaust in the seven religious studies examined. Nowhere does it state directly that Jews were killed.

Humanities—College Level

One textbook was available for examination offered through humanities courses which could conceivably include the Holocaust.[258] Other books, such as those dealing with ancient Greece or medieval art, were not included in this study. The one book examined does not include any reference to the Holocaust.

12
Conclusion

The textbooks used in American schools do not adequately treat the Holocaust. The books are faulted on three major counts: they do not give the Holocaust the treatment it deserves in its own right; they do not give students instruction in the lessons we need to learn from the Holocaust in order to safeguard our future; and they do not draw upon examples from the Holocaust which would enhance the instruction in the concepts of the various disciplines they are attempting to teach. There are a few bright spots, of course. A few texts do treat certain aspects of the Holocaust adequately, but no book is adequate in all aspects. For example, Paterson (college political science)[259] is quite good in describing American immigration policies, but is very weak on other aspects of the Holocaust.

A few elementary textbooks do have something on the Holocaust. They make brief reference with no explanation. There is a total of nine sentences in the nine books examined.

There is a great range of coverage in the secondary United States history texts. Some books ignore the topic completely, and the book with the greatest amount of coverage has 88 lines. A few texts do a good job on certain topics, but almost to the exclusion of other topics. They are especially faulted by their lack of explanation of the causes of the events—they seem to have just simply happened. They are faulted for omitting any role of the United States, especially our immigration policies.

The secondary world history texts give a better treatment than the United States history texts. The median coverage is 20 lines with one book having 278 lines. They are still generally inadequate in the same areas as the United States history texts, with the better of the books having weak areas.

Secondary government and civics textbooks are particularly poor. Only one of the ten books examined touches on the Holocaust. This book approaches the subject with the theme of civil disobedience.

The secondary sociology texts are also poor. Two of the three books have one line each, a slight, passing reference. These books are missing some golden opportunities to give effective instruction in certain concepts of sociology.

The secondary psychology textbooks do a little better. All four of the books examined include something, each on a different topic. As with the sociology texts, they could do much more to help illustrate certain principles of psychology. At least these books do not ignore the topic to the degree that the government and sociology texts do.

World geography texts, which include cultural and area studies, ignore the Holocaust almost completely. One of the five books studied has two brief references, on Israel and on migration.

One general social studies book was examined. It does not include any reference to the Holocaust.

The college textbooks show some interesting extremes. Four of the six books on American history do not contain any references. The books which focus on ethnicity rank very high in amount of coverage. This was perhaps the most pleasant surprise in the total study. The largest disappointment was, however, in the sparse coverage given in Western civilization texts—which would seem to be the most likely place to find a complete, lucid description of the events. However, these texts gave spotty and superficial coverage. The history textbook with a political science focus gives inconsistent coverage. Two of the six books have something: one deals with Eastern Europe while the other one has an extensive treatment on the role of the United States.

The college political science texts are also inadequate. Two of the four books on American foreign policy have something, but very little. Of the texts which focus on the American political and governmental scene, there is one sentence in the four books. Those with a focus on international politics are slightly better. Four of seven books have something, but very little. It would seem that the Holocaust would be of greater interest to international politics textbooks.

The college sociology texts are similar to the college history. A few do have a small amount of coverage, but the greatest coverage is found in those which focus on ethnicity. While this researcher believes that the Holocaust is an issue for everyone, the decent coverage given in texts of ethnicity, and not in college history or sociology books in general, seems to imply that interest in the Holocaust is limited to Jewish concerns.

Textbooks on religious studies usually do include references to the Holocaust in a passing manner. The references are not at all extensive, are included to illustrate a particular point, and assume that the reader is familiar with the details and implications of the Holocaust.

From what we have seen of the textbooks, this assumption may not be accurate.

The one humanities text examined had no reference to the Holocaust.

While a few textbooks do have something of value to offer on the Holocaust, the majority are woefully inadequate. If a student wanted to learn about the Holocaust, its place in history, the causes, the events, the implications, and the lessons for the future, he should read the best three high school United States history texts, the best three high school world history books, the college texts on ethnicity, and the one college text in history with a political science focus. These twelve books would teach him more than the other 196 books combined. There is good information in the textbooks but you must search for it. For a student to reach an understanding of the Holocaust from reading, he will need to go to sources beyond the textbooks.

In some areas, the student will be able to do exactly that. In spite of the generally inadequate coverage of the Holocaust in secondary textbooks, some communities have developed their own instructional material. In some cases these special programs were initiated by Jewish organizations, and in other cases by non-Jewish educators. A sampling of the special curriculum guides and materials is given below:

New York City has *The Holocaust: A Study of Genocide*, New York Division of Curriculum and Instruction, 1979, 587 p.

Philadelphia has *The Holocaust: A Teacher Resource*, Instructional Series of the School District of Philadelphia, 1977, 129 p.

Evanston, Illinois has *Teachers' Guide to the Holocaust*, 1977, 38 p.

Los Angeles has *The Holocaust: An Instructional Guide*, Instructional Planning Division, Los Angeles Unified School District, 1979, 67 p.

The state of New Jersey has a two volume set, *The Holocaust and Genocide: A Search for Conscience* produced in cooperation with the New Jersey State Department of Education, 1979.

The Brookline, Massachusetts Public School System has a program entitled *Facing History and Ourselves: Holocaust and Human Behavior*. They also have an extensive outreach program with in-service training and institutes. Perhaps the first major effort at developing materials for teaching about the Holocaust was conducted by teachers at Monument Mountain Regional High School in Great Barrington, Massachusetts. A collection of readings, *The Holocaust Years: Society on Trial* by Chartock and Spencer, was published by Bantam Books in 1978.

Most of the materials and curriculum guides have a broad scope of study and do not focus exclusively on the Holocaust. They usually include a study of the nature of people in general and other historical events. The units in the New Jersey set are illustrative of this idea: The Nature of Human Behavior, Historical Incidents of Genocide, The Rise of Nazism in Germany to 1933, Policy of Mass Murder, Resistance and Intervention, Related Issues of Conscience and Moral Responsibility. The guides usually include extensive and annotated books and audiovisual materials for use by students and teachers. Thus in reaction to the inadequacy of the traditional textbooks, groups of people around the country have done much work and have produced some excellent material for teaching about the Holocaust.

At the college level, each instructor selects the textbooks. While the usual texts do not include much on the Holocaust, a major change has taken place in recent years which have a direct bearing on Holocaust education. Many universities now offer a separate course on the topic. This change came about during the arousal of interest in the Holocaust during the late 1970s. Instructors for those courses have an array of excellent and scholarly books to choose as texts. Sample titles used are:

> Raul Hilberg's *The Destruction of the European Jews;* Nora Levin's *The Holocaust;* Lucy Dawidowicz's *The War Against the Jews,* and Randolph Braham's *The Politics of Genocide: The Holocaust in Hungary.*

What remains to be seen is the continued commitment of universities to offer the courses and students' enrollment in the courses.

Notes

1. Paul Goldstein, *Changing the American Schoolbook*, Lexington, Mass.: D.C. Heath and Co., 1978, pp. 43, 44.

2. Stella Dong, "Study Criticizes Coverage of Holocaust by 43 Current Textbooks." *Publishers Weekly*, New York, vol. 9, no. 216, Aug. 27, 1979, p. 296.

3. *Ibid.*

4. Frederick M. King, Herbert C. Rudman, Herbert V. Epperly and Ralph C. Cooke, *The Social Studies and Our Country*. River Forest, Ill.: Laidlaw Brothers, 1979, p. 353.

5. *Ibid.*, p. 355.

6. *Ibid.*, p. 311.

7. Frederick M. King, Herbert C. Rudman and LoDoris R. Leavell, *Understanding Our Country*. River Forest, Ill.: Laidlaw Brothers, 1979, p. 412.

8. Richard E. Servey, *Social Studies*. Glenview, Ill.: Scott, Foresman and Co., 1979, p. 267.

9. Muriel Stanek and Clinton Hartmann, *Americans All—A Nation of Immigrants*. Westchester, Ill.: Benefic Press, 1973, p. 127.

10. *Ibid.*, p. 130.

11. Leonard Berry and Richard B. Ford, *People, Places and Change: An Introduction to World Cultures*. New York: Holt, Rinehart and Winston, 1976, p. 126.

12. *Ibid.*, p. 134.

13. King, Rudman and Leavell, *op. cit.*

14. Berry and Ford, *op. cit.*

15. Larry Cuban and Philip Roden, *Promise of America: An Unfinished Story*. Glenview, Ill.: Scott Foresman and Co., 1971.

16. Charles Forcey and Ronald Posner, *A Strong and Free Nation*. New York: Macmillan Co., 1971, p. 587.

17. Richard C. Brown, Wilhelmina S. Robinson and John T. Cunningham, *Let Freedom Ring: A United States History*. Morristown, N.J.: Silver Burdett Co., 1980, p. 489.

18. John A. Garraty, *The American Nation: A History of the United States Since 1865*, 4th ed. New York: Harper and Row, 1979, p. 693.

19. James A. Banks and Sam L. Sebesta, *We Americans: Our History and People*. Boston: Allyn and Bacon, 1982.

20. Jack Abramowitz, *American History*, 5th ed. Chicago: Follett Pub. Co., 1979.

21. Norman Risjord and Terry Haywoode, *A History of the United States from 1877*. New York: Holt, Rinehart and Winston, 1979.

22. Leonard C. Wood, Ralph H. Gabriel and Edward L. Biller, *America: Its People and Values*. New York: Harcourt Brace Jovanovich, 1975.

23. Brown, Robinson and Cunningham, *op. cit.*

24. Lew Smith, *The American Dream*. Glenview, Ill.: Scott, Foresman and Co., 1977, p. 471.

25. Clarence L. VerSteeg and Richard Hofstadtler, *A People and A Nation*. New York: Harper and Row, 1977, p. 732.

26. Smith, *op. cit.*, p. 472.

27. Henry F. Graff, *The Free and the Brave*. Chicago: Rand McNally and Co., 1967, p. 660.

28. Banks and Sebesta, *op. cit.*, p. 211.

29. Henry Bragdon, Charles W. Cole and Samuel P. McCutchen, *Free People: The United States in the Twentieth Century*. New York: Macmillan, 1970, p. 346.

30. *Ibid.*, p. 355.

31. Risjord and Haywoode, *op. cit.*, p. 630.

32. Mitchell Okum and Stephen H. Bronz, *The Challenge of America*. New York: Holt, Rinehart and Winston, Inc., 1973, p. 669.

33. Bragdon, Cole and McCutcheon, *op. cit.*, p. 346.

34. Robert F. Madgic, Stanley L. Leaberg, Fred H. Stopsky and Robin W. Winks, *The American Experience*. Menlo Park, Ca.: Addison-Wesley Pub. Co., 1975, p. 478.

35. Glenn E. Hughes, Norman D. Miller and Stephen L. Volkening, *Reading American History*. Glenview, Ill.: Scott, Foresman and Co., 1978, p. 133.

36. Landis R. Heller, Jr. and Norris W. Potter, *One Nation Indivisible*. Columbus, Oh.: Charles E. Merrill Pub. Co., 1971, p. 522.

37. Henry F. Graff and Paul Bohannan, *The Promise of Democracy*. Chicago, Ill.: Rand McNally and Co., 1978, p. 504.

38. John Edward Wiltz, *The Search for Identity: Modern American History*. Philadelphia: J.B. Lippincott Co., 1978, p. 582.

39. Banks and Sebesta, *op. cit.*, p. 221.

40. Heller and Potter, *op. cit.*, p. 522.

41. Okum and Bronz, *op. cit.*, p. 686.

42. Jack Allen and John L. Betts, *History U.S.A.* New York: American Book Co., 1976, p. 576.

43. Risjord and Haywoode, *op. cit.*, p. 630.

44. Patricia Goldschlag and Jane Allen Clark, *Many Americans—One Nation*. New York: Noble and Noble, 1974, p. 357.

45. Lawrence J. Pauline, *Our America*. Boston: Allyn and Bacon, 1977, p. 421.

46. Jerome R. Reich and Edward L. Billen, *Building the American Dream*. New York: Harcourt Brace Jovanovich Inc., 1971, p. 677.

47. William G. Gardner, *Story of Our Country.* Boston: Allyn and Bacon, Inc., 1977, p. 441.

48. Okum and Bronz, *op. cit.,* p. 686.

49. Gardner, *op. cit.,* p. 441.

50. Banks and Sebesta, *op. cit.*

51. Bernard A. Weisberger, *The Impact of Our Past, A History of the United States.* New York: McGraw-Hill, 1976, p. 417.

52. Madgic, Leaberg, Stopsky and Winks, *op. cit.,* p. 478.

53. Social Science Staff of the Educational Research Council of America, *The American Adventure,* vol. 2. Boston: Allyn and Bacon, 1977, p. C-27.

54. Graff, *op. cit.,* p. 660.

55. Jack Abramowitz, *The American Nation: Adventure in Freedom.* Chicago: Follett Publishing Company, 1975, p. 638.

56. Herbert J. Bass, George A. Billias and Emma Jones Lapsansky, *Our American Heritage.* Morristown, N.J.: Silver Burdett, 1979, p. 686.

57. Banks and Sebesta, *op. cit.,* p. 211.

58. Leonard Pitt, *We Americans,* vol II. Glenview, Ill.: Scott, Foresman and Co., 1976, p. 771.

59. *Ibid.,* p. 773.

60. Bragdon, Cole and McCutchen, *op. cit.,* p. 394.

61. Graff and Bohannan, *op. cit.,* p. 508.

62. Social Science Staff of the Educational Research Council of America, *op. cit.*

63. Nancy W. Bauer, *The American Way.* New York: Holt, Rinehart and Winston, 1979, p. 631.

64. *Ibid.*

65. *Ibid.,* p. 634.

66. VerSteeg and Hofstadtler, *op. cit.,* p. 732.

67. Glenn M. Linden, Elizabeth Aston Wassenick, Dean C. Brink and Wesley J. Jones, Jr., *A History of Our American Republic.* River Forest, Ill.: Laidlaw Brothers, 1979, p. 558.

68. Okum and Bronz, *op. cit.,* p. 686.

69. Wiltz, *op. cit.,* p. 581.

70. *Ibid.,* p. 582.

71. Cuban and Roden, *op. cit.,* p. 89.

72. James I. Clark and Robert V. Remini, *Freedom's Frontiers—The Story of the American People.* Beverly Hills, Ca.: Benzinger, 1975, p. 455.

73. Risjord and Haywoode, *op. cit.,* p. 276.

74. *Ibid.,* p. 282.

75. Allen and Betts, *op. cit.,* p. 576.

76. Abramowitz, *op. cit.,* p. 638.

77. Brown, Robinson, and Cunningham, *op. cit.,* p. 523.

78. VerSteeg and Hofstadtler, *op. cit.,* p. 677.

79. Orrel T. Baldwin, *The Story of Our America.* New York: Noble and Noble Pub. Co., 1974, p. 398.

80. Risjord and Haywoode, *op. cit.,* p. 276.

81. Pitt, *op. cit.*, p. 624.

82. Graff and Bohannan, *op. cit.*, p. 504.

83. Boyd Shafer, Everett Augspurger, and Richard A. McLemore, *United States History for High Schools*. River Forest, Ill.: Laidlaw Brothers, 1977, p. 624.

84. Nelson Klose, *American History, Vol. 2, Since 1865*, rev. ed. Woodbury, New York: Barrow's Educational Series, Inc., 1973, p. 294.

85. Abramowitz, *op. cit.*

86. Wiltz, *op. cit.*, p. 583.

87. David B. Bidna, Morris G. Greenberg, and Jerald H. Spitz, *We The People, A History of the United States*. Lexington, Ma.: D.C. Heath and Co., 1977, p. 443.

88. Heller and Potter, *op. cit.*, p. 543.

89. Graff, *op. cit.*, p. 671.

90. Cuban and Roden, *op. cit.*

91. Bragdon, Cole, and McCutchen, *op. cit.*, p. 346.

92. Banks and Sebesta, *op. cit.*; Irving Barlett, Edwin Fenton, David Fowler and Seymour Mandelbaum, *A New History of the United States, An Inquiry Approach*. New York: Holt, Rinehart and Winston, Inc., 1975.; Joanne L. Buggey, Gerald A. Danzer, Charles A. Mitsakos, and C. Frederick Risinger, *American! America!* Glenview, Ill.: Scott Foresman and Co., 1977.; Madgic, Leaberg, Stopsky and Winks, *op. cit.*; Raymond J. Wilson and George Spiero, *Liberty and Union—A History of the United States*. Boston: Houghton Mifflin Co., 1972.; and Wiltz, *op. cit.*

93. Madgic, Leaberg, Stopsky and Winks, *ibid.*

94. Bauer, *op. cit.*

95. Bragdon, Cole, and McCutchen, *op. cit.*

96. Marvin Perry, Theodore H. Vow Lave, Jean Herskovitz, Donald M. Lowe, Donald Warren, Jr., and Joel H. Wiener, *Man's Unfinished Journey: A World History*. Boston: Houghton Mifflin Co., 1971, p. 698.

97. Michael P. Petrovich and Philip D. Curtin, *The Human Achievement*. Morristown, N.J.: Silver Burdett Co., 1970, pp. 704, 705.

98. Lefton S. Stavrianos, Loretta Kreider Andrews, John R. McLane, Frank R. Safford and James E. Sheridan, *A Global History*. Boston: Allyn and Bacon, Inc., 1979, p. 138.

99. *Ibid.*, p. 558.

100. Bertram L. Linder, Edwin Slezer and Barry M. Berk, *A World History*. Chicago: Science Research Associates, Inc., 1979.

101. Allan O. Kownslar and Terry L. Smart, *People and Our World: A Study of World History*. New York: Holt, Rinehart and Winston, 1981.

102. Perry, Vow Lave, Herskovitz, Lowe, Warren and Wiener, *op. cit.*

103. John Thompson and Hedberg, *People and Civilizations: A World History*. Lexington, Ma.: Ginn and Co., 1977.

104. Carl L. Becker and Kenneth S. Cooper, *Modern History*. Morristown, N.J.: Silver Burdett, 1977.; F. Kenneth Cox, Miriam Greenblatt and Stanley S. Seaberg, *Human Heritage, A World History*. Columbus, Oh.: Charles E.

Merrill Pub. Co., 1981.; Carlton J. H. Hayes and Margareta Faissler, *Modern Times: The French Revolution to the Present.* New York: The Macmillan Pub. Co., 1966.; Kownslar and Smart, *op. cit.;* Linder, Slezer and Berk, *op. cit.;* Mariah Marvin, Stephen Marvin and Frank J. Cappeluti, *The Human Adventure.* Menlow Park, Ca.: Addison-Wesley Pub. Co., 1976.; Perry, Vow Lave, Herskovitz, Lowe, Warren and Wiener, *op. cit.;* and Jean Reeder Smith and Lacey Baldwin Smith, *Essentials of World History,* rev. ed. Woodbury, N.Y.: Barrow's Educational Series, Inc., 1980.

105. Linder, Slezer and Berk, *ibid.,* p. 602.

106. Hayes and Faissler, *op. cit.,* p. 434.

107. Becker and Cooper, *op. cit.;* Mikiso Hane, James Neil Hantula, Norman Mysliwiec and Ralph Sandlin Yohe, *The World of Mankind: Cultures in Transition.* Chicago: Follett Pub. Co., 1973.; Kownslar and Smart, *op. cit.;* and William H. McNeill, *The Ecumene: Story of Humanity.* New York: Harper and Row Pub. Co., 1973.

108. McNeill, *ibid.,* p. 686.

109. Kownslar and Smart, *op. cit.,* pp. 678, 679.

110. Perry, Vow Lave, Herskovitz, Lowe, Warren and Wiener, *op. cit.,* p. 672.

111. Linder, Slezer and Berk, *op. cit.,* p. 608.

112. Jack Abramowitz, *World History.* Chicago: Follett Pub. Co., 1974, p. 452.

113. Linder, Slezer and Berk, *op. cit.;* Kownslar and Smart, *op. cit.;* and Perry, Vow Lave, Herskovitz, Lowe, Warren and Wiener, *op. cit.*

114. Perry, Vow Lave, Herskovitz, Lowe, Warren and Wiener, *ibid.,* p. 698.

115. Kownslar and Smart, *op. cit.*

116. Stavrianos, Andrews, McLane, Safford and Sheridan, *op. cit.,* p. 555.

117. Sol Holt and John R. O'Connor, *The New Exploring World History.* New York: Globe Book Co., 1977, p. 537.

118. Kownslar and Smart, *op. cit.*

119. Perry, Vow Lave, Herskovitz, Lowe, Warren and Wiener, *op. cit.;* and Suzanne Harris Sankowsky and Hirschfield, *Mainstreams of World History.* New York: Oxford Book Co., 1974.

120. Holt and O'Connor, *op. cit.,* p. 537.

121. Abramowitz, *op. cit.,* p. 518.

122. *Ibid.,* p. 678.

123. *Ibid.,* p. 697.

124. *Ibid.*

125. Linder, Slezer and Berk, *op. cit.;* and Kownslar and Smart, *op. cit.*

126. Frederick M. King, Herbert V. Epperly, Herbert C. Rudman and Ralph J. Cook, *The Social Studies and Our World.* River Forest, Ill.: Laidlaw Brothers, 1974, p. 308.

127. A. Wesley Roehm, Morris R. Buske, Hutton Webster and Edgar B. Wesley, *The Record of Mankind.* Lexington, Ma.: D.C. Heath and Co., 1970, p. 515.

128. William Johnson, Ira Peck, Francis Plotkin and William Richardson, *The Modern World.* New York: Scholastic Magazines, Inc., 1976, p. 160.

129. Becker and Cooper, *op. cit.,* p. 505.

130. Perry, Vow Lave, Herskovitz, Lowe, Warren and Wiener, *op. cit.,* p. 698.

131. John M. Good, *The Shaping of Western Society.* New York: Holt, Rinehart and Winston, 1968.; and Becker and Cooper, *op. cit.*

132. Linder, Slezer and Berk, *op. cit.*

133. Sankowsky and Hirschfield, *op. cit.,* p. 461.

134. Becker and Cooper, *op. cit.*

135. Perry, Vow Lave, Herskovitz, Lowe, Warren and Wiener, *op. cit.,* p. 698.

136. Hane, Hantula, Mysliwiec and Yohe, *op. cit.,* p. 182.

137. Paul Thoman Welty, *The Human Expression: A History of People and Their Cultures.* Philadelphia: Lippincott Co., 1977, p. 692.

138. Linder, Slezer and Berk, *op. cit.*

139. Perry, Vow Lave, Herskovitz, Lowe, Warren and Wiener, *op. cit.,* p. 697.

140. Smith and Smith, *op. cit.;* and McNeill, *op. cit.*

141. Stavrianos, Andrews, McLane, Safford and Sheridan, *op. cit.,* p. 558.

142. Marvin, Marvin and Cappeluti, *op. cit.,* p. 390.

143. Social Science Staff of the Educational Research Council of America, *Nations in Action: International Tensions.* Boston: Allyn and Bacon, 1977, p. 84.

144. Ralph Yohe, Sandlin, Gilbert A. Cahill, Herbert H. Gross and Charles F. Gritzner, *Exploring Our World: Eastern Hemisphere.* Chicago: Follett Pub. Co., 1977, p. 262.

145. Petrovich and Curtin, *op. cit.,* p. 704.

146. Holt and O'Connor, *op. cit.,* p. 553.

147. Becker and Cooper, *op. cit.,* p. 505.

148. Social Science Staff of the Educational Research Council of America, *op. cit.,* p. 101.

149. Perry, von Lave, Herskovitz, Lowe, Warren, and Wiener, *op. cit.,* p. 691.

150. Lester S. Rogers, Fay Adams, and Walker Brown, *Story of Nations.* New York: Holt, Rinehart and Winston, Inc., 1973; and Social Science Staff of the Educational Research Council of America, *op. cit.*

151. Linder, Slezak, and Berk, *op. cit.;* and Kownslar and Smart, *op. cit.*

152. Perry, Von Lave, Herskovitz, Lowe, Warren, and Wiener, *op. cit.*

153. Linder, Slezak, and Berk, *op. cit.*

154. Good, *op. cit.;* and Welty, *op. cit.*

155. Kownslar and Smart, *op. cit.;* Roehm, Buske, Webster, and Wesley, *op. cit.;* and Sankowsky and Hirschfield, *op. cit.*

156. Linder, Slezak, and Berk, *op. cit.*

157. Allen Schick and Adrienne Pfister, *American Government: Continuity and Change.* Boston: Houghton Mifflin Co., 1975.

158. Allan O. Kownslar and Terry Smart, *Civics: Citizens and Society.* New York: McGraw-Hill Book Co., 1980, p. 252.

159. *Ibid.,* p. 253.

160. R. Sprge Denisoff and Ralph Wahrman, *An Introduction to Sociology,* 2nd ed. New York: The Macmillan Pub. Co., 1979, p. 331.

161. *Ibid.,* p. 329.

162. Elgin F. Hunt, *Social Science: An Introduction to the Study of Society,* 4th ed. New York: The Macmillan Pub. Co., 1972, p. 344.

163. *Ibid.,* pp. 344, 345.

164. James O. Lugo and Gerald L. Hershey, *Living Psychology: Research in Action,* 2nd ed. New York: The Macmillan Pub. Co., 1976, p. 404.

165. Garlie A. Forehand, Althea J. Horner, Herbert Sorenson and Marguerite Malm, *Psychology for Living,* 4th ed. New York: McGraw-Hill Book Co., 1977, p. 425.

166. *Ibid.,* p. 332.

167. Rachel P. Ragland and Burt Saxon, *Invitation to Psychology.* Glenview, Ill.: Scott Foresman and Co., 1981, p. 431.

168. *Ibid.*

169. Elton B. McNeil, George D. Fuller and Jackie Estrada, *Psychology Today and Tomorrow.* New York: Harper and Row, 1978, p. 55.

170. *Ibid.*

171. *Ibid.,* p. 59.

172. Alan Beckler and Stuart Lazarus, *World Geography.* Chicago: Science Research Associates, Inc., 1981, p. 177.

173. *Ibid.,* p. 417.

174. William Stephen, *Social Studies.* Glenview, Ill.: Scott Foresman and Co., 1979.

175. Henry F. Bedford and Trevor Colbourn, *The Americans: A Brief History,* 3rd ed. New York: Harcourt Brace Jovanovich, 1972; John Blum, Edmund S. Morgan, Willie Lee Rose, Arthur M. Schlesinger, Jr., Kenneth M. Stampp and C. Van Woodword, *The National Experience: A History of the United States,* 4th ed. New York: Harcourt Brace Jovanovich, 1977; Paul K. Conkin, *The New Deal,* 2nd ed. New York: Thomas Y. Crowell Co., 1975; John A. Garraty (ed.), *Historical Viewpoints: Notable Articles from American Heritage,* vol. II, 3rd ed. New York: Harper and Row Pub., 1979.

176. Samuel Eliot Morison, Henry Steele Commager and William E. Leuchtenberg, *The Growth of the American Republic,* vol. II. New York: Oxford University Press, 1980.

177. *Ibid.,* p. 536.

178. Charles Sellers and Henry May, *A Synopsis of American History.* Chicago: Rand McNally and Co., 1966, p. 361.

179. *Ibid.,* p. 378.

180. *Ibid.,* p. 381.

181. Winthrop D. Jordan, *The White Man's Burden: Historical Origins of Racism in the United States.* New York: Oxford University Press, 1974.

182. Leonard Dinnerstein, Roger L. Nichols and David M. Reimers, *Natives and Strangers: Ethnic Groups and the Building of America*. New York: Oxford University Press, 1979, p. 175.

183. *Ibid.*, p. 257.

184. Leonard Dinnerstein and David M. Reimers, *Ethnic Americans: A History of Immigration and Assimilation*. New York: Dodd, Mead and Co., 1975.

185. Leonard Dinnerstein and Kenneth T. Jackson, *eds.*, *American Vistas: 1877 to the Present*, 3rd ed. New York: Oxford University Press, 1979, p. 188.

186. *Ibid.*, p. 190.

187. John Higham, *ed.*, *Ethnic Leadership in America*. Baltimore: The Johns Hopkins University Press, 1978, p. 30.

188. *Ibid.*

189. *Ibid.*, p. 28.

190. Edward McNall Burns, *Western Civilizations: Their History and Their Cultures*, 8th ed. New York: W.W. Norton and Co., 1973, p. 863.

191. Brian Tierney, Donald Kagan and L. Pearce Williams, *Great Issues in Western Civilization*, vol. II. New York: Random House, 1967.

192. *Ibid.*, p. 551.

193. *Ibid.*, pp. 572–574.

194. Donald Kagan, Stephen Ozmet and Frank Turner, *The Western Heritage Since 1648*. New York: Macmillan Pub. Co., 1979.

195. *Ibid.*, p. 909.

196. Mortimer Chambers, Raymond Grew, David Helaihy, Theodore K. Rabb and Isser Woloch, *The Western Experience*, 2nd ed. New York: Alfred A. Knopf, 1979.

197. *Ibid.*, p. 1033.

198. *Ibid.*, p. 1043.

199. Lloyd C. Gardner, Arthur Schlesinger and Hans J. Morgenthau, *The Origins of the Cold War*. Waltham, Ma.: Ginn and Co., 1970; Robert L. Heilbroner and Peter L. Bernstein, *A Primer on Government Spending*. New York: Random House, 1963; J.P. Nettl, *The Soviet Achievement*, New York: Harcourt Brace and World, Inc., 1967; and Daniel Yergin, *Shattered Peace: The Origins of the Cold War and the National Security State*. Boston: Houghton Mifflin, 1977.

200. Walter Laqueur, *ed.*, *Fascism: A Reader's Guide*. Berkeley: University of California Press, 1976, p. 151.

201. *Ibid.*, p. 155.

202. *Ibid.*, p. 200.

203. Thomas G. Paterson, J. Garry Clifford and Kenneth J. Hagan, *American Foreign Policy: A History*. Lexington, Ma.: D.C. Heath and Co., 1977, p. 401.

204. *Ibid.*

205. *Ibid.*, p. 403.

206. *Ibid.*

207. *Ibid.*, p. 405.

208. Geoffred Barraclough, *An Introduction to Contemporary History.* Baltimore: Penguin Books, 1967; Richard J. Barnet, *Intervention and Revolution.* New York: The World Publishing Co., 1968; and David Halberstam, *The Best and the Brightest.* New York: Random House, 1972.

209. Jean-Paul Sartre, *Anti-Semite and Jew.* New York: Schocken Books, Inc., 1948, p. 71.

210. *Ibid.,* p. 75.

211. *Ibid.,* p. 76.

212. *Ibid.,* p. 79.

213. *Ibid.,* p. 136.

214. Arnold A. Offner, *The Origins of the Second World War.* New York: Praeger Pub., 1975, p. 108.

215. *Ibid.,* p. 127.

216. *Ibid.,* p. 174.

217. James A. Nathan and James K. Oliver, *United States Foreign Policy and World Order.* Boston: Little, Brown and Co., 1976; and Barry B. Hughes, *The Domestic Context of American Foreign Policy.* San Francisco: Wilt Freeman and Co., 1978.

218. Charles W. Kegley and Eugene R. Wittkopf, *American Foreign Policy: Patterns and Process.* New York: St. Martin's Press, 1979, p. 373.

219. Bruce M. Russett, *No Clear and Present Danger: A Skeptical View of the United States Entry into World War II.* New York: Harper and Row, 1972, p. 42.

220. M. Glenn Abernathy, *Civil Liberties Under the Constitution.* New York: Dodd, Mead and Co., 1972; Richard C. Cortner, *The Supreme Court and Civil Liberties Policy.* Palo Alto, Ca.: Mayfield Pub. Co., 1975; and Michel Crozier, Samuel P. Huntington and Joji Watanuki, *The Crisis of Democracy.* New York: New York University Press, 1975.

221. Thomas Sowell, *Race and Economics.* New York: David McKay Co., 1975, p. vi.

222. Louis Rene Beres and Harry R. Targ, *Constructing Alternative World Futures.* Cambridge, Ma.: Schenkman Pub. Co., 1977; Thomas M. Franck and Edward Weisband, *Word Politics: Verbal Strategy Among the Superpowers.* New York: Oxford Univ. Press, 1971; and Fred A. Sondermann, William C. Olson and David S. McLellan, *The Theory and Practice of International Relations,* 3rd ed. Englewood Cliffs, N.J.: Prentice-Hall, 1970.

223. David W. Ziegler, *War, Peace, and International Politics.* Boston: Little, Brown and Co., 1977, p. 42.

224. Steven L. Spiegel, *ed., At Issue: Politics in the World Arena.* New York: St. Martin's Press, 1973, p. 114.

225. John G. Stoessinger, *Why Nations Go to War.* New York: St. Martin's Press, 1974, p. 46.

226. *Ibid.,* p. 173.

227. *Ibid.,* p. 195.

228. *Ibid.,* p. 176.

229. John G. Stoessinger, *The Might of Nations: World Politics in Our Time.* New York: Random House, 1961, p. 273.

230. *Ibid.*, p. 102.

231. *Ibid.*, pp. 242–244.

232. *Ibid.*, p. 299.

233. Louis E. Genevie, *ed., Collective Behavior and Social Movements.* Itasca, Ill.: F.E. Peacock Pub. Inc., 1978; William A. Gamson, *The Strategy of Social Protest.* Homewood, Ill.: The Dorsey Press, 1975; Hugh Davis Graham and Ted Robert Gurr, *eds., The History of Violence in America: Historical and Comparative Perspective.* New York: Frederick A. Praeger Pub., 1969; Francis Fox Piven and Richard A. Cloward, *Poor People's Movements: Why They Succeed, How They Fail.* New York: Pantheon Books, 1977; Barbara Salert, *Revolutions and Revolutionaries.* New York: Elsevier Scientific Pub. Co., 1976; Charles Tilly, *From Mobilization to Revolution.* Reading, Ma.: Addison-Wesley, 1978; and Michael Unseem, *Protest Movements in America.* Indianapolis, In.: Bobbs-Merrill Co., 1975.

234. Andrew M. Greeley, *The Demo national Society: A Sociological Approach to Religion in America.* Glenview, Ill.: Scott, Foresman and Co., 1972, p. 199.

235. *Ibid.*, p. 215.

236. Edward Simmen (ed.), *Pain and Promise: The Chicano Today.* New York: New American Library, 1972.

237. Charles F. Marden and Gladys Meyer, *Minorities in American Society,* 3rd ed. New York: American Book Co., 1968, pp. 121, 122.

238. *Ibid.*, p. 140.

239. Howard M. Bahr, Bruce A. Chadwick and Joseph H. Stauss, *American Ethnicity.* Lexington, Ma.: D.C. Heath and Co., 1979, p. 133.

240. *Ibid.*, p. 320.

241. *Ibid.*, p. 134.

242. *Ibid.*, p. 264.

243. Richard T. Shaefer, *Racial and Ethnic Groups.* Boston: Little, Brown and Co., 1979, p. 369.

244. *Ibid.*, p. 370.

245. *Ibid.*, p. 374.

246. *Ibid.*, p. 375.

247. *Ibid.*, p. 33.

248. Paul Tillich, *Dynamics of Faith.* New York: Harper and Brothers Pub. Co., 1957; and Sean Fagan, *Has Sin Changed?* Garden City, N.Y.: Doubleday and Co., 1979.

249. Andrew M. Greeley, *The Great Mysteries: An Essential Catechism.* New York: Seabury Press, 1976, pp. 128, 129.

250. *Ibid.*, p. 139.

251. Robert McAfee Brown, *The Spirit of Protestantism.* London: Oxford University Press, 1965, p. 25.

252. *Ibid.*, p. 43.

253. *Ibid.*, p. 237.

254. John L. McKenzie, *The Roman Catholic Church.* New York: Holt, Rinehart and Winston, 1969, p. 115.

255. *Ibid.*

256. Monika Hellwig, *What Are the Theologians Saying?* Dayton, Oh.: Pflaum Press, 1970, p. 73.

257. *Ibid.*, p. 91.

258. Morton White, *The Age of Analysis*. Boston: Houghton Mifflin Co., 1955.

259. Paterson, Clifford and Hagan, *op. cit.*,

Bibliography

The Selection of Textbooks

Association of American Publishers. *Limiting What Students Shall Read: Books and Other Learning Materials in Our Public Schools: How They Are Selected and How They Are Removed.* Washington, D.C., 1981.

Black, Hillel. *The American Schoolbook.* New York: William Morrow and Co., 1967.

Cole, John Y., and Sticht, Thomas G. (eds.) *The Textbook in American Society.* Washington, D.C.: Library of Congress, 1981.

Davis, James E. (ed.) *Dealing With Censorship.* Urbana, Illinois: National Council of Teachers of English, 1979.

Dong, Stella. "Study Criticizes Coverage of Holocaust by 43 Current History Textbooks." *Publishers Weekly,* 216 (August 27, 1979), 9, p. 296.

Goldstein, Paul. *Changing the American Schoolbook.* Lexington, Mass.: D.C. Heath and Co., 1978.

Elementary Social Studies Textbooks

Berg, Roger M. *Social Studies.* Glenview, Illinois: Scott, Foresman and Co., 1979.

Berry, Leonard and Ford, Richard B. *People, Places and Change: An Introduction to World Cultures.* New York: Holt, Rinehart and Winston, 1976.

King, Allen Y., Peters, Ida, Potter, Florence. *The United States and the Other Americas.* New York: Macmillan Publishing Co., 1978.

King, Frederick M., Rudman, Herbert C., Epperly, Herbert V., Cooke, Ralph C. *The Social Studies and Our Country.* River Forest, Illinois: Laidlaw Brothers, 1974.

_____ , Rudman, Herbert C., Leavell, LoDoris R. *Understanding Our Country.* River Forest, Illinois: Laidlaw Brothers, 1979.

Kownslar, Allan O. and Fielder, William R. *Inquiring About American History.* New York: Holt, Rinehart and Winston, 1976.

Parramore, Barbara M. and D'Amelio, Dan. *Social Studies.* Glenview, Illinois: Scott, Foresman and Co., 1979.

Servey, Richard E. *Social Studies.* Glenview, Illinois: Scott, Foresman and Co., 1979.

Stanek, Muriel and Hartmann, Clinton. *Americans All—A Nation of Immigrants.* Westchester, Illinois: Benefic Press, 1973.

United States History Textbooks

Abramowitz, Jack. *The American Nation: Adventure in Freedom.* Chicago: Follett Pub. Co., 1975.

―――. *American History.* 5th ed. Chicago: Follett Pub. Co., 1979.

Allan, Richard G., *et al. United States History.* vol. 4. San Juan Capistrano, California: Modulearn, Inc., 1976.

Allen, Jack, and Betts, John L. *History U.S.A.* Bicentennial ed. New York: American Book Co., 1976.

Baldwin, Orrel T. *The Story of Our America.* New York: Noble and Noble Pub. Co., 1974.

―――, and Vochatzer, Clyde. *Makers of American History.* New York: Nobel and Nobel Pub. Co., 1972.

Banks, James A., and Sebesta, Sam L. *We Americans: Our History and People.* Boston: Allyn and Bacon, 1982.

Barlett, Irving, Keller, Clair, and Carey, Helen. *Freedom's Trail.* Boston: Houghton Mifflin Co., 1979.

―――, Fenton, Edwin, Fowler, David, and Mandelbaum, Seymour. *A New History of the United States, An Inquiry Approach.* New York: Holt, Rinehart and Winston, Inc., 1975.

Bass, Herbert J., Billias, George A., Lapsanksy, Emma Jones. *Our American Heritage.* Morristown, New Jersey: Silver Burdett, 1979.

Bauer, Nancy W. *The American Way.* New York: Holt, Rinehart and Winston, 1979.

Bidna, David B., Greenberg, Morris S., and Spitz, Jerald H. *We the People, A History of the United States.* Lexington, Mass: D.C. Heath and Co., 1977.

Boyle, Donzella Cross. *Quest of a Hemisphere.* Boston: Western Islands, 1970.

Brady, Marion, and Brady, Howard. *Ideas and Action in American History.* Englewood Cliffs, New Jersey: Prentice-Hall, 1977.

Bragdon, Henry, and McCutchen, Samuel. *History of a Free People.* New York: Macmillan, 1978.

―――, Cole, Charles W., and McCutchen, Samuel P. *Free People: The United States in the Twentieth Century.* New York: Macmillan, 1970.

Branson, Margaret Stimmann. *Land of Challenge.* Lexington, Mass: Ginn and Co., 1975.

―――, and France, Edward E. *American History for Today.* Lexington, Mass: Ginn and Co., 1977.

Brown, Richard C., Robinson, Wilhelmena S., and Cunningham, John T. *Let Freedom Ring: A United States History.* Morristown, New Jersey: Silver Burdett Co., 1980.

Buggey, Joanne L., Danzer, Gerald A., Mitsakos, Charles L., and Risinger, C. Frederick. *American! America!* Glenview, Illinois: Scott Foresman and Co., 1977.

Chapin, June, McHugh, Raymond, Gross, Richard. *Quest for Liberty.* Menlo Park, Calif.: Addison-Wesley, 1974.

Clark, James I., and Remini, Robert V. *Freedom's Frontiers—The Story of the American People.* Beverly Hills, Calif.: Benziger, 1975.

Cuban, Larry, and Roden, Philip. *Promise of America: An Unfinished Story.* Glenview, Illinois: Scott Foresman and Co., 1971.

Current, Richard N., DeConde, Alexander, and Dante, Harris L. *United States History: Search for Freedom.* Glenview, Illinois: Scott Foresman and Co., 1974.

Eibling, Harold H., Jackson, Carlton L., and Perrone, Vito. *Two Centuries of Progress.* River Forest, Illinois: Laidlaw Brothers, 1977.

Forcey, Charles, and Posner, Ronald. *A Strong and Free Nation.* New York: Macmillan Co., 1971.

Friedel, Frank, and Drewry, Henry N. *America Is.* Columbus, Ohio: Charles E. Merrill Pub. Co., 1978.

Gardner, William E. *Story of Our Country.* Boston: Allyn and Bacon, Inc., 1977.

Garraty, John A. *The American Nation: A History of the United States Since 1865.* 4th ed. New York: Harper and Row, 1979.

Goldshlag, Patricia, and Clark, Jane Allen. *Many Americans—One Nation.* New York: Noble and Noble, 1974.

Graff, Henry F. *The Free and the Brave.* Chicago: Rand McNally and Co., 1967.

————, and Bohannan, Paul. *The Promise of Democracy.* Chicago: Rand McNally and Co., 1978.

Gross, Herbert, Follett, Dwight, Gabler, Robert, Burton, William, and Ahlschwede, Ben. *Exploring Our World—The Americans.* Chicago: Follett Book Co., 1977.

Heller, Landis R., Jr., and Potter, Norris W. *One Nation Indivisible.* Columbus, Ohio: Charles E. Merrill Pub. Co., 1971.

Hughes, Glenn E., Miller, Norman D., and Volkening, Stephen L. *Reading American History.* Glenview, Illinois: Scott Foresman and Co., 1978.

Klose, Nelson. *American History, Vol. 2, Since 1865.* Rev. Woodbury, New York: Barrow's Educational Series, Inc., 1973.

Leinwand, Gerald. *The Pageant of American History.* Boston: Allyn and Bacon, 1975.

Linden, Glenn M., Wassenick, Elizabeth Aston, Brink, Dean C., and Jones, Wesley J. Jr. *A History of Our American Republic.* River Forest, Illinois: Laidlaw Brothers, 1979.

Madgic, Robert F., Leaberg, Stanley L., Stopsky, Fred H., and Winks, Robin W. *The American Experience.* Menlo Park, Calif.: Addison-Wesley Pub. Co., 1975.

Okum, Mitchell, and Bronz, Stephen H. *The Challenge of America.* New York: Holt, Rinehart and Winston, Inc., 1973.

Pauline, Lawrence J. *Our America.* Boston: Allyn and Bacon, 1977.

Pitt, Leonard. *We Americans.* vol. II. Glenview, Illinois: Scott Foresman and Co., 1976.

Pulliam, William E., O'Neill, William L., and Bowman, Claire M. *America Rediscovered: Its Foreign Affairs*. Boston: Houghton Mifflin Co., 1977.

———. *America Rediscovered: Its People*. Boston: Houghton Mifflin Co., 1977.

———. *America Rediscovered: Its Political Life*. Boston: Houghton Mifflin Co., 1977.

Reich, Jerome R., Billen, Edward L. *Building the American Dream*. New York: Harcourt Brace Jovanovich Inc., 1971.

Risjord, Norman, and Haywoode, Terry. *A History of the United States from 1877*. New York: Holt, Rinehart and Winston, 1979.

Sandler, Martin W. *In Search of America*. Lexington, Mass: Ginn and Co., 1975.

Schwartz, Melvin, and O'Connor, John R. *The New Exploring American History*. New York: Globe Book Co. Inc., 1974.

Shafer, Boyd, Augspurger, Everett, and McLemore, Richard A. *United States History for High Schools*. River Forest, Illinois: Laidlaw Brothers, 1977.

Shaftel, George. *Decisions in United States History*. Lexington, Mass.: Ginn and Co., 1972.

Shenton, James P., Benson, Judith R., and Jakoubek, Robert E. *These United States*. Boston: Houghton Mifflin Co., 1978.

Smith, Lew. *The American Dream*. Glenview, Illinois: Scott Foresman and Co., 1977.

Social Science Staff of the Educational Research Council of America. *The American Adventure*. vol. 2. Boston: Allyn and Bacon, 1977.

Social Studies Curriculum Center, Carnegie-Mellon University. *The Americans*. New York: Holt, Rinehart and Winston, Inc., 1975.

Strong, Bryan. *America: In Space and Time*. Menlo Park, Calif.: Addison-Wesley Pub. Co., 1976.

Todd, Lewis Paul, and Curtis, Merle. *Rise of the American Nation*. New York: Harcourt Brace Jovanovich, 1977.

VerSteeg, Clarence L., and Hofstadtler, Richard. *A People and a Nation*. New York: Harper and Row, 1977.

Wade, Richard C., Wilder, Howard B., and Wade, Louise C. *A History of the United States*. Boston: Houghton Mifflin Co., 1972.

Weinstein, Allen, and Wilson, R. Jackson. *Freedom and Crises—An American History*. New York: Random House, 1974.

Weisberger, Bernard A. *The Impact of Our Past, A History of the United States*. New York: McGraw-Hill, 1976.

Wilder, Howard B., Ludlum, Robert P., and Brown, Harriett McCune. *This Is America's Story*. Boston: Houghton Mifflin Co., 1978.

Wilson, Raymond J., and Spiero, George. *Liberty and Union—A History of the United States*. Boston: Houghton Mifflin Co., 1972.

Wiltz, John Edward. *The Search for Identity: Modern American History*. Philadelphia: J.B. Lippincott Co., 1978.

Wood, Leonard C., Gabriel, Ralph H., and Biller, Edward L. *America: Its People and Values*. New York: Harcourt Brace Jovanovich, 1975.

World History/Western Civilization Textbooks

Abramowitz, Jack. *World History.* Chicago: Follett Pub. Co., 1974.

Becker, Carl L., and Cooper, Kenneth S. *Modern History.* Morristown, New Jersey: Silver Burdett, 1977.

Belasco, Milton Jay, and Kavunedos, Thomas G. *Our Western Heritage.* New York: Cambridge Book Co., 1970.

Cox, F. Kenneth, Greenblatt, Miriam, and Seaberg, Stanley S. *Human Heritage, A World History.* Columbus, Ohio: Charles E. Merrill Pub. Co., 1981.

Good, John M. *The Shaping of Western Society.* New York: Holt, Rinehart and Winston, 1968.

Hane, Mikiso, Hantula, James Neil, Mysliwiec, Norman, and Yohe, Ralph Sandlin. *The World of Mankind: Cultures in Transition.* Chicago: Follett Pub. Co., 1973.

Hayes, Carlton J. H. and Faissler, Margareta. *Modern Times: The French Revolution to the Present.* New York: The Macmillan Pub. Co., 1966.

Holt, Sol and O'Connor, John R. *The New Exploring World History.* New York: Globe Book Co., 1977.

Johnson, William, Peck, Ira, Plotkin, Francis, and Richardson, William. *The Modern World.* New York: Scholastic Magazines, Inc., 1976.

King, Frederick M., Epperly, Herbert V., Rudman, Herbert C., and Cooke, Ralph J. *The Social Studies and Our World.* River Forest, Illinois: Laidlaw Brothers, 1974.

Kownslar, Allan O., and Smart, Terry L. *People and Our World: A Study of World History.* New York: Holt, Rinehart and Winston, 1981.

Linder, Bertram L., Selzer, Edwin, and Berk, Barry M. *A World History.* Chicago: Science Research Associates, Inc. 1979.

Marvin, Mariah, Marvin, Stephen, and Cappelluti, Frank J. *The Human Adventure.* Menlow Park, CA: Addison-Wesley Pub. Co., 1976.

McNeill, William H. *The Ecumene: Story of Humanity.* New York: Harper and Row Pub. Co., 1973.

Perry, Marvin, Vow Lave, Theodore H., Herskovitz, Jean, Lowe, Donald M., Warren, Donald Jr., and Wiener, Joel H. *Man's Unfinished Journey: A World History.* Boston: Houghton Mifflin Co., 1971.

Petrovich, Michael B., and Curtin, Philip D. *The Human Achievement.* Morristown, New Jersey: Silver Burdett Co., 1970.

Roehm, A. Wesley, Buske, Morris R., Webster, Hutton, and Wesley, Edgar B. *The Record of Mankind.* Lexington, Mass: D.C. Heath and Co., 1970.

Rogers, Lester S., Adams, Fay, and Brown, Walker. *Story of Nations.* New York: Holt, Rinehart and Winston, Inc., 1973.

Roselle, Daniel. *A World History: A Cultural Approach.* rev. ed. Boston: Ginn and Co., 1969.

Sankowsky, Suzanne Harris, and Hirshfield. *Mainstreams of World History.* New York: Oxford Book Co., 1974.

Smith, Jean Reeder, and Smith, Lacey Baldwin. *Essentials of World History.* rev. ed. Woodbury, NY: Barrow's Educational Series, Inc., 1980.

Social Science Staff of the Educational Research Council of America. *Nations in Action: International Tensions*. Boston: Allyn and Bacon, 1977.

Stavrianos, Leften S., Andrews, Loretta Kreider, McLane, John R., Safford, Frank R., and Sheridan, James E. *A Global History*. Boston: Allyn and Bacon, Inc., 1979.

Thompson, John, and Hedberg. *People and Civilizations: A World History*. Lexington, Mass.: Ginn and Co., 1977.

Wallbank, T. Walter, Schrier, Arnold, Maier-Weaver, Donna, and Gutierrez, Patricia. *History and Life: The World and Its People*. Glenview, Illinois: Scott, Foresman and Co., 1980.

Weitzman, Rich, and Weitzman, Gross. *The Human Experience*. Boston: Houghton Mifflin Co., 1974.

Welty, Paul Thoman. *The Human Expression: A History of People and Their Cultures*. Philadelphia: Lippincott Co., 1977.

Yohe, Ralph, Sandlin, Cahill, Gilbert A., Gross, Herbert H., and Gritzner, Charles F. *Exploring Our World: Eastern Hemisphere*. Chicago: Follett Pub. Co., 1977.

Government and Civics Textbooks

Abramowitz, Jack. *Foundations of Freedom: The Declaration of Independence and the Constitution*. Chicago: Follett Pub. Co., 1976.

Diamond, Stanley E. and Pflieger, Elmer F. *Civics for Citizens*. Philadelphia: J.B. Lippincott Co., 1970.

Ebenstein, William and Mill, Edward W. *American Government in the Twentieth Century*. Morristown, New Jersey: Silver Burdett Co., 1973.

Feder, Bernard. *The Process of American Government: Cases and Problems*. New York: Noble and Noble Pub., 1972.

Hartley, William H. and Vincent, Williams S. *American Civics*. 2d ed. New York: Harcourt Brace Jovanovich, Inc., 1974.

Kownslar, Allan and Smart, Terry. *Civics: Citizens and Society*. New York: McGraw-Hill Book Co., 1980.

Kownslar, Allan O. and Smart, Terry. *American Government*. New York: McGraw-Hill Book Co., 1980.

McClenaghan, William A. *Magruder's America Government*. Boston: Allyn and Bacon, Inc., 1981.

Patrick, John J. and Remy, Richard C. *Civics for Americans*. Glenview, Illinois: Scott, Foresman and Co., 1980.

Schick, Allen and Pfister, Adrienne. *American Government: Continuity and Change*. Boston: Houghton Mifflin Co., 1975.

Sociology Textbooks

Denisoff, R. Serge and Wahrman, Ralph. *An Introduction to Sociology*. 2d ed. New York: The Macmillan Pub. Co., 1979.

Hunt, Elgin F. *Social Science: An Introduction to the Study of Society.* 4th ed. New York: The Macmillan Co., 1972.
Levin, Jack and Spates, James L. *Starting Sociology.* 2d ed. New York: Harper and Row, 1979.

Psychology Textbooks

Forehand, Garlie A., Horner, Althea J. Sorenson, Herbert, and Malm, Marquerite. *Psychology for Living.* 4th ed. New York: McGraw-Hill Book Co., 1977.
Lugo, James O. and Hershey, Gerald L. *Living Psychology: Research in Action,* 2d ed. New York: The Macmillan Pub. Co., 1976.
McNeil, Elton B., Fuller, George D., and Estrada, Jackie. *Psychology Today and Tomorrow.* New York: Harper and Row, 1978.
Ragland, Rachel G. and Saxon, Burt. *Invitation to Psychology.* Glenview, Illinois: Scott, Foresman and Co., 1981.

World Geography/Area Studies Textbooks

Beckler, Alan and Lazarus, Stuart. *World Geography.* Chicago: Science Research Associates, Inc., 1981.
Danzer, Gerald A. and Larson, Albert. *Land and People: A World Geography.* Glenview, Illinois: Scott, Foresman and Co., 1979.
Farah, Mounir A., Flickema, Thomas Orin, Hantula, James Neil, Johnson, Ellen C.K., Kane, Paul W., Karls, Andrea Berens, Leppeat, Ella C., and Ratcliffe, Robert H. *Global Insights, Peoples and Cultures.* Columbus, Ohio: Charles E. Merrill Pub., Co., 1980.
Versteeg, Clarence L. *World Cultures.* Glenview, Illinois: Scott, Foresman and Co., 1977.

Social Studies Textbook

Stephen, William. *Social Studies.* Glenview, Ill.: Scott Foresman, 1979.

History—College Level Textbooks

Barnet, Richard J. *Intervention and Revolution.* New York: The World Publishing Co., 1968.
Barraclough, Geoffrey. *An Introduction to Contemporary History.* Baltimore: Penguin Books, 1967.
Bedford, Henry F. and Colbourn, Trevor. *The Americans: A Brief History.* 3rd ed. New York: Harcourt Brace Jovanovich, 1972.
Blum, John, Morgan, Edmund S., Rose, Willie Lee, Schlesinger, Arthur M. Jr., Stampp, Kenneth M., and Woodward, C. Van. *The National Experience:*

A History of the United States. 4th ed. New York: Harcourt Brace Jovanovich, 1977.

Burns, Edward McNall. *Western Civilizations: Their History and Their Cultures.* 8th ed. New York: W.W. Norton and Co., 1973.

Chambers, Mortimer, Grew, Raymond, Healihy, David, Rabb, Theodore K., and Woloch, Isser. *The Western Experience.* 2d ed. New York: Alfred A. Knopf, 1979.

Conkin, Paul K. *The New Deal.* 2d ed. New York: Thomas Y. Crowell Co., 1975.

Dinnerstein, Leonard and Jackson, Kenneth T. (eds.) *American Vistas: 1877 to the Present.* 3rd ed. New York: Oxford Univ. Press, 1979.

Dinnerstein, Leonard, Nichols, Roger L., and Reimers, David M. *Natives and Strangers: Ethnic Groups and the Building of America.* New York: Oxford Univ. Press, 1979.

Dinnerstein, Leonard and Reimers, David M. *Ethnic Americans: A History of Immigration and Assimilation.* New York: Dodd, Mead and Co., 1975.

Gardner, Lloyd C., Schlesinger, Arthur, and Morgenthau, Hans J. *The Origins of the Cold War.* Waltham, Mass: Ginn and Co., 1970.

Garraty, John A. (ed.) *Historical Viewpoints: Notable Articles from American Heritage,* vol. II. 3d ed. New York: Harper and Row Pub., 1979.

Halberstam, David. *The Best and the Brightest.* New York: Random House, 1972.

Heilbroner, Robert L. and Bernstein, Peter L. *A Primer on Government Spending.* New York: Random House, 1963.

Higham, John (ed.) *Ethnic Leadership in America.* Baltimore: The Johns Hopkins Univ. Press, 1978.

Hirschfeld, Charles. (ed.) *The Modern World.* New York: Harcourt, Brace and World Inc., 1964.

Jordan, Winthrop D. *The White Man's Burden: Historical Origins of Racism in the United States.* New York: Oxford Univ. Press, 1974.

Kagan, Donald, Ozment, Steven, and Turner, Frank. *The Western Heritage Since 1648.* New York: Macmillan Pub. Co., 1979.

Laqueur, Walter. (ed.) *Fascism: A Reader's Guide.* Berkeley: Univ. of Calif. Press, 1976.

Morison, Samuel Eliot, Commager, Henry Steele and Leuchtenburg, William E. *The Growth of the American Republic,* vol. II. New York: Oxford Univ. Press, 1980.

Nettl, J.P. *The Soviet Achievement.* New York: Harcourt, Brace and World, Inc., 1967.

Offner, Arnold A. *The Origins of the Second World War.* New York: Praeger Pub., 1975.

Paterson, Thomas G., Clifford, J. Garry, and Hagan, Kenneth J. *American Foreign Policy: A History.* Lexington, Mass.: D.C. Heath and Co., 1977.

Sartre, Jean-Paul. *Anti-Semite and Jew.* New York: Schoken Books, Inc., 1948.

Sellers, Charles and May, Henry. *A Synopsis of American History.* Chicago: Rand McNally and Co., 1966.

Tierney, Brian, Kagan, Donald, and Williams, L. Pearce. *Great Issues in Western Civilization*, vol. II. New York: Random House, 1967.

Yergin, Daniel. *Shattered Peace: The Origins of the Cold War and the National Security State*. Boston: Houghton Mifflin, 1977.

Political Science—College Level Textbooks

Abernathy, M. Glenn. *Civil Liberties Under the Constitution*. New York: Dodd, Mead and Co., 1972.

Beres, Louis René and Targ, Harry R. *Constructing Alternative World Futures*. Cambridge, Mass: Schenkman Pub. Co., 1977.

Cortner, Richard C. *The Supreme Court and Civil Liberties Policy*. Palo Alto, California: Mayfield Pub. Co., 1975.

Crozier, Michel, Huntington, Samuel P, and Watanuki, Joji. *The Crisis of Democracy*. New York: New York University Press, 1975.

Franck, Thomas M. and Weisband, Edward. *Word Politics: Verbal Strategy Among the Superpowers*. New York: Oxford University Press, 1971.

Hughes, Barry B. *The Domestic Context of American Foreign Policy*. San Francisco: Wilt Freeman and Co., 1978.

Kegley, Charles W. and Wittkopf, Eugene R. *American Foreign Policy: Patterns and Process*. New York: St. Martin's Press, 1979.

Nathan, James A. and Oliver, James K. *United States Foreign Policy and World Order*. Boston: Little, Brown and Co., 1976.

Russett, Bruce M. *No Clear and Present Danger: A Skeptical View of the United States Entry into World War II*. New York: Harper and Row, 1972.

Sondermann, Fred A, Olson, William C., and McLellan, David S. *The Theory and Practice of International Relations*. 3d ed. Englewood Cliffs, New Jersey: Prentice-Hall, 1970.

Sowell, Thomas. *Race and Economics*. New York: David McKay Co., 1975.

Spiegel, Steven L. (ed.) *At Issue: Politics in the World Arena*. New York: St. Martin's Press, 1973.

Stoessinger, John G. *The Might of Nations: World Politics in Our Time*. New York: Random House, 1961.

Stoessinger, John G. *Why Nations Go to War*. New York: St. Martin's Press, 1974.

Ziegler, David W. *War, Peace, and International Politics*. Boston: Little, Brown and Co., 1977.

Sociology—College Level Textbooks

Bahr, Howard M., Chadwick, Bruce A., and Stauss, Joseph H. *American Ethnicity*. Lexington, Mass.: D.C. Heath and Co., 1979.

Gamson, William A. *The Strategy of Social Protest*. Homewood, Illinois: The Dorsey Press, 1975.

Genevie, Louis E. (ed.) *Collective Behavior and Social Movements*. Itasca, Illinois: F.E. Peacock Pub. Inc., 1978.

Graham, Hugh Davis and Gurr, Ted Robert (eds.) *The History of Violence in America: Historical and Comparative Perspective.* New York: Frederick A. Praeger, Pub., 1969.

Greeley, Andrew M. *The Denominational Society: A Sociological Approach to Religion in America.* Glenview, Illinois: Scott, Foresman and Co., 1972.

Marden, Charles F. and Meyer, Gladys. *Minorities in American Society.* 3d ed. New York: American Book Co., 1968.

Piven, Frances Fox and Cloward, Richard A. *Poor People's Movements: Why They Succeed, How They Fail.* New York: Pantheon Books, 1977.

Salert, Barbara. *Revolutions and Revolutionaries.* New York: Elsevier Scientific Pub. Co., 1976.

Schaefer, Richard T. *Racial and Ethnic Groups.* Boston: Little, Brown and Co., 1979.

Simmen, Edward (ed.) *Pain and Promise: The Chicano Today.* New York: New American Library, 1972.

Tilly, Charles. *From Mobilization to Revolution.* Reading, Mass.: Addison-Wesley, 1978.

Unseem, Michael. *Protest Movements in America.* Indianapolis: Bobbs-Merrill Co., 1975.

Religious Studies—College Level Textbooks

Brown, Robert McAfee. *The Spirit of Protestantism.* London: Oxford University Press, 1965.

Fagan, Sean. *Has Sin Changed?* Garden City, New York: Doubleday and Co., 1979.

Greeley, Andrew. *The Great Mysteries: An Essential Catechism.* New York: Seabury Press, 1976.

Hellwig, Monika. *What Are the Theologians Saying?* Dayton, Ohio: Pflaum Press, 1970.

McKenzie, John L. *The Roman Catholic Church.* New York: Holt, Rinehart and Winston, 1969.

Tillich, Paul. *Dynamics of Faith.* New York: Harper and Brothers Pub. Co., 1957.

Humanities—College Level Textbooks

White, Morton. *The Age of Analysis.* Boston: Houghton Mifflin, 1955.

Contributors

RUTH FIRER is associated with the School of Education of the Hebrew University of Jerusalem. A specialist in Israeli education and textbooks, she is the author of *Agents of Zionist Education* (Tel Aviv: Ha'Kibbutz ha'Meuchad, 1985) and of several studies in professional journals, including *Massua* and *Kivunim*.

GLENN S. PATE is Associate Professor at the College of Education of the University of Arizona, working primarily in teacher education. His main research area is the reduction and prevention of prejudice. He is the author of several reports on education and also the co-author of *Designing Classroom Simulations* (Belmont, Cal.: Fearon Publishers, 1973.

WALTER F. RENN is Professor of History at Wheeling College, Wheeling, West Virginia. A specialist on the Holocaust and the Third Reich, his studies appeared in *Contemporary Views on the Holocaust* (New York: Institute for Holocaust Studies of The City University of New York, 1983), *Dimensions*, and *Shoah*. He is currently investigating German wartime awareness of the Holocaust.